Places and Purposes of Popular Music Education

Places and Purposes of Popular Music Education

Perspectives from the Field

EDITED BY

Bryan Powell and Gareth Dylan Smith

Bristol, UK / Chicago, USA

First published in the UK in 2022 by
Intellect, The Mill, Parnall Road, Fishponds, Bristol, BS16 3JG, UK

First published in the USA in 2022 by
Intellect, The University of Chicago Press, 1427 E. 60th Street,
Chicago, IL 60637, USA

A catalogue record for this book is available from
the British Library.

Copy editor: MPS Limited
Cover designer: Aleksandra Szumlas
Cover image: Compiled collage of *Purposes and
Places of Popular Music* chapter authors, 2022.
Images courtesy of authors.
Frontispiece image: Photo credit to Virginia Wayman Davis.
Production manager: Sophia Munyengeterwa
Typesetter: MPS Limited

Hardback ISBN 978-1-78938-628-8
ePDF ISBN 978-1-78938-629-5
ePUB ISBN 978-1-78938-630-1

To find out about all our publications, please visit our website.
There you can subscribe to our e-newsletter, browse or download our current
catalogue and buy any titles that are in print.

www.intellectbooks.com

This is a peer-reviewed publication.

Contents

CONTENTS

vii

Acknowledgements

This book is dedicated to Steve, Abbey and Luna – the most steadfast of editing companions.

Special thanks to Sol Elisa Martinez Missena for her work in copyediting and proof-reading this text. Thank you also to the entire Intellect team for their assistance throughout this process, especially Tim, Sophia and Jess. And we extend our humble gratitude to Lucy Green and Libby Allison for their feedback and critique during the review process.

Introduction

Gareth Dylan Smith and Bryan Powell

This book arose from what felt like an urgent need. The journey to publication began in about 2015 when at a board meeting of the Association for Popular Music Education (APME) it was suggested that as the organization positioning itself as the primary body in popular music education – or at least the most highly visible one – we really ought to make some sort of a statement about what popular music education is. It would help, presumably, to know (and, moreover, to let others know) precisely for what we were 'the association'.

At that meeting, we decided that APME should produce a white paper to define for ourselves and others what we meant by 'popular music education'. With one exception we were all from the United States, and all of us were White. All but one of the task force members were cisgender males. We all worked in higher education, and about half of us had doctoral degrees. A year later, we brought our messy first draft to another APME board meeting, and Gareth Dylan Smith was assigned to finish it off in as cogent a fashion as possible, send it to the task force and then to the rest of the board for sign-off and publication. The white paper, 'Popular music education: A white paper by the Association for Popular Music Education', was posted on the APME website, and was later published in volume 2, issue 3 of the *Journal of Popular Music Education* (*JPME*); the white paper included a good chunk of text that we initially wrote for the editorial introduction to the first issue of *JPME*. The executive summary of the white paper follows below and can be found at https://www.popularmusiceducation.org/about-apme/white-paper/ (accessed 10 May 2022).

Introduction

The Association for Popular Music Education (APME), founded in 2010, is the world's leading organization in popular music education, galvanizing a community of practice, scholarship and innovation around the field. Popular music education (hereafter PME) is exciting, dynamic and often innovative. Music education – meaning formal schooling in music – has tended most of the time to exclude almost all forms and contexts of music, and therefore has also elided most models of music learning and teaching. Popular music is among these excluded musics. The report is based on the knowledge, perspectives and experience of APME Board members, and therefore reflects the Anglophone and largely US American orientation of the contributors. We recognize that popular music is as diverse as the world's cultures, and that writing on popular music education is as nuanced as the languages in which it is communicated.

What is Popular Music Education?

Popular music is qualitatively different from other forms of music, in function and aesthetics (although there are areas of commonality). PME, therefore, may also be understood as necessarily different from Western Art Music (WAM) education. However, APME does not intend to construct or to construe PME as existing or working in opposition to existing music education programs and paradigms. PME, like popular music, is highly complex, problematic and challenging, as well as being inspiring and deeply meaningful to many people, individually and collectively. This is true of all musical traditions, their associated hierarchies, embedded practices and assumptions, and attendant educational practices. APME recognizes that change, stasis and tradition all constitute the lifeblood of popular music. As such, and to reflect that ongoing change, the authors assert that popular music education practice and scholarship must remain reflexive, allowing for and embracing constant revision and re-contextualization. As such, this paper marks a moment in time but is not intended to codify, define or delimit PME. Popular music has a growing presence in education, formal and otherwise, from primary school to postgraduate study. Programs, courses and classes in popular music studies, popular music performance, songwriting, production and areas of music technology are becoming commonplace across higher education and compulsory schooling. In the context of teacher education, classroom teachers and music specialists alike are becoming increasingly empowered to introduce popular music into their classrooms. Research in PME lies at the intersection of the fields of music education, ethnomusicology, community music, cultural studies and popular music studies.

Who are the Popular Music Educators?

The following quotes and borrows from the editorial article introducing the issue 1, volume 1 of the *Journal of Popular Music Education*. [1] The popular music education world is populated by two largely separate but far from discrete communities. One of these groups comprises mostly school music teachers and those who work in higher education institutions to 'train' teacher/musicians for the workplace. For them, music education is a high art and prized craft; PME is one part of the jigsaw puzzle of a schoolteacher's diverse portfolio of approaches to learning, teaching and assessment. The other community primarily teaches popular music studies (including popular music performance, business and songwriting) in institutions of higher education. For them the goal is to learn (about) popular music; 'education' is implicit in the fact that this activity takes place in a college or university. These two communities (crudely bifurcated as they are here, for the purposes of this short paper) collide and collaborate at APME conferences. They rarely seem to bump into one another, however, at meetings of IASPM (frequented primarily by members of the popular music studies community) or ISME (attended mainly by music teachers and music teacher teachers). People's experiences of education are frequently self-defining and life-changing – affirming, uplifting, crushing, celebratory and (dis)empowering by turns; the same can be said of people's encounters with music. Humans' engagement with popular music and experiences of education are vital to people's understanding and tolerance of themselves and one another. APME believes in the necessity and transformative power of deep educational experiences that critique and enable, challenge and transform. Popular music exists at the intersection of folk and celebrity cultures, combining the everyday with the exceptional and fantastic. It merges commerce, community, commodity and the construction of meanings. People live their lives both as popular musicians and through popular musicians, realizing identities as fans, consumers and practitioners. Popular music scenes, communities and subcultures are local, regional, national and international. PME thus takes place at the cross-sections of identity realization, learning, teaching, enculturation, entrepreneurship, creativity, a global multimedia industry, and innumerable leisure, DIY and hobbyist networks – online, and in physical spaces. Popular music education is business and social enterprise. It is personal and it is collective. It is vocational and avocational, and it builds and develops communities. Popular music stands as a vital part of our modern lives. A valuable form of artistic expression, it embraces all facets of the human experience. It blends art with contemporary culture and tradition to make relevant the ever-changing now.

(Smith et al. 2018: n.pag.)

One day in late 2018, this book's editors were discussing APME's white paper and we realized that we probably ought to seek some responses to it. On the one hand, it seemed entirely necessary that this organization should articulate its focus and frame its field, while on the other hand, we were keenly aware that almost everyone involved in popular music education worldwide had been excluded from the process of arriving at our definitions and purview of popular music education; the text of the APME white paper also acknowledges this shortcoming. In the spirit of humility, gross inadequacy and inclusion, we began making a list of people who we would invite to write short responses to the white paper in a forthcoming Special Issue of the *JPME*. In about five minutes it became abundantly clear that this could not be a single journal issue; if we were to include anything like the number of perspectives we felt were necessary to fill in even the obvious gaps in expertise among the white paper authors, we would need to start work on a book.

We also realized that we could not presume to know who should be on the list. We had begun our list with convenience sampling, but convenience is not likely to be representative. So, we needed a very relaxed timeline for this book project, that would allow us to put out a call for chapters, hear back from the profession (necessarily limited to the type of people who read and feel they can or want to respond to a call for book chapters), invite colleagues and contacts who we felt should be involved, and have conversations with others who would point us towards people and perspectives we did not know. As such, this book has been approximately four years in the making since our conversation in the winter of 2018. We are beyond grateful for the commitment, patience, enthusiasm and tenacity of the authors in this book.

The balance of the book's chapters still reflects the editors' respective contacts lists. But these lists have grown with the word-count limit of the book since our initial conversation about it with our publisher (thank you, Intellect, for your flexibility and for your belief in the book!). We are delighted that roughly two-thirds of contributing authors are not the 'usual suspects' writing on popular music education inasmuch they do not have doctoral degrees.

When introducing the first issue of the *Journal of Popular Music Education* back in 2017, and as quoted above in the white paper excerpt, we wrote about how:

> [T]he prospective audience for and contributors to *JPME* seemed to come from two largely separate but far from discrete communities. One of these groups tends to see *JPME* as the 'Journal of (Popular) Music Education'; this group comprises mostly school music teachers and those who work in higher education institutions to 'train' teacher/musicians for the work-place. For them, music education is a high art and prized craft; PME is one part of the jigsaw puzzle of a schoolteacher's diverse portfolio of approaches to learning, teaching and assessment. The other community views *JPME* as the 'Journal of Popular Music (Education)'; this group primarily teaches popular music studies (including popular music performance, business and songwriting) in institutions of higher education. For them the goal is to learn (about) popular music; 'education' is implicit in the fact that this activity takes place in a college or university.
>
> (Smith and Powell 2017: 4)

While that reflected our experiences at the time, it now seems rather narrow and parochial a view. It was based on our sense of the potential 'markets' for the journal, which seemed important for generating discussion, finding an audience and garnering article submissions. Even for these purposes, though, that seems inadequate and outdated. Popular music education is bigger than us. It is bigger than scholarship on the topic. And it is bigger than the phrase implies. Indeed, outside the narrow confines of music education scholarship, the notion of *popular music education* at all probably sounds a little silly. However, among the community of scholars and students for whom this book is primarily intended, the phrase serves a purpose and has meaning and frames a variety of practices and perspectives. Which brings us to the question:

Does the world already need another *edited book about popular music education?*

We have both been involved as editors of recent handbooks on popular music education. Those books reflected the respective editorial teams' different approaches to collating writing on current thinking and practices in the field. *The Routledge Research Companion to Popular Music Education* (2017) is, as the title suggests, mostly research orientated. It was written and edited by researchers for an intended audience of principally researchers, including professional academics and students. *The Bloomsbury Handbook of Popular Music Education: Perspectives and Practices* (2019) contains chapters by high-profile thinkers in the field, as well as many more chapters by practitioners; the key aim in conceptualizing that book was to frame the book's sections with scholarship and then to contextualize and add meaning to that scholarship by including examples from practitioners who would not ordinarily write for a 'handbook'-type publication. One of the problems with academic publishing is that it frequently excludes the voices of those who, arguably, the profession needs most to hear from. Of course, producing scholarship is not for everyone, nor is reading it. The framing and citing and pontificating and philosophizing to which we two author/editors and our ilk are professionally prone, while providing succour and provocation for our higher education peers, can be alienating for colleagues in the 'real world' beyond the ivory tower.

This book is one attempt to provide a manuscript-megaphone for a variety of perspectives, including those we do not usually hear from, but who are doing far and away from the coolest, most relevant and most interesting things. It also includes contributions from many of the aforementioned 'usual suspects' in higher education, but we have tried hard to get these folks to write differently than they ordinarily would. We asked for rants, manifestos and pieces that are pithy and punchy and poignant; this request has resulted in a wide tonal variety among chapters, from more traditionally scholarly pieces replete with citations and references, through descriptions of practice, to straight-up polemics. We were careful about keeping contributions below a 2000-word threshold. Academic writing is not known for getting straight to the point – for good reason, as research is meticulous and careful, and writing about it requires diligence and precision. So, this book is intended for academics of all ages and stages, but the writing is often deliberately *non*-academic in tone. It is more about beliefs, experiences and motivation, about frustrations, aspirations and celebrations. We hope the authors leave readers wanting more. The writers betwixt these covers are each intriguing and awesome, each in their own ways. The chapters are intended to whet appetites, prime pumps, open eyes and start cogs turning. As editors, we are beyond humbled that these people took the time to write and revise (and revise and revise!) their ideas for this collection.

This book is organized into four parts of roughly equal size: (1) beyond the classroom, (2) identity and purpose, (3) higher education and (4) politics and ideology. Inevitably, some chapters could have fitted easily under two or more of these headings, but we are hopeful that readers will nonetheless find a sense of cohesion in the way the volume is structured; scholarly contributions rub shoulders with more personal and polemical pieces, and in places we have paired chapters on similar themes while in other locations we have opted for deliberate changes of tone, topic or tempo. And of course, no one is under any obligation to read the chapters in the order they are presented, or to consume the book cover to cover.

Thank you to everyone in this book. And thank *you* for opening it.

Gareth and Bryan, October 2021

REFERENCES

Smith, Gareth Dylan and Powell, Bryan (2017), 'Welcome to the journal', *Journal of Popular Music Education*, 1:1, pp. 3–7.

Smith, Gareth Dylan, Powell, Bryan, Fish, David Lee, Kornfeld, Irwin and Reinhert, Kat (2018), 'Popular music education: A white paper by the Association for Popular Music Education', *Journal of Popular Music Education*, 2:3, pp. 289–98.

PART 1

BEYOND THE CLASSROOM

In this opening section of the book, the authors present diverse perspectives on the places and purposes of popular music in a wide range of settings outside of school classrooms. Authors take us to cities and community centres in the US American Midwest, Northeast, Southwest and Great Plains, to the streets of Edinburgh, prisons in the United Kingdom and United States, schools in New Jersey, a home in South London, and to extra-curricular programmes in the Republic of Ireland.

Sergio Alonso,
music educator

Krystal Prime
Banfield,
Berklee College
of Music

Natalie Betts,
Weston College

1

Abigail D'Amore,
independent
consultant

Eva J. Egolf,
New York
University

Jason Hanley,
Rock and Roll
Hall of Fame

Niklas Lindholm,
Rockway Ltd
and Arcada
and Metropolia
Universities of
Applied Science

Tobias Malm,
Stockholm Univer-
sity and Royal
College of Music

Bryce Merril,
Bohemian
Foundation

Stuart Moir,
Moray House
School of Educa-
tion and Sport,
University of
Edinburgh

Roshi Nasehi,
musician

Joseph Michael
Pignato,
State University
of New York

Eleanor Rashid,
freelance music
practitioner,
songwriter and
performer

Tiger Robison,
University of
Wyoming

Kayla Rush,
Dublin City
University

Martin Ryan,
Kent State
University

Tom Scharf,
novelist, painter
and musician

Kenrick Wagner,
social entrepre-
neur and hip-hop
artist

1

'Something to Talk About': Intersections of Music, Memory, Dialogue and Pedagogy at the Rock and Roll Hall of Fame

Jason Hanley

Jason Hanley is Vice President of Education and Visitor Engagement at the Rock and Roll Hall of Fame in Cleveland, Ohio, USA, where he oversees the museum's award-winning programmes.

This chapter focuses on how popular music education is designed and experienced at the Rock and Roll Hall of Fame in Cleveland, Ohio, USA. It explores the intersections between history, sound, people, place, culture and meaning, integrating them into a popular music pedagogy through the practice of dialogue.

I work, study, listen, learn and teach at a place of intersections. It is an institution invested in *history*, containing its own Library and Archives, partaking in the creation of a historical narrative and the creation of a specific musical canon. It is an organization fully invested in the concept of *popular music*, and more specifically in the roots, branches, connections, attitudes and sounds of rock and roll. It is a gathering place (physical and virtual) that seeks to serve as a locus for *community*, for diverse and distinct voices to be heard, to converse, to share and to celebrate. It is a stage for *performance*, where practitioners share their art, discuss their process and interact with fans. It is above all an arena of *education* where rock and roll serve as an incubator/tool/convener for conversations about the sound, context and meaning of the music. I work at the Rock and Roll Hall of Fame (aka 'Rock Hall') in

Cleveland, Ohio, USA, where our mission is to 'engage, teach, and inspire through the power of rock and roll'.

That mission compels us to connect with every visitor and engage them as students. Some come specifically for a Rock Hall education programme on school field trips, as part of a college class or early years Head Start programme, on a tour (edutainment), or for scheduled adult programming.[1] Even more guests visit the museum on vacation or as part of a business trip, and are of all ages, often in multi-generational groups. It is important in this environment for us to ask, 'what does it mean to practise popular music education?' As a museum, the Rock Hall provides opportunities for visitors to interact with the subject of rock and roll in the form of artifacts and exhibits.[2] As an educational institution we can consider our work within developing academic fields such as public musicology or applied ethnomusicology (both variations on public history), or we can place it within a more traditional western Art music approach to music appreciation. We could discuss educational methods that use music as a cultural lens to investigate other academic subject areas such as math, science, language arts or history, or look at it from the perspective of performance practice and consider how an entire generation is learning to play music via a rock and roll oral tradition (think about *School of Rock*, Little Kids Rock, or the Rock Hall's own *The Garage* exhibit). When we ask what popular music education is at the Rock Hall, the answer is: all of those and more. It is all about *intersections* – between the many ways we understand our physical space and the museum's mission and the way we understand and interact with our students/audience, making sure that rock and roll is made relevant to them all. One key concept that allows us to navigate this, while also honouring the 'popular' in popular music, is *dialogue*.

Dialogue and memory

I started considering the importance of dialogue in popular music education when I began working at the Rock Hall in 2004. My co-worker Susan Oehler and I were tasked with reformulating the museum's education programmes. We took the knowledge base from our academic backgrounds and worked to connect it to the public experience of a museum. In 2009, we published a pedagogical philosophy of popular music in the *Journal of Popular Music Studies*, based on our rubric of 'Sound–Context–Meaning':

> Because popular music is cultural and often encompasses vernacular knowledge, we assert that popular music study can be a valuable component for sustaining arts education that is democratic and pragmatic in nature. [...] The programming we

create allows for people to bring both the knowledge and voices of their communities into dialogue with the historical narratives, authorities, and resources of the Rock and Roll Hall of Fame and Museum.

(Oehler and Hanley 2009: 9, 13)

Back then we were championing the value of popular music in education (both within music and more broadly) and suggesting a foundational approach based on concepts that worked in and out of the academy. In the remainder of this short essay, I want advocate for dialogue at the core of any pedagogy of popular music – that a true understanding and embrace of 'popular' music lies at the intersection of multiple conversations.

First conversation: The work in dialogue with history

Past, present and future all potentially exist in a work of music. It draws from the past: the works that have come before it, the story of the songwriter/performer/producer, the sounds of the music and cultural historical context at the time of creation. It lives in the present where it comes to life in a moment, within current events and musical styles – always moving forward – while also encountering its own history. A song projects itself into the future where it will one day be interpreted again, in a new context, by new ears and with a new understanding of the song's multiple and eventual 'present' moments. This is one aspect of what makes popular music so unique – the meaning of any song or album can and *will* change over time. The music itself has an experience, a *memory* and one or more larger contextual connections. This is at the core of the Sound–Context–Meaning pedagogical rubric – a method of listening to a song's sonic attributes, placing them in a context and examining the multiple meanings.

Second conversation: The work in dialogue with its creator

Popular music exists in dialogue with its creators. Songwriters, performers and producers frequently discuss their work and the creation process with music journalists, in public forms, in oral histories and more, including events at the Rock Hall.[3] Their stories contribute to our understanding of the genesis and authorial intent of a song, the songwriting process, and how an artist's relationship with a song changes over time. We can allow artists' voices to participate in the dialogue about the music. These conversations are an invaluable part of my own interaction with the study of popular music and my work as an educator. In a recent conversation with Mavis Staples during the 2019 Rock Hall Honors event honoring her life and work, Staples discussed her commitment to social justice that began during the 1950s with the Staple Singers and continues today in her solo records. She described how she views music as a tool, a delivery system for her message – and as such the difference between popular music and gospel is inconsequential if she can reach an audience:

> When I hear a song with a message that I think can help move the world forward, move us forward, make us happy, it's just better than anything. Music is better than anything. [...] If you sing from your heart, you'll reach the people, they'll feel you. What comes from the heart reaches the heart. When you sing from your heart, you'll get your message across.
>
> (Staples 2019: n.pag.)

Staples' words help us better understand her career and the impact her music continues to have, especially when put into dialogue with the other artists interviewed that week discussing her impact on their music including Valerie June, Taylor Goldsmith and Jackson Browne. These conversations are an invaluable resource when one examines the sounds of Staples' gospel, freedom songs, soul, disco, funk, pop and Americana music.

Third conversation: The work in dialogue with the audience

Any study of popular music needs to consider the audience, who allows us to better understand how a song is received, how meaning is constructed in diverse communities and why. Historical events and the words of the creator can define the 'meaning' of a work, but sometimes this can also happen on its own as a song travels from one community to the next, is received and re-appropriated by new audiences. Consider the case of Martha Reeves and the Vandellas' 1964 hit for Motown Records, 'Dancing in the Streets'. It was written by Marvin Gaye, William 'Mickey' Stevenson and Ivy Jo Hunter as a feel-good slow groove song, and later recorded as an up-tempo dance song by Reeves in two takes, as she described in a 1996 Hall of Fame interview at the Rock Hall: 'it's fun to dance in the streets [...] and I said can I sing it my way?' (Reeves 1996). The song took on an entirely new meaning during the civil rights protests across the United States in the coming years. 'Dancing in the Streets' became a message about protesting in the streets, for making sure the message of the movement spread. The original lyric that was about dancing became a clarion call to action: 'Calling out around the world, are you ready for a brand-new beat?'

Fourth conversation: The teacher in dialogue with the student (and vice versa, and beyond)

As educators, we must view students as engaged participants whose personal experiences serve vital roles in the transfer of knowledge. Paulo Freire describes this dialogic model of education in his seminal 1970 book *Pedagogy of the Oppressed* saying: 'The teacher is no longer merely the one-who-teaches, but one who is himself taught in dialogue with the students, who in turn while being taught also teach. They become jointly responsible for a process in which all grow' (Freire 1970: 53). Popular Music Education should always be a dialogue between educator, creator, audience and history. This creates a space for multiple forms of knowledge and for students to share personal stories. We embrace this model at the Rock Hall in all our programming by listening to students from early years to higher education and using their feedback to update our programmes, making connections to new artists that the students are listening to. In the course we teach at Cuyahoga Community College, students teach the final classes focusing on contemporary music while using the models of critical thinking we have laid out throughout the semester. This work becomes more powerful when we allow music they care about to come into dialogue with the history about which we teach them. In public programming, adult learners can bring their own life experiences, specific contextual moments or knowledge and even an understanding of how a song or artist may have been understood within a particular location at a specific time. As Freire says: 'Education is thus constantly remade in the praxis. In order to *be*, it must *become*' (Freire 1970: 57, orginal emphasis).

The power of popular music and education

At the Rock Hall, we equip students with tools to understand the intersections of music, lyrics, artifacts and the history of rock and roll while allowing them to apply their *own* knowledge. This is very different from what Freire calls the traditional *banking* model of education where the educator pours a predetermined history into the student to accept and memorize. The banking version of popular music history, and specifically rock and roll history, typically resorts to the facts, dates, and 'important' artists (which almost always defaults to Elvis, the Beatles, Zeppelin, etc.). But teaching popular music using dialogue positions the facts of rock and roll as only one part of the equation. The goal is to help students understand *what* they hear, which is very different from telling them the *right way* to hear. The educators at the Rock Hall are always students. We learn how a song/artist can be understood in a new light, by a new set of students, how to teach

9

that music moving forward and how we can place it into our ever-evolving narrative about rock and roll. The history of rock and roll is always changing so that forgotten stories can be reclaimed (Sister Rosetta Tharpe), established stories can be reframed (Queen and Freddie Mercury), and new art can reexamine the old (John Legend performing Bill Withers' music). The key in dialogue is to make sure we listen – that the music we discuss is also the music that connects to the audience, their generation, their tastes and especially their story.

NOTES

1. Programmes such as the college class we teach in connection with Cuyahoga Community College and the Head Start based Toddler Rock programme are extended engagements over an entire semester. We also reach hundreds of thousands more via our online offerings and our digital learning platform Rock Hall EDU. To learn more about the Rock Hall's onsite and online programming, see https://www.rockhall.com/education. Accessed 19 January 2022.
2. I've discussed this topic in detail in Hanley and Metz 2020.
3. The Rock Hall makes video and audio of interviews, performances and events available at the Library and Archives: https://library.rockhall.com/home. Accessed 19 January 2022.

REFERENCES

Freire, Paulo (1970), *Pedagogy of the Oppressed*, London: Penguin Press.

Hanley, Jason and Metz, Kathryn (2020), 'Scenes from a music museum: The piano man's notebooks in the Rock and Roll Hall of Fame', in R. Banagale and J. Duchan (eds), *We Didn't Start the Fire: Billy Joel and Popular Music Studies*, Lanham: Lexington Books.

Oehler, Susan and Hanley, Jason (2009), 'Perspectives of popular music pedagogy in practice: An introduction', *Journal of Popular Music Studies*, 21:1, pp. 2–19.

Reeves, Martha (1996), 'Hall of Fame Series – Martha Reeves on "Dancing in the Street" (June 1996)', YouTube, https://www.youtube.com/watch?v=zvGmu5T9ocs. Accessed 28 April 2022.

Staples, Mavis (2019), interview with the Rock and Roll Hall of Fame, Rock Hall Honors, 20 September.

2

Learning to be Active:
The Formative Power of Music as
a Catalyst for Political Activism

Stuart Moir

Stuart Moir is a bicentennial education fellow at Moray House School of Education and Sport, University of Edinburgh, where he teaches on the community education programmes.

This chapter draws attention to the transformative power of music in helping people learn about democracy and supporting their development as active and critical citizens. Writing from a Scottish context, but with international relevance, the author challenges all educators to recognize we are not neutral in the face of injustice.

Introduction

Over the last 40 years, the discourse about the purpose of education has shifted from an emphasis on *'learning to be'*, to *'learning to earn'* (Biesta 2006: 172, original emphasis). For Woodford (2008), popular music education is no exception. This increasingly exclusive emphasis on the development of 'homo economicus' for employability as the key outcome has a profound effect across education and in particular on our students. It positions them as self-seeking 'lone wolves' (Walker 2012), primarily valorized for their role as producers and consumers. Ultimately, this approach reinforces the neoliberal status quo, with all its inherent injustices and inequalities, as education becomes *'adaptive rather than transformative'* (Walker 2012: 386, original emphasis), leading to the corrosion of our students' character (Sennett 1999).

As educators, we should remember we are not neutral, even if we try to be. In our work, despite the range and complexity of our approaches to the learning encounters with students, as a final outcome we continually face what Freire (1985) would assert, is ultimately a binary choice between working towards the adaptive or transformative purposes of education. Therefore, as the chorus of the song made famous by Pete Seeger (Seeger 1998) asks, which side are you on? Popular music educators could just work with their students to focus on developing their performance skills and musical knowledge to make them industry ready and employable. This may provide individual benefit, but ultimately is adaptive. Or, they can still do this, but at the same time, use music as a medium to engage their students in a critical dialogue about the 'pubic issues' in society and help them think of better ways to organize it, focused on democracy and social justice, thus promoting citizenship and activity in civic and political affairs as well as employability. This is the choice I face as an adult and community educator,[1] yet this is just as pressing and crucial for popular music educators as education always has a wider social and democratic purpose beyond just an individual's economic utility, important though that is. For example, Jackson (2009) argues that there is a powerful pedagogical relationship between music and political activity.

Political socialization

The sustainability of any democratic polity relies on the active participation of its citizens in civic and political affairs. Therefore, if we value democracy, being clear about how people become active participants is important and the concept of political socialization is used to explain how people become politically active (Neundorf and Smets 2017). It is the mainly informal social learning process, usually situated in young peoples' formative life experiences, which results from their interactions with a range of socializing agents such as family background, schooling, peer relationships or mass media. Yet music is overlooked and so largely absent from most of the literature on political socialization (Jackson 2009).

Nevertheless, others recognize that the transformative role music can play in people's lives. Music (including song lyrics) can scaffold people's political learning, influence their identity formation and raise their critical awareness of issues, offering new perspectives to help them make sense of their lived experiences (Eyerman and Jamison 1998; DeNora 2010). Yet, music's transformative power should not be a surprise. Music involves feelings and emotions connecting people to ideas and beliefs shared by wider social movements. It is a combination of all of these factors that help some people develop political beliefs and become active.

Young people and their engagement with music

The data discussed in this chapter are drawn from my doctoral study (Moir 2020). I conducted interviews with people between 19 and 27 years old, who were already critically conscious citizens committed to social justice and active in the Communist, Labour or trade union movement in Scotland. For the two activists discussed in this chapter, music was a vital socializing agent. Their names are pseudonyms and I have presented their words in the Scots dialect they spoke in.

Harry cites music as a significant socializing agent, but his family background helped him develop key values which became important in his political development:

> **Stuart:** But would you be interested in things like fairness and equality and injustice?
>
> **Harry:** Oh aye, well ... very vague notions o' equality, I wanted everybody tae be okay and do well and have access to opportunity ... I think that's obviously, in terms o' how they've rubbed off on me, that's impacted my values, the idea that you treat people wi' fairness. I'd definitely say that was instilled by my family, tae treat people how you'd like tae be treated.
>
> (cited in Moir 2020: 154)

The result of this enculturation process on Harry's political identity was that he became 'vaguely left wing [...] wanted the best for everybody'. A link can be made between his developing sense of values and political identity, and the music he became interested in – popular Irish Republican or rebel songs associated with his football team, Glasgow Celtic. However, this genre of musical expression is controversial, particularly in the context of Scottish football, as it is associated with sectarianism in the wider Scottish society between Catholic and Protestant communities.

Harry recognizes the sectarian nature of some of these songs, as he acknowledges; '*I make a distinction between Irish rebel tunes and the sorta, the bigoted ones*' (cited in Moir 2020: 154, orginal emphasis). Yet, many of the songs Harry listened to and that developed his political awareness depict the history of the Irish people and their relationship and struggles with the United Kingdom. These songs draw on and deal with themes such as injustice, inequality, anti-oppression, anti-colonialism, sedition and the struggle for freedom. The following quotation

13

both hints at his developing intellectual curiosity and highlights the impact that this music had on his political socialization:

> a lot of the tunes I like just had a lot o' history behind it and I liked to read about history and I read about the history of the IRA, and I read the history about the troubles. The impact that the British Empire had had across the world. And that, towards the later stages crystallised my view o' imperialism and crystallised my view o' how we're perceived in the world and again how the class differences and ... that really, really sorta opened things up tae me.
>
> (cited in Moir 2020: 155)

Harry's experience is representative of some of the activists I studied. Harry's experience and encounters with music help to illustrate how different socializing agents can interact with music to enhance political socialization. In particular, the family background of all will have made them more likely to be open to the awareness raising possibilities of some politically informed music.

Another young activist's experience shows that if a politically nurturing family environment is not present, then music can be a crucial and primary source of political socialization. Freddy's family background played no part in his socialization. Music was the crucial factor for him. His introduction to music was the result of the peer relationships he developed at school:

> [Y]ou know I grew up with them [his peers] so to speak and so what's quite relevant here is not so much their personal political leanings but actually strangely enough the music they were listening to. So, they were the only ones in our school that were listening to a type of music called grime rap, which obviously I got into as well.
>
> (cited in Moir 2020: 156)

One of the rappers important in Freddy's politicization was Akala (real name Kingslee James Daley), a male British rapper, poet and political activist. Freddy explains:

> Akala raps quite a lot about Malcolm X and his influence on him. So eventually I started to read Malcolm X and I think that was the first ever politically active writings that I started to read, so I think that was really the start of my political awakening so to speak.
>
> I went to go on, about 12, 13 I think, to start looking more at the Black Panther party and then Marxism, Leninism and stuff like that, and you know that's eventually how I got into reading Marx. [...] 'cause I think I was trying to learn just as much as possible at this time ... So I was looking at that and obviously from reading

Malcolm X, Marxist books were right up on my list [...] the rest is history so to speak, I'm a Communist now.

(cited in Moir 2020: 156)

For these young people, the themes and ideas portrayed in the lyrics of the songs they listened to stimulated their intellectual curiosity and for some inspired an autodidactic process. The music acted like a gateway to the development of their political awareness. They moved from just listening to the music, to being interested in studying what the music introduced them to.

Conclusion

As educators, our work with students can either lead them to adapt to the way things are or encourage them to question and look for alternatives that strengthen democracy and advance social justice. As Woodward (2019) argues, music and music education are powerful tools to develop in students the dispositions essential to democratic citizenship. For the young people discussed in this chapter, music was a vital means of political socialization. They moved from just listening to music, to a deeper hermeneutical engagement with it. The political awareness of these activists was developed by listening to music, and it helped them, 'read the world' (Freire 1985), enabling them to connect their own lived experiences and material conditions with wider political and social movements for social justice. In the process, they became critically conscious, engaged citizens willing to become active in the struggle to make our society more socially just. For these young people, this process was exclusively peer- and self-directed, without the involvement of popular music educators. For the benefit of democracy, popular music educators need to recognize and assert the power the music has in helping people become politically active and in promoting awareness of alternative ways of seeing and acting. This will help their students critically examine mainstream music culture and question its tight relationship to market and consumer rationality (Van Heertun 2010), and thus contribute to challenging the injustice and inequalities that characterize contemporary market-based capitalist societies.

NOTE

1. I am not a musician nor a popular music educator. Before working in academia, I worked as community educator and I now work in a school of education on a professional preservice degree programme for those wishing to enter the field of community education.

REFERENCES

Biesta, Gert (2006), 'What's the point of lifelong learning if lifelong learning has no point? On the democratic deficit of policies for lifelong learning', *European Educational Research Journal*, 5:3&4, pp. 169–80.

DeNora, Tia (2010), *After Adorno: Rethinking Music Sociology*, Cambridge: Cambridge University Press.

Eyerman, Ron and Jamison, Andrew (1998), *Music and Social Movements: Mobilizing Traditions in the Twentieth Century*, Cambridge: Cambridge University Press.

Freire, Paulo (1985), *The Politics of Education: Culture, Power and Liberation*, London: Bergin & Garvey.

Jackson, David (2009), *Entertainment and Politics: The Influence of Pop Culture on Young Adult Political Socialization*, New York: Peter Lang Publishing.

Moir, Stuart (2020), 'How did young left wing political activists learn to become active and critical citizens', EdD thesis, Edinburgh: University of Edinburgh, https://era.ed.ac.uk/handle/1842/37112. Accessed 28 April 2022.

Neundorf, Anja and Smets, Kaat (2017), 'Political socialization and the making of citizens', in *Oxford Handbooks Online*, Oxford: Oxford University Press, https://doi.org/10.1093/oxfordhb/9780199935307.013.98. Accessed 28 April 2022.

Seeger, Pete (1998), 'Which Side Are You On?', *If I had a Hammer: Songs of hope and Struggle* [SF CD 40096], Washington DC: Smithsonian Folkways Recordings.

Sennett, Richard (1999), *The Corrosion of Character: The Personal Consequences of Work in the New Capitalism*, London: W.M. Norton & Company.

Van Heertun, Richard (2010), 'Empowering education: Freire, cynicism and the pedagogy of action', in *Revolutionizing Pedagogy*, New York: Palgrave Macmillan, pp. 211–34.

Walker, Melanie (2012), 'A capital or capabilities education narrative in a world of staggering inequalities', *International Journal of Educational Development*, 32, pp. 384–93.

Woodford, Paul (2008), 'Fear and loathing in music education? Beyond democracy and music education', *Action, Criticism, and Theory for Music Education*, 7:1, pp. 105–38.

3

Mariachi Master-Apprentice Program: *Familia* During the COVID-19 Pandemic

Sergio Alonso

Sergio Alonso is a high school and community music educator in San Fernando, California, USA, where he teaches mariachi music.

This article describes how Mexican American students from a northeast San Fernando Valley, California community music education programme created a virtual mariachi concert amidst surging COVID-19 cases. Programme instructor and community member, the author documents how communal familism among mariachi musicians helped foster togetherness and unity in the face of adversity.

Framed against the backdrop of a global pandemic, we draw on the collective strength of *familia* ('family)' to transform challenge into opportunity. In doing so, we reveal the immeasurable degree of student initiative, fortitude and agency.

After twenty years of serving the San Fernando community, the Mariachi Master Apprentice Program (MMAP) temporarily ceased operations in spring 2020 as COVID-19 began to spread throughout California. State public health officials implemented legislation prohibiting mass gatherings, and after-school educational programmes halted in-person instruction. Although MMAP staff resumed classes through a fully distanced model, they cancelled all live public performances. In lieu of in-person activities, MMAP students created a virtual concert[1] to celebrate MMAP's twentieth anniversary. MMAP's instructional team called on *familia* to help support this ambitious endeavor.

For people of Mexican ancestry, *familia* can serve as a resource of support when facing challenges (Hipolito-Delgado 2018). Among Mexican American adolescents, *familismo* ('familism') is a source of inspiration during adversity and can help bolster resiliency (Morgan Consoli and Llamas 2013). Hipolito-Delgado

(2018) maintained that in Mexican culture, *familia* is often extended to include grandparents, aunts, uncles, cousins and close family friends. I posit that the notion of *familia* may broaden to include a community of practitioners who express a shared desire for solidarity, strength and solace during times of uncertainty. This chapter draws on testimonials to illustrate how *familia* may support Mexican American musicians adversely impacted by COVID-19. By examining MMAP's twentieth-anniversary virtual concert, I aim to demonstrate how recontextualized mariachi education cultivates a sense of communal *familismo* among students.

Creating a virtual community

The city of San Fernando is located within the northeast San Fernando Valley region of Los Angeles County, California. Situated within this historically underserved community of 93.2 per cent Latinx ancestry, the MMAP operates under the city's Recreation and Community Services Department. Established in 2001, MMAP unites members of the highly celebrated Mariachi Los Camperos with community youth to study the popular mariachi music forms. Togetherness is foundational to MMAP pedagogy and consistent with the philosophy of programme co-founder, the late mariachi pioneer Natividad 'Nati' Cano. A powerful force in shaping mariachi music and ardent advocate of mariachi education, Cano founded Mariachi Los Camperos in 1961, an institution widely regarded as one of the world's finest mariachi ensembles (Jaquez 2000). In discussing Cano's teaching method, Rodriguez (2006) articulated that, instead of dividing students into separate instrument groups, Cano believed in keeping everyone together.

Drawing on Cano's vision, Campero facilitators sought to design an online learning project that conveyed an atmosphere of togetherness. The preconcert narrative presented this objective: 'This presentation reflects our desire to express music, culture, and community together, even when we can't be! This grassroots project was conducted entirely at a distance' (Mariachi Tesoro de San Fernando 2020). Showcasing MMAP's advanced ensemble, Mariachi Tesoro de San Fernando, the virtual concert consisted of three primary components: (1) multimedia recordings, (2) thematic community performance and (3) alumni testimonials. Student digital recordings required the use of various computer software and phone applications. MMAP facilitators utilized Finale notation software to arrange music and create digital guide tracks. In addition, facilitators conducted bi-weekly rehearsals via Zoom and employed the *BAND* mobile application to exchange documents and multimedia. Furthermore, students utilized a variety of multimedia recording applications to produce their individual audio and video files. Production software also included Wondershare Filmora and Final Cut Pro video editing software, and Pro Tools digital audio workstation.

Creating a sense of community involved placing students at preselected historical markers within San Fernando. Mariachi Tesoro instrumentalists individually recorded their videos on location to create various performance themes. The contextual backdrops included:

- Las Palmas Park Mural: The mural depicts the history of San Fernando.
- Cesar E. Chavez Memorial Park: The Cesar Chavez Memorial is the nation's first monument that celebrates the life of the American Civil Rights Leader.
- Misión San Fernando Rey de España: The San Fernando Mission is the namesake of the city of San Fernando.
- Commercial Landscape: Many local businesses have served San Fernando for generations and continue to form part of our community's commercial identity.
- Lopez Adobe: The Lopez Adobe is one of the oldest private residences in the San Fernando Valley.
- Historic Schools of the Los Angeles Unified School District: San Fernando Middle School and Morningside Elementary School are two of the oldest school buildings in the LAUSD.
- San Fernando Gateways: The gateways mark the entryways to the city of San Fernando (Mariachi Tesoro de San Fernando 2020).

Rounding out the twentieth-anniversary celebration were former students who shared personal stories. Many alumni are university graduates who lead successful careers across diverse professions. MMAP alumni also perform within the ranks of some of the world's most revered mariachi ensembles, including Mariachi Los Camperos, Mariachi Sol de Mexico and Mariachi Reyna de Los Angeles. In view of the fact that Mexican American high school students from this underrepresented sector of Los Angeles County often do not continue to higher education and the arts, alumni role models helped to inspire MMAP students and nurture cross-generational unity.

The influence of familia and community

For many Latinx people, collectivism and *familismo* play an essential role in guiding socialization practices (Ruiz 2005). Latinxes often view their achievements as being dependent on the outcome of others. As such, individuals grow within the context of their relationships. Rooted in collectivist orientation, Mexican-origin families embrace interdependence and group collaboration (Caldera et al. 2014).

Mexican American community members also value the notion of *familismo*: the importance of family unity, togetherness and well-being. Virtual concert students and alumni participants revealed the importance of *familia* on their desire to study and perform mariachi music. Jose, a Mariachi Tesoro *vihuela* player, expressed how his parents and grandparents influenced him:

> The shaping of my musical identity at my home has a great impact on why I play mariachi music. Mariachi music has always been played in my house. The support provided from my parents and my grandparents are a big influence in playing mariachi music.
>
> (Castillo 2021: n.pag.)

Romina, an alumna and violinist for Mariachi Reyna de Los Angeles, explained how mariachi music was part of her everyday home life:

> I truly believe they fostered my love for music at home. I grew up listening to trio and mariachi music every day at home. Every day my mom and dad played music for about an hour while they prepared dinner, and I would hear them sing along to some of my now favorite songs.
>
> (Huerta 2021: n.pag.)

Students also described how community impacted their musical interests. Jorge, Jose's older brother and Mariachi Tesoro trumpetist, spoke of his experience as a Latino community member:

> My community definitely has had an impact on my identity as a Latino. In the San Fernando Valley, I see many Hispanic people, and it makes me feel close and connected to my people and culture. Since I was young, I had the desire to play the trumpet, and the first genre I were to ever play was mariachi.
>
> (Castillo 2021: n.pag.)

Romina expressed how the mariachi community helped shape her multidimensional identity:

> I'm a daughter of Mexican immigrants, so I identify as a Mexican American woman. I often consider myself more 'Mexican' than American, and mariachi has played a huge part in that. Growing up in a mariachi community allowed me to really explore and feel proud of my Mexican roots and traditions. I also identify as a feminist, and I believe that mariachi has played a role in that too.
>
> (Huerta 2021: n.pag.)

Testimonials illustrate the significance of *familia* and community on ethnic and musical identity. Through their shared beliefs and values, mariachi musicians form mutually dependent relationships and create a sense of *familia* among their community of practitioners; this communal *familismo* serves as a source of strength when faced with adversity.

Strength in communal familismo

Analytical studies illustrate the county-level disparities among racial/ethnic groups in COVID-19 cases and deaths in the United States (Khanijahani 2020). Findings conclude that COVID-19 cases and deaths were disproportionately higher in Latino and Black neighbourhoods. Among those infected in Los Angeles County, Latinx's were the most negatively impacted ethnic community with over 60 percent of the confirmed cases and 50 per cent of the total deaths (County of Los Angeles Public Health 2020). Four Latino-predominant cities within the northeast San Fernando Valley were among the top 25 communities in the county with the highest COVID-19 rates.

The pandemic ravaged many Mexican American families in San Fernando, and the MMAP *familia* did not go unscathed. Jose and Jorge lost their grandfather, and Romina lost both her grandmother and mother to COVID-19. For Jose, Jorge, and Romina, coping with loss entailed reflecting on how mariachi music helped form emotional and spiritual bonds between them and their loved ones. Jorge explained how mariachi took on new meaning:

> My *abuelo* [grandfather] passing away has made a huge impact on my life and what I do. It has made me appreciate mariachi even more as I feel I am motivated by my abuelo to continue on and play for him.
>
> (Castillo 2021: n.pag.)

Romina expressed her difficulties in working with COVID-19-positive patients and as a professional mariachi musician:

> I began working full time as a speech-language pathologist at a rehab hospital. Around the same time I started that job, my mom contracted COVID. She passed away three weeks later. I am now working with COVID-positive patients, and it is so difficult at times because it is so personal. I also could not play mariachi music for two months after my mom passed; it reminded me too much of her.
>
> (Huerta 2021: n.pag.)

Dedicated to students' family members who lost their lives to COVID-19 during the making of the project, the 70-minute virtual concert premiered on 17 December 2020 (Mariachi Tesoro de San Fernando 2020) amidst a surging COVID-19 outbreak. Notwithstanding the personal hardships and educational challenges resulting from the pandemic, MMAP students individually carried out the online learning project and collectively created a space of togetherness. Mariachi music students' cultural concept of *familia* and community within the context of adversity served to create a fellowship founded on interconnectedness, unity, mutual dependency, and well-being, here termed *communal familismo*.

NOTE

1. The concert is available online: https://www.youtube.com/watch?v=IoPOKkZnZQY&t=3s. Accessed 28 April 2022.

REFERENCES

Caldera, Yvonne M., Velez-Gomez, Paulina and Lindsey, Eric W. (2014), 'Who are Mexican Americans? An overview of history, immigration, and cultural values', in Y. M. Caldera and E. Lindsey (eds), *Mexican American Children and Families: Multidisciplinary Perspectives*, London: Routledge, pp. 3–12, https://doi.org/10.4324/9781315814612. Accessed 14 March 2022.

Castillo, Jorge (2021), email to author, 1 January.

Castillo, Jose (2021), email to author, 1 January.

County of Los Angeles Public Health (2020), 'COVID-19 locations & demographics', http://publichealth.lacounty.gov/media/Coronavirus/. Accessed 14 March 2022.

Hipolito-Delgado, Carlos P. (2018), '*Cultura y familia*: Strengthening Mexican heritage families', in P. Arredondo (ed.), *Latinx Immigrants: International and Cultural Psychology*, Cham: Springer, pp. 147–67, https://doi.org/10.1007/978-3-319-95738-89. Accessed 14 March 2022.

Huerta, Romina (2021), email to author, 10 January.

Jaquez, Cándida Frances (2000), '*Cantando de ayer* (singing of yesterday): Performing history, ethnic identity, and traditionalism in United States-based urban mariachi (Publication No. 9963818)', ProQuest dissertations and thesis, Ann Arbor, MI, USA: University of Michigan.

Khanijahani, Ahmad (2020), 'Racial, ethnic, and socioeconomic disparities in confirmed COVID-19 cases and deaths in the United States: A county-level analysis as of November 2020', *Ethnicity and Health*, https://doi.org/10.1080/13557858.2020.1853067. Accessed 14 March 2022.

Mariachi Tesoro de San Fernando (2020), '20th Anniversary virtual concert', 17 December, 2020, YouTube, https://www.youtube.com/watch?v=IoPOKkZnZQY&t=3s. Accessed 11 March 2022.

Morgan Consoli, Melissa L. and Llamas, Jasmin D. (2013), 'The relationship between Mexican American cultural values and resilience among Mexican American college students: A mixed methods study', *Journal of Counseling Psychology*, 50, pp. 617–24, https://doi.org/10.1037/a0033998. Accessed 11 March 2022.

Rodriguez, Russell C. (2006), 'Cultural production, legitimation, and the politics of aesthetics: Mariachi transmission, practice, and performance in the United States (Publication No. 3219648)', ProQuest dissertations and thesis, Santa Cruz: University of California.

Ruiz, Elizabth (2005), 'Hispanic culture and relational cultural theory', *Journal of Creativity in Mental Health*, 1:2 pp. 33–55, https://doi.org/10.1300/J456v01n0105. Accessed 11 March 2022.

4

People and Popular Music in an English Prison: Transforming Criminal Justice

Natalie Betts

Natalie Betts is a music and creative arts lecturer for Weston College. She teaches a non-accredited music course at Her Majesty's Prison and Young Offenders Institute Portland, England.

This chapter explores how music can be used within prison to give people access to a community to which they can add value, and asks whether transformative narratives from the music classroom be used to demand transformation in our wider society?

A criminal sentence is a judgement, a summative assessment of an individual's inability to follow the law. It is a marker that highlights anti-social behaviour and consequently leaves a person tagged with a statement of their past, rather than a means to their future. As a teacher working in prison, it is my responsibility to challenge this label and recognize that a criminal conviction does not define a person. Instead, a prison sentence can be used positively, as the start of a formative process of reflection to support meaningful transformation in a person's understanding and direction. Using popular music as a tool, practitioners in prison education can offer people opportunities for development. At the same time, the prison music educator can voice their experiences to highlight the requirement for a transformation in the ways in which wider society views criminal justice.

People in prison

As a demographic, people in prison exhibit multiple complex needs, disproportionate to the general population; with greater incidents of exclusion from school

(Prison Reform Trust 2019), higher prevalence of learning difficulties (Crabbe 2016), mental health problems and drug and alcohol addiction (Tyler et al. 2019). As the histories of many people in prison are characterized by disadvantage and marginalization (Baybutt et al. 2018), they are predisposed to social stigma; 'dehumanization, threat, aversion, and sometimes the depersonalization of others into stereotypic caricatures' (Dovidio et al. 2000: 1). Stigma can cause self-stigma whereby the stigmatized person internalizes prejudice and discrimination causing 'a redefinition of the self, based on negative characteristics recognized by society' (Bosco et al. 2018: 136). Notably, this can diminish a person's motivation and self-confidence to achieve (Corrigan et al. 2009).

I deliver a popular music course at Her Majesty's Prison and Young Offenders Institute (HMP/YOI) Portland on the south coast of England. The prison holds a population of up to 530 adult and young adult males. It is a resettlement facility, which provides people with opportunities to develop skills in order to gain employment on release. I have been a Music and Creative Arts lecturer at Portland for four years, working as a member of the education team. Before I started this role, I had never set foot in a prison. I had no idea what to expect. I found that the community of people that I was introduced to within the classrooms in prison was not dissimilar to any other group in society. HMP/YOI Portland's education department provides a positive place within the prison, characterized by respect and friendliness, used for socializing, learning and creativity, revealing the varied, extensive and often extraordinary talents and strengths of different people in the prison. Although the prison environment is an inherently cold, restrictive and often hostile place, an alternative narrative exists within the music classroom.

Popular music in prison

Since being in prison, I've been able to find my shine and rebuild my life. See, when I get out, I think it's time to change my grind [...] Since being in jail, I've had opportunities to better myself. And these opportunities I may not have had, if I was still in the community.

(see Note, PRISON – Spoken Word)[1]

My music course at Portland runs for four weeks, full-time, with groups of six people and two peer mentors, people in prison who assist with or lead classroom activities. The music course offers those in prison an environment where stigma is suspended; participants in the class are referred to by their names or as learners, teammates and musicians. Pro-social labelling aims to support the development of non-criminal behaviours and builds social capital as people in prison practice different identities (McNeill 2016), whilst counteracting the negative effects that criminal classification and stigma can have on a person's well-being, confidence and aspirations.

Music allows me to engage the different learners in my classroom. I practice inclusivity by replacing 'deterministic views of ability with a concept of transformability' (Florian and Spratt 2013: 124), that is, the understanding that every person has the potential to learn, regardless of learning difficulties or background. The responsibility for individual progression lies with the teacher who must alter their pedagogical approach (Loreman 2017). In contrast to other areas of the prison that are characterized by dynamics of control, authority and power, the music classroom allows learners in prison to experience an environment that supports their autonomy. Autonomy support is fulfilled when a learner in the classroom engages in a task that is meaningful to them, allowing them to adopt their own perspective which is valued by others, and gives the learner the opportunity of self-initiation, choice and exploration within the learning topics (Niemec and Ryan 2009). Learners are respected as self-determined people, qualified to make their own decisions, and my role is to work in equal dialogic relation to them. This means adopting language that is open and proleptic, '(giving advice, proffering possible solutions, using model verbs [may, would, could] [...]) [orientating] students towards possibility' (Vossoughi and Gutiérrez 2017: 157); encouraging the learners to feel confident to engage in transformative action.

I offer an unaccredited, personal, social and emotional development (PSED) course rather than delivering a route to a music qualification. This gives learners the opportunity to participate in popular music practices in a number of ways such as instrumental skills development, digital music production, songwriting, performance and/or recording. The critical approach to music education that I adopt rejects the 'the linear and elitist face of the music curriculum' and recognizes the value of learning that relates to 'the realities of individuals and communities in which it engages' (Schmidt 2005: 3, 4). Learners are given the freedom to explore any genre of popular music that they enjoy. They regularly engage in creating UK rap, grime and trap music to express their feelings and write socially and politically conscious lyrics. Ipsative assessment is used to address the discriminations of systematic assessment; individuals evaluate their own progress against personal targets rather than external standards (Fautley 2015).

Although the learners in my classroom have been socially excluded from their wider communities, popular music-making encourages the people in prison I work with to feel that they belong to a community that they can add value to. This is achieved through group songwriting and performance. Whilst each group member focusses on the independent element they bring to a performance, the interdependent nature of a unified music performance encourages interaction. Musical activity not only helps group members to experience the well-being benefits of social engagement and connection but also engages individuals in positive exchanges, allowing them to practice social awareness and pro-social identities. Autonomy-supportive relationships exist between the learners, operating on a level of mutual power. This helps individuals in the class to receive support from their peers that can stimulate transformation while providing opportunities for them to give encouragement back and nurture a social responsibility to others.

Transformation and criminal justice

The transformation of a learner in prison is inherently hard to prove. For this reason, I believe that prison educators should focus on the 'process rather than outcome' of transformative education (Behan 2014: 28). This will encourage them to continue to pave the way as leaders of social change and criminal justice, challenging outdated notions of punishment and retribution. I am also cautious that claims of transformative education in prison can assume that learners in prison need transformation (Ginsberg 2019). My suggestions therefore, are grounded in the knowledge that as a free educator I should avoid adopting a saviour mentality believing that all people in prison need or want to be transformed. Instead, I promote a transformative approach because the foremost goal of a prison educator 'must be not to change people in prison, but to change the landscape of the prison itself' (Karpowitz 2017: 12), by offering opportunities for self-determined transformation.

Whilst notions of transformation should continue to challenge and impact prison education in positive ways, there is also a necessity for practitioners in prison to voice the change that is essential in wider society. The criminal justice system extends way beyond the perimeter of the prison, the cells which the people in prison inhabit and the classrooms wherein prison educators work tirelessly to empower their learners. It is a system that encompasses every part of society; criminal justice is the responsibility of the community beyond the walls. What teaching popular music in prison demonstrates is that it is possible to create a community of care and development within the prison. If this can be achieved in a hostile environment, where resources are limited and people typically have complex histories, challenging day-to-day lives and an unknown future, we should be encouraged that we can make change within our wider communities too. There is a requirement for a transformation of understanding within our society that insists we have a shared responsibility for criminal justice.

NOTE

1. PRISON – Spoken Word

   Follow the link to listen to an audio recording of a learner who engaged in my music class in prison, along with other educational courses. He describes, through spoken word, what prison means to him and the opportunities it has given him. Recording available at: https://soundcloud.com/user-76427803/prison-spoken-word/s-LFdIG. Accessed 19 January 2022.

REFERENCES

Baybutt, Michelle, Dooris, Mark and Farrier, Alan (2018), 'Growing health in UK prison settings', *Health Promotion International*, 34:4, pp. 792–802.

Behan, Cormac (2014), 'Learning to escape: Prison education, rehabilitation and the potential for transformation', *Journal of Prison Education and Reentry*, 1:1, pp. 20–31.

Bosco, Nicolina, Giaccherini, Susanna, Petrini, Fausto, Castagnoli, Stefano and Meringolo, Patrizia (2018), 'Fighting stigma in the community: Bridging ties through social innovation interventions', in B. A. Cunningham and H. A. Cunningham (eds), *Deconstructing Stigma in Mental Health*, Hershey: IGI Global, pp. 133–68.

Corrigan, Patrick, Larson, Jonathon and Rüsch, Nicolas (2009), 'Self-stigma and the "why try" effect: Impact on life goals and evidence-based practices', *World Psychiatry*, 8, pp. 75–81.

Crabbe, James (2016), 'Education for offenders in prison', *Journal of Pedagogic Development*, 6:3, pp. 3–7.

Dovidio, John, Major, Brenda and Crocker, Jennifer (2000), 'Stigma: Introduction and overview', in T. F. Heatherton, R. E. Kleck, M. R. Hebl and J. G. Hull (eds), *The Social Psychology of Stigma*, New York: The Guildford Press, pp. 1–30.

Fautley, Martin (2010), *Assessment in Music Education*, Oxford: Oxford University Press.

Florian, Lani and Spratt, Jennifer (2013), 'Enacting inclusion: A framework for interrogating inclusive practice', *European Journal of Special Needs Education*, 28:2, pp. 119–35.

Ginsberg, Raphael (2019), 'The perils of transformation talk in higher education in prison', in R. Ginsberg (ed.), *Critical Perspectives on Teaching in Prison: Students and Instructors on Pedagogy Behind the Wall*, New York: Routledge, pp. 60–67.

Karpowitz, Daniel (2017), *College in Prison: Reading in an Age of Mass Incarceration*, New Jersey: Rutgers University Press.

Loreman, Tim (2017), 'Pedagogy for inclusive education', Oxford: *Oxford Research Encyclopedia of Education*, https://oxfordre.com/education/view/10.1093/acrefore/9780190264093.001.0001/acrefore-9780190264093-e-148?print=pdf. Accessed 10 June 2020.

McNeill, Fergus (2016), 'The fuel in the tank or the hole in the boat? Can sanctions support desistance?', in J. Shapland, S. Farrall and A. Bottoms (eds), *Global Perspectives on Desistance: Reviewing What we Know and Looking to the Future*, Oxon: Routledge, pp. 265–81.

Niemec, Christopher and Ryan, Richard (2009), 'Autonomy, competence, and relatedness in the classroom: Applying self-determination theory to educational practice', *Theory and Research in Education*, 7:2, pp. 133–44.

Schmidt, Patrick (2005), 'Music education as transformative practice: Creating new frameworks for learning music through a Freirian perspective', *Visions of Research in Music Education*, 6, pp. 1–14.

Tyler, Nichola, Miles, Helen, Karadag, Bessey and Rogers, Gemma (2019), 'An updated picture of the mental health needs of male and female prisoners in the UK: Prevalence, comorbidity, and gender differences', *Social Psychiatry and Psychiatric Epidemiology*, 54, pp. 1143–52.

Vossoughi, Shirin and Gutiérrez, Kris (2017), 'Critical pedagogy and sociocultural theory', in I. Esmonde and A. Booker (eds), *Power and Privilege in the Learning Sciences: Critical and Sociocultural Theories of Learning*, New York: Routledge, pp. 139–61.

5

Popular Music Pedagogy in
a United States Prison:
Lessons from a Western Rural Facility

Tiger Robison

Tiger Robison, Ph.D., is assistant professor of music education at the University of Wyoming. Tiger writes about classroom management and plays electric bass.

In this chapter, the author provides a personal reflection on the politics and pedagogy of creating music with prison inmates. He presents three lessons learned on visits to prison and touches on the transformative potential of music making in carceral institutions.

There is a saying in prison education that, 'once you know one facility, you know one facility', meaning that assumptions and generalizations across prisons are usually unwise. However, the construct of prison is uniquely human (compared with consequential exile or death in the animal kingdom), and they all involve to varying degrees isolation from loved ones and large amounts of time during which reflection is the only possible activity. Such conditions make for ripe opportunities to make sincere, original music in the popular music tradition, and that is exactly what goes on in the state penitentiary of one rural state in the western United States. The penitentiary has a full rock-band infrastructure thanks in large part to an inmate identified as 'James' based on his favourite musician James Hetfield of Metallica. His advocacy and persistence coupled with administrators who see value in prisoners' self-betterment have led to a facility that houses popular music pedagogy in a place that arguably needs it most.

The first visit

My first observation of the inside of the penitentiary was the lighting: bright, fluorescent and oppressive. Given safety concerns about some inmates and events that unfolded later, I realized its purpose after my first visit. There was a short reprieve from that lighting when James showed me the small storage room for the programme's instruments. Some instruments were in disrepair, but others were respectable Jackson guitars and basses, Randall amp heads and an electronic drum set matched with a speaker. We started jamming under the occasional watchful eye of a very professional staff member who clearly trusted James to a degree. After a short while, we paused for a moment as we switched instruments and I listened to the circumstances of his life. It is worth noting that prisoners pay all the money they have as fines for going to prison and are generally very busy working full-time jobs at far under minimum wage to pay reparations each month to parties they have been convicted of harming. They then purchase their own hygiene products with the remainder of their wages. I remember thinking that those conditions make James' advocacy for this programme all the more impressive. Another staff member then politely interrupted us, 'There's been an incident. Mr. Robison, this man [guard] will escort you out.'

'No band rehearsal tonight?' James asked.

'No, sir', she replied.

'Yes, ma'am. I understand', James said as he waved a brief goodbye to me and set down his guitar.

I sidestepped a pool of blood on the way out of the facility. As soon as I left penitentiary grounds in my car, I pulled over to the side of the road and wrote down my impressions. In particular, I wrote about how much I wanted to return to the facility and how much James had already taught me in my short time there. I texted my colleague who arranged the visit, 'Just left the penitentiary, I'm absolutely hooked, thank you so much for the introduction'. 'I'm so glad!' she replied. Then, my instinct was and still is to share James' wisdom (through my admitted biases) with music education stakeholders while simultaneously advocating for popular music education programmes in prisons. This short chapter is my first step in a line of publications towards those aims.

The second visit

'Hey, you're back!' James said two weeks later when I arrived in the gym for my second visit. 'He didn't think you'd be back', said James while pointing to the respectful staff member, 'but I knew you'd be back. That stuff doesn't happen often, generally frowned upon since we all have to go into lockdown, but it does happen. That one was particularly brutal'.

I replied, 'Good to see you, man. What are you working on?'

'I wrote a song for my mom', James said.

'Sweet, let's get to it!' I said, and we were off to the instrumental storage room. As a musician, I was drawn to James' careful song construction and innate ability to match chords and articulations with his lyrical content. As a researcher, and similar to our first visit, I was drawn to every sentence James uttered in his casual way because they were all gold for any social science researcher, yet they were his day-to-day habits of speaking. The juxtaposition still makes me smile.

The lessons

The following lessons are my interpretations of James' candid remarks, which I believe will resonate with stakeholders in popular music pedagogy.

Ambition and persistence rule the day. If James had stopped trying to better the rock band programme after its modest start, he would not have the impact on his fellow inmates and the outside world (including me) that he has today. He is masterful at writing to manufacturers for instruments or replacement parts, writing to non-profits for any kind of support, making reasoned arguments for what he wants (e.g. advocating for steel strings on guitars was a prolonged effort because of the potential security issue), and including others in his efforts. The lesson here for popular music educators is clear.

Many people reading this text are in positions of power compared to James, and that includes me. Respectfully, James' ambition and persistence for music education as he knows it far outweigh that of any other educator I know. If we coupled our collective power with James' level of persistence, we could multiply our impact ten-fold. I will never forget the look on James' face when I donated some older music textbooks to the penitentiary library during my second visit. I will be chasing that feeling and trying to match James' level of ambition for the rest of my career.

'Play the Game' if doing so helps people. James will often remark about 'playing the game' to get what he needs to make music and mentor younger inmates. I see similarities between his advocacy efforts and those of music educators more broadly. He knows better than most people that the ultimate music advocacy is its inherent value. However, he is also very skilled at marketing the non-musical benefits of music making in a correctional setting (e.g. lower amounts of violent incidents, artistic products that reflect well on the prison, efficient use of staff member time through musical activities that occupy more inmates, and many more examples). James is comfortable posing for a photo opportunity if it means he can 'put a guitar in

another kid's hand, so he stops breaking the sprinkler heads and getting in trouble'. He concedes that advocating for the music programme is 'exhausting' when employing the non-musical benefits, but that he needs to 'speak their [prison administrators'] language'. James' lesson is nuanced for popular music educators in my view.

There is value in extolling the virtues of music for music's sake, and that those parties who do not understand it need to do so before any meaningful change happens. For example, it is a tried and true practice to include sceptical school administrators in artistic performances and/or gather testimonials from respected community members who are enlightened on the topic in order to communicate the significance of our sonic art to those in power. However, when faced with the choice of employing solely these tactics and possibly receiving no support, or marketing the non-musical values of music education and possibly receiving support, the value of the former approach becomes less clear. Wherever one's philosophy on the issue is, at a bare minimum, James' tactics of having multiple advocacy strategies for a diversity of audiences is a wise practice and one from which we can all learn.

Be grateful for the intrinsic value of music and self discovery. 'I don't really need money if I have music', was one of the first golden sentences James uttered on my second visit. He continued, 'I mean especially in my context now, but that was true before all this [prison].' To hear James talk about music in this way continues to be refreshing to me and I imagine to any music educators reading this. Music education is not an easy field nor business. We can become susceptible to the pressures of our profession and lose sight of why we committed our professional and/or personal lives to this pursuit. However, those sentiments are the farthest they ever are from my mind when I hear James talk about how music helps him cope with his time. James makes the most of the small amount of time he is afforded to enter musical introspection, under the close but respectful and professional supervision of the facility employees. Those of us not in that situation could benefit from the reminder that our opportunities to make music may be fleeting and that we should take advantage of any chance to do so.

Concluding thoughts

I hope that this short chapter has encapsulated just a few of the lessons James and other prisoners have to offer the greater public about music making. Anyone reading this is always welcome to contact me at Tiger.Robison@uwyo.edu, but there are organizations that have been helping make the arts in prisons more widespread for a long time. Consider contacting Jail Guitar Doors (https://www.jailguitardoors.org/), the Justice Arts Coalition (https://thejusticeartscoalition.org/music/), or like-minded organizations if these lessons or stories have piqued your curiosity.

6

Developing a Certifiable and Relevant Popular Music Curriculum for Early School-Leavers in Ireland

Martin Ryan

Martin Ryan is a music educator from Limerick, Ireland who specializes in teaching popular music through technology. He is a doctoral student of music education at Kent State University.

In this chapter, the author discusses the challenges, pitfalls and successes of developing a certified popular music education course aimed at early school leavers in Co. Clare, Ireland.

The guitar, touring and teaching

My path to becoming a musician began at 10, when a brief but negative first experience with a musical instrument shaped my life profoundly. In 2001, a year in which the Irish charts were filled with guitar-based music by bands including The Strokes, Slipknot, Blink 182 and Ash, I asked my father to teach me guitar. He sat me down at the kitchen table, placed a very large Italian acoustic guitar in my lap and opened a book entitled *10 Traditional Irish Folk Ballads*. I hated everything about that experience and assumed music was not for me. It was not until five years later, once internet access was established in our household that I picked the guitar up again, this time armed with the ability to seek out and learn the type of music that I enjoyed. The fact that I was able to 'teach myself' at a pace that suited me, and more importantly, in a way that catered to my own musical interests, gave me a feeling of self-expression I had never experienced before. Shortly thereafter, I started my first band and began touring the country exploring my true passion. This path of chasing self-expression through the guitar and song-writing has brought me to the present day, where I have released four albums and toured the world a number of times while also working every position imaginable within the music industry. These experiences have also led me to teach an array of programmes with an organization called Music Generation.

Music Generation is a nationwide Irish non-profit music education initiative created by U2, designed to deliver accessible, creative and inclusive music programmes throughout Ireland (Flynn & Johnston 2016: 11). These programmes are based around a popular music pedagogy which aims to support children and young people to express themselves in whatever form they desire, whether writing and performing songs, playing an instrument, practising as part of an orchestra or jamming with a band. There are currently 25 Music Generation regional areas across Ireland. Whilst these are founded on the same shared values, each area has the flexibility required to imagine and create programmes that respond to local community needs.

I currently work with Music Generation Clare. The programmes I have worked on with Music Generation Clare include instrument, songwriting and music technology lessons. The content and structure of these classes vary dramatically but the primary focus of each lesson is on students' personal creative goals. These could be as simple as playing an instrument along with their favourite track and finding other similar music, or as complex as writing, recording and releasing their debut album with ambitions of navigating the music industry as a professional. I value this approach to music education and it takes me back to the reason my first musical experience with those ten traditional Irish folk ballads was a negative one; my own musical interests and creative goals were not recognized at the time.

After three years of teaching with Music Generation in County Clare, I was assigned the position of lead Youthreach tutor. Youthreach is a public academic programme for students (typically ages 15–18) who have left school early without any qualifications. It provides these students with basic education, personal development skills, vocational training and work experience. Up until this point, Music Generation Clare has provided creative workshops that have strictly omitted any elements of the school music curriculum. All Music Generation work had acted as alternative and additional music programmes within public schools to enrich students' lives. This has led to a difficult situation where school administration boards and governing bodies have struggled to understand the importance and validity of a creative programme where students' self-expression and personal development are the primary foci. In an effort to bridge the gap between what school administration deems of sufficient value to a students' school programmes and modern day musical interests of students in County Clare, I was tasked with developing Music Generation Clare's first certified programme that would be delivered in Youthreach centres throughout the county.

Towards certification

In the context of the Irish education system, Music Generation and creative musical expression, in general, have been viewed as extra-curricular. At the request of the Education Training Board (the governing body of the Irish schooling system), Music Generation Clare was tasked with developing a certified programme in Youthreach centres in County Clare which was a new endeavour for the organization. Certification is required to give students enough official academic credit to progress with their educational journeys after they leave Youthreach. For Music Generation to receive teaching hours in Youthreach classrooms and to justify its importance within the education system, a certified Level 3 QQI (Quality & Qualifications Ireland) music appreciation programme was to be developed. In Ireland, further and higher education contains ten levels, beginning with level 1–5 certificates. This is then followed by an advanced certificate for level six, an ordinary bachelor's degree for level seven, an honours bachelor degree for level eight, master's for level nine and a doctoral degree for level ten.

My job was to develop the music generation level three QQI music appreciation programme. Strict criteria had to be met in development and implementation. First and foremost, the programme had to be based around a popular music pedagogy with creativity at its core, per the mission statement of Music Generation. It needed to cater to and engage students with no prior experience playing musical instruments. It also needed to be quantifiable, so that it could be graded by tutors and verified by the Education Training Board (ETB) to grant certification. In my experience, delivering workshops that are creative in nature and in which outputs are intangible is often difficult to quantify, especially through the eyes of examiners and internal verifiers who may not have musical backgrounds.

Compromise while maintaining relevance

Popular music is influenced by factors including the music industry, technology, texts and genres, mediation, consumption, subcultures and politics (Shuker 2010: 3). As a result of these numerous factors, popular music evolves rapidly. In order for a popular music education programme to remain relevant and captivating, it must keep pace with changes in popular music. Education, however, is slow to change. In Ireland, legislation and education policy from the Penal Laws of the nineteenth century can still be observed in the education system today. Whilst educational change today remains slow, the concepts of progressive education and educational change are not new. Over 100 years ago, John Dewey noted the importance of relevance within education where reflection and inquiry are employed to develop a curriculum (Dewey 1916: 107).

This stark contrast between popular music's constant reinvention of itself and education's desire to remain constant presented a barrier for the development of this music appreciation programme that held students' own interests and creativity at the core. A compromise would have to be met in relation to maintaining relevance for learners while being consistent enough to be understood, graded and certified by the ETB. I liaised closely with the ETB, Music Generation staff and Youthreach students. The programme structure is centred around discovery, listening, identifying and analyzing. The specific elements that would be discovered, listened to and compared are led by the learners. This allows for creative, relevant input from the class and gives learners ownership over the musical direction, which can then be discussed, analyzed and noted consistently.

The programme consists of ten topic areas that have been designed to give students a complete immersive learning experience in the music and the music industry. These topic areas – 'learning outcomes' in ETB terminology – include the following:

(1) Musical style identification;
(2) Music and genre characteristics;
(3) Musical vocabulary;
(4) Music production processes;
(5) Live performance processes;
(6) Contrasting pieces of music;
(7) Instrument identification;
(8) Rhythmic patterns;
(9) Artist analysis;
(10) Personal impact of music.

An example of an exercise undertaken in topic three (musical vocabulary) is where students are asked to select three pieces of music. They must then listen to and analyze these pieces under the predetermined assessment criteria of rhythm, mood, melody, timbre and instruments used. This is a simple exercise when analyzing a rock band but more challenging in the context of electronic-based music. The programme is flexible enough to open up dialogue on synthesized instruments, discussing how they sound and identifying similar synthesizer sounds in other artists' music. This helps use students' voices to further inform their own musical interests. This exercise is typical of the format delivered throughout the certified programme, where the musical direction of exercises is decided upon by students but the criteria for analyzing them are predetermined.

Challenges

One of the greatest challenges faced in developing this programme was having it structured and rigid enough to be verified internally by ETB staff who may not have musical backgrounds while remaining flexible enough to stay relevant to learners. I believe a good compromise and methodology have been achieved in implementing this dynamic between student-focused flexibility and structural rigidity. In doing so, unfortunately a number of assessments within the programme require the completion of comprehension-based questions, atypical of music programmes. This may present a barrier to learners, especially given that the programme is aimed at early school leavers.

From a structural perspective, developing a codified popular music education programme has entailed facing the challenge that students today develop music skills and abilities informally. In my opinion, popular music is flooded with self-taught musicians because it gives the ultimate level of self-expression. Every single aspect of a student's journey is their own when self-taught. Developing a structured music education programme goes against this ideal, even if it is a popular music education programme. Overcoming this challenge once again lies in the flexibility of the programme and using the voices of students wherever possible, giving them a broad, base level set of skills that can be taken away and applied to achieve their creative goals beyond the classroom.

Successes and a look towards the future

The first year of the programme took place in the academic year of 2019/20. The programme was delivered to five classes across four Youthreach centres in County Clare. Students who completed the work and minimum requirements for the programme received certification for completing the Level three QQI Music appreciation programme. These students also gained credit towards their overall Level three QQI certification. As a result of the positive impact of the programme and successful rollout, the ETB granted permanency to the programme within Music Generation Clare, guaranteeing delivery of the level three QQI music appreciation programme across all County Clare Youthreach centres for years to come. This has demonstrated the validity of the programme while also providing a level of security to Music Generation and programme tutors. Currently, in its second year, a significant review of the programme involving the surveying of participating students will be completed, with the aim of identifying further improvements of the programme from the students' perspectives.

REFERENCES

Dewey, John (1916), *Democracy and Education: An Introduction to the Philosophy of Education*, London: Macmillan.

Johnston, Thomas and Flynn, Patricia (2016), *Possible Selves in Music, Dublin: Music Generation*, pp. 11–13, November, https://www.musicgeneration.ie/content/files/17012020Possible-SelvesinMusicfulldocument2016.pdf. Accessed 21 November 2020.

Shuker, Roy (2010), 'Popular music', in M. Ryan (ed.), *The Encyclopedia of Literary and Cultural Theory*, Abingdon: John Wiley & Sons, Ltd., pp. 2–6.

7

Project Gametime:
Hip-Hop and After-School Programmes

Kenrick Wagner

Kenrick Wagner is a social entrepreneur and hip-hop artist with over
fifteen years of professional musical experience as a music educator,
performer, recording artist, published author and producer.

*This chapter is about an after-school initiative in the United States,
dedicated to providing top-quality youth programming and building
a generation of leaders who will use creativity to learn and thrive.*

Introduction

I like to call myself a coach, as someone who guides young people to find what
they're most passionate about creatively. The way that I do that, or practise that,
is being able to create a culture or an environment where young people can feel
safe to express themselves. That's kind of at the base level of what it looks like, or
what I strive to create every day as an educator–coach.

I've found in my practice as a coach–teacher–facilitator, that music, and popular music more specifically, has been a great platform to engage students. Coming
from a background of being a hip-hop practitioner, a recording artist and a musician, I discovered my own talent and my own creative force. My music and teaching started with learning traditional concert band music, growing up playing the
saxophone, and being interested in just expressing myself. I picked up the saxophone in middle school and started to play whatever it was the conductor said
we were going to play, which was usually western European music – really *in the
box*. And as I learned how to use that instrument and that tool to express myself,
I found that I gravitated more towards the popular music of my time, which was

hip-hop because it surrounded my culture – it's what I listened to. I woke up, it was on the radio. I liked the idea of people mastering words over beats. And that led me to feel very confined with the saxophone and very restricted in the concert band setting regarding what I was allowed to play and how I could approach my creativity.

During band rehearsals, in the small pockets of time before we got into actually playing what was on the sheets – that little practice time where we were supposed to be warming up – I would take that to play popular tunes or try to learn them. I would learn small riffs from rap music. I would play show tunes. I remember being so hung up over the John Williams *Superman* theme and trying to play that and learn that on my own. But again, this was small pockets of time where I was able to do that, or if I took my instrument home, I had more time. There was no outlet for me to even express myself the way I wanted to as a child who was in love with and passionate about hip-hop music.

So now as an educator, I seek to be able to create that – that small pocket of time – I seek to create that environment for students today so that they don't have to do it in private or restricted moments. I aim to draw out that time and expand that time by drawing that music out. I strive to make popular music accessible to young people so that they can feel comfortable creating and expressing themselves. I think at the very least, we need to be able to appreciate young people's creativity as much as they are told to appreciate our musical and creative history. And through that creation of that environment, we create a *restorative culture*, which derives from restorative practices, which talks about how we create an environment where students can create their own expectations within the community and also be held accountable, so they can set themselves up for success based on their own ideas. In that environment, the educators are just guides. We don't teach and restrict but we guide them with our expertise and our history so that they can shape the future creatively. For me as a hip-hop coach and educator on leadership, it's all about *how do we get these young people to be young people?*

Project Gametime

Project Gametime (for more information, check out projectgametime.com) started as a professional development, team-building company to help facilitate and guide educational leaders and school teachers with how to teach in a fun and engaging way. I talk a lot about creating culture and creating environments because I feel like that's probably the base of it. From the moment you walk into a space, what is it? How do you feel? What are you drawn to? What makes you want to be here? And at the very basic level, it's about how do we create this safe space in a safe environment? That's how you get access to everything else from education – restorative practice, music, creativity and leadership.

Project Gametime started as a place that wanted to teach teachers how to create safe spaces, and it has developed into a company that also goes into schools and works directly with them to create these safe spaces. From creating that safe space, we then started to do direct service after school, creating safe spaces for young people there. In our programme, kids can be kids and they don't have to worry about being adults, because they live in this world where they have to be adults at twelve, which I call the *speed of life*. This is especially true for students in marginalized communities. I'm a product of that – I was affected by the speed of life as well. My older sister (God rest her soul) had to take care of me because my mom was working double shifts and overnight shifts. And so at twelve years old, we had to learn how to cook and clean, we had to learn how to manage an entire household.

With Project Gametime I wanted to create at least this pocket of time, where for these three hours you can be a kid here, you can explore, you can be creative, you can have fun. You don't have to worry about being an adult for these three hours of your life. And we have always used pop culture and pop music in our training and in the after-school programme. One of the staples of our programmes is all of the group leaders get a bluetooth speaker, and they're trained on how to curate playlists of pop music or pop instrumentals. So as soon as the kids go into the room, there's music playing everywhere; they walk into this environment where it's like, oh, music is playing now!

The kids are coming straight from school, eight hours of this instruction and when they walk into this environment when music is playing – they can be a little more relaxed. They can free their minds a little bit. They can relax a little bit and they can have a real conversation. And the language we use when we're in training with doing team building, we use a lot of things that are associated with pop culture. We use a lot of examples of memes that are on Instagram, or whatever the current event is; we keep these conversation starters and use them as teachable moments.

We started to build on top of our after-school, which started from just basically having this space where they get homework help and a snack and then they may have an enrichment activity or two. We now focus our programming around a lot of creative arts. We do music making and we do dance, we do movement. We do what we call trap yoga where kids are doing yoga using trap music in the background, which is cool. It's just building on top of buildings, that's what I call it. We're building on buildings. Project Gametime is a people development company now, right, because at the base of it we're trying to build people, we're trying to build positive, great citizens who are carving out a future.

8

In Conversation with Eleanor Rashid, Music Practitioner

Eleanor Rashid and Gareth Dylan Smith

Eleanor Rashid works as a freelance music practitioner, songwriter and performer throughout London, England. She founded and presents On Repeat, a weekly podcast that explores genre and music hierarchy.

In this chapter, Eleanor speaks about her freelance work with London-based arts charity, Creative Futures, United Kingdom. She describes her Seeds Creative project, which explored the use of popular music in early years education, where she researched and practised an original participant-led model with a focus on rap and Bollywood.

The following is the edited transcript of an interview between Eleanor Rashid and Gareth Dylan Smith.

GARETH DYLAN SMITH (GDS): Hi Ellie. What do you do?

ELEANOR RASHID (ER): It's hard explaining what I do it because it's different every day and the projects change all the time, but my musical values tend to stay the same and seep into all of the work I do. I look at genres of music from different cultures and music from the home. I wouldn't say that I teach. What I do is more practitioner based. I specialize in early years, nought to five. I've been working with babies quite a lot over the last few months with their parents, and with refugees in London. I go into nurseries, and to schools sometimes, and basically see what's needed creatively. With children, for example, helping them to develop their own voices, and with staff because there is this huge problem, I think, with the idea or the term *musicality*. It's something that people have drilled into them for whatever reason from quite a young age – adults just have this idea that they are not musical, so I'm trying to give some tools for them to be able to use music creatively in their classroom or children's centre or whatever. And it's not just about like, here's a song like you can use; it's more like here's how you can adapt it depending on the needs of the children.

A lot of my work explores eliminating the genre hierarchy and considers why we ought to validate people's musical tastes. If I'm leading staff training on genre, I'll ask everyone what they listen to. There'll be people from 19 to 65/70, and often they say like disco, reggae, rock and go out of their way to say how much they hate opera or how much they don't identify with it. They might use other classical music to help them calm down, like a winding down thing. But people shy away from classical otherwise because that's what they've been taught equates to musicality. And that has a direct correlation to privilege in education, especially in the United Kingdom, where things are based on grade systems and ABRSM and you needing money to learn a western orchestral instrument. So what I do is validate things like rap, songwriting, lyric writing, and I encourage using different beats and rhythms from different genres.

GDS: What does a typical day look like for you?

ER: On a Wednesday, for example, I run all the music at a few nurseries around Kensington in west London. I work with the children and use that space to experiment with new early years ideas. My job is basically to develop a really good relationship with the staff and teachers and figure out what the gaps are, and it can take getting to know them quite personally. Something I like to find out is where they stand like on a personal level with music. And it's always really interesting. I'm here to build upon what they already have rather than teach them songs or whatever. You can find out quite a lot! I was working at this one school in Harrow, and the teachers had this idea that classical music was the most important thing but one of them wanted to do Bollywood stuff. And once I said this is so cool that you like Bollywood music – you've got dance and now you've got interesting rhythms. A lot of the kids in the class listen to Bollywood at home. I would try and find out what the children listen to at home and bring that into the nursery or school space because I'm not sure how relevant it is just to be teaching kids, say, nursery rhymes.

I've got into heated debates with people because it can be quite conservative and traditional and people get stuck there. Some people are happy to sing 'Twinkle,

Twinkle Little Star' for the rest of their career but I think we can do better than that because I don't think it's relevant. I'm not saying get rid of nursery rhymes (people feel quite threatened by that), but I just think, why wouldn't we introduce rap? I found a book of nursery rhymes recently and it was 100 or something years old and it was just horrendous! Like I can't even say some of the stuff that was in it, some of the words that were used. They're racist, they're really not relevant today, and on a musical level kids can actually be challenged a little bit more.

Another company I work for is Creative Futures – a charity that delivers artistic programmes in communities and settings across London. One of the programmes I was a part of was Sound Communities, where I worked in settings such as nurseries. It was actually more of a staff project and a chance to explore how music could be used to enhance learning as well as how it could be used more for its own sake.

I also work for Girls Rock London, for 11–16-year-olds. They're great because they challenge genre as well and that can really help some people integrate into the group. You get people from different backgrounds. I think there are about 50 young people and probably even more staff, which is good. Something I've found is that even with the good intention of getting people together from different backgrounds, people don't seem to mix, so you can use genres to integrate people. Most of the stuff we're playing is sort of disco and jazz and stuff like that and there were some groups who just weren't identifying with it at all, so validating their music choices and what they like was really rich for them and for everybody else.

We used to do this kind of circle where we'd be playing a song and everyone would get into pairs, and they would dance to the song and then everybody else would copy that dance. I remember there were a group of girls who didn't want to pick a song because they thought that their music was inappropriate because it was Afrobeat and I thought that's crazy – if anything, Afrobeat is even better to dance to! But they were like, well, everyone here's White so they won't understand and they'll feel like it's not good and inappropriate and whatever. And then you've already got people sort of separating into groups. It's difficult because we didn't have a lot of staff who really knew anything about Afrobeat, grime, drill or even hip-hop. I think it's so important to put our own preferences aside and try to understand different genres and why people like to listen to different things that we might not be so familiar with. In doing this, we welcome respect and an acceptance of different cultures, which helps us to integrate and understand each other.

9

Reciprocal Benefits of Music Cities and Modern Band

Bryce Merrill and Tom Scharf

Bryce Merrill is the music programmes director at Bohemian Foundation in Fort Collins, Colorado. He is a musician and advocates for popular music as a public good in his free time.

Tom Scharf is a novelist, painter and working musician in Denver, Colorado. He runs rivers, and sometimes they chase him.

The authors are active in the Music Cities and modern band movements discussed in the chapter because they believe in the power of popular music to improve lives, strengthen communities and challenge systemic inequalities. They have witnessed this power in rural communities in Colorado and urban centres throughout the world.

Introduction

Governments, non-profits, musicians and music businesses worldwide have begun to advocate for commercial music as a public good. This Music Cities movement focuses almost exclusively on the economic, social and cultural value of commercial music to communities. In doing so, music education in the United States, which is most often associated with western art music and the non-profit infrastructure that supports it, is left out of the conversation. In this chapter, we identify logical points to connect music education with commercial music to enhance educational opportunities for children. We believe these connections will support relevant educational engagement for students, build stronger and more integrated Music Cities, and further the case for commercial music as a public good.

Music Cities: Background

The term 'Music Cities' has gained popularity in the twenty-first century as a way to describe efforts by musicians, music advocates, government and business leaders and others to demonstrate the importance of music to communities. Music Cities now refers less to actual municipalities and more to strategies that communities can use to capitalize on or preserve music as a social, cultural and economic asset.[1] The music industry, the argument goes, drives local economies by creating employment and a tax base. The creation and consumption of music also brings social and cultural value to cities, improving social cohesion through public concerts, for example, or enhancing shared historical identity through music heritage projects.

Through the Music Cities movement, the conversation has shifted to distinctly embrace commercial forms of music as vital and relevant influences on the social and economic well-being of communities. Public dollars (governmental or philanthropic) have commonly been focused on supporting classical music forms such as symphony and opera. Communities of all sizes across the United States, for example, have long lobbied that no city is complete without a local symphony orchestra. The Music Cities movement, particularly because it relies heavily on economic development arguments, secures investment in the broader music industry and ecosystem beyond just visible markers of 'high culture'. The movement views musicians, record labels, venues, promoters, agents, managers, technologists and many others as sources of public good and thereby also worthy of public investment. While many communities have recognized the power of contemporary music to enhance social experience and cohesion, there have been few intentional financial interventions beyond market forces to support them. Supply and demand in commercial music (a band who plays a club show for ticket revenue, for example) have been the norm while traditional (principally western classical) musical forms earn subsidies from government and philanthropy. This is changing: commercial genres like rock, hip-hop, EDM, punk, Americana and others are lauded for their community value, and policies and programmes are continually being developed to support their growth.[2]

Music Cities organizations, policy think tanks, non-commercial radio stations, government and universities are developing strategies that inform 'best practices' for successful Music Cities.[3] Unfortunately, these organizations have either forgotten or inadvertently moved away from music's educational value, focusing on music *business* rather than music *education*, or have narrowly construed music education as housed in schools rather than intrinsically connected to commercial music scenes. Either way, there is a path – and there are good reasons – for connecting commercial music to music education to increase the overall value that music brings to cities.

Adding modern band to the Music Cities conversation

Modern band pedagogy, which emphasizes teaching contemporary music in a student-centred and inclusive manner, is perhaps the most obvious connection point between music education and Music Cities in the United States.[4] If cities are to thrive musically, they need to cultivate the next generation of musicians and music lovers. Modern band teaches students everything from the basic structures of commercial music to its social and cultural dimensions. In school districts around the United States – including in global Music Cities like Los Angeles and New York – students can form a band in the first grade and continue their modern band educational journey into high school.[5] Imagine the musicianship and creativity of a future music scene where this is commonplace. Because modern band emphasizes expanding access and participation in music, it also increases the number of students with a lifelong love of popular music. Is there a more successful audience development strategy? Music Cities supporters should view this educational movement as uniquely aligned with their own interests. Modern music teachers, like working musicians, should be positioned as invaluable assets to, and integral parts of, a vital music community.

Likewise, modern band proponents should see the Music Cities movement as a new and potentially powerful ally in advocating for popular music. This movement has the attention of mayors and governors, business leaders and musicians of all levels.[6] While it is common for world-famous musicians to advocate for music education, the Music Cities movement, with its emphasis on *all* musicians in a community, could bring a significant number of voices – and votes – to conversations regarding policy, advocacy and funding. Musicians at all levels have the potential to move audiences to action, and Music Cities advocates and music education supporters could develop a 'cradle to stage' approach to advocating for the value of music to communities (Grohl 2017).

Music Cities engaging local communities

The Music Cities movement positions working musicians as critical resources to the vibrancy of Music Cities. The educational potential of these musicians who work in popular genres such as hip-hop, rock, electronic music and others is currently underutilized. Again, modern band in schools seems to offer a perfect connection. Teachers offering lessons in, for example, rap or beat-making should look to current hip-hop artists for best practices and inspiration. In the classical music world, guest (or 'teaching') artists are commonplace. Teaching is a common way for many musicians to supplement their income. Commercial artists, because of the divide between music education and business, do not have regular access to training resources to prepare them to teach in schools. Creating this infrastructure, which could easily be added to existing teaching artist support systems, would be essential to realizing the educational potential of commercial musicians.

In the summer of 2018, libraries around the United States used music to encourage reading with the theme 'Libraries Rock!' The connection of music to libraries is growing beyond thematic programming to include musical equipment check out and even recording studios.[7] However, most libraries lack instructors, particularly those who can teach the styles of music most students are interested in. Libraries serve broad, diverse communities and develop programming to meet the needs of their populations. Commercial musicians with some training in teaching and student engagement can fill this need and offer relevant, hands-on and impactful instruction.

Another connection point for Music Cities' and music education can be found in the *Declaration on Equity in Music for City Students* (Yale School of Music 2018). The text puts forward the idea that an 'active music life' is a basic human right for all students and can be defined as the following:

(1) Accessible, sequential, and robust music instruction in schools;
(2) Outside-of-school opportunities that provide services that schools do not provide; and
(3) Music-making in less formalized contexts (at home, at places of worship, with family and friends).

The text also acknowledges that limiting who is included as educators (be it by genre or educational background) constrains our ability to create the kind of music ecosystem that can offer more students an active music life. Meeting students 'where they are' means connecting them with music forms that are the most culturally relevant and inspiring to them. Educators and mentors need continually to expand the definition of what music is, and how it is being created, experienced and taught. Being a music educator is 'far less about being an adept performer of the western 'classical' canon and far more about teaching and inspiring students to make music' (Yale School of Music 2018). It seems to us that commercial music-making and learning would satisfy criteria two and three for an active music life; add modern band instruction in schools and students could more fully realize their active music life. If, as the text poignantly argues, an active music life is an *inherent right* akin to human dignity, then those responsible for finding and advancing the ways that students can realize this should grow to include commercial musicians teaching in multiple community contexts.

Music Cities proponents should embrace this equity position and advance the educational role that commercial music plays in communities.[8] Music educators of all stripes should consider ways that commercial music can be leveraged to provide students with an active music life. The intention is to 'grow the pie' for all students, rather than divide the already small pie of music education between classical and commercial musicians. This is a 'yes/and' proposition.

Music Cities and music education success in Colorado

In Colorado, a consortium of funders and educators is beginning to forge connections between Music Cities work and its emphasis on commercial music and music education. Through a project called 'Take Note Colorado', funders support commercial music programming for students in libraries and community centres. It is important that instructors have some pedagogical training. Commercial musicians have few opportunities to learn how to teach, so specific curricula and training regimens tailored to commercial musicians are being developed.[9] Commercial musicians are paired with classroom teachers to expand and enrich existing offerings. It is early in the process of connecting music education to commercial music, but there are signs that there is value in this approach, both for students and musicians. Students who may lack access to an active music life are given new opportunities that meet them 'where they are' culturally and physically. Commercial music and musicians increase access points and entice students who may not be drawn to traditional school music provision. In Colorado, there is evidence that educational uses of commercial music create opportunities for specific populations of students, such as recent immigrants and refugees, who are underserved by traditional music education. Commercial musicians are also benefiting – developing new sources of income through teaching and finding individual and social fulfillment in education. In the music business, such fulfillment is in short supply.

Commercial music creates many demonstrable impacts on communities. It drives economies, connects people to places and history, and improves quality of life. The argument that music is good for cities would only be enhanced by adding the educational value of commercial music. Likewise, in commercial music, education can find a strong ally in providing students an active music life.

NOTES
1. Statewide music strategies (Colorado, TX) and regional music strategies (South Australia, Northwest Arkansas) are increasingly common, and communities of all sizes and political geographies are embracing the Music Cities approach.
2. One policy that has become popular is the designation of 'loading zones' for musicians, which are designated parking spaces for loading and unloading gear in front of commercial venues.

3. The *Mastering of a Music City* report by the nongovernmental organization, Music Canada, provides an overview of Music City policies throughout the world.

4. We assume readers of this book are familiar enough with modern band pedagogy to avoid describing it.

5. The 'modern band pipeline' from elementary through high school is not available to all students, in part due to differences between school districts and prevailing inequities therein (e.g. racial, gender, socioeconomic and geographic disparities).

6. The UNESCO Cities of Music project lists prominent Music Cities globally: https://citiesofmusic.net/; Sound Diplomacy lists recent music city reports: https://www.sounddiplomacy.com/insights (both accessed 19 September 2020).

7. Music programming is beginning to occur in various community settings, such as Boys & Girls clubs and city recreation centres.

8. A recent Music Cities conference in Memphis was themed around education and equity; the former was not particularly well represented; the latter focused on equity in the industry and communities, but not educational equity. See https://musiccitiesconvention.com/memphis-information. Accessed 26 January 2017.

9. Denver-based nonprofit Youth on Record recently launched its Musicians in Community (MIC) programme to teach musicians trauma-informed pedagogy that prepares them to work with vulnerable populations.

REFERENCES

Grohl, Virgina (2017), *From Cradle to Stage: Stories from the Mothers Who Rocked and Raised Rock Stars*, Seattle: Seal Press.

Yale School of Music (2018), *Declaration on Equity in Music for City Students: A Report on the 2017 Yale Symposium on Music in Schools*, https://www.declaration.yale.edu/about-the-declaration. Accessed 19 September 2020.

10

Berklee City Music Programme: Teaching and Learning Through Contemporary Popular Music

Krystal Prime Banfield

Krystal Prime Banfield is Vice President for Education Outreach, Social Entrepreneurship at Berklee College of Music in Massachusetts, USA, and supervises Berklee's international creative youth development programme, Berklee City Music.

This chapter documents the author's observation experience in Boston, Massachusetts, that exhibits teaching approaches infused with the social–cultural contexts of contemporary music, and with elements of creative youth development that excites youngsters, making a positive learning environment, motivating urban youth.

A community of musical practice

On a chilly March, Saturday morning in Boston, I entered a modest-sized classroom within an urban high school. It felt more like a one-room schoolhouse with multiple groups of children, approximately twenty in tight-knit clusters using every inch of the space, actively engaged in music learning. Each group of enthusiastic beginners studied one of six different instrument groupings, which included woodwinds, brass, percussion and strings. Groups played simultaneously. The youngsters represented a beautiful garden variety of cultures and ethnicities with an average age of eight years old. Their instructors ranged from upper elementary, middle and high school youth, to Berklee college students, public school music teachers, Berklee college professors and alumni. The public-school teachers taught and coached the college students who were teaching the middle and high schoolers as they introduced new skills to the beginners. For every instrumental song and skill being taught the historic and current sociocultural contexts were being discussed – making meaning and enlivening their experience. The music instructors teaching contemporary popular music looked like the students they taught. They originated from the cultures in which the music was formed, providing authentic perspectives by way of storytelling their lived experiences. Their knowledge base further informed music practice and understanding, inspiring and motivating the youngsters. It was an inclusive and safe space. There was overwhelming joy in the music making environment. This is how teaching and learning *can* be.

Amidst a sweet cacophony, tunes emerged: Latin jazz melodies played on trumpets, a German folk melody played on woodwind instruments, and a group of bassists playing the bass line from Michael Jackson's 'Beat It'. The instructional approaches were clearly working as I watched the body language of each child emerge into the physical characteristics of trained musicians. All were focused for the two-hour morning session. The lead K-8 teacher, Mr Camen Bernard shared with me how he constructed his accelerated learning approaches with the beginners who had only been on their instruments for a month but were motivated to play. Mr Bernard said: 'Although we see them only once per week, we are in regular contact with the children through their caregivers (families). Their caregivers are held responsible for their daily study and are encouraged to engage with their children.' Sunday through Friday, students use Berklee PULSE[1] for home study, accessing beginner theory exercises and are also given homework assignments to listen closely to the music they hear everywhere they go, noticing when and how music is used. They then share what they observed with their families and in class. Mr Bernard explained,

> We talk about what music means – its cultural contexts and meaning, how it functions, what they hear and like, what others are listening to and what effect it has on them. We talk to them and work with them not as if they are beginners, but as musicians. This approach increases their enthusiasm for learning.

Mr Bernard expressed that they also communicate the kinds of music they would like to learn. He said: 'We exchange ideas on music we know we will teach them and that will help them to grow. But, we meet them half way by teaching them some of the tunes they listen to and want to learn'.

Teaching and learning music at BCMP

The highest-income families spend seven times more on enrichment activities for their children than low-income families. This creates achievement and opportunity gaps (McCombs et al. 2017). In Out-of-School Time (OST) programmes, young people, in particular those who are marginalized, thrive and can accelerate learning in most any discipline, given the focused and tailored instructional time is in something they enjoy that validates who they are and what they represent. My observation and conversation with Mr Bernard are only a snapshot of the approaches to teaching and learning in the Berklee City Music Program (BCMP). With over 25 years in educating and motivating thousands of youth, BCMP, Berklee College of Music's creative youth development contemporary popular music and performing arts programme; has advanced equity by increasing access to a well-rounded education in music for youth from underserved communities. This is achieved by engaging young people and their families with what is most familiar – their culture and music. The programme utilizes our web-based tool called Berklee PULSE that allows all students to engage in adaptive learning, which provides effective pathways for all styles of learning. The programme welcomes young people from ages 8 to 19, to participate as beginners and grow to advanced learners. As an urban based programme, learners arrive at all ages and engage in positive youth development, music practice, music literacy comprehension and understanding. Many adolescent beginners come with instruments, having performed in religious services or neighbourhood community centres, but seek more.

As a popular music institution, BCMP remains an important part of realizing the Berklee mission that states the institution is 'founded on jazz and popular music rooted in the African cultural diaspora […] embracing the principal music movements of our time' (Berklee n.d.: n.pag.). In the words of philosopher Raymond Ruble, contemporary refers to the 'common culture', thereby, referring to the common music of their surrounding communities – thus, speaking in a musical 'tongue' that is understood (Ruble 2005: 69). This equity work is especially important given our vision is to help all children, but especially those most in-need of support. The BCMP approach embraces contemporary music and performing arts and the social–cultural contexts in a manner that represents the more current, lived experiences. The contemporary popular music being studied is rooted in the African cultural diaspora.

Our young people are always plugged-in to music and the latest trends, excited to engage as performers, creators, teachers, producers and/or entrepreneurs. Their learning and capabilities accelerate from their passion to study, read, understand the contexts and perform music that stems from their culture in a supportive environment with committed teachers.

Over the years, BCMP has become more refined and intentional in approaches that are infused with youth development and has broadened the scope to include more international contemporary and folk-infused traditions. BCMP has established partnership network programmes across North America, in the Caribbean and in Quito, Ecuador. Collectively all programmes strive to provide culturally enriched contemporary popular music and performing arts instruction inviting youth into spaces and to concepts they could not have previously accessed, to foster their development in purpose and enhance their understanding and sense of responsibility to themselves and their communities as artist citizens. While many of the students self-identify by excelling in developing mastery in music, the programme has become an effective means for preparing and educating all youth to cope with the realities that life brings. Some might argue that youth development and pursuing excellence in music cannot simultaneously be achieved. This is not true, as both pedagogical approaches complement each other. There is much that can be learned from this model and always room for enhancements. There are numerous successful creative youth development models that exist. I encourage readers to explore OST partnerships and placed-based educational approaches to enhance instruction.

Youth development approaches to teaching and learning support healthy mental attitudes. This has been especially important for the majority of BCMP youth and teachers who identify as black skinned and brown skinned people, who experience daily racial polarization heightened by racially motivated violence. This racial violence occurs in their communities and is witnessed nationally by the public. This racial polarization is also currently amidst the impact of the COVID-19 pandemic. Students need safe spaces to have conversations and to share creative ideas. These spaces can incorporate music to address isolation, mental health and social justice issues. This practice motivates our youth to be active participants in creating meaning, constructing their own realities, and understanding the social contexts of themselves and others. This also informs choices in music expression and creation. Teaching the skill of discernment within a positive youth development framework also results in students understanding the power of contemporary music and being responsible persons to the artistry they emulate and/or create. An example of discernment can be found in musics with lyrical content that are demeaning or harmful, examples of which can be found in every genre of music. BCMP conducts critical and comparative analysis of the words and music of all tunes. This is endeavoured among teachers, youth and youth development staff who together discuss the impact of what is being stated and the role music in it. Teachers and students work collaboratively to change the lyric content, but maintain much of musical elements. This is achieved by deriving their own original tunes or seeking other works responsibly, realizing the impact they can make when others experience their music.

BCMP model rests comfortably in the African cultural diaspora and Berklee College's framework, where traditionally the experiences of music and the education of a strong community are seamless. In the words of Dr Ysaÿe Barnwell:

> [L]ooking from an African worldview, music exists because it does something.
> It never is the art-for-art's sake phenomenon, because music is so integrated into

every aspect of life activity for African people. We can see how that applies to all who embrace contemporary popular music idioms. Evidence of functionality is seen in how it is created and how it is used – it touches, its vulnerable and is accessible.

(Banfield 2003: 153)

Observing our Boston campus programme and BCMP Network of urban community partners, I have experienced the tremendous and positive impact of contemporary music study and performance. These kinds of phenomena happen mostly when children feel validated and can see 'themselves' through the learning experiences and in the instructional materials used to reach them. Although I have witnessed similar responses among the urban youth who are successful in classical music instruction, children engaged in a serious study of contemporary music do not have to make the leap from their identity in their home communities and school. Musical elements stemming from contemporary popular music traditions are the most pervasive in popular music worldwide. While contemporary popular music is an embodiment of these elements, all music requires discernment. Music teachers can validate and strengthen the muscles of discernment within music instruction. Beginning with articulating your own values and experiences with contemporary popular music is a first step in understanding how deeply your students' value and hold specific musics with a high esteem and/or significantly impacts them.

It is important to provide an education in contemporary popular music. In the midst of racial and inclusion biases, class disparities, and lack of equity in K12 education, creativity in contemporary music and the arts provides youth a space where they can be confirmed and heard. Contemporary popular music genres rooted in the African cultural diaspora are among the most familiar among youth within the US, which also impacts on youth worldwide. Given this circumstance, more music education programmes should provide instruction in contemporary and popular musics. Teachers who aspire to have an inclusive classroom instruct in music and curricula that fully embrace the cultural voices among students. How can we say that we are authentic in our approaches to teaching if we are not embracing the social–cultural contexts that inform music practice? Imagine what learning is being missed.

NOTE

1. Berklee PULSE → stands for Pre-University Learning System Experience and is an online music education portal that provides resources for playing music, practicing and learning music theory.

REFERENCES

Banfield, William C. (2003), *Landscapes in Color: Conversations with Black American Composers*, Lanham and Oxford: The Scarecrow Press.

Berklee (n.d.), 'Mission and philosophy', https://www.berklee.edu/about/mission-and-philosophy. Accessed 2 May 2022.

McCombs, Jennifer Sloan, Whitaker, Anamarie and Youngmin Yoo, Paul (2017), *The Value of Out-of-School Time Programs*, Santa Monica, CA: RAND Corporation, https://www.rand.org/pubs/perspectives/PE267.html. Accessed 19 January 2022.

Ruble, Raymond (2005), 'Popular culture and philosophy', in R. B. Browne (ed.), *Popular Culture Studies Across the Curriculum: Essays for Educators*, Jefferson and London: McFarland & Company, Inc, p. 69.

11

A New Generation:
An Intrinsic Case Study of a Club DJ's
Formal Learning Experiences

Eva J. Egolf

Eva J. Egolf earned a Ph.D. from New York University. She lives in Bronx, New York, USA, where she teaches music in school and university settings.

This chapter presents a case study that examines initial music learning experiences of a club DJ in New York. When an aspiring artist enrolls in a local DJs school, insight is obtained regarding formal and solitary learning practices.

Introduction

This chapter presents an intrinsic case study (Stake 1995) of the learning experiences of a New York club DJ. Significant findings include: lack of enculturation time associated with participation as a club patron, solitary learning practices that were distinctive and access to colleagues and work through the DJ school. Notably, this DJ recognized his positioning at a crux of generational change: a time when older DJs learned through informal means, and his positioning in a new generation who could access knowledge and work through a DJ school. I present this case to illuminate an experience of learning at the cusp of the transition from an informal process to a formal one.

I met the participant in 2011. He worked as a professional DJ and instructor. He was in his mid twenties, and of self-described Hispanic descent. In 2012, I began conducting interviews and observations as part of my doctoral dissertation fieldwork, and, at that point, there was an initial interview and subsequent observation of a DJ set (Egolf 2014). In 2014, I communicated with the participant as I expanded my initial research. At that point, he informed me that he had left the DJing profession to pursue another career. I use the pseudonym DJ M for the participant.

Learning practices overview

DJ M was attracted to shows on local radio where DJs mixed long sets. He described wanting to be a DJ, but not knowing how to pursue this knowledge. At a minimum, he knew he needed equipment to practise. As a young teen, with the help of an uncle, he purchased and setup a single turntable in his bedroom. He would listen to hip-hop on a local radio station, and practise scratching along with the radio. In this initial informal learning time, he described an extensive amount of listening and copying. These early practice sessions were solitary in nature both in the sense that he was practising alone, and that he was practising without outside direction from a teacher about what to do. Frustrated by not knowing what to do, DJ M purchased a book about how to DJ. While DJ M reported that it was a little helpful, he was unsure of how things should look. At this point, he was not going to clubs, as he was still underage. The sense of how DJing should look or sound in live performance was elusive. All that informed him were what he could read in a book or hear on the radio.

Wanting more guidance about how to DJ, in high school DJ M sought the help of a hip-hop-oriented, community-based organization. While this organization had ties to the music industry, and DJ M found this learning related to recording technology and music business informative, he was disappointed that he could not learn how to DJ through this organization. He learned of a newly formed DJ school from an advertisement on the radio and found out that they had a scholarship programme. He applied, secured the scholarship and began courses at the DJ school. DJ M attended for three semesters. He described what he learned in the classes as largely an affirmation and confirmation of what he was practising at home. He valued the contribution of his instructors in correcting what he described as 'form'. He described being able to practise alone in ways that were categorically different since receiving instruction. Now he had seen and heard real DJs and had a sense of what his 'form' should look like.

While DJ M valued the classes, he thought he learned the most later when he became a DJ instructor and employee of the school. During this employment be developed professional contacts and friendships that would help launch his DJing career. DJ M (2012) recalled: 'I became an employee. The classes were all good. They revealed all the stuff to you because it was a set curriculum in a certain way. But it wasn't until I was an employee that I felt that I advanced' (n.pag.). As an employee, DJ M became friends with the other DJ instructors. They informed him of what he called 'tricks of the trade' that were not covered in the curriculum. DJ M also was able to get encouragement, and other employees were able to watch and help him DJ in a one-on-one setting, differently than a class.

In addition, to help with technique and encouragement, the other DJ instructors at this school referred DJ M for gigs. They would ask DJ M to cover gigs for them if they were double booked for gigs or unavailable. This referral system was crucial, as it helped DJ M launch his career working in clubs. By the time DJ M graduated high school, he had enough work as a club DJ to move out of his mother's house and sustain an independent living. When I met DJ M he had been a professional DJ for at least five years.

Solitary learning practices

As noted above, practising for DJ M was a solitary endeavour. In the beginning, his efforts were largely informal. Upon entering the DJ school DJ M's learning and practising became shaped by formal instruction. To describe these practices, I characterize solitary learning experiences as self-taught solitary learning (STSL) and teacher-directed solitary learning (TDSL). I use STSL to describe learning processes associated with DJ M's early experiences, in which he determined what he wanted to learn and tried his best to teach to himself. He described this time as involving a lot of trial and error and listening and copying. This approach is not significantly different from other findings, especially those of Bell (2018). Similarly, the practice of listening and copying is prevalent among other informal popular music learners, as described by Green (2002). DJ M is the only DJ I have interviewed who described extensive listening and copying as part of a practising routine. This might be because his focus was primarily on hip hop. As described by DJ M, the hip-hop technique of scratching is well suited to learning through listening and copying. Other DJs, I met do not report listening and copying, perhaps because they focus on house music, which emphasizes the technique of long blends as opposed to scratching. During these initial learning experiences, DJ M's only guide was what he could hear on the radio, or read in a book. These guides were both inadequate because reading about DJing or listening on the radio do not capture the complexity of live DJ performance. He was underaged and did not experience being able to watch DJs as a club patron or by hanging out in DJ booths – both hallmarks of the enculturation processes of other DJs I encountered.

I contrast STSL with TDSL, which accounts for solitary practising that is organized or heavily influenced by a teacher. In TDSL, even though the teacher is not physically present, the ways in which DJ M practised, and what he practised, were influenced by a teacher. After engagement with the DJ school, DJ M's practising turned toward the more formally oriented TDSL. Having teachers to show him 'form', critique, and guide his musical efforts shaped his solitary practising. In this shift, DJ M's practising evolved from an informal to a more formal orientation. Aspiring DJs engaging in formal instruction through a DJ school is new to DJ M's generation.

A new generation of learning

DJ M came of age when there was a possibility to secure formal instruction in DJing at community schools in New York. DJ M understood that his access to this type of formal instruction was different from other DJs. As an employee of the DJ school, DJ M engaged in conversations with more experienced DJs. In these conversations, it became apparent to DJ M that he was learning differently from how older DJs had learned. DJ M (2012: n.pag.) recalled these conversations:

> If you would speak to a lot of DJs who were older than me [...] they would all tell you that they learned from someone else. They knew someone who was a DJ. They carried records, you know, which is a lost thing right now. Where you carry a laptop, you don't have anybody with you. Before you needed a group, and I remember this talking to my father. He would say, 'Oh yeah. I remember when my cousin used to DJ in the parks. We would have like, ten to twelve of our friends with us all of the time'. Because one person needs to carry the speakers, one person needed to carry a crate of records. But say there was, six or eight crates of records, you need six or eight different people to carry each of those records plus the turntables plus everything. And they are jumping on the train to wherever they're going. And that's where everybody learned. Because it was like okay, we're all here at the party, we're going to get on also. But I also think that it is neighbourhood-wise. If you did not grow up in a place where there were other people for you to learn from, you're not going to learn.

DJ M described a different type of informal learning than what he encountered as a solitary bedroom DJ, and later as a student in a DJ school. In addition to recognizing the learning of another generation might be different in that particular nature, DJ M (2012: n.pag.) also mentioned the internet:

> Nowadays, if you have access to the internet you can look up videos. And you can do all this stuff. But I wasn't able to do that. [I] had to listen to the radio and make sure I learned. And then I had that confirmation later on when I went to a DJ school.

Conclusions

I present the intrinsic case of DJ M because of his formal learning at the DJ school, and his generational positioning. While I do not mean to suggest the informal learning practices of the prior generation are extinct, it is significant that the new generation represented by DJ M are able to access formal instruction and professional benefits associated with the school. Interfacing with the DJ school shaped DJ M's solitary practising as he moved from more informal STSL to more formal and structured TDSL.

In addition to formal instruction shaping practising approaches, DJ M benefitted from affiliation with the DJ school as a means to launch his professional career. What is noticeably absent from DJ M's learning was a period of enculturation as a club patron. Many other DJs use this enculturation time for purposes that are twofold: as an effort to learn how to DJ, and to develop professional contacts to pursue work. Instead, DJ M found help finding work, and opportunities to learn through the DJ school.

With help finding work and access to formal instruction, a new generation of DJ learners emerge that can access a DJ community music school. I am left wondering about the other DJs who DJ M described as learning 'another way'. The extensive period of enculturation – hanging out in booths, carrying records to parties, patronizing clubs – could that be replaced with the benefits of professional contacts and formal instruction associated with a DJ school? Can these modes of formal and informal learning coexist? I have lingering questions about how relationships between informal and formal learning will develop over time with future generations of DJs, and what implications this may have for the larger conversation related to popular music education.

REFERENCES

Bell, Adam (2018), *Dawn of the DAW: The Studio as Musical Instrument*, New York: Oxford University Press.

DJ M (2012), in-person interview, Brooklyn, 31 May.

Egolf, Eva (2014), 'Learning processes of electronic music club DJs', Ph.D. thesis, New York: New York University.

Green, Lucy (2002), *How Popular Musicians Learn a Way Ahead for Music Education*, Burlington: Ashgate.

Stake, Robert (1995), *The Art of Case Study Research*, Thousand Oaks: Sage Publications.

12

Playing with Vocal Processing Technologies: Fostering Interaction with Children with Special Educational Needs

Roshi Nasehi

Roshi Nasehi is a Welsh-born, London-based musician of Iranian parentage with a track record in performance, theatre, recording, cross arts collaboration workshops, public art and social intervention projects.

This chapter presents a reflection on using vocal processing technologies in workshops for people with special educational needs and disabilities and from refugee backgrounds. The author also discusses her experiences trying these approaches at home during lockdown with her own rambunctious, autistic 5-year-old.

Music and my autistic son

For some years, I have explored the creative and educational possibilities afforded by using vocal processing technologies to make music for theatre, film and in creative workshops. The results in special education needs and disabilities (SEND) and refugee workshops, in particular, have been quite astonishing. Over the years, I have supported children with speech delay and selective mutism, helping to break their silence, using effects like looping and putting their voices through echo and robot voice settings for self-expression, role-play and storytelling.

My own 5-year-old boy is autistic, which manifests in significant language delay and social communication difficulties. Inevitably, I wondered how he would respond to these workshop approaches at home, and lockdown seemed the right moment to test them out. With the help of bursaries from UK-based organizations Sound Connections and Sound and Music, I was able to create a portable studio set up to explore this.

As with other parents, I sang to my boy every day from when he was born: every nappy change, toothbrush time or bedtime seems fitting for a lively or soothing song with a baby. I think these song interactions served a deeper purpose for my child because he sang before saying anything at all. Music continues to be a major source of communication and expression between us. Every day, I cherish the way his little fluttering soprano voice effortlessly adapts to a wide range of material. This encompasses songs he remembers from wonderful music sessions with Becky Dixon at Beanstalk Arts, tunes from nursery days and his new song-punctuated schedule in reception class. These are interspersed with melodic fragments from Raffi, Pete Seeger, Bob Dylan, Simon and Garfunkel, Daft Punk, Laurie Anderson, Ella Fitzgerald, The Mills Brothers, Rose Royce and more.

Recently, my son became enchanted with various Kraftwerk tracks we play him at home. I notice him trying to mimic the timbral effect and melodic lines when he recreates the records. I wondered how he would respond to a microphone put through effects. Though he can be prescriptive about how I join in with him ('mummy copy'), he has learnt that there is a reward in connection and interaction. Music and play have been the key supports for reinforcing this.

Vocal processing at home during lockdown

It's a rainy lockdown morning. We have had a little jam with ukulele and hand percussion already as we do most days. My son's favourite song at the moment is a version of 'Ten in the Bed' which involves stuffed animals flying around the room, complete with elaborate routines about where they each hurt themselves, how we should cuddle and comfort them better, and how they should cuddle and comfort each other better. On this particular day, following this routine and our repertoire of other favourite songs, I introduce the idea of 'play with the microphone'. From the moment, I begin setting up the vocal processor, he seems intrigued. Inevitably it takes a while to realize that the ice cream-shaped Beta 58 does not need to go right in his mouth. It also takes him a while to realize the microphone will do its job of amplifying him without the need to shout down it, though there is of course the visceral thrill of this kind of flagrant noise-making as with most children presented with a microphone! The excitement of hearing his voice, larger-than-life state, bouncing around the room, makes him surge with joy and energy.

I show him different effects settings like echo and delay, and see him using his voice really creatively, deploying whispers and animal sounds to make soundscapes. These are the kind of bright, opulent compositions that can only come from children's voices. I soon see that, ironically, the delay effect needs to happen quickly. He needs to feel his voice swimming in it soon after vocalizing. However, a longer delay (than the preset) makes it easier to pass the microphone back and forth between us and create layers of soundscape that linger for longer. Of course, he finds it difficult to pass the microphone back to me at all, but a slower rate of decay makes this more advanced stage of interaction more possible. The harmonizer and radio effects encourage role play ('telephone, who's there?') and the robot effect makes him fall on the floor with laughter. He does what every kid seems to do with the robot effect: unnecessarily putting on a mechanical voice when talking through it. He itches to say as much as he can into the robot effect: repeating phrases from our diary, CBeebies television shows and favourite songs. But most importantly, he is sharing the enjoyment with me. There is lots of eye contact and he wants me to be in on the joke. When he sees that I share his joy, he beams.

My son recently started doing DIR®Floortime™ therapy and I am conscious of what his therapist said about his desire for me to join in with various scripts again and again: 'he's trying to recreate the connection with you'. My son needs help pushing the loop pedal but pushing it is also very pleasing for him. We do not use screens much at home but in this digital age when buttons are becoming obsolete, the simple pleasure of pushing is very satisfying. This applies to both of us but it is especially gratifying for him as a sensory-seeking child with tactile, vestibular (relating to movement) and proprioceptive (relating to body position) sensory needs.

We continue to 'play with the microphone' at times throughout lockdown. The soundscapes get longer and sharing becomes easier. He seems to realize that the echo sound offers more scope for experimenting and he asks for this setting first, spending longer exploring his voice through this effect than any other. The experience seems to stay with him. One morning, from his seat in the back of my boyfriend's car he sings 'hello, hello, hello', fading his voice with each greeting until they dissolve into a whisper. Under the live, reverberating bridge in Ladywell Fields where we usually clap and exchange spoken and sung vowel sounds and funny faces, he now includes a shout out of the word 'echo'. He has made the connection with what we were doing at home. And now he knows there is a snazzy bit of kit waiting that can recreate our under-the-bridge play.

Vocal processing in other settings

In the past, I used this technology with children exhibiting a range of difficulties including selective mutism, notably when working in Cherry Trees School in East

London on projects for Sing Up and Spitalfields Music. The teachers there were the most inspiring and dedicated group of educators I have ever worked with, supporting primary-aged boys with complex behavioural, emotional and social difficulties (BESD). One might assume these children would be full of rage and have frequent outbursts. While there were such instances, there were as many examples of children shying away and hiding under tables and chairs. The vocal processor seemed to make expressive vocalizing 'safe' for children like these. Their voices could be transformed to sound like robots or aliens. They did not have to expose their real voices and could safely role-play. Vocal processing beautifully taps into a stage of imaginative play on which many children in BESD and SEND settings may have missed out. It is an opportunity to transform and escape into a new space sonically and emotionally. I would interview children assuming robot characters. Sometimes they played the role of benign, helpful robots, and at others they were mischievous robots. They could be 'safely naughty' in this guise.

In an episode of the WNYC Radiolab show *Juicervose*, Geraldine Dawson and Simon Baron-Cohen (2014) talk of how 'music activates emotional centres in our brains'. They explain that brain scans of people with autism spectrum condition (ASC) show that the experience of listening to music activated the emotional centres of their brains in a way that is comparable to neurotypical people. This did not happen in regular interactions for autistic people. Time and again studies show the 'music effect' as being a real, tangible thing. Autistic children also seem to have higher incidences of musical aptitude. Academic music therapists like Adam Ockelford put the perfect pitch rate in autistic children at 5–8 per cent (vi)-In the wider population it is one in 10,000. My son appears to have perfect pitch.

I am also reminded of how well vocal processing worked to break the ice with refugee groups in both community settings and UK immigration removal centres (IRCs), Brook House and Tinsley House. IRCs are bleak places for anyone. Detainees are often shackled. There is little privacy or contact with the outside world. Detainees usually have no idea how long they are going to be there. Psychotherapists widely report a range of mental health difficulties like PTSD, depression and suicidal ideation. Often the only medical care available is painkillers. Several detention centres in the United Kingdom have been subject to journalistic investigations and exposed as being abusive. I am realistic about how much a music workshop achieves in such horrible circumstances but always felt that disrupting grim routines with something creative was worth doing. From time to time something more happens – seeming moments of connection and cultural exchange. On a project for Music in Detention (MID), I encouraged a shy young male detainee to have a robot voice conversation with an older male staff member. I sensed them viewing each other differently afterwards.

On another MID project with Syrian families in Bedford, the group became strikingly playful and adventurous quickly after introducing vocal-processing activities, offering up impassioned solos and electing to sing entire traditional songs through enhanced delay effects. The desire to play, explore and ultimately transform and transcend was strong within the group and the sonic possibilities of vocal processing seemed to support this perfectly. In 2018, I composed a piece derived from recordings of a husband and wife singing the song 'Lama Bada Yatathanna', though echo effects and time-stretched it for seven minutes to represent each year of the war.

Vocal processing technology and interaction

Studies suggest that PTSD and autism are frequently misdiagnosed as each other. There is definitely some crossover: social withdrawal, rigidity, anxiety among other features. Autism could even be framed as playing out like a response to trauma, and it stands to reason that support activities for children and young people negotiating PTSD may also work for children negotiating autism. Ultimately my little boy is not ready for more than occasional, brief interactions with the technology. Usually, it is something I use with junior and senior-aged children rather than rambunctious infants for whom these new sonic toys may be too much. Even with older ones, I rarely introduce it straight away to avoid it becoming too dominant and gimmicky. It can be a wonderful development, even a game changer, but generally if introduced after we have already interacted through some other means: a sharing activity involving movement, clapping, whispers, shouts, call and response or singing.

For now, the technology is a little too exciting for my boy. I get frustrated by him diving onto the pedals, throwing around the microphone I use for gigs and recording, and making trip hazard loops out of the XLR lead. But there is something worth revisiting and re-creating. If I say his 'hello, hello, hello' when he is splashing in the bath, it elicits a playful, interactive response. According to the SCERTS model the more children on the autism spectrum spend in isolated, self-absorbed, repetitive play, the deeper they retreat into that world. So, every interaction and extension of play counts, especially when children are young, like my little boy.

REFERENCE

Dawson, Geraldine and Simon, Baron-Cohen (2014), *Juicervose*, 18 September, https://www.wnycstudios.org/podcasts/radiolab/articles/juicervose. Accessed 6 May 2022.

13

The Oneonta Hip Hop Collective:
Students Owning the Moment

Joseph Michael Pignato

Joseph Michael Pignato, professor at the State University of New York, Oneonta, teaches music industry, beat production, experimental music and improvised rock.

This chapter describes the Oneonta Hip Hop Collective (OHHC), a student founded organization at a rural university campus in the United States. The author relied heavily on participant expressions to illustrate ways in which the agency of young people can articulate their purposes and created places for music teaching, learning and community.

This chapter derives from a study that employed qualitative methods including interviewing founding members of the Oneonta Hip Hop Collective (OHHC), transcribing those interviews, coding the resultant data and analyzing those data through the framework of a *community of response*. The chapter relies heavily on participant expressions in the hope of telling the stories in *their* voices as much as possible. In taking this approach, I hope to illustrate ways in which young people articulate their purposes and places in music teaching and learning and in their communities.

The State University of New York, Oneonta is a four-year, post-secondary institution of higher education. The bucolic campus, located in the foothills of New York State's historic Leatherstocking Region, offers bachelor's degrees in some 60 major areas of study as well as a limited number of post-baccalaureate certificates and master's degree programmes (SUNY Oneonta 2020). The Music Department at the college offers quite a diverse range of musical genres for students to study, create and perform. The department offers a BA in Music and a BA in Music Industry. The latter degree programme features multiple pop, rock, electronic music and jazz ensembles as well as theory, literature and history courses exploring these genres. At the time of the OHHC's founding, hip-hop was notably absent from those offerings, with a few exceptions. Karina, a founding member of the OHHC, explained how students understood the absence of hip-hop in the curricula:

At Oneonta, but also elsewhere, everyone likes hip-hop but they don't respect is an *art form*, which is why in an academic setting, the offerings are going to be [...] I don't know, I guess more of what people think of as artsy. Like the academicians, the professors, they're going to focus on the performances they *know*. Also, this music has its own culture and dynamics. I feel like geographically speaking, this school, is mostly, I think we have a lot of students who are not exactly, well they're not the minority population. That population is smaller, the African American population, the Hispanic population is smaller and, I guess, those are the people that are going to be most attracted to hip-hop be it courses, ensembles, or campus events. Frankly, the whole college just assumes that people won't like rap and I think it leads to an effect that people who do like hip-hop, who feel it's a part of their life, of their culture, end up feeling like they're not welcome. Like, there's not a lot of diversity in the music courses, or any of the courses for that matter, which is problematic given the college's history.

(Karina 2015: n.pag.)

Although the confines of this chapter do not allow full discussion of the history to which Karina referred, I will point readers to the excellent documentary, *Brothers of the Blacklist* (Gallagher 2014). Suffice to say, in the early 1990s an egregious violation of student civil rights on the part of the campus administration and the City of Oneonta police, led to the longest litigated civil rights case in US History (New York Civil Liberties Union n.d.).

The implications of the Blacklist incident reverberated on campus for some time. In the second decade of the 2000s, SUNY Oneonta committed to recogniz-ing the impact of the original incident, offering an official apology ceremony and instituting numerous programmes to diversify the campus. Consequently, students began openly addressing issues of race, equity and exclusion. At the time, the campus was buzzing with common reads, discussion groups, assemblies, cultural programming and demonstrations. Armand, a student of colour, problematized the new initiatives:

It was like we [students of colour] always talked about it but now it was okay for White students, faculty and administrators to do so. It was weird because we were kind of having the conversation all along but for them it was like, 'no, we're starting the conversation now'. So even then, we kind of felt excluded from this thing that really affected us, not them. It was like, 'hey, be quiet! We're apologizing here'.

(2015: n.pag.)

Another consequence of the campus efforts to atone for the Blacklist incident was an immediate and problematic backlash targeting students of colour. Kellin, a founding member of the OHHC, described an infamous exchange on the then popular social discussion platform *Yik Yak*:

> I helped organize a peaceful protest in the quad in response to police brutality. It was there that I learned they were cutting the funding for the ALS Department [Africana and Latino Studies]. I'm not saying that it goes hand in hand but like that's a pretty significant thing. I mean people losing their jobs in the ALS department? And you know like racial profiling on campus and the whole thing that happened so long ago. I don't want to get into that with the blacklist, but it's just, it's ridiculous. Like it's 2015. But still, on top of it all, there were these statements on *Yik Yak*, racial things being said, and they're anonymous so you don't know who they are but, at the same time, it's clear that racism is alive on campus. Stuff like this made a lot of us feel like we didn't fully belong here. Like it was okay to talk about race but not say anything that made the majority of people uncomfortable.

(Kellin 2015: n.pag.)

According to Armand (2015: n.pag.), the OHHC was formed to give the founders a 'forum for learning, supporting, and growing in hip-hop'. It also served as a support group, one in which Oneonta students, a few alumni and some members of the local community expressed 'a shared vision' to 'help each other out', to create comfort through music. Caia (2015: n.pag.), a singer, dancer and OHHC founding member, described the group as a place where 'we belong and feel welcome, regardless of who we are or where we're from'.

At first, the group began meeting to share knowledge specific to hip-hop, things like a weekly cypher, beat production demonstrations, MCing, DJing and hip-hop performance. The founding members wanted to 'fill a hole in the music curriculum on [their] own terms' (Jones 2015: n.pag.). Armand, a founding member described the group's genesis:

> There was just a bunch of people in Oneonta who were kind of rapping, doing their own thing. It goes back to hip-hop not really being supported around, let alone given the time of day. So we started the OHHC to bring those people together, to make our own community within the larger community.

(Armand 2015: n.pag.)

Caia described the sense of community in particularly poignant terms:

> We tried to create an environment where hip-hop was accepted and where *we* were accepted. Where we didn't feel judged or ridiculed or out of place. I can honestly say, I don't know where I'd be right now without the OHHC. It's so engrained in my life. They're like family to me.
>
> (Caia 2015: n.pag.)

Eventually, the OHHC evolved to encompass much more. It became a politically minded organization that had hip-hop, the culture of the cypher and communal performance at its core.

Collectively, the OHHC formed an unofficial campus club that operated outside the official channels of Student Association funded clubs, grew rapidly, became prominent in the community and, at its peak, included dozens of members. Founding member MC Kellin explained:

> It needed to be ours. The SA [Student Association] is cool but this had to be for the students and community members who started it and, if we were going to be marginalized, might as well use that as a strength, you know what I mean? Let's face it, Oneonta is not the most forgiving, let alone welcoming place, towards hip-hop. On campus, hip-hop has been vilified. If people see it or hear it, they assume it's the party rap that's popular: rapping about drugs, or girls, or gangs, or money, or whatever. We wanted to be represented better than that, as more than that.
>
> (2015: n.pag.)

The earliest days of the OHHC can be understood as a *Community of Response*, a term I developed while teaching about popular music to describe the ways in which fans come together around an artist, a musical genre or a subcultural movement (Pignato 2017). The members of the OHHC came together for a kind of 'gather round' experience, connecting based on their interests in hip-hop, and in search of a feeling of belonging. Communities of response represent a precedent step to what Jean Lave and Etienne Wenger (1991) have called 'communities of practice'. Communities of response are yet to be fully understood by those who form them, often starting as one thing and morphing into another. In the case of the OHHC, that progression is well summed up by Talia, a DJ and founding member of the OHHC:

> It was like we came together because, 'hey, you like hop hop? Me too'. But then, it became more. The group, our weekly cyphers, the way we handled the stuff with yik yak and the protests, we allowed people to just forget about stuff for a while. In that

71

environment you don't really feel pressured to do something one way or another, you're just going with the flow, not to make a bad pun about flow, but I think when you're in that moment, everything else fades away.

(2015: n.pag.)

The weekly cyphers were essential to the membership of the OHHC, providing them with opportunities to express themselves, practice their rhyming skills, support one another, experience fellowship and build feelings of belonging. Jones, a founding member discussed the cathartic and comforting role of the cypher in his life and in the life of the OHHC:

Being part of the cypher kind of bonds you with the others. You get things out. You can learn certain things, although it can be a competition, at the same time, you're all even. When you're next to rap or whatever or do poetry, that moment is *yours*. You *own* that moment. Everyone, they respect what you're doing. No one is judging you so you're open. You're free to do and say what you please. The circle, your committee, your group. That kind of thing is life or death important, especially in the big picture of everything else going on at that time. It literally saved me.

(2015: n.pag.)

The founding members of the OHHC provide an example of how, devoid of places and purposes for music teaching and learning that speak to them, young people will create their own, on their own terms, within or without institutional recognition or support. In addition to rectifying a dearth of hip-hop music and culture on the university campus and in the surrounding community, the founders of the OHHC grappled with larger issues, some long-standing and others more recently embroiling their campus. By forming the OHHC, a community of response, the members created inclusion where they felt exclusion, equity in the face of inequity, and representation for students of colour at a time and place when such students felt as if they 'didn't really matter at all'.

REFERENCES

Armand (2015), Skype interview with author, 5 June.
Caia (2015), Skype interview with author, 5 June.
Gallagher, Sean (dir.) (2014), *Jonathan Demme Presents, Brothers of the Blacklist* [documentary film], UK: Whatnot Productions.
Jones (2015), Skype interview with author, 5 June.
Karina (2015), Skype interview with author, 5 June.
Kellin (2015), Skype interview with author, 5 June.

Lave, Jean and Wenger, Etienne (1991), *Situated Learning: Legitimate Peripheral Participation*, New York: Cambridge University Press.

New York Civil Liberties Union (n.d.), 'Brothers of the black list film screening', https://www.nyclu.org/en/events/brothers-black-list-film-screening. Accessed 2 March 2022.

Pignato, Joseph Michael (2017), 'Situating technology within and without music education', in R. Mantie and A. Ruthmann (eds), *The Oxford Handbook of Technology in Music Education*, Oxford: Oxford University Press.

SUNY Oneonta (2020), 'About SUNY Oneonta', https://suny.oneonta.edu/about-oneonta. Accessed 2 March 2022.

Talia (2015), Skype interview with author, 5 June.

14

Rockway and Formal–Informal Online Music Learning in Finland

Niklas Lindholm

Niklas Lindholm is co-founder and CEO of Rockway Ltd and has taught music technology and video-based pedagogy courses in Arcada and Metropolia Universities of Applied Science.

This provides a description of how the for-profit, online music education platform, Rockway, has bridged formal and informal learning paradigms in Finland to serve music learning purposes at home and in schools.

Background

Rockway is a small private company that has provided video-based online music learning since 2006. Aimed at adult Finnish consumers who wish to learn to play an instrument, it is the largest online school in Finland with 140 teachers and over 14,000 video lessons. Over the years, Rockway has been adopted in schools, and courses can be borrowed through libraries nationwide. Rockway's position between formal and informal education is somewhat unique, and as such its services have been adopted in formal education all the way up to teacher training in universities, replacing some in-person classes. This way of learning has proven to be effective and resource saving. As co-founder of Rockway, I feel that it points to new and exciting possibilities for what being a teacher or learner looks like in the future.

Formal education

In Finland, music education has traditionally been rooted in a somewhat Germanic, western European classical music education. Although the first music school focusing on popular music education was founded in the 1970s, most music schools maintained a largely classical curriculum up to the late 1980s. During the 1990s, popular music education spread and became more commonplace throughout Finnish schools and music schools.

The Finnish education system has received a lot of praise globally over the past several years, usually ranking at or towards the top of league tables since the year 2000.[1] In Finland, the concept of private schools does not exist. There are only public schools, which makes the educational system equally accessible to all regardless of socioeconomic background. Elementary school teachers in Finland often teach everything from biology to languages, mathematics, music and even gymnastics. The role of the teacher as a kind of generalist has its origins in two things; the small size of the economy and the low population density. Both of these factors drive up education costs per capita and hence call for teacher efficiency.

One major differentiator from many other education systems around the world is the freedom elementary school teachers in Finland have when teaching. They are not bound by strict guidelines; rather, they follow quite loosely stated goals that give them freedom, as well as expectations, to teach in their own way. This way of thought also projected itself on to music education in elementary schools as early as the 1980s. Popular music was pouring into the classroom via demands from students and teacher preferences. I remember getting to try songwriting when I was a student in the third grade. The songs we came up with were really simple, but it still was an introduction to that creative process. This kind of environment also presented music as something approachable, fun and easy to access. Since then, Finnish elementary school education has evolved and is now focuses on phenomenon-based learning, where one focuses on the bigger picture and paints that picture through the different subjects being taught, e.g. writing a song in English might involve music (basic chord progression, melody and composition) mathematics (learning how music is built up of numbers), English language studies (produce the lyrics to the song), computer science (creating/recording a demo of the song), history (how music has evolved), religion (the role music has and has had in different religions), geography (the roots of popular music), etc.

All this puts a demand on teachers and creates a need for assistance in many areas, not least of which are music and music technology, all while keeping costs down. This in turn raises the need for new tools and ways to support the teachers in the multitude of expertise they need to master. The need for quality instruction at a lower price calls for online solutions to support teachers. In order to have digital tools widely spread, there needs to be major pedagogical change. This change is slow because there are few if any established best practices using digital means in music education. At least in Finland, there is also a lack of research on the subject.

Rockway has been used in different kinds of formal education for the past decade, from elementary schools to universities. The platform has been adopted in teacher training; as public resources are becoming more scarce, students are studying music through Rockway. We at Rockway are also doing research together with universities on how the courses that Rockway provides compare to traditional one-on-one learning. Through this kind of research, we hope to gain insight into how to develop didactics and pedagogics for how best to use online and digital means in different classrooms.

Informal education

Traditionally, people have learned to play music on their own, or through a master–apprentice relationship before music schools were established. I would propose most people still learn music informally rather than formally (notwith-standing formal learning of, for example, classical music). The tools for informal learning have improved over the last decades, with the internet providing previously-unheard-of possibilities. Rockway is a good example of such a tool, not to mention YouTube. YouTube is of course the largest source of information for music learning. When trying to learn to play an instrument on YouTube there are some major obstacles, namely finding the right material and trusting that it is accurate. It is rather time consuming, hacking one's way to a good 'curriculum' on YouTube. Also finding accurate sheet music such as transcriptions can be difficult. This is where the value proposition of Rockway lives – in its offer of curated and structured material provided by music education professionals. Rockway has brought a professional touch to informal (self-directed) learning.

The adult population in Finland is increasingly playing musical instruments. About 40 per cent of the adult population in Finland play, or have played an instrument. Many of those who played as children or young adults would like to come back to playing, but they feel either they do not have time or cannot be bothered to find a teacher. Young people with excess time on their hands would prefer to search YouTube for free content rather than pay for online learning. Working adults increasingly value their free time and want to focus on learning instead of searching. A lack of time is the most common reason we hear for why someone is not playing or practising. Since new musicians might not know what to do and when to move forward, we suggest using Rockway as little as fifteen minutes per day with 100 per cent focus. When learning online, using less time might even be better. If you spend hours at a time online, the temptation to binge on lessons is big. Instead of actually playing and learning what is being taught in the lessons one might stay passive, only watching. This is a quite typical behaviour and something many do not even realize they are doing. They feel they have learned what is taught and while that might be true on a theoretical level, a student's skill in actually playing an instrument may not be evolving.

In addition to this, getting feedback is crucial for knowing when to proceed to the next task at hand and when not to. Understanding the importance of assessment is nothing new, but it presents challenges in online contexts and is an area for future development. Rockway offers assessment through well-organized online coaching, where learners are given feedback and advice as they return given tasks via video. This is one way in which possible issues, not evident through audio-only assessment methods (e.g. posture, technique) – can be addressed. Video-based assessment also drives possibilities for peer-to-peer learning and assessment, potentially building community and togetherness.

Becoming one

I predict that in the near future, informal and formal education will melt together in Finland. The need to cut back on costs will affect creative subjects in school curricula and force schools to find new ways of providing education in these areas. The quality of more informal learning materials, that do not follow formal curricula and pedagogies and are often mainly made for consumers, in many ways exceed the potential of formal education provision, because competition in the consumer market is much fierce. Also, trends towards life-wide and lifelong learning encourage companies and schools to work together in order to provide cost-effective and flexible possibilities for anyone to earn diplomas or a degree.

So, is the teacher taken out of the picture? No, but the teacher's role is changing. Already now teachers are becoming more facilitators of learning, than the sole source of knowledge in a classroom. This is a big mind-shift and not all teachers are onboard. In the future, the role of the teacher will shift more to content-producer and facilitator because learning will happen through problem-solving and creative thinking that requires the teacher to produce creative tasks and solvable problems through different media, as fewer and fewer students will be in any kind of live classroom, but rather learn on their own and return assignments for assessment. This will give the word 'school' a new meaning. A school will no longer be a building or a physical place. A school will be a name on a diploma.

That has been the most important role of many schools already. In Finland, I see this change starting to happen.

NOTE

1. https://www.weforum.org/agenda/2018/09/10-reasons-why-finlands-education-system-is-the-best-in-the-world. Accessed 19 January 2022.

15

How Do We Get Girls and Non-Binary Students to Play Guitar Solos?[1]

Kayla Rush

Kayla Rush is an anthropologist and a Marie Skłodowska-Curie research fellow based at Dublin City University. Her current work examines private, fees-based rock music schools.

This chapter examines gender inequality in guitar soloing in private rock music organizations in the United States and Ireland. It discusses some socio-cultural factors that influence this gender imbalance, and ways that well-intentioned teachers might inadvertently perpetuate it. It makes several suggestions for ways in which teachers can actively encourage female and non-binary guitarists to solo.

The guitar solo, particularly the improvised, virtuosic guitar solo, has been gendered as masculine almost since the first emergence of the electric guitar in the early twentieth century (Walser 1993; Waksman 1999). This type of performance is also frequently upheld as the epitome of rock – the most 'rock' that rock music can be – and in this way popular understandings of guitar solos play a key role in perpetuating the gendering of the entire genre. For a girl or non-binary student to solo, then, is to disrupt deep-rooted gendered understandings of rock.

With the explosive growth of popular music education over the past two decades, and thus the readier availability of guitar learning to students of all genders, we might expect the status quo to have begun shifting. And yet, in my hundreds of hours of research with private, fees-based rock schools in Ireland and the United States, I have yet to see a girl play a guitar solo in these settings.[2] This chapter is an attempt to think through the social processes and practices behind this observed phenomenon. I invite readers to think alongside me and consider ways in which gender expectations shape popular music learning experiences.

Barriers

I have already touched upon the first, and perhaps earliest, barrier: the ongoing perception of the guitar as a masculine instrument (Björck 2011; Powell 2019; Waksman 1999). The musical status quo reproduces itself: prospective students see boys and men playing guitars in popular culture and among their peers, while girls and women are more likely to be cast as singers (Bayton 1997: 37). As a result, more boys pick up guitars, so the pool of potential girl and non-binary guitarists is simply smaller. This is further exacerbated by the gender distribution of popular music teachers, at least in the private organizations in which I have worked, where nearly all of the educational staff are cisgender men (and nearly all White men at that), and the few women employed are most often vocalists.

The dearth of girl and non-binary guitar soloists, however, is not only the product of underrepresentation. For even when classes or bands have both boy and girl guitarists, boys typically 'shred' – play virtuosically and soloistically – while girls 'strum' – accompany the other musicians by strumming chords in a steady, set pattern. I have found this to even be the case in bands where the girl guitarist – and there is rarely more than one in a group – is noticeably more skillful or experienced than her male peers. Girls and women in North American and European contexts are often socialized to be more disciplined, more reserved and less willing to put the spotlight on themselves. This is a tricky process to overcome, as gender expectations are felt and passed on from very early ages, and they come from numerous sources – family, peers, educational settings, popular culture, etc. (Brown et al. 2020). Gender expectations also intersect with race, class, disability, sexual orientation and other identities (Hess 2016). While space precludes me from discussing intersectionality in popular music education here, we must always remember that gender identities are not monolithic categories, but one component of students' complex, multifaceted identities.

Research has demonstrated that boys are far more likely to take charge and determine what sort of music is made in popular music education settings, while girls 'most often adopted a wait-and-see attitude' (Lindgren and Ericsson 2010: 46); this has been reported at both secondary and tertiary levels of study (Georgii-Hemming and Westvall 2010: 29; Ahlers 2015: 190). I have found boys far more likely to volunteer to play a solo or to initiate the addition of a solo to a song. They are also more likely to practice soloing during band downtime, whereas girls tend to sit quietly waiting for instruction.

Ferm Almqvist (2016) writes that teenage girl guitarist students often find themselves expected to take on organizational tasks, while their male peers claim the flashiest or most technically complicated solo parts, thus receiving more credit for their ostensibly more visible (but less labour-intensive roles). I have also found this among adolescents with whom I research, with girls as young as ten and eleven assuming the unofficial role of keeping their bands disciplined and focused, at times even to the extent of keeping their (nearly always male) teachers on track.

Teacher expectations based on student gender are also crucial. While there is a broad spectrum of approaches to popular music education, generally speaking the movement has been away from a top-down 'formal' model, toward a more 'informal learning' approach in which teachers facilitate the students' own initiative and creativity. This is a welcome change with many benefits for learning. However, without some level of facilitation or intervention from teachers, students tend to reproduce the gender status quo. Ferm Almqvist (2016) argues that a higher level of instructor intervention is vital for achieving a greater level of gender equality, and I am inclined to agree (Rush 2021). But for intervention to be successful, popular music teachers must be aware of how gender socialization shapes their students' everyday lives, and of their own unconscious biases as individuals who live in gendered and gender-unequal societies. Green, for example, demonstrated that school music teachers tend to perceive boys as more inherently creative and imaginative, particularly in their approaches to composition (Green 1997: 196–200; 2002: 139–41) – that is, with regard to the skills seen as necessary for improvised soloing.

Suggestions

Gender-specific popular music education programmes like girls rock camps and schools offer a potential solution, aimed as they are at both elevating female and non-binary musical role models and challenging the socialization processes whereby girls and women learn to present themselves as less confident. But addressing and rectifying gender inequality is not, and should not be, only the responsibility of these dedicated programmes and spaces. It is also vital to address and think through the impacts of gender socialization in more mainstream spaces, including schools and private extracurriculars.

I believe that an excellent place to start within these spaces is consciously considering how teachers recruit guitar soloists for particular songs or performances. I have found that, unless an individual student has initiated or offered to play a guitar solo unprompted when popular music teachers look to add a solo to a song they are most likely to phrase it as an open invitation: 'Does anyone want to play a solo here?' (a phenomenon also reported by Georgii-Hemming and Westvall 2010: 29). Based on what I have detailed so far, we can surmise that boys are likely to be first to respond to such invitations. If no one responds to the open call for solos, teachers most often begin asking individual students, starting with whomever they perceive to be the most confident – and this perception appears to be based on which students feel the most comfortable soloing unprompted during band downtime, who are nearly always boys. Occasionally the teacher will then proceed to ask all of the guitarists one by one, but more often they will stop once they have solicited one or at most two solos. This means that girls are either never asked, or they are third, fourth or fifth down the list, which could make them feel like an afterthought rather than as valued and desirable soloists.

One potential way forward, then, is to invite girls and non-binary students to play solos *first*, rather than as an addendum to the list of their male peers. Another possible tactic is for instructors to spend class time teaching students simple, straightforward routes into soloing – for example, the pentatonic 'shapes' on which many guitarists rely for basic solo structure. At present, it seems the 'how' of soloing is most often assumed to have been learned outside the classroom, which can make soloing seem like an inaccessible type of knowledge for those who have not already received this training, who in my experience are disproportionately girls. Teaching soloing basics in the classroom context could be one step toward levelling the playing field. This is even more so if instructors take time to teach basic soloing techniques on *all* instruments, including voice, as this can undermine the traditional understanding of the guitar as the top of the rock hierarchy, perhaps removing some of the 'lesser' value assigned to stereotypically feminized instruments. Teaching improvisation as a skill to be learned, rather than as something that happens 'naturally' (but only for those experienced or confident enough to do it), allows space for girls and non-binary students 'to be allowed to be mediocre and to make mistakes, just as men [and boys] are' (Hill 2016: 168).

Simple interventions such as the two I have suggested will by no means solve the problems of gender inequality in popular music and popular music education. But they can be steps toward making instructors more conscious of how gender socialization affects their students' engagement in the learning environment, and of how their own social identities and unconscious biases can affect the opportunities afforded to students in these spaces. Equipping popular music teachers with greater consciousness of gender inequality and gender socialization is vital for training up more girl, women, and non-binary guitarists and eliciting solo performances from these players, and indeed for changing gendered perceptions of rock music and musicians.

NOTES

1. This project has received funding from the European Union's Horizon 2020 research and innovation programme under the Marie Skłodowska-Curie grant agreement No. 844238,

and from the Department of Further and Higher Education, Research, Innovation and Science (DFHERIS) of Ireland, via the Higher Education Authority (Cost Extensions for Research Disrupted by COVID-19).

2.   In both of the locations in which I have conducted intensive research, none of the students openly identified as transgender or non-binary. As such I can only speculate as to how these young people experience rock learning, particularly as my own perspective is limited by my experiences as a cisgender woman. Given the discrimination and transphobia that trans and non-binary people face, I believe they too experience barriers to guitar soloing, barriers that may overlap with, but will not necessarily be the same as, those experienced by cisgender girls and women.

REFERENCES

Ahlers, Michael (2015), 'Opening minds: Style copies as didactical initiators', *IASPM@Journal*, 5:1, pp. 181–94.

Bayton, Mavis (1997), 'Women and the electric guitar', in S. Whiteley (ed.), *Sexing the Groove: Popular Music and Gender*, London: Routledge, pp. 37–49.

Björck, Cecilia (2011), 'Claiming space: Discourses on gender, popular music, and social change', Ph.D. dissertation, Academy of Music and Drama, Gothenburg: University of Gothenburg.

Brown, Christia Spears, Biefeld, Sharla D. and Tam, Michelle J. (2020), *Gender in Childhood*, Cambridge: Cambridge University Press.

Ferm Almqvist, Cecilia (2016), 'Becoming a guitar playing woman: The risk of unequal gender role conservation in non-formal ensemble music education', in R. Wright, B. A. Younker and C. Beynon (eds), *21st Century Music Education: Informal Learning and Non-Formal Teaching Approaches in School and Community Contexts*, Waterloo: Canadian Music Educators' Association, pp. 21–38.

Georgii-Hemming, Eva and Westvall, Maria (2010), 'Music education – A personal matter? Examining the current discourses of music education in Sweden', *British Journal of Music Education*, 27:1, pp. 21–33.

Green, Lucy (1997), *Music, Gender, Education*, Cambridge: Cambridge University Press.

Green, Lucy (2002), 'Exposing the gendered discourse of music education', *Feminism and Psychology*, 12:2, pp. 137–44.

Hess, Juliet (2016), '"How does that apply to me?" The gross injustice of having to translate', *Bulletin of the Council for Research in Music Education*, 207–08, pp. 81–100.

Hill, Rosemary Lucy (2016), *Gender, Metal and the Media: Women Fans and the Gendered Experience of Music*, London: Palgrave Macmillan.

Lindgren, Monica and Ericsson, Claes (2010), 'The rock band context as discursive governance in music education in Swedish schools', *Action, Criticism, and Theory for Music Education*, 9:3, pp. 35–54.

Powell, Bryan (2019), 'Breaking down barriers to participation: Perspectives of female musicians in popular music ensembles', in Z. Moir, B. Powell and G. D. Smith (eds), *The Bloomsbury Handbook of Popular Music Education*, London: Bloomsbury Academic, pp. 337–49.

Rush, Kayla (2021), 'Riot grrrls and shredder bros: Punk ethics, social justice, and (un)popular popular music at School of Rock', *Journal of Popular Music Education*, 5:3, pp. 375–95. https://doi.org/10.1386/jpme_00054_1. Accessed 9 May 2022.

Waksman, Steve (1999), *Instruments of Desire: The Electric Guitar and the Shaping of Musical Experience*, Cambridge: Harvard University Press.

Walser, Robert (1993), *Running with the Devil: Power, Gender, and Madness in Heavy Metal Music*, Middletown: Wesleyan University Press.

16

Learning to Become a Band, Learning Popular Music

Tobias Malm

Tobias Malm is a Ph.D. in education at Stockholm University and Royal College of Music in Stockholm, Sweden, where he teaches learning and organization theory, and teacher training courses.

This chapter aims to show how learning popular music involves often-overlooked processes of learning to become a band, it discusses implications for educators and calls for more research. Based in Sweden, a small country with relatively large impact on popular music, the author currently sets out to answer that call.

Introduction

A band, undisputedly, is a place for popular music education (Green 2002), which, for many musicians, constitutes the necessary form for creativity and performance (Behr 2010). Musicians without a band in many cases give up playing at all (cf. Bennett 1980). A band may be thought of as a situated social setting in which people 'realize' identity as a musician (Smith 2013) and thus is strongly connected to a practitioner's motivation to play and learn popular music (cf. Lave and Wenger 1991; Karlsen 2010).

However, a band is not a given or some a priori social context of popular music. On the contrary, organizing a band in all its informal and leisure-based terms (Mantie and Smith 2017) constitutes many challenges. There are many band-threatening social tensions inherent within the structures and logics of a band, including play vs. work, friendship vs. collegiality and creativity vs. commerce (e.g. Cohen 1991; Berkaak 1999; Weinstein 2004; Malm 2017,

2020). Unfortunately, these essential 'micro- organizational' (Bennett 2001) and interpersonal aspects of music-making still seem underemphasized within the fields of popular music and music education. Perhaps the emerging area of popular music education will lead the way in opening up for a more holistic view on popular music practices.

With this short essay, I wish to highlight that a band in itself is something that is learnt. To illustrate this, I describe some general features of band members' learning processes of becoming a band, based on a selection of band research.

Learning to become a band

Finnegan ([1989] 2007) argues that band members' coordination and administration of themselves as an organization is an important learning process within a band. Weinstein (1991) adds that this process takes place 'the hard way' meaning that members gradually learn to differentiate between their individual self-fulfillment and the common work by trial and error, learning from mistakes and experiences. Moreover, Weinstein (2004) argues that the formation of a band as a workgroup requires the development of different types of leadership. Some bands develop a more hierarchical and asymmetric power structure, while others agree on a certain division of labour. In this process, Weinstein (2006) identifies that members learn to divide work between necessary roles linked to performance, creativity, business and social relations. In general, these band structures are learnt as informal, as well as more pronounced band norms for the joint work (Groce 1991a).

Furthermore, research indicates that band members learn to work together by developing certain conceptions on both a collective and an individual level. First, Finnegan ([1989] 2007) argues that bands mould together by a collective sense of community that goes beyond each individual member and bridges the internal tensions. She exemplifies this process with a sense of togetherness that playing live shows may result in. Behr further argues that the band members' ongoing negotiation in the 'micro-field' – i.e. internally in the band – develops a cohesive internal culture that, together with being recognized as a collective actor publically, forms a community-founding 'character':

> In building relationships not only with each other in the micro-field but, as a collective agent, with the outside world a band forms a 'character'. In learning, socializing, and negotiating creative decisions together, the band members become entwined in an enterprise whose outward face incorporates musical, performative, and

image-related features. Logos, performing style, lyrics, musical style, haircuts, cloth-
ing, and numerous other details form part of this mix.

(2015: 17)

Behr points out that a band's bridging sense of a 'we' forms in a combination of
the members' interaction and the collective characteristics they are attributed in
their outgoing activities by outsiders.

Second, Berkaak (1999) argues that bands that survive the internal tensions
consist of band members who individually have learnt to 'disentangle' the inherent tensions. In line with Groce (1991b), this means that the members adopt a
pragmatic professionalism and a realistic view of the industry and their careers,
and that the band activities are structured and kept separate from the rest of the
members' social lives. In this way, the individual musician learns to relate to music
as a kind of technique and only something that one is engaged in, rather than something existential and self-defining that easily may become sensitive in relation to
the band's activities and band mates.

Taken together, becoming a band involves three foundational learning
processes. In a first learning process, the band is formed as a micro-organization
based on the band members learning to separate their own persons from the
collective, and on their development of more or less formal structures of division
of labour, hierarchies and collegiality. In a second learning process, the band's
outgoing activities as a collective actor contributes to the development of a notion
of being a common 'we' shared by the members. This group identification in itself
bridges internal tensions. In a third learning process, the members develop professional identities and alignment with the music industry, which, through a less
sentimental and more pragmatic view of the band activities, may reduce internal
tensions further.

However, there is still relatively little research on the learning processes of
becoming a band. Existing research on these complex processes seems of age
and somewhat under-theorised, idealized and rough-cut. It appears as if a band
may succeed if only the members learn to become a formal small business where
communality and solid professional identities dissolve individuality and tensions.
Such an ideal situation hardly exists in any band, regardless of the level of ambition and commercial success. One may also wonder how the identified learning
processes take place over time more precisely in terms of situations, phases and
periods. Moreover, it may be questioned whether the development of the band
always goes in the same direction, that is, from less organization, community and
professionalism, towards more. Perhaps the band members' learning may result in
the band also diminishing its ability or desire to establish these conditions. Furthermore, one may wonder if a band that has reached a certain state remains in that

state or if the band and its members may switch dynamically between different states and identities.

Conclusion

In this chapter, I have illustrated how a band is a product of learning processes, briefly described as they are identified in a selection of band research. Since a band constitutes a central place for learning popular music (cf. Green 2002), learning popular music in many regards, and for many musicians, interconnects with organizational learning processes. Becoming a band provides authenticity (cf. Karlsen 2010; Behr 2015) and identification (cf. Bennett 1980; Smith 2013), which may motivate musicians for sustained engagement in, and further mastery of, popular music practices (cf. Lave and Wenger 1991). Popular music practices thus feature organizational aspects that academics and practitioners may consider as integral parts of informal educational processes of popular music. In addition, I have argued that there is a need for more theoretically informed research into micro-organizational and interpersonal aspects of music-making and learning. Such research may contribute to a more encompassing understanding of the practices and development of popular music, and, particularly, contribute to the development of the research area of popular music education.

Considering the proposed centrality of learning to become a band in learning popular music, popular music educators – and especially in formal school settings – face a number of challenging trade-offs. These trade-offs include balancing between, on the one hand, the formal educational logics of generalism and individualism, and, on the other hand, the situated and collective logics of becoming a band (cf. Westerlund 2006; Lindgren and Ericsson 2010). Educators could reflect upon issues such as; what skills are necessary for students to be able to participate independently and fruitfully in a band? Do the students spend enough time in a band in order to start developing band structure and identification? What are the benefits and hindrances of repeatedly changing band constellations and subgenres, and how does that differ between students with different experiences? How does individual assessment and grading affect students' learning to separate their band's collective performance from their persons, and their development of an authenticating common 'we'?

REFERENCES

Behr, Adam (2010), 'Group identity: Bands, rock and popular music', dissertation, Stirling: University of Stirling.

Behr, Adam (2015), 'Join together with the band: Authenticating collective creativity in bands and the myth of rock authenticity reappraised', *Rock Music Studies*, 2: 1, pp. 1–21.

Bennett, Andy (2001), *Cultures of Popular Music*, Buckingham: Open University Press.

Bennett, H. Stith (1980), *On Becoming a Rock Musician*, Amherst: University of Massachusetts Press.

Berkaak, Odd Aare (1999), 'Entangled dreams and twisted memories: Order and disruption in local music making', *Young: Nordic Journal of Youth Research*, 7:2, pp. 25–42.

Cohen, Sara (1991), *Rock Culture in Liverpool: Popular Music in the Making*, Oxford: Clarendon Press.

Finnegan, Ruth ([1989] 2007), *The Hidden Musicians: Music-Making in an English Town*, Middletown: Wesleyan University Press.

Green, Lucy (2002), *How Popular Musicians Learn*, Aldershot: Ashgate Publishing.

Groce, Stephen B. (1991a), 'What's the buzz?: Rethinking the meanings and uses of alcohol and other drugs among small-time rock 'n' roll musicians', *Deviant Behavior*, 12:4, pp. 361–84.

Groce, Stephen B. (1991b), 'On the outside looking in: Professional socialization and the process of becoming a songwriter', *Popular Music & Society*, 15:1, pp. 33–44.

Karlsen, Sidsel (2010), 'BoomTown music education and the need for authenticity – Informal learning put into practice in Swedish post-compulsory music education', *British Journal of Music Education*, 27:1, pp. 35–46.

Lave, Jean and Wenger, Etienne (1991), *Situated Learning – Legitimate Peripheral Participation*, Cambridge: University Press.

Lindgren, Monica and Ericsson, Claes (2010), 'The rock band context as discursive governance in music education in Swedish schools', *Action, Criticism, and Theory for Music Education*, 9:3, pp. 35–54.

Malm, Tobias (2017), 'Becoming a rock band: The challenges of group identity', *Journal of Popular Music Education*, 1:2, pp. 165–82.

Malm, Tobias (2020), 'Learning to develop as a rock band: The contradiction between creativity and entrepreneurship', *Learning, Culture and Social Interaction*, 25, p. 100379.

Mantie, Roger and Smith, Gareth Dylan (ed.) (2017), *The Oxford Handbook of Music Making and Leisure*, New York: Oxford University Press.

Smith, Gareth Dylan (2013), *I Drum, Therefore I Am – Being and Becoming a Drummer*, Farnham: Ashgate.

Weinstein, Deena (1991), *Heavy Metal: A Cultural Sociology*, New York: Lexington Books Macmillan, Inc.

Weinstein, Deena (2004), 'Creativity and band dynamics', in Eric Weisbard (ed.), *This Is Pop: In Search of the Elusive at Experience Music Project*, Cambridge: Harvard University Press, pp. 187–99.

Weinstein, Deena (2006), 'Relations in The Kinks – Familiar but not fully familial', *Popular Music and Society*, 29:2, pp. 167–87.

Westerlund, Heidi (2006), 'Garage rock bands: A future model for developing musical expertise?', *International Journal of Music Education*, 24:2, pp. 119–25.

17

Popular Music is Not the Answer

Abigail D'Amore

Abigail D'Amore is an independent consultant specializing in music education, youth voice, professional development of teachers and musicians, evaluation and impact and strategic planning.

While popular music appeals to the majority, its inclusion in formal institutions can exclude students if the teaching and learning approaches are tokenistic. The author shares a perspective on context and learning styles as well as content, the role of the 'teacher' in popular music education and implications for recruitment and training.

Popular music, in its various forms, has always appealed to the majority of young people. However, if the inclusion of popular music in schools is tokenistic, the very music that young people identify with has the potential to alienate and exclude. Music is more than a subject in school for young people. We know that music has a positive impact socially, psychologically, emotionally and in some cases academically, at a time when mental health issues among children and young people are dramatically rising. Yet as a school subject in England it is on the brink of crisis. At the heart of this is a diminishing workforce of music educators who are often not enabled by the institutions in which they work to make popular music learning a fully inclusive experience for all young people.

Popular music can play an important role in school music education. It has the potential to draw young people into learning through a medium they are familiar with, and to demonstrate to them that their musical interests are valued. It provides an opportunity to meaningfully engage with youth voice, agency and co-creation of musical learning due to young people being experts in their own right in popular music beyond the classroom.

As an independent music education consultant, I have often observed a position amongst music educators (whether teachers, headteachers, policymakers, examination boards, etc.) that western classical music has a degree of superiority over popular music and other musical styles, genres and cultures. In 2001, Lucy Green identified that while popular music has been present in schools for years, the practices and processes through which it is learned are not. This remains the case in many settings today. If popular music education in schools is taught using the same methods and teaching approaches drawn from western classical music, by teachers who are classically trained, its value for young people is significantly diminished. Popular music in itself, therefore, is not the answer. We need to look to how it is 'taught' in formal institutions.

What versus how

When planning music learning experiences, there is often a default towards content over context and learning styles. What should be learnt, what do they need to be able to do, and what learning will be evidenced? This often becomes the discourse rather than *how* will they learn, *how* will they create, *how* do we draw on prior musical experiences and interests and most importantly, *why* are they going to be learning in this way. Ideologies informing how music should be taught are often based on the learning experiences of the people in power making these decisions.

Assumptions are made about how young people themselves learn popular music, leading to a one-size-fits-all approach. Yet we know that young people all have different starting points, interests and learning styles, often informed by cultural context, family and social environment, and the influence of the media. Some learners prefer structure and clear progression routes, some want to be encouraged to be creative, some like to be led, others like to lead, some prefer learning notation, most are able to learn by ear and so on. At the heart of this set of often complex and multifaceted decisions, in a formal setting, is the educator. If there is little or no empathy, understanding and interest towards learners' existing musical interests and passions, it can take away ownership from the young people.

The role of the 'teacher' in popular music education

I want to share two examples of leadership in popular music education. Neither is from a formal institution.

The first is a film of a 2-year-old child rapping with an adult, that we can assume to be a family member: https://bit.ly/2Hp901o. The second is a film about a project developed in South London 'Roadworks' that trialled applying a critical thinking approach to drill music with a group of young musicians: https://bit.ly/3nOflmw (accessed 27 May 2022).

These videos represent both ends of the age spectrum from early years to late teens. The experiences of the child/young people range from joy, pride and collaboration to critical thinking and reflection. The leadership in both situations is compelling, engaging, natural and authentic. It involves repetition, modelling, encouragement, coaching, standing back and enabling the child and young people to learn in their own way, immersing them in a musical genre that they are deeply connected to. What does this tell us about the role of an educator in popular music? What qualities of effective musical leadership – aspects of which are present in these examples – transcend training programmes, and are effective due to an individual's style, musicianship and personality?

Through working as an evaluator and critical friend on a Youth Music funded project run by the City of London Sinfonia[1] and sound artist Gawain Hewitt in a hospital school for children and young people with a range of mental health issues, I was involved in conducting some exploratory work around the qualities of effective leadership needed to work with vulnerable young people. The aim of the project is to engage young people in group music-making activities during a potentially difficult time of their lives. The approach involved a series of workshop-style sessions, led by Gawain with the City of London Sinfonia, combining minimalism with electronic music, beat making, technology and live instrumentation to co-create new music with the young people.

Our discussions involved analyzing which aspects of Gawain's leadership could be described as generic, and which aspects were highly specific to his personality and individual style. After a workshop exploring and unpicking this, we established that the following attributes of leadership were particularly effective with this group of young people:

1. *Structuring an environment for creativity:* Considering what the learning space will look, feel and sound like. A creative 'informal' environment is often highly structured and planned by the leader, even if what you see and hear feels like chaos.
2. *Having a command of your craft (instrument, voice, technology):* Being bold and confident with musicianship, and able to openly demonstrate this to young people. Sharing your own drive and passion for music.
3. *Modelling learning:* Showing rather than telling, and being confident to take a step back and let students absorb information without jumping in and doing it for them.

4. *Helping young people understand and master their own abilities:* Tapping into prior experiences, knowledge and understanding of the young people and incorporating this into the learning.
5. *Aiming for high quality musical outcomes:* Recognizing that outcomes may differ for all young people. Have a strong commitment to your role of making a difference in young people's lives through the process of making music with them.
6. *Have a breadth and depth of understanding of the range of needs of children and young people:* Don't make assumptions. Notice, listen to and value everyone.
7. *Being reflective:* Reflecting on problems and why things are not working, and then finding solutions.

It struck me that all of these should be present in any music education setting, particularly in popular music learning. Combined with an individual's unique personality, musicianship and style, an empathetic, supportive and highly musical approach to learning inevitably emerges. This approach is often at the heart of community music practice, which typically happens outside of schools (as do the two video examples above). How can we bring this style and approach of learning more into mainstream education settings? We are in a situation where some of the most dynamic, engaging, accessible and inclusive popular music education is happening *away* from formal settings.

Implications for recruitment and training

In a survey (68 responses) conducted for Sound Connections,[2] we asked our network (including musicians, freelance workshop leaders, primary and secondary school teachers, and grassroots community organizations) an open question about what skills, knowledge and behaviours they needed to do their job, in whatever context they were working in, as a way of identifying and responding to training needs.

These were some of the most common responses:

- Communication skills,
- Teaching and learning strategies,
- Relationship/partnership building skills,
- Curriculum design/planning,
- Workshop planning/leading,
- Music education sector knowledge,
- Inclusion and diversity,
- Working with young people with Special Educational Needs (SEND),

- Child development,
- Empathy,
- Patience,
- Passion,
- Engaging,
- Authenticity,
- Commitment,
- Curiosity,
- Encouragement,
- Energy,
- Entrepreneurship.

Many of these focus on the 'how', rather than the 'what'. Developing music educators is an ongoing process that cannot necessarily be done in a short-term initial training course. It has led me to question how accessible the routes into formal training programmes are to musicians from a wider range of backgrounds and cultures, who would be effective role models, coaches and leaders for young people.

In England, the music education workforce in the formal sector (primary teachers with a music specialism, secondary classroom teachers, visiting instrumental and vocal teachers for example) are majority White, with a western classical training. This can only be an anecdotal observation – based on regularly visiting schools, attending conferences, and having professional conversations – because there is little available data or research on the diversity and identity of our music teaching workforce, which in itself is a concern.

Formalized systems and structures can present barriers preventing popular musicians from working in these environments – for example, unconscious bias, concerns over psychological safety, minimal representation of people of colour in senior leadership positions, recruitment and retention practices, cost and length of training programmes for example – where we should be nurturing and encouraging a much more diverse workforce. Mentoring, shadowing, coaching, providing structured feedback and ongoing reflective practice are potentially more effective professional development approaches for encouraging more popular music role models into the education system.

Reflect and act

The way that young people are able to access popular music education is evolving rapidly, but organizations and the workforce are not necessarily keeping up with this rate of change by adapting methods, approaches and attitudes. Popular music itself is a key part of the solution as it engages so many young people, whether as passive consumers or active participants. But it does this anyway, regardless of organizations and teachers. Through the COVID-19 pandemic, we have seen a necessary shift to remote and online learning and collaboration, altering the way that we think about how, where and with whom popular music learning happens.

Therefore, who are music educators for? Arguably they are needed more than ever, but in their roles as coach, mentor, supporter, encourager and role model rather than as a transmitter of content. If music educators are truly for the young people (rather than for the system), then it is increasingly critical that the 'how' of learning is as important as the 'what'. Alongside this we must constantly reflect on how we can make our workforce in schools less homogenous, make routes into music teaching more accessible, and ensure that the twenty-first century classroom popular music teaching reflects the innovative, real and engaging popular music learning that happens beyond the school.

NOTES

1. https://cityoflondonsinfonia.co.uk/. Accessed 19 January 2022.
2. Sound Connections (www.sound-connections.org.uk [accessed 9 May 2022]) is a London-based music education sector support organisation.

REFERENCE

Green, Lucy (2001), *How Popular Musicians Learn: A Way Ahead for Music Education*, Abingdon: Routledge.

PART II

IDENTITY AND PURPOSE

While ideas around identity and purpose pervade this book, in this section the authors consider the purposes that popular music has played in their own lives and how this intersects with their developing identities as musicians, educators and thinkers. Several North American music teacher–educators consider how aspects of popular music and associated pedagogical approaches enable and enabled them to re-imagine teaching practices, and authors from India, Paraguay and Sweden present details of their personal journeys in and with popular music in a range of styles. Authors explore ways in which constructing and construing identities are important facets of praxis.

adam patrick bell, Western University

Aixa Burgos, Passaic Preparatory Academy

Christopher Cayari, researcher

Matthew Clauhs,
Ithaca College

Shane Colquhoun,
music educator

Sheena
Dhamnsania,
elementary music,
songwriting and
rock band teacher

Jabari Evans,
University of
South Carolina

James Frankel,
musician, music
educator and very
proud Deadhead

Felix Graham,
educator

Steve Holley,
Arizona State
University

Mia Ibrahim,
middle-school
music teacher

Erik Lundahl,
Ystad Gymnasium

Roger Mantie,
University
of Toronto
Scarborough

Nina Menezes,
University of
Tampa

Sol Elisa Martinez
Missena, Boston
University

Jared O'Leary,
BootUp PD

Meghan K.
Sheehy,
Hartwick College

Shree Lakshmi
Vaidyanathan,
The Bangalore
School of Music

Martina Vasil,
University of
Kentucky

Andy West,
Leeds
Conservatoire

18

Life as a Cabaret:
Singing Our Ideal Self into Being

Felix Graham

Dr. Felix Graham (singwithdrfelix.com) is a NYC-based educator whose practice focuses on vocal health and retraining, while guiding clients in reconciling their voice and personal identity.

Musical interaction – and particularly performing – is well understood as a vehicle for self-discovery and identity development, but there are relatively few secure performance environments for singers to explore. This chapter explores how singing, voice and identity intersect, and the potential cabaret performance holds for trans and cis-gender singers' individual self-development.

An identity is always already an ideal, what we would like to be, not what we are [...] But if musical identity is, then, always fantastic, idealizing not just oneself but also the social world one inhabits, it is, secondly, always also real, enacted in musical activities [...] In this respect, musical pleasure is not derived from fantasy – it is not mediated by daydreams – but is experienced directly: Music gives us a real experience of what the ideal could be.

(Frith 1996: 123, emphasis added)

Introduction

The image of the traditional concert performance is one of a near-religious formality and stodgy ritual performed by highly trained professionals. By contrast, the image of a *cabaret* is its direct opposite: loud, raucous, informal, irreverent. Instead of formal performances given by acolytes in the gleaming temple of the concert hall, cabaret is performed by anyone who wants to share their music with an audience, often in venues where 'shabby' is a generous way to describe the ambience. Cabaret is the illegitimate sibling of the vocal world – showing up tipsy at the family reunion, openly speaking all the things everyone thinks but dares not say.

As a musical/theatrical form, cabaret can run the gamut from amateur variety show to the professional vocalist's take on the solo autobiographical performance. In this chapter, however, I am defining cabaret as a loosely themed collection of vocal performances from an array of musical genres, by performers of disparate backgrounds and levels of experience. These performances are usually organized and presented by an Emcee, whose role is to keep the show on track and manage the atmosphere with off-the-cuff banter and humour.

This looseness of format can result in chaos, but it's also what gives cabaret its power: everyone can participate, everything goes and every *body* is welcome. It's an environment in which vocational and avocational performers alike can explore themselves, their gender and their sexuality. There's even room for performers to work out their place in the world, in an environment that is usually composed of friends, family or supportive outsiders. No performance environment is ever completely safe, but a sympathetic space in which to try on new emotions, new identities, new pieces of the puzzle that are our *self* is as secure as such experiences can be.

Generally, when we talk about music and identity development in avocational musical education, the focus is on musical *listening* – the consumption of music performance. In my experience as a trans-identified musician and music educator, however, it is *performance,* and *singing* in particular, that has been the most useful path for identity development and self-discovery in avocational musicians. Cabaret, with its openness and its chaos, has been the perfect vehicle for this kind of self-defining performance – both for my students *and* for myself.

Who am I? Performance as identity development

Identity development is movement; a sometimes-constant, sometimes-erratic progression towards an idealized self. It's also a movement towards an idealized self that is itself shifting and changing as we're exposed to new ideas, new opportunities and new ways to be in the world.

A marker of human advancement could be described as the freedom – materially and spiritually – to explore new facets of self. Certainly, one of the most remarkable shifts in twenty-first century social development has been the explosion of possibility in personal identity, particularly around the intersection of gender and sexuality.

Musical interaction has long been recognized as an important vehicle for identity development. This is, in part, because it offers the participant an opportunity to 'try on' new facets of identity, sometimes referred to as *provisional selves*. The idea of *provisional identities* is akin to trying on a new suit of clothes; we put on a new set of beliefs, behaviours or emotions to see how it 'fits' us. And, like new clothes, we might decide that it doesn't flatter us and reject it altogether, or we might love it and keep it and wear it every day. Conversely, we might initially dislike it, but keep coming back to it again and again, adjusting here and there, until we decide that not only will we keep it, we'll wear it at every available opportunity.

When we sing, we're not just trying on a new self in the metaphorical sense, we're experiencing it literally; we're stepping into that new role, experiencing those emotions in a real, intense way. In the process, we're also communicating our hesitation and/or eagerness, our uncertainty and/or surety, our worry and our joy in this new role to our audience. We are modelling this new, provisional self in the mirror *and* putting it out there in front of an audience, taking in their reaction and processing their reception of this potential ideal self.

Self-concept, identity and music education

What role does music education (and by extension, a music educator) play in a young student's personal development?

Self-concept, a person's perception of themselves, is as much social as it is personal. Our understanding of ourselves is strongly impacted by the information we receive about ourselves from other people. Whether or not we understand ourselves to be musical or even have the capacity for music relies in no small part on the musical interactions with have with our teachers and with our peers in musical environments during our developmental years. If others communicate to us that we are musical, then it is much more likely that we will integrate the label of 'musician' into our self-*concept* (Elorriaga 2011).

Things to think about

How did your early musical experiences influence your decision to be a musician?

Come to the cabaret: My trying-on story

I am a music educator now, but I have always been a performer. I have worked as a professional musician in many capacities, though primarily as a classical vocalist, where I have experienced a great deal of joy on the operatic and concert stage. While I would argue that there is room for personal exploration in that repertoire, given the level of scrutiny that accompanies classical vocal performance there is no room for the level of vulnerability intense self-discovery requires.

When I initially began to have questions about my gender identity, my career path precluded any sort of musical self-exploration, which I felt very acutely. As my gender identity collided with my professional, musical and vocal identities, I focused more on my academic career and began to perform less and less until I quit classical performance almost entirely for several years.

After leaving classical repertoire for a time, I realized that I needed some kind of outlet, not just to satisfy my artistic side, but to explore all of these new, uncertain and, frankly, *scary* new ideas that were swimming in my head. *Am I transgender? What does that mean? Do I really feel this or am I just pretending? What will people say? What will happen to my career? Will I lose my singing voice if I transition?*

I had so much to express, so many new selves to try on, and nowhere to do it … which is when I started to think about cabaret. In the cabaret environment, I realized I could sing whatever I wanted: musical theatre, jazz, pop, rock, R&B. If it could be played on a piano and sung by a singer, it was fair game. In this way, I could – and did – try on many, many different provisional selves. Even more importantly, I was able to do it in front of people who accepted me as whoever and whatever I was in that moment.

I did not keep every provisional self that I tried on in song, of course. In time, though, I was able to home in on the parts of a new gender identity that I wanted to retain. I became a brand-new man, quite literally, through cabaret; I do not believe I would have had such a clear transition if I had not had the time and space to sing my new self into being.

Musical vs. personal identity

How does singing intersect and influence self-development?

Research around music and identity suggests that voice is an integral part of self-identity – certainly, speaking voice is a large part of one's sense of self, but investigation has found that singing voice holds a great deal of weight as well, particularly for vocational and avocational singers. Musical vocalization can be an important part of the 'actual construction, maintenance and performance of self at various stages of personal, musical and psychological development' (Faulkner and Davidson 2004: 232; Graham 2019)

Things to think about

How does your speaking voice intersect with your own personal identity?

Would you be the same person you are today, if you had not picked up your instrument or begun singing at some point in your young life?

Your table's waiting: Stories looking for outlets

Since transition, I have started singing professionally again in my former area of expertise, but I have not quit singing casually in the cabaret environment. Having seen how powerful the experience was for me, I have even recently tried to bring some of that environment into my own classical performances. Further, in my applied voice studio, I encourage my students to use cabaret performances in this self-exploratory way, often with great results.

It has certainly been a useful tool for my trans, queer and other minority students, but it has also been a fantastic space for students who fit more easily within societal norms. Everyone has questions about themselves, everyone has doubts and fears to unpack. Occasionally, there are even students who discover an aspect of themselves through this kind of casual performance that they did not know they possessed.

While I have talked about cabaret in the context of allowing avocational musicians an outlet for expression and exploration, these singers are not the only group to benefit. An unexpected facet of cabaret performance has been the way in which it has helped the professional singers in my studio tackle their own issues with performance anxiety. Through low-stakes performance, in genres in which they have less experience (and thus, less emotional baggage), they have been able to find joy in performing that they previously lacked.

Good pedagogy is the art of facilitation, creating spaces where students can experiment, experience and work out new skills and new ways of understanding *for themselves*. And, in my experience, providing students with low-stakes, non-judgmental outlets to perform music from *all* genres is both good pedagogy in action and a critical part of creating confident, self-assured performers, regardless of whether they choose to pursue music vocationally or otherwise. Cabaret – with its openness, its joyous noise, the space it allows for imperfection – might just be the ideal environment for that ideal musician to flourish and come to life.

Self and performance anxiety

How do provisional identities and performance anxiety interact?

Literature on performance anxiety in musicians suggests that self-discrepancies (the perceived differences between one's current self and one's ideal self) are a high predictor of performance anxiety in musicians (Castiglione et al. 2018: 797–98).

Things to think about

How might exploration of self through low-stakes performance be a useful tool for vocational musicians?

Are the benefits of low-stakes performance different between vocational and avocational musicians?

REFERENCES

Castiglione, Claudia, Rampullo, Alberto and Cardullo, Silvia (2018), 'Self representations and music performance anxiety: A study with professional and amateur musicians', *Europe's Journal of Psychology*, 14:4, pp. 792–805.

Elorriaga, Alfonso (2011), 'The construction of male gender identity through choir singing at a Spanish secondary school', *International Journal of Music Education*, 29:4, pp. 318–32.

Faulkner, Robert and Davidson, Jane (2004), 'Men's vocal behaviour and the construction of self', *Musicae Scientiae*, 8, 231–55.

Frith, Simon (1996), 'Music and identity', in S. Hall and P. Du Gay (eds), *Questions of Cultural Identity: SAGE Publications*, Thousand Oaks: SAGE Publications, pp. 108–48.

Graham, Felix Andrew (2019), 'Singing while female: A narrative study on gender, identity & experience of female voice in cis, transmasculine & non-binary singers', doctoral dissertation, Teachers College, Columbia University, New York, https://academiccommons.columbia.edu/doi/10.7916/d8-mnh1-st58. Accessed 16 March 2022.

19

My Therapist Said It's FINE:
The Duality of Being a Music(ian) Teacher

Sheena Dhamsania

Sheena Dhamsania has taught elementary music, songwriting, and rock band in Wyoming for ten years. She is in the composer duo No Such Thing As Noise.

This chapter focuses on the duality and balance of being both an educator and artist. From Jackson, Wyoming, United States, Dhamsania shares anecdotes of her experience in teaching and performing realms. She discusses how she grappled with an evolving identity to expand her capacity to hold two worlds in one.

'So, there I am, on the tour bus …' Ah, an all-too-predictable opening to a story that winds in and out of debauchery, late nights and illicit adventurings. It is a badge of one's badassery in that (1) you've 'made it' to the point of having a tour bus and (2) you lived to tell the tale. As a nerdgoth, first gen, Indian bassoonist from the suburbs of Detroit, I pursued a classical/orchestral/WhiteAF music track as a way to be heard (ironic for a brown girl?), to get scholarship and to have a steady career in music. The tour bus end of the music spectrum seemed a distant dream, perhaps not even mine. But, nonetheless, there I was, on our Skullcandy-sponsored tour bus, playing bass in an outlaw country band, throwing afterparties for a snowboard film premiere in the ski-town American West. There was only one caveat. Instead of continuing on the road with the band for a couple more stops, my weekend was over. I would return to my polished cardigan aesthetic, teaching elementary general music on Monday.

My life has been a strenuous exercise in duality. It has taken many years of therapy (shoutout to Diana!) to recognize that this is not inherently a negative thing. Dialectical behavioural therapy has shown me that I can simultaneously exist as an elementary teacher role model and bass thumping, late-night gigging musician. I can hold space and thrive in both places. It has been revealed to me that I am not necessarily living with cognitive dissonance, but rather I am embracing the expansiveness of my capacity. This may sound obvious, but it took me a long time to come to terms with *all* facets of my being. When I play a public daytime show, I accept and expect to have a crew of littles looking up in equal parts confusion and awe as they see their teacher in performance mode. Perhaps I'll run into their guardian later that night at the bar gig.

My pontifications about identity as music educators and artists burgeons a few questions as we, as a field, evolve into more relevant caretakers of the profession: how do we stay authentic in our work as educators *and* artists? How do we embrace the many sides of ourselves in the classroom and on the stage? How do we express ourselves fully as artists without risking our reputations as teachers? The answers I am still ironing out. There have been times where I have felt restricted as an artist in serving as a public figure in my community. Other times where I have felt alienated at the state conference for not having the Orff Level XXXVIII certification because I played a gig that weekend instead. In an all too close encounter, I imbibed a shot bestowed upon me by an audience member at the bar. The crowd erupted in the chant, 'teacher of the year!', which I had, in fact, been awarded that year. I try not to hide aspects of my being, but there have been moments where I have had to seriously consider the repercussions of momentarily shirking responsibilities in my 'dual life'. In no way do I presume that my case is special. All teachers, regardless of subject specialism or grade level, face similar scrutiny. We all walk the line between our personal and professional lives. As music teachers, we are living with multiplicities with which we must come to terms as educators and artists. A clue, I have discovered, lies in finding integration and common ground to connect these seemingly divergent pathways of our existence.

Although the concept of using creativity and vernacular music in the classroom was not lost on me, having attended Michigan State University with some great minds on the topic (cue Dr John Kratus!), the first integration into my own teaching began in a selfish endeavour. When I began picking up bass to play gigs at the country music club with my roommate whose bass player dropped out, I desired an excuse to practice while I was teaching. Seems a little self-serving, eh? So what! Henceforth, the after-school rock band at Wilson Elementary commenced, where kids (and teacher!) could learn rock and electronic music instruments. They (we!) could also write original music and collaborate with friends. I would learn riffs and write lyrics in the afterschool rock band that I would then bring to my musician friends after hours. Does this seem like cheating? Maybe. Does it feel good to be bad? I won't say no.

Integrating popular music within the classroom does not merely live in performance and creating. One of the greatest pleasures of experiencing music with others, for me, exists in mutual listening. It is when I look around the room at students listening to a song that I have felt profoundly in my soul (e.g. Aphex Twin's 'Avril 14th' or Sam Cooke's 'A Change Is Gonna Come') and noticing how music *looks* in a child who appears to be feeling this music in a similar way. It is when a student shares with me a song they've choreographed a dance to, moving in time with pure joy. It's spiritual. It is the connective tissue I yearn for as an artist in connecting with other artists, with an audience and with students. And it is completely accessible to a five-year-old who can listen with an open heart. Listening together has been a big source of integration in my experience as a music(ian) teacher.

In the past ten years of teaching, I see choir teachers who can pick up a guitar. Band teachers who write their own songs and encourage their students to do the same. Elementary general teachers who carefully place protest music into their curricula, showing students at a young age that they, too, have a voice. As our field evolves, as WE evolve, into more capable, relevant and creative music(ian) teachers, we will have to confront our collective cognitive dissonance (expansiveness of our capacity) between our artist selves and our teacher selves. The richness will live in the moments where we can integrate our learnings in both worlds and come to terms with our duality. We can live in both spaces. We were born to create, emote and promote this process for the next generation.

20

Pursuing Popular Music Shapes Me as a Scholar, Musician and Human

Christopher Cayari

Christopher Cayari's (he/they) research focuses on mediated musical performance, YouTube, informal music learning, virtual communities, video game music, and online identity.

The music we perform shapes who we are as people, and this chapter explores the popular musics that influenced my identity as a scholar, musician, and human. Performing and listening to popular music as a teacher in my classroom as well as researching through qualitative methods shaped who I am.

I am a product of a music education system that privileges students who are western-classical-art-music-reproducers. However, my ability to perform the entirety of *Songs of Travel* by Ralph Vaughan Williams, my capacity to conduct large ensembles of singers and instrumentalists and my comprehension of the difference between French and German Neapolitan sixth chords are not what I love about being a musical scholar, performer and researcher. What I love about being a musical educator is being able to combine my love of popular culture with my passion for music. I am approaching this chapter as an autoethnography with a research question of, 'What inspires me to pursue popular music education?' The answer is simple: 'I like fun, cool, new things'. Throughout this chapter, I explain how popular music education provides me with opportunities to explore interests in varied musical contexts, how musical activities inspire aesthetically meaningful non-musical artefacts and how popular music empowers us to express ourselves as learners, musicians and, most importantly, humans.

Eclectic loves, compounding identities

When I was a classroom music teacher in the early 2000s, I was teaching full-time and holding 40 private music lessons a week. When my students asked, 'Mr. C! What type of music do you listen to?' I told them, 'I don't listen to music. I hate music.' We would have a laugh, and I would die a little more inside as I fought back a tear from escaping my eye. Like so many others who leave our profession before their fifth year of teaching, I was burnt out. Today, I could tell you a long string of music that I love listening to: EDM; alternative rock; dubstep; SKA! (it is not dead); Top 40, especially the type that is pumped at the dance club; video game music, which I affectionately refer to as VGM; folk rock; nerdcore; those stupid music videos on YouTube in which dogs bark your favourite tunes; and musical theatre. I have dedicated my scholarship to pursue being a person who researches things that are new, exciting and inspirational (at least to me). My eclectic tastes and styles inspire my research and propel me towards exploring musical phenomena.

Popular music allows me to pursue my varied musical interests while giving me a community in which I can interact. While I find listening to music helps me pass time while driving, concentrate while sitting at my writing desk, or feel energized at the gym, musical communities are what inspire me to be a better person. I love amateur music making that manifests in YouTube videos created by people who perform for a camera in their bedrooms and living rooms. My first YouTube case study was about Wade Johnston, whose first videos were of him playing with his high school graduation gifts – a new guitar, ukulele and laptop computer – at his kitchen table singing in a typical singer-songwriter style that resembled Elton John or Ben Folds. My most recent case study was inspired by Carlos Eiene, a jazz musician who made his bedroom one of the most recognized recording studios in the VGM cover community. While neither genre was something I enjoyed listening to before I conducted my research, after getting to know my research participants and the people who love the music they produced, I found myself incorporating those types of music in my life. For example, I had to listen to a cover of 'I'm Yours' by Jason Mraz over 100 times and it seeped its way into my heart. Watching that ukulele cover inspired me to develop my ukulele programmes at the schools in which I taught, and I have since worked with over 500 students from Grade 3 through college, helping them play popular tunes on the quirky four-stringed instrument. I even created a video tutorial series for ukulele players that is available on YouTube, which allows my reach to go far beyond my physical classroom.

Similarly, after getting to know the various VGM cover artists through my studies, I have developed research projects that explore how VGM can serve as a bridge between classical and popular genres with the use of technology and media. I have become a contributing member of the VGM community online and in the physical world. I have attended and spoken at conventions that have tens of thousands of attendees on topics like building musical communities and using video games as inspiration to perform. I often ruminate over whether an appreciation for video games inspired me to listen to VGM beyond the console, or whether people playing cool music inspired me to see the potential for learning and joy through popular music making. Similarly, did my love for the musical genres inspire my research, or did my research make me fall in love with the ways my participants made music?

Fandoms give me life!

Regardless of my variation on, *Which came first: The chicken or the egg?*, popular culture fandoms give me life, and one could argue that music is always implicated in any fandom. To say something gives me life is a vernacular saying that means it gives me a reason to live, get up in the morning and be a better person. I love online musical communities. Some especially inspirational fandoms that I have discovered through YouTube were Neil Cicierega's 'Mysterious Ticking Noise', an ostinati-layered chant featuring puppets inspired by *Harry Potter*; the a cappella worship music arranged by my friend and research participant, David Wesley François; and the EDM video game music of Ben Briggs, whom I discovered while searching for covers of the 'Tem Shop' featured in the wildly popular independent video game *Undertale*, created by Toby Fox. I have to be honest, while the music of each of these groups made me bop up and down in my chair as I listen to them while writing this chapter, it is not the organization of sound that continually inspires me but the communities that have developed around the fandoms of these songs that give me life.

The research I have done about popular music in the above examples has inspired me to teach in a way that privileges participation, and participatory music making abounds in all three examples. Do a YouTube search for 'Mysterious Ticking Noise' and see all the ways people have created a tribute to the silly song. Imagine Grade 5 students (9–10-year-olds) giggling as they prepare their own renditions. François has harnessed the joy of congregational singing online – a form of popular music that mirrors pop culture trends in music and brings people together in a participatory fashion, rather than separating performer and audience. He did this by providing resources and opportunities to join virtual choirs of worship, bringing together hundreds of singers and instrumentalists across the world to contribute to multitrack crowdsourced, collective ensembles online. A week before I wrote this chapter, I attended Super MAGFest 2020 (Music and

Gaming Festival) and witnessed Briggs jumping up and down on stage as I and thousands of others sang nonsense syllables during the DJ Block Party at 2 a.m. to his remix of the 'Tem Shop', which has been listened to countless times on the internet streaming sites. The sound of these musical examples being spewed from the Alexa-enabled device in my office not only affected me musically by putting me in a great mood but also the memories of the communities that have emerged from these popular music examples bring me inspiration to make music, conduct research and teach students.

Popular music empowers me: Coming out to my profession

This inspiration also empowers me. I am inspired to pursue music as a creator. I sit down at my piano and sight-read fan-transcribed scores and chord charts, and I delight over my classical guitar as I learn how to play music from *Undertale* by ear. I scroll through online forums in which avid fans of new musical theatre discuss how Zachary Noah Piser was cast as the alternate lead in the Broadway production of *Dear Evan Hansen* in New York City, making him the first Asian American to be cast in a role traditionally played by a White person. Hearing this inspired me to start learning the repertoire from the musical, a task I had not previously attempted because I did not see myself as one who might fit in that role. After buying a plane ticket to see him perform, I decided to learn the repertoire from the show to include in my next performative autoethnography research performance.

Performing popular music has empowered me to explore my intersectionality as a member of multiple minority groups, solidify my identity and propel me towards activism. Between 2015 and 2019, I toured a one-person musical theatre review I wrote using repertoire from some of my favourite shows. I have belted along with so many Original Broadway Cast (OBC) recordings throughout my life – in my bedroom, during car rides and for makeshift performances of the *Wicked* tour live in my friends' living rooms. Anyone who loves the feeling of singing or playing along with recordings knows how aesthetically gratifying 'performing' for an imaginary sold-out audience can be (imagine this book's co-editor Gareth Dylan Smith with headphones on while wailing on cymbals and drums! I have seen it at the Rhythm! Discovery Center in Indianapolis; it is a spectacle). These imaginary performances turned into actual sold-out audiences through my autoethnographic musical theatre performances, which deal with my experiences growing up as a queer person navigating school, being a teacher, and developing a career as a musical academic scholar. Learning musical theatre repertoire sung by and written for queer people empowered me to not only be proud of who I am but also become an activist for the marginalized communities to which I belonged. The popular music I chose to perform gave me the strength to come out to my profession and be a voice that insists on opportunities for sexuality-diverse and gender-diverse individuals like me to be represented and given opportunities to perform. Singing my favourite popular music gave me the courage to take a leap and stand up for a cause that was meaningful to me.

Whose music can empower you?

This chapter shines a light on how popular music inspired me to pursue academic research, popular music inclusion in classrooms, and musical performance. In (*unpopular?*) music education, especially in the United States where I live, we have been struggling with the question of, 'Whose music are we really teaching?' While it might sound like a broken record, I argue that there is no single right way to approach this inquiry. Educators can harness *popular* to appeal to the eclectic affinities students have; and getting to know someone else's music often leads to finding respect for, and even joy in new sounds. I return back to my initial statement in this chapter. While a predominantly-western art approach gave me a baseline for becoming a fully-fledged musical force not to be reckoned with, it was flinging myself into popular music that helped me develop my identity as a musician and allowed me to feel empowered as a human being. How might you empower your students in a similar way?

21

I've Learned Three Chords. Now What?

Roger Mantie

Roger Mantie is an associate professor at the University of Toronto Scarborough. His teaching and research focus on music, education and leisure.

Drawing on the personal experience of someone with musical training who learned basic guitar strumming later in life, I argue that the field of popular music education needs to move past pleas for curricular inclusion and start grappling with the paradigm of formal music learning as the 'teleology of technique'.

Deep down, I have always envied guitarists. Inevitably, they are the cool kids who cop tunes from the radio or lead informal ad hoc rock and pop anthem sing-alongs. There is just so much more cachet in the guitar than there is in my instrument, the saxophone. Even though the saxophone became somewhat popular in radio hits of the 1980s, I never found much satisfaction in belting out 'Careless Whisper' (nor did anyone find it particularly impressive that I could do so). There just didn't seem to be as much point to playing a short, single-line melody on my saxophone as there was in being a guitarist sitting around with a bunch of people launching into 'Don't Stop Believing' or 'Brown-Eyed Girl'.

Admittedly, there was a period in my life when I convinced myself that the guitar wasn't so cool. During my undergraduate years, I was decidedly snobbier. Against my will, I was forced to learn some guitar in General Music Methods, a required course in my music education degree. I somehow managed to get through 'Lean on Me' well enough to pass the course, but the experience was far from satisfying. The student-quality classical guitars probably had something to do with it, although I still remember feeling like the whole exercise was a waste of time. I had *serious* practising to do. Even if the saxophone was a second-class citizen in the school of music, I was still studying *real* music, not strumming through some pop schlock (even if in the eyes of some of my classical musical peers I was in the same camp as the popular music crowd because I played jazz). I knew I was never going to teach guitar or 'general music', and I certainly wasn't going to teach *popular* music. (The horror!) My destiny was to teach music of worth; music of educational *quality*.

Over the course of my school teaching career, I somehow ended up with at least one really good guitarist among my students each year. No doubt there were many of them, but, as the guitar was not a band (i.e. wind band) instrument, I only encountered the guitarists 'talented' enough to play in the jazz bands (where guitarists were acceptable because they were learning 'real' music). Inevitably this was always something of a struggle for me pedagogically, because, as every guitarist who has attempted to do jazz finds out very quickly, there is a steep learning curve between the basic strumming and tab playing of folk, rock and pop, and the sophisticated harmonic voicings of jazz guitar (not to mention the idiomatic Freddie Green downstroke staccato style of big band guitar playing).

As a teacher, I did my best of course, but, unlike in the concert band where my wind instrument doubling abilities allowed me to quite literally pick up any instrument and demonstrate it reasonably well, all I could do for the guitarists (at a time before YouTube, remember) was to tell them to find a good guitar teacher. Fortunately for me, the students were always diligent and seemed to figure things out on their own (like so many guitarists seem to do). This, however, always left me feeling rather inadequate as a music educator. It wasn't just that I couldn't play jazz guitar; I couldn't play *any* guitar. It's pretty hard to thumb one's nose at 'guitarists' and their lack of musical sophistication (with their simple three-chord rock music) when you can't even play one basic chord on the instrument. I could demonstrate basic piano chords, basic drum patterns and even play basic walking bass lines, but the guitar: *nothing*.

I never learned the guitar in my youth even though we had one in the house. I suspect it was because we had a big hollow-body (rather than a Strat or Tele) and my dad played it to accompany old-time fiddle tunes. Playing folk and trad has become somewhat fashionable today (many young people are doing it), but it was definitely not cool in the 1980s when I was growing up. The last thing I wanted to do was pick up *that* guitar. It was only many years later, in my forties, that I felt compelled to finally confront my deep-seated envy and my lifelong failings as an educator. With the assistance of a knowledgeable other (thanks, Jesse) I went out and bought a guitar. And not just any guitar. Here I was, 30 years later, buying a guitar not that dissimilar from the one my father played so I could strum along to the fiddle tunes my daughter was playing. (Oh, the irony.)

Learning and/or education

If it wasn't for the lack of calluses that limited me to about ten minutes a day, I think I probably could have learned to strum along, at a rudimentary level, to about 75 per cent of the popular music canon in a day or two (minus any barre chords, which I still find next to impossible). This was both a revelation and a disappointment. On the one hand, how wonderful! I could now do what had seemed like such a mystery to me. I could finally play guitar! (Kind of.) On the other hand, I could not shake a dual sense of regret. First, why had I waited so long to do something so relatively simple (by which I merely mean that strumming basic chords is easy, not that the guitar itself is easy)? Why had I missed out on so many years of doing something so musically and personally rewarding? Second, this was just a little *too* easy. Yes, my progress was aided by my existing musical abilities. I wasn't a musical beginner starting from scratch; I was simply adapting a lot of embodied knowledge to a new instrument. But still, was this all there was? E, A, D, G and C chords (only three or four of which were necessary on any given tune)?

I am exaggerating, of course. Learning to strum on the guitar is a bit more complicated than I'm implying – though not *that* much more. Learning to play rock guitar riffs and tunes beyond the I-iv-V-vi framework, especially beyond the keys of E, A, D and G does require an investment of time and energy, even for experienced musicians – just as learning other instruments in the typical western popular music ensemble (keyboards, bass, drums) becomes more difficult as one moves beyond entry-level playing. The point, however, is that almost anyone with a basic sense of beat competency, coordination and fundamental knowledge of form and harmonic progressions *can*, relatively quickly, learn to play basic popular music tunes on keyboards, bass, drums and guitar (to which one might today add the even easier strumming instrument, the ukulele). Unlike so many wind and bowed string instruments (and piano) that require years and years of study in order to go beyond a rudimentary level, most popular music instruments have a *low point of entry*. This is, in part, what helps to make them 'popular', of course.

None of this is news to anyone, I realize. The point of my autobiographical oversharing is simply to lay the groundwork for the very modest sketch of a much larger argument, which is that popular music education has been so obsessed with curricular justification and the celebrated (but under-examined) issue of 'informal learning' that it has yet to pay sufficient attention to larger matters of what it means to be educated in and through popular music. This is in no way to overlook or dismiss any of the fine scholarship in popular music education to date (a good deal of which is provided in the excellent bibliography of the Association for Popular Music Education (APME) white paper).[1] Rather, I merely wish to add my voice to those who advocate not for (or against) popular music, but for educative experiences that contribute purposefully to meaningful and rewarding living.

The title of this chapter is intended to draw attention to institutionalized music learning and teaching's obsession with technique and virtuosity as educational aims. Because many instruments require long periods of study in order to 'perform' adequately, it seems reasonable to equate the achievement of executive skills with 'education'. This phenomenon is exacerbated by classical and jazz (and now, increasingly, 'trad') repertoire that is typically predicated on a 'teleology of technique', whereby student progress is marked by the ability to perform repertoire of increasing virtuosity. What happens, however, when virtuosity has no truck with a musical practice? Or more precisely for my argument here: what is educative about music outside of the achievement of virtuosic technique?

The answer to the *executive skills equals learning* question depends, in part, on the context for the word 'educative'. The purposes of secondary and tertiary education are understood by many people to be quite different. Whereas the secondary level of mandatory schooling typically implies an accepted notion of 'general' education – even among elective and specialized courses – the purposes of the tertiary level, as many scholars in popular music education are wont to point out, take many forms. Parkinson and Smith (2015) frame this in terms of 'authenticity', whereby curricular and instructional practices should reflect potential use value. Regardless of the level of instruction, however, there is, in institutionalized teaching structures generally, an implicit and explicit expectation for teachers to demonstrate 'development', 'progress' and 'learning'. It is questionable, for example, to equate musical development as simply being able to perform more and more songs of equivalent difficulty – at least within current norms and expectations of many educational institutions that increasingly adopt 'outcomes based' accountability models as part of the inexorable march of a neoliberal human capital agenda.

To put a finer point on my argument, it would seem inevitable that, in order to conform to institutional norms in education, popular music education is eventually going to have to develop method books and 'graduated repertoire' lists that emulate that of the existing conservatory structure. I do not mean to suggest that such teaching does not already exist. Rather, I am predicting that popular music education is going to have to contend more directly than it has to date with the issue of 'development'. For example, a potential problem with Parkinson and Smith's argument about authenticity is that use value in the sense of applied music making (creating, producing, recording) in popular music implies something bounded or closed based on a student's or teacher's imagined futures – *unless* conceived according to a teleology of technique whereby students are 'prepared' for virtually any application in the popular music field (i.e. the ability to create/ perform all forms of popular music, from hip-hop to prog rock to EDM to the black sheep of popular music education: country). Musical training of this sort, however, would seem to run somewhat contrary to the spirit and ethic of popular music interests.

Personally, I think one of the most interesting and compelling aspects of popular music education lies in its potential to undermine the notion of music education as simply the teleology of technique. With thoughtful and rigorous theorization, popular music education could move beyond its current pleas for curricular inclusion and challenge what it means to be musically educated. As now-ubiquitous ukulele jams highlight, almost anyone with sufficient finger dexterity, beat competency and a basic sense of pitch can participate in popular music making. The low bar of entry opens the door to so many people who might otherwise be shut out of music making (especially instrumental music making) opportunities. These jam sessions fulfill a valuable function in society. When placed in the context of formal education, however, participatory music making faces a problem: I've learned three chords. *Now what?*

NOTE

1. https://www.popularmusiceducation.org/about-apme/white-paper/. Accessed 19 January 2022.

REFERENCE

Parkinson, Tom and Smith, Gareth Dylan (2015), 'Towards an epistemology of authenticity in higher popular music education', *Action, Criticism & Theory for Music Education*, 14:1, pp. 93–127.

22

Intersections and Roundabouts: Connecting In-School and Out-of-School Experiences to Teaching Practices

Steve Holley

Steve Holley is a Ph.D. candidate in music learning and teaching at Arizona State University. His research focuses on experiences of professional musicians-come-teachers in popular music classrooms.

This chapter considers the influence of in-school and out-of-school performing and teaching experiences through a first-person narrative. The discussion is approached in reflective and reflexive manners as the author explores how their varied experiences inform and influence their teaching practice in the context of a popular music classroom.

Music learning should enable learners to move toward a degree of independence and autonomy in music. Music learning should empower learners with music understanding so they can become musically proficient and eventually musically independent of their teachers.

(Wiggins 2001: 39)

Background

I entered teaching from a somewhat unorthodox path. While attending college in Memphis, I focused on securing degrees in jazz and classical bass performance and made a resolute decision to not pursue music education. You see, my mother was a highly regarded band director, and I had no desire to follow in her footsteps. Because of her profession, I was a 'band kid' before I joined the band; Friday night football games, festivals, parades and band camps were regular features throughout my childhood. While I went on to experience a traditional, secondary school band experience, my path to teaching had many twists, turns, and the occasional, sometimes confusing roundabout. It was this long, winding path that, despite my attempts to steer clear of my mother's vocation, eventually led me to the only plausible route.

With the benefit of hindsight, I am now developing a better understanding of the beginnings of my pedagogy and how over time, my experiences as a 'band kid' began to mesh with my out-of-school musical self, forming a sort of mashup of these seemingly disparate happenings, what Parkinson and Smith (2015) refer to as hybridized learning experiences. Later, I began teaching with the impressions of this hybridity underpinning my emerging practice, but without the foundations of any formal training in music education. I am now discovering that this multiplicity of musical situations, what Tobias (2015) calls 'dynamic intersections' – a remixing of formal (in-school) and non-formal (out-of-school) environments with my knowledge and understanding of music in multiple performative and educative facets – formed the foundation of my pedagogical approach to music learning and teaching. On this point, I wonder, 'Are my experiences in music learning and teaching really so different from those of my colleagues who experienced, perhaps, a more conventional music education?'

Looking back to my time performing in a variety of musical settings, I often wonder why there was not a deeper pedagogical crossover between how on- and off-campus musical groups operated when there seemed, at least to my eye and ear, to be a wealth of approaches that could be shared and applied across the various formats, with each manner of musical setting informing the others. Green (2002) reinforces this idea of a disconnect when noting 'formal music education and informal music learning have for centuries been sitting side by side, with little communication between them' (216). I certainly experienced this disconnect throughout my college tenure as I became aware that a majority of my classmates pursuing classical music studies only participated in the more traditional ensembles and thereby only experienced that paradigm. On the other hand, I also noticed the majority of my classmates pursuing jazz studies participated not only in the requisite jazz ensembles but also in several off-campus groups focusing on a number of musical genres including the blues, soul and R&B (it was Memphis, after all). I was lucky that I was able to participate in a range of musical situations: an orchestral rehearsal in the afternoon, a jazz trio gig later that evening, followed by a late-night show with a rock band. It was in and through this musical 'grab bag' that these outwardly dissimilar musical settings began to reveal their possible connections. It was these intersections that began to establish an unconscious footing and where the groundwork of my pedagogy took shape.

From teacher to producer

Upon accepting my first teaching position at a school in Colorado – directing two jazz ensembles, one middle school and one high school – I initially conducted rehearsals in a somewhat traditional manner that seemed appropriate given the in-school setting; that being a more director-centred style. As the programme expanded to include bands focusing on R&B, soul and salsa, I continued to explore and incorporate some of my acquired out-of-school, less-formal attitudes into our somewhat conventional rehearsal environment. Over the course of our collective discovery, I grew to a deeper understanding of how a hybrid learning environment – an atmosphere that encouraged a collaborative, co-learning spirit as well as a blending of formal, non-formal, and informal pedagogies – allowed me to explore a shifting of my roles and responsibilities within the ensemble (Holley 2019). Additionally, this approach not only served as a crossroads between my in-school and out-of-school musical experiences (as our emerging Commercial Music Program began offering additional ensembles and courses focusing on production and entrepreneurship) but also doubled as an on-ramp for inclusion of students varied musical experiences (modern pop, hip-hop, neo-soul and EDM). Kruse (2016; following Tobias 2015a) explains that this crossfading[1] of music education, of these in-school and out-of-school experiences, could be blended in varying amounts depending upon the changing needs of the musical situation (Folkestad 2006, following Green 2002, 2006). Further, this flexibility also allowed the collective to consider how the music and artists we studied and performed were locked in a circular pattern of influence with culture, history and current events, thereby affording us the opportunity to employ the 'students' culture to help them create meaning and understand the world' through music (Ladson-Billings 1992: 106).

My initial forays beyond the world of teaching how I was taught consisted of simply asking the drummer to count off the tunes in rehearsal and performances. From there, I increasingly ceded song selection to students and eventually exited the stage entirely during performances. As the students took on additional responsibilities, we realized a deeper engagement with the music – arranging songs, creating segues and offering suggestions to the other musicians as to how they might improve their parts; this, in turn, improved the song and the overall experience of the collective. As the students became more enmeshed in the management and organization of the rehearsals and performances, my role in the ensemble further shifted to that of facilitator or guide; to offering my experiences as a support to their musical journey. This shift away from my serving as the sole source of knowledge in the classroom nurtured a more democratic environment where student agency, ownership, autonomy and self-confidence could grow and flourish (Wiggins 2001). The students, whether they realized it or not at the time, were exploring their agency and taking ownership of their band, their rehearsals, their performances and their learning process.

As time went on, I soon withdrew from using the label of 'teacher' or 'director' and settled on 'producer', as I viewed my role in the rehearsal process as similar to that of a producer in a recording environment, offering sage-like advice now and again when needed, helping to negotiate conflicts when they arose and asking provocative questions in an effort to press the students to think more deeply, more critically about the music (Randles 2012). My function was to facilitate the student learning process vis-à-vis the diversity of experiences I brought to the classroom; to support students as they wrestled with various problems – musical and otherwise – one might find in any professional setting. Scott affirms this position when noting the primary role of the music teacher is to 'model the thinking processes and tools of musicians and to facilitate each student's learning as they explore musical questions or problems' (2007: 36). As we explored this co-learning environment, I continued to alter my role in rehearsals based on the needs of individual students balanced with the desires of the ensemble as a whole. Opfer and Pedder (2011) discuss how a teacher's orientation – that is, their beliefs, perceptions and preconceived notions with regard to teaching and learning – has a strong influence on how and what they *learn*. I would offer a teacher's orientation has an equal, if not greater, impact on how and what they *teach*, as the totality of our intramusical and extramusical background has a lasting impact on our approaches towards, and attitudes in, the music classroom.

Takeaways

I felt then, as I do now, that my pan-musical experiences afforded me the flexibility to alter my orientation, to modify my concept of music teaching as it was not clearly aligned with one particular style of pedagogy or musical genre. It was these multiple paths, side trips and the occasional backtrack that afforded me this breadth and depth of experience I might have missed had I taken a more conventional teacher training route. It was through these intersections of music and life that my teaching self, and the various roles I take on and hats I wear within the classroom, emerged. It is this shifting and remixing of identities and roles, and becoming what Abramo and Reynolds (2015) call a 'creative pedagogue', that has helped me to grow reflectively and reflexively. In an effort to meet the needs of students, my orientation dictates I approach music education in the only way I know how; through applying what I have learned from my experiences in an array of musical settings as a teacher, performer, director, arranger and audience member and by affording students these same opportunities. I maintain my hybridized approach to popular music pedagogy is inherently practical and appropriate within the context of a music rehearsal or, realistically, any classroom setting. It is this 'bridging the gap' (Rodriguez 2004) between in-school and out-of-school experiences, of both students and teachers alike, that guides my path in the classroom. In the end, it seems, I exited the final roundabout precisely as intended.

NOTE

1. Crossfading, when used in a recording environment, is a means of blending two audio tracks by decreasing the volume of one track while, at the same time, increasing the volume of another.

REFERENCES

Abramo, Joseph M. and Reynolds, Amy (2015), '"Pedagogical creativity" as a framework for music teacher education', *Journal of Music Teacher Education*, 25:1, pp. 37–51.

Folkestad, Göran (2006), 'Formal and informal learning situations or practices vs formal and informal ways of learning', *British Journal of Music Education*, 23:2, pp. 135–45.

Green, Lucy (2002), *How Popular Musicians Learn: A Way Ahead for Music Education*, Burlington: Ashgate.

Green, Lucy (2006), 'Popular music education in and for itself, and for "other" music: Current research in the classroom', *International Journal of Music Education*, 24:2, pp. 101–18.

Holley, Steve (2019), *Coaching a Popular Music Ensemble: Blending Formal, Non-formal, and Informal Approaches in the Rehearsal*, Denver: McLemore Ave.

Kruse, Adam J. (2016), 'Toward hip-hop pedagogies for music education', *International Journal of Music Education*, 34:2, pp. 247–60.

Ladson-Billings, Gloria (1992), 'Culturally relevant teaching: The key to making multicultural education work', in C. A. Grant (ed.), *Research and Multicultural Education: From Margins to the Mainstream*, London: Falmer Press, pp. 102–18.

Opfer, V. Darleen and Pedder, David (2011), 'Conceptualizing teacher professional learning', *Review of Educational Research*, 81:3, pp. 376–407.

Parkinson, Tom and Smith, Gareth D. (2015), 'Towards an epistemology of authenticity in higher popular music education', *Action, Criticism, and Theory for Music Education*, 14:1, pp. 93–127.

Randles, Clint (2012), 'Music teacher as writer and producer', *The Journal of Aesthetic Education*, 46:3, pp. 36–52.

Rodriguez, Carlos Xavier (2004), 'Popular music in music education: Toward a new conception of musicality', in C. X. Rodriguez (ed.), *Bridging the Gap: Popular Music and Music Education*, Reston: MENC, pp. 13–27.

Scott, Sheila (2007), 'Multiple perspectives for inquiry-based music education', *The Canadian Music Educator*, 49:2, pp. 35–38.

Tobias, Evan S. (2015), 'Crossfading music education: Connections between secondary students' in-and-out-of-school music experience', *International Journal of Music Education*, 33:1, pp. 18–35.

Wiggins, Jackie (2001), *Teaching for Musical Understanding*, New York: McGraw-Hill.

23

Different from the Norm:
Teaching Band in Alabama

Shane Colquhoun

Shane Colquhoun, Ph.D. is a Grammy-nominated music educator. He currently teaches band and general music at Loachapoka High School located in Auburn, AL, USA.

The author of this chapter teaches band and general in a small rural town seven miles out of Auburn, Al, which is located in the southeastern United States. In this chapter, he discusses how a traditional wind band ensemble can function by playing primarily popular music.

Discovering popular music education

In a room full of preservice or in-service music educators at conferences or during guest lectures, one of my favourite questions to ask is, 'can music programmes survive on popular music alone?' After the question, the tension in the room is usually tangible. Although no one typically responds, you can sense that most music educators believe popular music cannot be the dominant genre in a traditional western classical music ensemble (wind band, choir or orchestra). For decades, western classical music has been the chosen – even default – genre in United States music education. Even in general music classes, students who do not participate in the traditional ensembles and are taking a music course for credit towards graduation are typically subjected to a music curriculum dominated by classical music.

I genuinely believe that many music educators realize the gaping hole in our profession and are either struggling to find legitimacy in popular music or do not know where to start. In 2008, I was 23 years old and was offered my first band director position at a small rural school seven miles outside of Auburn, Alabama. Five years into my career, I vividly remember wanting to abandon the field of music education – not because I no longer loved music, but because I was frustrated with the traditional approach to teaching music in the United States. I was tired of the struggle to keep students motivated, the festival ratings, and the narrow expectation of what musicianship is. My teaching practices strongly reflected my formal musical training and experiences in secondary school, undergraduate and graduate school, where my musical interests were not acknowledged. Unfortunately, I replicated the same experience with my students.

In 2015, I attended the *Association for Popular Music Education Conference* in Miami. From the knowledge I obtained there, my music education perspective and my role as a music educator drastically changed. From that conference, I learned that it was possible to meet students where they are as musicians while incorporating their music and addressing the standards of the curriculum. As a music educator, I believe my job is to create lifelong independent musicians capable of creating and recreating music without my presence. As a Band director who is responsible for leading and directing the concert and marching band, and an advocate for popular music, my approach to music education differs in three ways: (1) I do not limit popular music to the marching band, and I prioritize student interest and input over traditional performance routines, (2) I embrace the idea that popular music can be utilized formally and informally, and (3) I do not focus on virtuosity on a primary instrument.

Working as a band director

To avoid generalizing, I will speak specifically about my experiences as a band director in Alabama who understands how most secondary band programmes operate in my area (and, by and large, the southeast region of the United States). The typical format for a high-school band programme is the marching band in the fall, then shift to concert band that would start with a holiday concert. When students return from break, the focus typically turns to state music assessment and Solo and Ensemble in the late winter and early spring, and a spring concert a few weeks before summer vacation. The winter concert typically consists of holiday music; state assessment and Solo and Ensemble consist of traditional wind band literature. Spring concerts are a mixture of traditional band literature and may include multicultural pieces, songs from movies or popular music tunes.

During the fall, popular music is used heavily with the marching band. In the Southern United States at all levels, American football is king, and a huge part of the American football experience is the marching band (high school and college). Many schools will play several popular music songs on the field during their halftime performance and while sitting with the band in the stands to provide motivation and excitement for the football team on the field and the fans in attendance. However, once the marching band season is over, generally, so is the usage of popular music repertoire.

In the Southern United States, after the holiday performances, it is common for students who participate in their school band, choir or orchestra to attend their state music performance assessment. These events are also known as Music Festivals. Attending a music performance assessment for many programmes is the accepted status quo. In some districts, ratings and attendance at these assessments determine if a band director will receive their stipend or extracurricular bonus pay for the semester or even decide if they get to keep their job. For music educators, these state-sponsored music festivals are equivalent to high-stakes testing for math, English, and science teachers. Many band directors build their entire programme around attending not only these performances but also the results. At these festivals, students perform three pieces from a list of repertoires selected by the state for a panel of three judges and are assessed on their performance. The highest rating a performing group can receive is 'one' or a Superior, followed by a 'two', which is a rating of excellent, a 'three', which is a rating of good, and a 'four', which is a rating of fair. Typically, popular music is not allowed or encouraged. These festivals can also be sponsored by the state music education organization or by an independent company that usually ties the music festival to an activity such as a theme park.

As a band director, I have decided not to limit popular music to marching band season and place students learning and interest over the heavy performance culture and the over-emphasis on superior's ratings and concert band festivals. The conscious effort of making music relevant to my students does not mean performance is not essential. I believe that performance and assessments are essential; however, I believe that student learning supersedes both performance and assessment. I am willing to skip a performance if my students lack interest or for a more extensive learning goal set by my students and me. For example, in the spring of 2018, I gave the students a choice to perform in a local Battle of the Bands at a nearby Historically Black College or to travel to Atlanta to perform in an independently run music festival called the Trills and Thrills Music Festival. The Battle of the Bands event was at a local high school in Marietta, Georgia. These battle of the band's events are very popular in the southern United States. They are usually hosted by a Historically Black College and University (HBCU) and often are great avenues for college recruitment. At the battle of the bands, we would have to play a twelve to fifteen-minute set of popular music songs. In contrast, the trip to

Atlanta would have been a traditional music festival where we would play three concert band selections for a panel of three judges and receive a rating of superior, excellent, good, or fair. We would also stay overnight in Atlanta, and after the performance, go to the theme park Six Flags Over Georgia.

Although my students are very motivated by receiving 'Superior' ratings, after taking a poll, they overwhelmingly voted to skip the festival and attend the Battle of the Bands. Over the years, I have learned that although they have grown to appreciate traditional band literature, the class environment and motivation levels are at the highest when students are playing the music that they identify with and choose. One of the biggest and most commonly heard arguments against popular music is that teachers should expose students to more 'aesthetically pleasing' music. Unfortunately, what is viewed as 'aesthetically pleasing' is typically set by the band director with little regard to students' musical interests. My question or response to that is, should we expose students to what we proclaim as more 'aesthetically pleasing' music while suppressing the music that is culturally relevant to them? I believe that as music educators, we should teach music appreciation and expand our students' horizons. However, that appreciation starts with us educators appreciating the music of the students. Over my twelve years of teaching, I have found that students are far more enthusiastic when they like the music that they are playing. Although the traditional approach is not wrong, the way most traditional band directors use popular music inherently minimizes popular music and subconsciously tells our students that popular music is either not worthy of being performed outside of entertainment value or not meaningful enough to be studied as serious music.

In my music teaching, I embrace the performance of popular music, both formally and informally. I believe that developing both formal and informal music skills are valuable and worth developing. Musicianship should not only be based on a person's ability to read music staff notation. However, I understand that for music to be a viable option for college scholarships, they have to be able to read music staff notation at a high level. On the other side of the coin, my students' musical activities outside of school do not always include reading music. As an educator, I should value, foster and encourage those experiences. Students should have opportunities to express musicianship in natural, familiar and comfortable ways. Conversely, popular music should not only be limited to being learned informally and by ear. I preach to my students: the more music skills you have, the more opportunities you will potentially have. There is a wealth of popular music arrangements available for wind bands that are educational and can be studied in the same way we study traditional band literature.

Another important element of my teaching is that I value comprehensive musicianship over virtuosity on one instrument. I believe that student musicians should have opportunities to learn multiple musical instruments and musical genres. I encourage my students to learn about music recording, playing a modern instrument, songwriting, DJing and any other musical activities they are open to. In addition to the encouragement, I also use class time to cultivate these skills.

Final thoughts

Although I believe that I am a respected band director in my area, I have been ridiculed by some of the band director in my district for not taking part in the state music festival. Even with receiving many accolades for our marching band and receiving 'superior' ratings for four years straight (2015–18) at independent music festivals, some of my colleagues doubt my music education approach. However, I have decided that my number one goal as a teacher is student interest and student learning. I see my approach as a necessary and quality education.

In closing, to answer my favourite question, can music programmes survive on popular music alone? My answer to this question, without hesitation, is 'yes!' It does not mean I advocate moving entirely away from traditional large ensembles and classical music. I believe that it is necessary to expose students to the music of many genres and cultures, but this should not occur at the expense of their own culture, identity and musical preference. Just because the traditional model has worked for you does not mean it is the most viable option for students. As a profession, we want music to be relevant to our students, so why wouldn't we value the music they value? Embrace it.

24

Popular Music Education as a Place for Emergent Pedagogies

Meghan K. Sheehy

Dr. Meghan K. Sheehy is an assistant professor and director of Music Education at Hartwick College in New York, USA. She loves playing horn, piano, and singing to her son!

In this chapter, the author reflects critically on their past teaching practices, examines the impact of personal music experiences and colour-blindness on their students' experience, and concludes with ways to evolve from colonial practices towards anti-racist pedagogy through popular music education practices.

Music education in the United States is being called on to evolve (Powell et al. 2019). Classrooms and music teacher education programmes, so commonly filled with colonial curriculum and privileged educators, are now being provided with numerous open-source resources for incorporating antiracist pedagogy. Popular music education provides some of the most underutilized resources available to challenge colonialism and promote antiracism.

A first-year teacher's experience

Over a decade ago, I began my first job as a music teacher in the United States. Hired by a secondary school in South Carolina as their band director, my responsibilities included concert band, general music and marching band. This school was in an area known as the I-95 'Corridor of Sham' based on a 1993 lawsuit, Abbeville County School District vs. The State of South Carolina, where 34 school districts came together to sue South Carolina for failing to provide equitable education resources (Crain 2016). The student demographics of the school that hired me in 2005 were similar to present-day data: 66 per cent Black, 25 per cent White, and 9 per cent Hispanic, Asian or other (Institute of Education Sciences 2020). My music classroom demographics for the marching and concert bands were more than 90 per cent Black, significantly different from the national average of 15.2 per cent (Elpus and Abril 2011).

Like most high school band directors and music teacher educators in the United States, I am White (Hewitt and Thompson 2006). I also attended a primarily White institution for my bachelor's and master's degrees. The band I inherited in my first job had been through several tough years. There were no seniors in the group and the rest of the students in grades 9–11 had been without a middle school band director as that position went unfilled during their sixth–eighth-grade years. The instrumentation of the group was primarily trumpet, clarinet, flute and percussion, and about half of the students learned through rote instruction. Readers may imagine the work required to arrange music for this group; no easy feat for a first-year teacher trying to get her classroom and curriculum organized! So, imagine your surprise upon learning students volunteered to arrange pop music for the marching band to play.

There I was, a first-year teacher with non-traditional band instrumentation, and students offering to arrange pop music so we could perform current songs during our (American) football games. I said imagine *your* surprise because I did not feel surprised. I felt guarded and unsure. I did not come from a background of playing modern pop songs in marching band. I had already chosen our football crowd's entertainment: songs that I performed during my time as a student, just like my band directors had done before me. In the end, I allowed the students to arrange exactly one pop song to perform in the bleachers. I later realized what a tremendous missed opportunity that was for them and for me.

Anti-racism in the music classroom

I wrote this chapter at an extraordinary moment in history during the spring and summer of 2020. People around the world have joined together in protest to speak out against systemic racism, racist policies and police violence. As of this writing, in one month of protesting, we have seen many points of progress in the United States, including police departments banning the use of choke holds; introduction of federal legislation on police reform in Congress; upgraded charges against the police officers involved in George Floyd's death; reopening several murder investigations into the deaths of people of colour; and much more (Ankel, 2020). Black,

Indigenous and People of Colour (BIPOC) are speaking out on all platforms to continue their long conversation to generate awareness of racist policies and the need for change while guiding their allies to resources related to antiracism allyship and pedagogy.

The call for antiracist pedagogy has gone out across the field of education via social media and is permeating social media teaching group pages, public posts and curricular development. There are many conversations investigating how to integrate antiracist pedagogy in all aspects of a music student's learning experience, paired with numerous online resources to guide educators in effecting these changes. This movement feels international and urgent, and the field is responding. As an example, blogger Douglas Yeo outlined the inherent racism in Henry Fillmore's *The Trombone Family*, highlighting how they were 'born and marketed in a crucible of racial stereotyping, minstrelsy, racism, and Jim Crow' (2020: n.pag.). In the past, similar socially relevant posts earned few interactions. But at this moment, followers in music education were ready to receive this news and make changes accordingly, with many pledging to remove the works from their libraries immediately. Music educators are ready to integrate antiracist practices into their spaces.

Music students often have personal experiences of growth, friendship, safety and comfort in our school music spaces. At the secondary and university levels, students often spend more time with music teachers and classmates than with any other group of people (Morrison 2001). This unique relationship may provide outstanding opportunities for music teachers to integrate anti-racism and allyship pedagogy into their classrooms, as these spaces can generate a meaningful culture among participants (Adderley et al. 2003). in an environment where there is often already a comfortable space for discourse.

Antiracist pedagogy – including topics of racism, White supremacy, White privilege, code-switching, decolonizing, allyship, appropriation and more – can be integrated in music classrooms by taking advantage of teachable moments, or creating curricular experiences and concert programming explicitly designed for students and teachers to access a specific antiracist topic. For example, an instrumental conductor could programme Mayhew Lake's 'Slidus Trombone' in place of Fillmore's 'Lassus Trombone' (Yeo 2020) and engage students in discourse about the programming decision. A music teacher educator could have students learn about the context of a song from a member of a local American Indian tribe, as opposed to performing an appropriated version of an American Indian piece with little or no context. Furthermore, curricula that seem to be designed to limit students' experience to western classical and folk musics can be expanded to include music representative of a culture's change and growth – popular music.

The role of popular music education:
A ninth-year teacher's perspective

Revisiting my first year as a teacher, I feel disappointed over missing the opportunity to let my students arrange pop music for marching band. I could have helped guide them in exploring a culture of music arrangement and composition, but instead, I was colour-blind in my attempts to make *their* band experience look like *mine*. I did not honour what students valued. Deborah Bradley (2015: 197) describes colour-blindness as 'a mask for racist thoughts [and] actions [...] allowing White people to appear reasonable, even moral'; she continues, 'By teaching only "the best" music, one can easily hide behind a misguided sense of providing children with an equitable music education, overlooking the fact that such musical curricular choices represent a specific and narrow cultural perspective.' I wore that mask, completely unaware of the impact my privilege had on existing and potential learning opportunities for my students. In my unacknowledged racism and privilege, I failed my students deeply.

The silver lining is, that moment was such a powerful experience for me that I have used it to help guide my teaching and philosophy in a healthier, more inclusive and antiracist direction. I have grown to prioritize the integration of popular music education in my classrooms here at Hartwick College. Examples include:

- Incorporating popular music education conversations, techniques and lesson development into several courses within our music education sequence;
- Organizing regular visits to local teachers who incorporate popular music education into their classrooms;
- Hosting guest speakers who specialize in popular music education;
- Hosting monthly popular music 'hangs' for local youth and young adult programmes;
- Integrating a required Vernacular Music course for all music education majors.

It will no longer be enough for my students to understand the difference between equity and equality, or to learn about democracy in the classroom and social justice in education. With BIPOC around the world unifying their voices behind this momentous protest and call to action, I am learning about the value of moving further into the specifics of antiracism and allyship. Through these efforts, I hope Hartwick music education graduates will seek to create classes for popular music when they begin their own music teaching careers, integrating popular music concepts and activities into their varied music classrooms.

ACKNOWLEGMENTS
My deepest thanks to my middle school band director, Joe Kasmark, the Governor's School for the Arts in Norfolk, Virginia, and my trombone-playing dad who sat next to the piano with a metronome and a clock. I am here because you were there.

REFERENCES
Adderley, Cecil, Kennedy, Mary and Berz, William (2003), '"A home away from home": The world of the high school music classroom', *Journal of Research in Music Education*, 51:3, pp. 190–205, http://drora.me/wp-content/uploads/2014/04/a-home-away-from-home-the-world-of-the-high-school-music-classroom.pdf. Accessed 10 May 2020.

Ankel, Sophia (2020), '30 days that shook America: Since the death of George Floyd, the Black Lives Matter movement has already changed the country', *Business Insider*, 24 June, https://www.businessinsider.com/13-concrete-changes-sparked-by-george-floyd-protests-so-far-2020-6. Accessed 1 July 2020.

Bradley, Deborah G. (2015), 'Hidden in plain sight: Race and racism in music education', in C. Benedict, P. K. Schmidt, G. Spruce and P. Woodford (eds), *The Oxford Handbook of Social Justice in Music Education*, New York: Oxford University Press, pp. 190–203.

Crain, Adam (2016), 'Learning is a joy: The "Corridor of Shame"', *Palmetto Promise*, 10 August, https://palmettopromise.org/learning-is-a-joy-a-court-order-the-corridor-of-shame/. Accessed 17 March 2020.

Elpus, Kenneth and Abril, Carlos (2011), 'High school music ensemble students in the United States: A demographic profile', *Journal of Research in Music Education*, 59:2, pp. 128–45, https://www.jstor.org/stable/pdf/23019481.pdf?refreqid=excelsior%3A3f613d60d3b32bc270eb24f13e908cb1. Accessed 29 April 2020.

Hewitt, Michael P. and Thompson, Linda K. (2006), 'A survey of music teacher educators' professional backgrounds, responsibilities, and demographics', *Bulletin of the Council for Research in Music Education*, 170, pp. 47–61, https://www.jstor.org/stable/pdf/40319348.pdf?refreqid=excelsior%3A11ce54afe891b7434be0b3e21baa8256. Accessed 29 April 2020.

Institute of Education Sciences (2020), 'Common core of data: Search for public school districts', *National Center for Education Statistics*, https://nces.ed.gov/ccd/schoolsearch/schooldetail.asp?Search=1&InstName=Manning+High+School&City=Manning&State=45&County=Clarendon&SchoolType=1&SchoolType=2&SchoolType=3&SchoolType=4&SpecificSchlTypes=all&IncGrade=-1&LoGrade=10&HiGrade=13&ID=450177000327. Accessed 17 March 2020.

Morrison, Steven J. (2001), 'The school ensemble: A culture of our own', *Music Educators Journal*, 88:2, pp. 24–28, https://doi.org/10.2307/3399738. Accessed 4 May 2020.

Powell, Bryan, Smith, Gareth Dylan, West, Chad and Kratus, John (2019), 'Popular music education: A call to action', *Music Educators Journal*, 106:1, pp. 21–24, https://doi.org/10.1177/0027432119861528. Accessed 29 April 2020.

Yeo, Douglas (2020), 'Trombone players: It's time to bury Henry Fillmore's "Lassus Trombone", The Last Trombone', Word Press, 28 June, https://thelasttrombone.com/2020/06/28/trombone-players-its-time-to-bury-henry-fillmores-lassus-trombone/?fbclid=IwAR2UvUWGqnEj4tcG0VBXyCm2gHOd40L2MCwrtmTrn5qWEJ5MUXVt6FaVvjI. Accessed 29 June 2020.

25

Think Big, Start Small: Enacting Change in Higher Education

Martina Vasil

Martina Vasil is an associate professor of music education at the University of Kentucky, USA, and is president of The Association for Popular Music Education.

Martina describes how she brought popular music education (PME) to the University of Kentucky, USA by thinking big and starting small. She now provides annual training in PME for K–12 teachers, has established practica in local schools that teach PME, and revised her college course curricula to teach PME.

One of the most successful strategies I have employed in my fifteen-year career as a music teacher and music teacher educator is taking big ideas and projects and breaking them down into manageable chunks that I can get started on right away. This essay details my journey of enacting change in higher education – I first share my educational and teaching background, then describe what led me to integrate popular music education into the college courses I teach and how I brought popular music education training to my university. Through small, meaningful steps, I was able to enact larger, curricular changes in my institution. Through sharing my story, I hope I can encourage and enable others to reach their goals.

The journey

When I decided to pursue music education as a career, I knew I should know something about western European art music and that I had to audition on my clarinet.

I eagerly purchased classical music CDs, the book *Classical Music for Dummies*, and Alfred's *Essentials of Music Theory*. Once I was admitted to a music teacher education programme, I completely stopped listening to the radio. I quickly cast aside listening to any other kind of music except classical music. Success in classical music was reinforced from all sides, and even my original plan to become a music teacher was shaped and twisted into something else. I soon became hell-bent on becoming an orchestral clarinetist and clarinet studio professor. This state of mind did nothing to prepare me for the realities of teaching.

Teaching made me question everything I had learned in my programme. Throughout my six years working in Pittsburgh, Pennsylvania, I changed jobs four times, worked in Catholic and public charter schools, and taught general music,[1] wind band and bowed strings to children and adolescents (ages 6 to 13). It felt like a roller coaster ride, and my biggest struggle was teaching general music to adolescents; they did not want to learn about classical music. When I began teaching in 2005, students were obtaining Apple iPods and seriously curating their own libraries of music and developing their musical tastes. I had no idea what they were listening to or how to connect to their interests.

I was at my wits' end and desperate to find ways to connect to my students' musical interests. I knew two things that they loved: dancing and R&B music. I had learned next to nothing about either in my music teacher education programme but had been salsa dancing for a few years at the time. I took what felt like a risky step. I curated a list of songs that blended R&B songs with salsa beats and designed a series of lessons that led students through basic salsa steps to creating their own dance routine to perform at the end-of-year concert. The response from students was heartening; they loved it. I broke more fragile ideals that year and tried things I never learned in my collegiate education – student-composed raps using GarageBand, drumming units and students researching their favourite music artists.

What I did not realize at the time was that I was dipping my toes into popular music education (PME). That first salsa lesson I taught was the initial step. Even though I chose the music, it was informed by student interest in R&B music. I unwittingly engaged students in informal learning. Students imitated me modelling the dance moves; later, I gave students time to practise salsa steps on their own or with partners and often returned to a group step practice to review or to introduce a new step. I often wandered around the room giving individual help. Students helped to shape the final dance routine and I could see the pride in their faces when they performed for their parents at the end-of-the-year school showcase, a programme where students shared what they learned in their music and dance classes. Teaching PME was a small, 'revolutionary action' (Deleuze and Foucault 1977) that brought my attention to the power and hierarchies

I had learned through my music teacher education programme, and it changed my trajectory into music teacher education forever.

Enacting change in higher education

Bresler (1998) stated that there are three kinds of contexts within which change occurs: (1) a micro context – teachers' beliefs and practices in the classroom, (2) a meso context – the structures and goals of the school, and (3) a macro context – the more generalized policies, systems and cultural views that influence the curriculum. The day I brought salsa dancing and PME into my classroom, I was enacting change in a micro context. As I moved into higher education, I saw PME as a way for me to help evolve the curriculum for music teacher education as well. Again, I began within a micro context, my own classroom and curricula; after five years I began to see changes within my school of music (meso context).

Within the micro context of my classroom, I integrated PME throughout the two general music methods courses I had inherited. In particular, I revised the curriculum of my second general music methods course in just three years; it is now focused on general music for grades five to twelve with PME and Orff Schulwerk at the core of the pedagogical approaches being studied and applied. I added a hands-on popular music ensemble component to this class as well. Not only are my college students learning how to use PME in their future general music classrooms through designing lessons and practising their pedagogy at local schools, but they are forming their own popular music ensembles, running rehearsals, learning new instruments (e.g. drum kit and electric bass) and putting on a show open to the public. At the graduate level, I also offered a new course on PME with a similar popular ensemble experience using an existing course shell meant for special topics.

The changes I made to my curriculum were met with no resistance from my administration or colleagues. Why? I think largely because I was tinkering with my own classroom. I was able to make my changes first, then move the official documentation through 'the system' – this includes a formal proposal for a course change that is submitted to the college-level curriculum committee for review, then to the university undergraduate curriculum committee for review, and a final approval from the university senate. Perhaps another reason I did not face resistance was that my college students were immensely pleased and excited by these experiences as evidenced from verbal and informal feedback and positive comments in formal course evaluations. Seeing their classmates at a bar performing popular music only heightened the expectations of my incoming classes and increased excitement.

How did these small changes spill over into meso contexts? I caught the attention of my administrators and colleagues in a positive way. From the beginning,

I was intentional about inviting my college dean, school of music director and teaching colleagues to attend my students' public performances, and I shared what was going on in my classroom via social media. I also showed support to my colleagues and students through attending dozens of student and faculty recitals and orchestra, wind band and choral concerts. After seeing my graduate students perform popular music at a bar, my dean asked me to create an interactive rock band experience to welcome students to our community at the college open house, an event for prospective students that includes music performances and question-and-answer-opportunities. I teamed up with my music theory colleague (who wrote a theory book based on popular music and performs popular music in the community) to teach the students our university fight song using ukuleles, a drum kit, electric and bass guitars and vocals. The hour-long session was successful and widely broadcast on our college social media platforms. From there, my director began inviting me to attend recruitment weekends for the school of music, where I provided a ukulele hour for prospective students and their parents to actively participate. Further, workshops I had been organizing for PME through non-profit funding began to be financially supported by my director. Because of these workshops, local area teachers began incorporating PME and continue to view the University of Kentucky as a hub for professional development in PME. In the past year, my dean chose my proposal for popular music programming (along with just one other colleague's proposal) to represent the college as we applied for a $50,000 grant from the university. My director has also hired two new tenure-line professors in PME – an electroacoustic composer/arranger and an audio engineer who has resurrected the rock band at the school. With these new instructors in place, my director then formed a committee (which I am on) to create admissions guidelines and a 'track' for music education majors to enter our programme with computer as their main instrument.

Over the past six years, I have felt momentum at my university and, overall, I feel a slight shift in the culture, which indicates to me that perhaps change is beginning to stir within macro contexts. I think this change is partially due to work I have done – my curriculum, my sharing and the bonds I have forged – but some of it is also serendipitous. I happen to have a dean and director who are open-minded, invigorated by new ideas and innovative curriculum, and willing to put their support behind such efforts.

Conclusion

Enacting change in higher education can be and has been difficult – particularly with centuries-old curricula based on western European art music and seemingly immovable structures in place. The small changes I made within my micro context charted the way for larger changes to occur. Changing one's classroom practice *can* make a difference in music teacher education and can lead toward larger changes within meso and macro contexts. This is an idea that has been corroborated in the research (Fullan 2007; Hargreaves 1994; Randles 2013) and bears repeating – effective change in education begins with small-scale efforts initiated internally – with teachers.

NOTE

1. In the United States, 'general music' is used to describe classes that are 'designed for *all* students' and are not traditional performance ensembles (e.g. wind band, choir or orchestra). It also includes short-term exploratory courses that are labelled 'general music' but excludes those that are specialized (e.g. steel drums and electronic music lab). General music is usually compulsory for children ages 5 to 11 and becomes optional as children grow older and can choose amongst specialized arts classes in which to participate.

REFERENCES

Abril, Carlos and Gault, Brent Michael (2016), *Teaching General Music: Approaches, Issues, and Viewpoints*, New York: Oxford University Press.

Bresler, Liora (1998), 'The genre of school music and its shaping by meso, micro, and macro contexts', *Research Studies in Music Education*, 11:1, pp. 2–18.

Deleuze, Gilles and Foucault, Michel (1977), 'Intellectuals and power', in D. F. Bouchard (ed.), *Language, Counter-Memory, Practice: Selected Essays and Interviews by Michel Foucult*, New York: Cornell University Press, pp. 205–17.

Fullan, Michael (2007), *The New Meaning of Educational Change*, 4th ed., New York: Teachers College Press.

Hargreaves, Andy (1994), *Changing Teachers, Changing Times: Teachers' Work and Culture in The Postmodern Age*, New York: Teachers College Press.

Randles, Clint (2013), 'A theory of change in music education', *Music Education Research*, 15:4, pp. 471–85.

26

Becoming a Popular Music Educator:
A Personal Journey

Matthew Clauhs

Matthew Clauhs is an assistant professor of music education at Ithaca College in Ithaca, NY, USA, where he teaches courses in music education and instrumental methods.

This chapter follows my transformative journey in popular music education, moving through careers as a music teacher, district-level coordinator and college professor, inspired by learning more about my students' motivations and musical interests, working to better serve minoritized populations in school music programmes in the United States.

Many academics, particularly those engaged in qualitative research, maintain 'we live storied lives', and these stories help us make sense of our world and affect how we navigate through life. As I consider the places and purposes of popular music education in my own life, I realize how different institutions, students, teachers, municipalities and communities have strongly influenced my perspectives on teaching and learning. My journey of becoming a popular music educator has been transformative; I began teaching as a high school band director and unexpectedly found a place in the popular music education space. Recognizing that many others have similar roots, I thought my story may be useful to music educators and teacher educators who are going through transformations of their own. Therefore, this chapter highlights various places that shaped my perspectives on popular music education and describes how my experiences with teachers and students at each location contributed to a larger purpose of broadening school programmes to provide more equitable and accessible music education for all learners.

Boston Arts Academy – Boston, MA (2006–10)

One of my first teaching positions was at a performing arts high school, the Boston Arts Academy in Boston, Massachusetts. Relatively fresh out of college, I was excited to apply the skills and understandings I learned as an undergraduate music education student in a vibrant and musically rich school setting formed by a consortium of colleges which included Berklee College of Music. Within weeks of starting this position, however, I realized my expectations about how students *should* participate in school music did not match my students' goals for how they *wanted* to take part. I learned that my own experiences in a large middle-class suburban school district could not be broadly applied across all contexts. Specifically, the way I learned the saxophone through method books emphasizing five-line stave notation and music theory, and the way I participated in ensembles directed by a teacher using western classical pedagogies, was not a one-size-fits all approach to music education.

Many of my students in Boston learned to play their instruments by ear and performed outside of school in salsa bands, jazz combos, R&B ensembles, hip-hop projects and church worship bands. I learned that my definition of success – participating in honour ensembles and becoming a school band director – was not the only definition of success for a young musician. Instead, I had a group of high school students who toured with Kris Allen (winner of the eighth season of American Idol), a pair of young men who signed a contract with Def Jam records, and another student who was working with Sean 'P. Diddy' Combs on the MTV series, *Making the Band*. These achievements may not have been celebrated or recognized by our state-, regional- or national-level music education associations, but these students were just as musical as the 'motivated ones' who participated in honour ensembles along with me as a student. I needed new (to me) pedagogies and approaches for teaching that better matched the musical goals and aspirations of the learners at the Arts Academy.

Berklee College of Music – Boston, MA (2007–10)

While working at the Boston Arts Academy, I was offered an additional position teaching music theory and ensembles for the Berklee College of Music City Music programme, a preparatory school for students aspiring to go to Berklee. The curriculum at the preparatory school aligned closely with the Berklee College curriculum, which had a longstanding tradition of preparing students for careers in jazz and commercial music. I was fortunate to have colleagues at Berklee College of Music who mentored me and shared their teaching strategies. Berklee held annual conferences, *Berklee Teachers on Teaching*, that showcased best practices for teaching in learning in contemporary music settings. I enrolled in courses at Berklee's Boston Campus and online at online.berklee.edu that focused on arranging, sound recording and music production, and later studied guitar with a professor in the Performance Studies division. I found that Berklee has a formalized approach to teaching popular music, with a sequential curriculum, method books and expert teachers. Many popular music artists and producers learned, or at least furthered, their craft in formal classroom settings at this institution.

In addition to having conversations with faculty members and studying course materials, I learned a great deal about popular music education by observing some of Berklee's City Music high-school ensembles, which performed jazz, R&B, rock and pop music repertoire on a typical instrumentation of guitar, bass, drums, keyboard and technology. These ensembles were directed by Berklee faculty members with significant industry experience. I observed how ensemble directors would facilitate rehearsals, placing the responsibility of learning material on the students, but providing expertise and guidance when needed. I had never observed middle school and high-school students performing in rock, pop and R&B ensembles before, and I was inspired by how these groups provided opportunities to students who were less interested in performing in orchestras, wind bands and choirs. As I was beginning to understand how popular music education could broaden access to school music programmes, I was learning from my students, particularly students of colour, how they were marginalized – and at times blatantly discriminated against – by the very same things that I celebrated a music student myself: competitive school music festivals and traditional honour ensembles.

Temple University – Philadelphia, PA (2010–13)

I moved to Philadelphia to pursue a doctorate in music education at Temple University, determined to better understand how race, gender, access and equity intersected with music education. I wanted to learn how traditional music pedagogies and practices might not be inclusive of all learners, or might altogether block them from participation in school music, as many of my Boston students had explained to me. Temple University was, for me, the perfect place to examine these questions, as the university was located in Philadelphia and allowed me to study a cognate area of urban education in addition to my music education coursework.

It was during this time that I learned of the influential work of Lucy Green and applications of informal music learning at Musical Futures programmes in England. However, at the end of my graduate studies, I visited music classrooms that had misinterpreted the works of Green and poorly instituted pedagogies of

Musical Futures. These teachers attempted to engage students in informal music learning without the proper support; they provided students with rehearsal spaces and instruments, but no guidance or instruction. Students were plugging electric guitars into bass amplifiers with speaker cables; drum kits were not properly assembled and the rehearsals seemed to lack any sense of purpose or direction. I had had some experience with learner-led ensembles in Boston, and many of them thrived and significantly outperformed teacher-directed ensembles, but I did not see this style as a one-size-fits all approach; it seemed especially inappropriate for learners who lacked a fundamental knowledge of instrument technique. I understood the idea and purpose of informal learning but did not believe popular music *must* be taught this way in all settings and situations. The curriculum and instruction at Berklee College of Music after all, were highly formal – and Berklee prepared many successful popular musicians and producers in the United States (e.g. Quincy Jones, Terri Lyne Carrington, Melissa Etheridge, John Mayer). To suggest popular musicians must learn through informal methods was obviously incorrect, and was an assumption that Lucy Green herself rejected, but it seemed many music educators seemed to think this way. I had learned techniques for teaching popular music to high school-aged students through the Berklee City music programme, but was less familiar with school programmes that had developed popular music curricula, which broadened school music at the school or district level.

Johnson City School District – Johnson City, NY (2013–16)

After completing my Ph.D., I accepted a position as a music teacher in upstate New York, eventually becoming the music coordinator of Johnson City School District. Johnson City was a GRAMMY Signature School District and had received a NAMM Best Community for Music Education award every year in a recent decade. However, enrolment data revealed that the music programme disproportionately served white students and students from higher socioeconomic backgrounds. Drawing on experiences from Boston and my graduate studies, I wondered if contemporary music offerings might appeal to a more representative population of students, with a richer diversity of musical preference, race and economic class. I had attended training sessions held by Little Kids Rock and wondered how the inclusion of modern band and music technology classes might attract students less interested in wind band, orchestra and chorus. Representing Little Kids Rock, Bryan Powell visited our high school to deliver a day-long professional development workshop on modern band to all twelve of our district's music teachers. The department agreed to implement a new popular music curriculum, with electives at the high school and new approaches to general music from elementary to middle school. The response was overwhelming and enrolment data showed that students of colour and students who were eligible for free/reduced-price lunch were more likely to participate in these new electives than white students and those who did not qualify for free/reduced-price lunch. Including popular music classes and ensembles in the school district led to a music department that better reflected the racial and economic diversity of our school district.

Ithaca College – Ithaca, NY (2016–today)

The current place in my popular music education journey is the Ithaca College School of Music. Since joining the faculty in 2016 my perspectives about popular music education have been strengthened through observations of colleagues doing incredible work in this space. My colleagues on- and off-campus have challenged my bias towards a teacher-led approach to popular music and demonstrated successful models of learner-led ensembles and classes, unlike the misguided attempts at informal learning I previously observed as a graduate student.

One of the most profound experiences of my brief career in higher education to date was a Modern Band Fellowship led by Little Kids Rock at Montclair State University in the summer of 2018. The fellowship was comprised of several university faculty members from around the country who were similarly interested in popular music education for the purpose of broadening school music and increasing access. The fellowship led to collaborative projects and presentations that would continue to bring my understanding of popular music education into focus. I brought these experiences back to campus and created a music education course titled 'Modern Band', which included students from all around campus. It is unusual for students outside of the department to participate in a music education course, but the enrolment in this class is an example of how school music at any level, including the tertiary level, can be broadened to increase access to more learners. Additionally, I supervise student teachers whose field experience is primarily in a popular music setting. Students at the college are increasingly interested in becoming popular music educators themselves, as they see the opportunity it provides for providing culturally responsive music education for all students.

Continuing the popular music education journey

Although I did not initially seek to become a popular music educator, I have been inspired by the current modern band movement in the United States and educators

146

who have been able to create inclusive school music programmes. My experiences in Boston, Philadelphia, Johnson City and Ithaca have provided a multitude of perspectives and models for popular music education that prove there is not a singular pedagogy for this field, but instead many pedagogies. My experiences as a learner, practitioner, administrator, graduate student and currently as a music teacher educator, have shown me how various stakeholders of school music in the United States may view the benefits of popular music education, and the opportunities it provides for inclusive music education. I look forward to creating new stories as the field – and my understanding of it – continues to evolve and adapt to meet the needs of contemporary students.

27

Confessions of a Deadhead Music Educator: Connecting Worlds

James Frankel

James Frankel, EdD, is a life-long musician, music educator and very proud Deadhead. He is the founder and director of MusicFirst.

This chapter is about reconciling the expectations of a formal music education and teacher training in the United States, with the author's personal music preferences. Through reflection, many parallels are drawn between the Grateful Dead and the key tenets of becoming a music educator, incorporating popular music into modern music education.

For many music educators, there are two distinct musical worlds that brought them from an avid middle-school and high-school musician and music lover to taking the big step on deciding to major in music education. Those two worlds are what I would call the *academic* music world and the *popular* music world. For me, these two worlds were both very important to me and completely separate. Throughout my childhood I played piano as well as a variety of brass instruments – starting on trumpet in fourth grade, moving to baritone horn in seventh grade and finally the tuba in eighth grade. At the same time, my piano skills shifted to the synthesizer/keyboard world in ninth grade after I had saved up enough money to buy my first synthesizer – the Roland Juno 106. I made the shift when I realized that it was infinitely more fun for me to play the keyboard parts from the music I loved (The Beatles, Pink Floyd, Rush and Yes) rather than the classical piano canon that I dreaded practising. Right around ninth grade, the divide between academic music and popular music became quite distinct to me. One world was what I did in school (tuba), and the other was what I did the second I got home from school (synthesizer). Reminiscing on that time in my life, I can remember vividly separating the two – never discussing with my high-school band direc-tor what music I liked, and never discussing with my popular-focused keyboard teacher what I did in school. My band director had no idea I played keyboards, and my keyboard teacher had no idea I played the tuba. At the time I probably didn't think anything of that, but looking back I think that many, many other music students and future music educators may have had that same experience.

In tenth grade, I got introduced to the Grateful Dead. While my path to becom-ing a fully-fledged Deadhead took a little while, I know the reasons why I liked them the second I heard them – the music was amazing and the people who listened to them were really cool. I wanted to be one of those people. I went to my first Dead show and was absolutely floored by the community that followed the band around and the carnival-like atmosphere of the shows. This was my tribe. Meanwhile, my entire social existence in high school revolved around the music programme. I was a quintessential band geek during the day and at football games and parades. The marching band programme was my other tribe. My outward transformation from a band geek to a tie-dye wearing patchouli smelling Deadhead took about a year. By the time I was in eleventh grade, I was a full-on Deadhead – a long haired, peace loving, crystal wearing hippy. Even still, my two musical worlds were totally separate. Around that time I started taking tuba lessons with Don Butterfield, a very well-known tuba player and teacher. Between Don and my high school band director, they probably judged me on my tuba playing first, and my sense of fash-ion second. In all the years I studied with Don, he never asked me about the music that I liked – he only focused on my learning the standard tuba repertoire and my technique in lessons. I was also well aware of the stigma surrounding Dead-heads – largely that they smoked pot and did psychedelic drugs. Regardless of whether that stigma was true or not, I got the impression that I could not be open about my own musical taste with my teachers because I wouldn't have been taken seriously as a musician. I didn't think that any of my music teachers even liked popular music – that was certainly the impression that they gave me. Until very recently, I never shared the fact that I am a Deadhead with the tens of thousands of educators to whom I have presented sessions at conferences, nor the thousands of educators that I have trained – probably for the same reasons as when I was high school. This prompted me to ask several important questions of myself and of my profession: Why is it that we compartmentalize these two worlds? Isn't all music worthy of being taught? Shouldn't music educators be interested in what their students listen to? When you become a music educator do you have to stop liking popular music and plunge head first into the academic music world to be considered a serious music educator? What is it about popular music that makes it seem like it can't be taken seriously in formal music education? Is it the sex, drugs and rock and roll? Or something more sinister?

These questions all came into focus for me in 2010 when I gave a talk at a university music education programme on my predictions for the future of music education. As part of the talk, I predicted that popular music would be not only included in general and performance-based methodologies, but would eventually become the primary direction of curriculum in order to remain relevant to the students. I made the bold claim that if Jimi Hendrix were alive at the same time as J. S. Bach, they would more than likely have been good friends, and would probably have partied together. I remember distinctly that the students clapped and cheered at this, but some of the faculty members openly bristled – folded arms, stern looks, shaking heads and audible gasps. At the time I chalked it up to maybe being too progressive for the institution. Since then I have come to realize that this attitude is very common at the university level. I have also realized that not only are the musical aspects of why I love the Grateful Dead the exact same five reasons why I am a musician, they are also fundamental to who I am as a music educator.

1. *Innovation*
   It can easily be argued that the Grateful Dead pushed music technology more than any other rock band in history. They basically invented the concept of a high quality sound system for their live shows. The famed Wall Of Sound that they toured with in the early 1970s was, and remains, a marvel of technology. They had the first ever monitors on stage and used the first noise-cancelling technology. Jerry Garcia, the lead guitarist and vocalist of the band, was one of the first people to use a MIDI guitar in the mid 1980s. The band was famous for allowing people to record their live concerts and disseminate the tapes for free. Even today, anywhere members of the Grateful Dead play, you can expect to see a huge array of technology in their personal setups. This openness to adopting and innovating technology is central to my own teaching.

2. *Improvisation*
   The Grateful Dead started and continue to embody the 'jam band' scene. Every member of the band was an extremely talented improvisor. Most songs take well over ten minutes to perform, often extended by numerous and lengthy solos. The members of the band were huge jazz fans and tried to emulate musicians like John Coltrane, Miles Davis, Thelonious Monk and others by exploring every note of melody within a song. The reason that most Deadheads love the music is that they never hear a song played the same way twice. In fact, the Dead never played the same setlist in the thousands of concerts that they performed over 50 years. While many aspects of improvisation are essential for music educators to be successful, it is no surprise that teaching jazz ensemble was my favourite part of my teaching job at the middle-school level.

3. *Master musicians*

Few would argue about how incredibly talented the musicians of the Grateful Dead were/are. Jerry Garcia is considered one of the greatest guitarists in history. Bob Weir is one of the most innovative rhythm guitarists, employing some wildly original chord voicing and inversions. Bill Kreutzmann and Mickey Hart, the drummers of the band, pushed the envelope of what drums and percussion meant to rock – which included a fifteen to twenty minute drum solo at every concert. Phil Lesh is widely considered one of the most original bass guitar players, and the numerous keyboard players who played with the band over the years were incredible musicians. For me, I know that the pure dedication to being the best musician possible was inspiring and certainly pushed me to also be the best musician and teacher that I could be. As I was always inspired by their performances, I wanted to inspire students through my teaching.

4. *Music theory*

While I didn't realize it until very recently when I began playing the music of the Grateful Dead on my keyboards, there is a lot to be learned from the music that the band played. Jerry Garcia explored all kinds of modes in his extended improvisations, especially mixolydian, and used chromatic passing tones, major pentatonic scales, and a lot of blues and bluegrass to provide audiences with some of the most amazing and surprising music ever to come from a guitar. The band often used odd time signatures, syncopated rhythms, modulations, a wide variety of musical styles (everything from folk to disco) and displayed a fervent desire to always make original music – never bending to what mainstream music labels and audiences wanted. Analyzing their music using the music theory skills that I have acquired over the past few decades made me realize just how original and talented the band was. There is almost any aspect of music theory that can be taught using their music – from half steps to German sixth chords.

5. *Building a community*

For me, the most special aspect of being a Deadhead is belonging to a community. Whenever I meet a fellow Deadhead, regardless of who they are, where they come from or what they look like, I can instantly strike up a conversation find a common bond over the music. The Grateful Dead were absolute masters of creating a community around their music – whether intentional or not. That sense of belonging is a central part of being a musician – whether as a member of the marching band, concert choir, string orchestra, mariachi band, steel drum band or iPad ensemble – and it is one of the most special aspects of a school music programme. From my experience teaching, all students want is a place to fit in, feel comfortable and call home while at school – united in purpose and interests.

You can easily swap out the Dead for any musical artist – from Buddy Holly to Dr. Dre. With some possible exceptions, the five reasons that I listed above are the same reasons many people love the music that they love. Talent, meaningful songs, unique musical qualities, musical form, infectious rhythms and a community of dedicated fans – isn't that why we love the artists we love? Taking that energy and using it to inspire students in our classrooms is what it's all about in my opinion. It is essential to remember that the students in our classes are most likely having those very same experiences with musicians they love. To discount that, to not try to incorporate the music that our students love to teach the same musical concepts that we have been teaching for decades using musical examples far removed from the music that is in their earbuds is missing an amazing opportunity. Embrace the music that your students love and use it to teach and inspire. I can only imagine what would have happened if my music teachers had done the same for me.

28

A Personal Journey with Popular Music in Paraguay

Sol Elisa Martinez Missena

Sol Elisa Martinez Missena is a DMA student and research assistant in Music Education at Boston University, from Asuncion, Paraguay. Her work experience includes teaching piano, accompanying and choral conducting.

In this chapter, the author describes her experiences with learning popular music as a classically trained pianist in Asuncion, Paraguay, and her struggles in finding her own musical self-identity.

Popular music, classical music and growing up in Paraguay

Most Paraguayans' first direct contact with popular music happens in family gatherings. It is common to celebrate birthdays and holidays with the whole family, including cousins, uncles, aunts and grandparents from both sides. Usually, there is an 'uncle' playing the guitar singing old ballads or traditional Paraguayan music, and everybody starts singing and dancing if the music is joyful. These events mark the first involvement with popular music for many Paraguayans, alongside listening to the radio, attending live concerts and/or in youth camps. If you happen to have been raised in the capital or big cities of the country, you are more likely to have been exposed to pop, Latin music, Argentinian rock, metal, reggaeton and jazz (to a lesser degree) since most radio stations in these areas promote these styles of music. In most rural settlements, people tend to listen to traditional Paraguayan music, reggaeton, pop ballads, cachaca and vallenato.

Unfortunately, I did not share these typical musical experiences as a child growing up in Paraguay. From when I was very young, my mother and maternal grandmother influenced my sisters and me to learn classical music, and more specifically, to learn 'classical' piano. Important aspects of this influence were my grandmother's nationality and upbringing. She was born in Uruguay and raised in Argentina where western classical music was more widespread than in Paraguay. Since my grandmother did not experience Paraguayan culture in her youth, she brought with her western musical culture and strongly inculcated her family to learn piano. Back in the 1990s when I started learning classical piano, people who practiced it in Paraguay always had some sort of foreign influence or started because someone from their family already played classical piano. Because of this strong influence, my contact with popular music in my childhood was mainly through listening to the radio or watching television rather than through performance.

It was not until I built friendships with popular music fans during my teenage years that I started to have a deeper understanding and appreciation for it. In the context of friendship, I learned about their passion about these music's since I began spending more time with them. After a while, I started singing and performing with them which broadened my perspective about popular music. Another important group of experiences in this period was youth camps. It was common to gather around the fire to sing popular songs of the time, and there was always a guy dedicating a song to a girl. Most of the songs we sang were Latin music, rock, pop and ballads, mostly in Spanish since not many knew English well enough to know famous songs' lyrics. Since I was part of my school's choir and chamber orchestra my exposure to gospel music and ballads increased. Moreover, I started regularly attending services for teenagers at a Baptist Church, where I met incredibly talented musicians, passionate about gospel music and rock and roll from the 1980s, who played worship music in these styles.

I kept on practising classical piano and violin during my teenage years, but at the same time, started playing popular music, especially at weddings and in school graduation ceremonies. People heard I was studying music, and asked me to play in their events, but they did not know I was a complete amateur in popular musical styles. At these events, I mostly sang or played violin, performing pop music, Disney music, romantic ballads like those from the Mexican singer Luis Miguel or guaranias (traditional Paraguayan music). Since I did not have popular music training, I had to learn on my own by listening to recordings or from cover versions on YouTube. I listened to the videos over and over until I knew the songs. While I loved classical music, I always felt freer when playing popular music.

Competition and self-expression

In my experience as a piano soloist, there was an unspoken air of competition. Maybe some people like this, but I am not a competitive person at all and I enjoy making music with other people in a more collaborative environment. Popular music thus gave me that refreshing break I needed from the perfectionism of the classical music culture and provided the balance I craved between performance excellence and creativity. Unlike my more informal popular music-making experiences, classical concerts were much more structured as the expectations were significantly higher for when interpreting a piece. It is expected that you play the notes exactly as they are on the score and a certain type of playing is expected according to the period in which a given piece was written. Although I understand the relevance of playing a piece exactly as a composer intended, I always wanted to make music that I felt that was my own; that had original, creative input from me. I could do that with popular music.

The pursuit of creativity and performance freedom in popular music made me feel like an outsider among my classical piano peers. My classmates were really into learning music from the classics such as Beethoven, Mozart, Rachmaninoff, Chopin and other famous composers of piano music. Still, I was always choosing contemporary music, atonal, prepared piano pieces and music based on popular music such as Piazzola's work, pieces that were not usually 'popular' among classical pianists. This preference was an effort to introduce a bit of improvisation, or a 'piece of me', into my performances.

Ultimately, my training as a classical musician became an obstacle to feeling completely comfortable improvising or playing popular music. I am not sure how the experience was for others learning classical music, but I had strict piano teachers who focused on playing the correct notes or having a 'perfect' performance. Later, this translated to stage fright in instrument exams and performances. I struggled to 'let myself go' with the music, and just play from the heart. Deep down, I knew classical music was a separate element in my life. It was the music I played in institutions, but not the music to which I was exposed every day or the music to which I listened. Therefore, my goal became honing musical skills that would help me make music I enjoy, inside and outside of institutions.

Popular music allowed me to be me

Learning popular music has been a journey of identity self-discovery. At the beginning of my musical life, I learned conservatoire music (western classical music), but after I grew up, I started wondering 'why am I playing this? Does this music truly represent me? Do I want to keep playing this after graduating?' These questions made me realize that it is the music you enjoy listening to, and the music you are surrounded by daily, that is the stronger part of your identity. In some way, I feel that all those years of devotion to classical music were a mask that I wore. Not because I have not found beauty in it, but because with popular music I could be myself.

29

From Bowing My Double Bass to Pushing My Push: A Swedish Journey from Music Education to Popular Music Educator

Erik Lundahl

Erik Lundahl is an assistant principal and music teacher at the aesthetic programme at Ystad Gymnasium in Ystad, Sweden, where he teaches the EDI and other music courses.

In this chapter, Erik describes his journey through Swedish music education leading up to a professional career in music education and as a freelance musician, music producer and songwriter. He discusses the potential imbalance between how one teaches and how one approaches creativity in a traditional popular music education setting

I believe there is an imbalance in how people study tradition vs. creativity in popular music education. This is a highly subjective opinion based on my own experiences, but maybe there is something to it – is it not the combination of creativity *and* the pursuit of challenging traditional thoughts, ideas and ways to operate what makes popular music exciting?

Musician and music learning

I have always identified myself as a broad musician. Genre, style, sound, by ear or sight reading, it does not matter, I have always thought it was fun. I started somewhat involuntarily as an 8-year-old singing in a boys' choir. It was very traditional and stuffed with clear expectations and ideals. At about the same time, I started playing double bass in combination with an otherwise full focus on becoming a basketball professional one day. Everything was going on in parallel, I thought it was fun with the music lessons, but the focus was on sports; music only caught me in shorter, intense moments.

About five years later, I first got hold of an electric bass. It was without expectations and with a commitment stereotypical to a teenager that I got to plug in and play 'Smoke On The Water' by Deep Purple. It caught me. I started to rehearse with my first 'real' band in a port area in the city of Malmö and got to perform live with our original music in the course of a year. Life was open and without the need for decisions and defined priorities. I went to school, in my spare time I played basketball and music – because it was fun.

When it was time for me to choose a high school, the scale had tipped in music's favour and I started to study on the aesthetic programme at Spyken in my home-town of Lund. There, for the first time, I met other young people of the same age on a daily basis who in many ways had the same burning interest in music as me. The next three years were the best of my life so far. I was given the opportunity to play pop music along with others who also liked it. When I entered the third and final year, my classmates and I were in a Swedish nationwide music competition where we won a tour to southern Africa. I guess you can imagine what it did for the motivation for a 17-year-old like me.

When I started high school, I had also started to think about the path of music probably being something I would like to work with in the future. Even though it felt impossible for me as a teenager to see this road, it actually existed, both in our educational system and also in the Swedish and global music business. After I graduated high school, I continued with a pre-university music course and spent a whole year playing with others – no mathematics, no Swedish, just music. I got to try living away from home for the first time and made all the mistakes and discoveries that one should at that age.

In 2008, I entered the Academy of Music in Malmö (part of Lund University) to start my undergraduate music studies. What only four years earlier had felt like an extraordinarily difficult goal to achieve had happened! In Sweden, there are six music colleges and they provide the highest form of music educa-tion in the country. At the time, the Academy in Malmö offered courses and programmes for musicians, music teachers, composers, arrangers and music producers, with different genre orientations. The programme I studied was 'Instrumental and ensemble teacher with a specialization in rock music'. I spent four and a half years of studies with electric bass as my main instrument, which ultimately resulted in the degree of Master of Arts in Music Educa-tion, but above all provided me with invaluable knowledge, experience and a big professional network. I further supplemented the eighteen months after graduating with a one-year course in music production. These years shaped me enormously.

Since graduating from university in 2013, I have been professionally active as a musician, band leader, teacher, music producer and songwriter. I am also the first teacher in Sweden to ever educate in the Electronic Digital Instrument (EDI). An EDI consists of a computer, a digital audio workstation and a control unit (for example an Ableton Push). The latter has required a tremendous thought process and has in many ways influenced how I think about popular music education. My thoughts are very much about the balance, or maybe the imbalance, between tradition vs. creativity in popular music education, authentic assessments and how to more clearly relate the theoretical elements of music to the performance of music.

Musician and music teacher

Nowadays I am back on an aesthetic programme, this time on the other side as a teacher at Ystad Gymnasium. Since I started working, I have taught a number of different courses, such as electric bass, the arts and society, music theory, live performance workshops, music production and aesthetic communication, which have all gradually slipped over into becoming more and more a purely service as a teacher in the EDI. In addition to teaching, I work with programme development and within the framework of my Lead Teacher Assignment, I also work on educational development for the programme. Since 2017, Ystad Gymnasium, with me as a teacher, is the first school in Sweden to train in the EDI, a journey that I started two years earlier.

At that time, my professional focus was on my career as a freelance musician, songwriter and music producer. I played in a variety of constellations and was responsible for music with international artists, in hotel and spa facilities, I played in cover bands, a classical orchestra and in a number of different original music projects. I've played at clubs, festivals, on radio and TV and toured most parts of Europe, Russia, Africa and South and Central America. In my role as an educator, I had also been active in London at that time and lectured at university conferences in Sweden, Norway and the United States. As a music producer and songwriter, I am published and still working at Cardiac Records, where, through a close collaboration with Sony Music Sweden, we release music with national and international artists. These experiences have shaped me and characterize me a lot in my role as a popular music educator.

When I was 15 and younger, people got together when playing music. And so did I. Either in someone's basement or in a rehearsal complex; possibly in the school's regular music hall sometimes. The point here is that everything revolved around the physical meeting. The years I am referring to are around 1998–2003 and we certainly lived in a partly digital society back then, but neither processor power, stable internet connection nor digital music consumption was to any great extent available to ordinary people at a reasonable cost. We met and played with each other and had always done so in some form. But as the internet infrastructure grew, became more stable and a reasonably good computer with a music programme that did not have too high of a gateway became available, new doors opened for enthusiasts and non-professionals. In the mid 2000s, we read about artists who produced albums at home in their bedrooms, how they recorded and mixed everything themselves and how music consumption pushed further towards streaming.

In the early 2010s, we found ourselves in the middle of the golden age of EDM music, with Swedish artist Avicii at the forefront. He was admittedly from a family with a musical background but still in the traditional sense musically untrained. He jammed with ideas and produced day and night in his room. He was not a rehearsal complex musician; he was something else. At the time you could also see at stages around the world how the computer was becoming more and more like a faithful servant to pop acts of various kinds. If you had not tuned in to backing tracks, you could manoeuvre a synth or control the light show using music impulses via the computer. The uses were, and are, many and varied. Around 2015, I was wondering what it would have been like if Avicii had been musically schooled. If he had played the EDI and used it both in the studio and live, perhaps we would have seen him in other contexts outside of his daily music performance. What would then have happened with his music? In some cases, perhaps it would have led to undesirable outcomes and bound him to rules, obstructing his creativity. Imagine, similarly, Bob Dylan with three years of song coaching; it might not have resulted in the same sound. But that is not really my point either. Rather, if we have relevant and appropriate popular music education conducted in a professional and thoughtful way, would these and similar issues and examples become non-issues?

I would like to return to my opening: I think there is an imbalance in how to study tradition vs. creativity in popular music education. One issue is partly based on the fact that, for example, one can see a 'creative risk' with a trained Avicii or Bob Dylan. But if popular music education cannot improve and be a resource for an artist and music producer, what is the purpose and justification of the education? As a counter, I was told a story about a school in Stockholm where last year, students played 'I Wish' by Stevie Wonder during a live performance workshop. I was told how the students kindly did what they were told and played the song from beginning to end, but the glow was missing. Nobody scheduled an extra rehearsal or wanted to push the project beyond the lesson. Instead, the same students went away and jammed completely different things on their break, wrote songs together and had great sessions. This is an example of a pattern I see happening in environments I teach in. My vision is to enable creative magic to happen during lessons and help students get better in the eye of the storm, where creativity flows, and they make or arrange music that challenges and sets trends.

In conclusion, one should never exclude the other. I think there is an imbalance between tradition and creativity in popular music education, and as an educator I am in pursuit of inclusion.

30

From A. R. Rahman to Ed Sheeran: How Informal Learning Practices can Inform Music Teaching

Shree Lakshmi Vaidyanathan

Shree Lakshmi Vaidyanathan teaches kindergarten music at a private school and is a part-time faculty member at The Bangalore School of Music in Bangalore, India.

Realizing that some of her musical skills do not come from her classical music training, the author delves into her childhood in Indonesia and adolescence in India, recognizing that her experiences in informal music learning vastly contributed to her overall musicianship and her music teaching today.

Introduction

At the turn of the millennium, the internet was a luxury for students like myself living in a lazy coastal college town in southeast India. Visiting overpriced internet cafés was considered splurging at the time, and the engineering college I attended allowed internet access only for academic purposes. So, during my second year, when I was unwillingly thrust into the role of music arranger of the college band, I spent my free time figuring out chords, riffs and interludes sans Google or Yahoo. YouTube did not yet exist.

Green observes that 'just because the musicians are not necessarily able to talk about or name musical procedures and elements [...] it does not follow that they should conceive of themselves as 'not knowing' about them. Rather, they have 'tacit' knowledge of them' (2017: 97). Indeed, although my band members could not read any conventional notation systems other than chord names, I like to think we made reasonably good music together. We not only participated in (and won!) inter-college competitions but were also invited to play in public spaces during community events. Our setlist included popular songs from Bollywood and Kollywood[1] movies dating from the 1970s to the early 2000s with the odd instrumental number like the *Mission: Impossible* theme thrown in. It was during this time, I realized that my early unsupervised and informal music learning had more of an impact on my musicianship than my classical piano training.

In 2003, on deciding that coding in a cubicle was not the life for me, I defied all logic and chose to become a music teacher instead. This essay describes my early informal experiments with popular music, which unwittingly nurtured my musicianship and eventually led me to establish my career as a music educator.

How to create a musician? Listen. Play. Rinse. Repeat.

At the age of 5, I was living with my parents and sister in a middle-of-nowhere village in West Java, Indonesia; green fields sprawled around as the majestic Mt. Geulis stood watch over us. Both Indian and Indonesian musical traditions are primarily aural/oral systems. Any notation forms are rudimentary, recently developed and serve as learning aids, rarely used during performances. So, when my parents bought me a wooden toy piano, I was naturally expected to play by ear, because nobody around me knew any different. Soon, with my father's help, I was pecking away charming Indonesian nursery rhymes like '*Balonku ada lima*' ('I have five balloons') and '*Saya punya topi*' ('I have a hat') on the toy piano with the painted-on black keys. My father, whose only musical training as a young boy in southern India came from eavesdropping on his neighbours every time they tuned into *All India Radio* or *Radio Ceylon*, was determined to make me play all his favourite songs using only my index finger. And I delivered.

By the age of ten, I was fairly proficient in the art of single-finger-playing on the minute keys of my new tiny-but-functional Casio VL-1; my repertoire comprising not only popular Tamil and Hindi golden oldies from the 1950s to 1970s but also random British or American hits thrown in for good measure. The recording feature on this antiquated device (which for some reason, doubled as a calculator) was instrumental, literally, in honing my aural skills. Dad's critical ear would spot slip-ups and I would have to correct pitches and/or rhythms without quite understanding what I was doing. At this stage, I was not only playing C major-based songs like 'Do-Re-Mi' from *The Sound of Music* but also those based on complex Indian *ragas* or modes. I vividly remember playing '*Konjum Purave*'[2] ('Cuddling Doves') and the very depressing *Jaane kahan gaye voh din?*[3] ('Where have those days gone?') on this instrument.

At the age of 11, I moved to India and started formal piano lessons – a novelty for an Indian girl from my ethno-religious background. At fifteen, my parents bought me a Yamaha PSR-620 electronic keyboard, which turned out to be a significant influence on my musicianship. With not only hundreds of instrument voices, built-in styles and a floppy-disk drive, this keyboard had chord display and multi-track recording. This meant that I was at least attempting to reproduce two-time Academy Award winner A. R. Rahman's early masterpieces[4] as well as Disney renaissance hits like 'Circle of Life' track for track. Yanni introduced me to the wonderful world of orchestration. In listening to syrupy love songs by sappy boy bands like Boyzone, Backstreet Boys and Michael Learn to Rock on my Sony Walkman (and later, Discman), I understood song structure and replicated common chord progressions, modulations and harmonies long before I studied them in a theory class. Theory classes soon became my favourite because I finally understood what I was doing intuitively. This music-making was mostly for myself and my family. While I did perform often at school events or at my piano school, the music I played in those contexts was not popular music.

Indian popular music, like Indian classical music, is learned by ear albeit under more relaxed circumstances. On observing some of my acquaintances over the years who have learned Indian popular music outside of a school setting, I noticed that almost all their learning came from watching, listening to and repeating what their teacher played. They may write out broad instructions in a notebook, such as what note to start on and the overall song structure. They may also write out note names or note numbers as recommended by their teachers, to aid them during practice, but almost never while performing. This was the kind of support I gave my band mates while at college. Typically I would have to show them a riff or an interlude once or twice, and they would just pick it up by ear. I almost never had to write out instructions other than chord names.

Jaffurs brings up the question of what constitutes musicality in the context of the intersection of formal and informal music learning practices (2004: 191). There was a time when I haughtily thought that people who had never taken music lessons and who could not read notation could never be musical. But my experiences with my college band quickly put that silly notion out of my head. Similarly, I was by no means a good piano student; I never mastered the art of sight-reading, nor do I have a western classical repertoire to write home about. But I came to realize this did not necessarily mean I was not musical.

Work hard. Play harder.

Between 2003 and 2020, I worked several teaching jobs. I have taught, among other things, general music and choir for school children aged 3 to 17. Relevantly,

I have taught music theory and I run an annual twelve-week aural training session for the Associated Board of Royal Schools of Music (ABRSM)[5] students at an exclusive western classical music school in Bangalore. The realization that my early experiences have greatly impacted my musicianship has drastically changed the way I teach my own students. I now tend to approach all my lessons from a place my students are comfortable in, and using music they are comfortable with – usually popular music, hopefully enhancing the authenticity of the learning experience (Green 2006: 115). I can trace almost every skill I now use in my classes back to my informal learning experiences as a school and college student.

During that phase of my life, I experimented with how different types of riffs on different instruments could dramatically alter the style of music being played. I have used this knowledge to teach a Musical Styles and Periods module in my senior aural training class. Listening to the bass line of different kinds of music has helped me tackle a Chords and Inversions module and I encourage my students to do the same with their favourite songs long before I teach that module. Often, when I am asked to accompany children while they sing songs unfamiliar to me, it is my knowledge of riffs, built-in keyboard styles, transposition, harmonization, instrumentation and chord progressions that helps me to accompany them instantly. Yes, my piano and music theory lessons have helped, but not as much as the hundreds of sleepless nights spent on musical experimentation in my bedroom.

In my general music classes, I have allowed middle and high school students, aged ten to fifteen to pick songs to learn on their own and perform during the music period. Some songs I knew, like 'Believer' by Imagine Dragons, and some I did not, like 'Appu dance' from the 2017 Kannada hit movie *Raajakumara* ('Prince'). Since the schools I have worked in are not equipped with adequate instruments for all students, we have improvised using classroom instruments (shakers, triangles, tambourines, etc.), bongos, buckets, wooden boards and *dandiya* sticks.[6] On one occasion, I wanted to give some of my students aged 12 to 14 an experience of performing Indian classical music, specifically south Indian Carnatic music – a genre I myself am not trained in and one that most students would consider boring and meant for old people. We agreed on Indian Raga's fusion version of Ed Sheeran's 'Shape of you',[7] provided they did all the groundwork, watched the instrumentation instruction video (Jimmy Fallon and The Roots' classroom instruments version of the same song) and practised on their own with little input from me. Given that only a quarter of the students was musically trained, I was quite impressed by the motivation levels and the end result. The students were obviously thrilled that they were allowed to perform a 'clean version' of this pop song in front of the school. When some of the students from this group later approached me expressing interest in forming an informal school band in the forthcoming academic year, nothing could wipe the smile off my face the entire day.

Conclusion

I do not identify as a popular musician. I do, however, recognize that my competency as a music educator is heavily influenced by my informal learning experiences with popular music during my youth. I found purpose in my work, staying out of trouble and setting goals for myself, learning the importance of discipline, patience and persistence without realizing that I was not only training myself for a future career but also to be a more productive human being.

NOTES

1. Kollywood is a film industry based in Chennai in southern India that releases films for the Tamil speaking people of India and Sri Lanka, and the Tamil diaspora around the world (see Getter 2014). Bollywood is based in Mumbai and releases Hindi films. Over a dozen regional language film industries exist in India.

2. From 1952 Tamil film *Thai Ullam* ('Mother's heart'). I later learned that the melody first appeared in *Thandi Hawayein* ('Cool breezes') from the 1951 Hindi film *Naujawan* ('Youth').

3. From 1970 Hindi film *Mera Naam Joker* ('My name is Joker').

4. A. R. Rahman's early movie albums like *Roja* ('Rose'), *Thiruda Thiruda* ('Thief! Thief!') and *Bombay* (well, Bombay) from the 1990s, along with India's 2002 Oscar entry, *Lagaan* ('Tax'), are deserving of international accolades by themselves. In my opinion, him winning the Oscars for *Slumdog Millionaire* could be compared to Beethoven winning a Grammy for his *Bagatelle no. 25*.

5. The Associated Board of Royal Schools of Music (ABRSM), based in the United Kingdom, is an examinations board that conducts music exams around the world.

6. *Dandiya* sticks are a pair of sticks, made of wood, metal or recycled paper used in traditional Indian folk dance. They are not drumsticks but we used them on buckets and wooden boards.

7. Video of my students singing the Carnatic fusion version of Ed Sheeran's 'Shape of You' can be found on YouTube using the search string 'Shape of You Carnatic North Hills' or by clicking this link: https://www.youtube.com/watch?v=vafAyngx8GI. Accessed 19 January 2022.

REFERENCES

Getter, Joseph (2014), 'Kollywood goes global: New sounds and contexts for Tamil film music in the 21st century', in G. D. Booth and B. Shope (eds), *In More Than Bollywood: Studies in Indian Popular Music*, Oxford: Oxford University Press, pp. 60–73.

Green, Lucy (2006), 'Popular music education in and for itself, and for "other" music: Current research in the classroom', *International Journal of Music Education*, 24:2, pp. 101–18.

Green, Lucy (2017), *How Popular Musicians Learn: A Way Ahead for Music Education*, London: Routledge.

Jaffurs, Sheri E. (2004), 'The impact of informal music learning practices in the classroom, or how I learned how to teach from a garage band', *International Journal of Music Education*, 22:3, pp. 189–200.

31

What's Words Worth:
A Short Polemic on the Citation of Lyric

Andy West

Andy West is a professor at Leeds Conservatoire, where he is the head
of postgraduate studies and oversees the MA Music programme.

*This chapter is written from the author's perspective as a listener
and songwriter. With reference to current and historical examples,
it focusses on the extent to which lyrics can be separated from song
recordings, and aims to prompt reflection on the evaluation and
study of lyric writing.*

It's a warm afternoon in late July 2020, and I am at home reading a newspa-
per review of Taylor Swift's new album *Folklore*. It is written by a journalist whose work I admire very much, who frequently captures the energy of
new recordings in her writing, and whose reviews I consider to be a reliable
conduit to the record itself. When Margo Price brings out a new record, this
music journalist makes me feel like I'm by the Cumberland River in East Nash-
ville. When The Unthanks release an album I can smell the breeze coming in
off the Northumbrian coast. Best of all, unlike the vast majority of her contemporaries, she never pulls any punches; if a record is flawed, she tells it like it
is. At various points in the review of *Folklore*, however, I find myself switch-
ing off, leaping over lines to catch the next wave of descriptive verve, the next
stretch of neatly drawn critical subjectivity. The reason for my skipping?
Tracts of lyric extracted from *Folklore*; couplets and phrases from the mighty pen
of Taylor Swift intended to add dimension to detail, derailing my train of thought.

For me, this is an unexpected development; to paraphrase the old joke about the
beer drinker, I never met a lyric I didn't like. From Duke Ellington to Kasey Chambers,
from Alex Turner to Patti Smith, there are an endless number of songwriters

I consider to be great lyric writers. So why should I be so quick to overlook lyric in this instance? Fellow authors of books on songwriting have written at length and in depth on the subject of lyric; those who spring to mind have enhanced countless musicians' lives with their popular texts on how to make song words 'work'. Days earlier I had audited a degree programme where one of the modules focused exclusively on lyric writing; 87 per cent of the cohort expressed satisfaction with the programme. Clearly, the exclusive focus on lyric writing is more of an issue for me than it is for others. Why is that?

Well, I don't have anything against Taylor Swift. She's good. It's just that over the years, time has told me it would be a mistake for me to equate lyric with the written word. When Diana Ross sings 'Where Did Our Love Go?' or when Morrissey delivers 'William, it was Really Nothing', I love the way the words orbit at a remove from the music, delight at the duality of implied meaning. When the needle lands on the groove, the commonplace turns complex, and suddenly, what on paper aches with misery is replete with suggestion, aflame with the inference of ulterior motive. Despite her desperate words, could it be that Diana Ross is secretly overjoyed? Is Johnny Marr's guitar telling us something beyond the mask of Morrissey's words? If I cast my mind back to a time before I heard these songs, I am certain I would have misunderstood the words without the music. Worse still, if I had seen the lyrics to a record like 'Woodface' by Crowded House in advance I may well have avoided it; it's not really a lyric album and Neil Finn is not really a 'lyric on the page' writer. But what a melodicist! What a voice! What a band! What feel!

Is there another end of the spectrum, a place where the music interferes only minimally with words, where lyric can project unhindered from the page? Dylan's lyrics for *John Wesley Harding* were apparently mostly written in bed as he recovered from a motorcycle accident. They look incredible on paper. Maybe he didn't have a guitar with him at the time and was forced to work within the constraints of the poet. Hours and hours laid up in the luxury of time; reading back and forth, repeating phrases, pausing to think about what is being said, what is to be absorbed. Sure enough, the music fades into the background of *John Wesley Harding*, the rustic plainness of its harmony and melody foreground the lyric on each track, helping us to hear the words as Dylan heard them in his head.

Lesser poets, i.e. everyone else, are obliged to control the repetition, to find music that can create spaces within the words; gaps in language where we can dream ourselves in. Performance is important too; the same song can sound entirely different in a different voice. When I hear Elkie Brooks sing 'Lilac Wine' it sounds to me like someone trying to tell her story to the world. When I hear Nina Simone sing 'Lilac Wine' the voice I hear is one of quiet desperation, of an embittered lover singing quietly to herself, alone. The words are the same, the meaning not the same at all. The voice brings the lyric to life. Without Paul Weller's accent and manners, how would I know 'Going Underground' was a youth song and not a poem by Adrien Henri or Roger McGough? The relative absence of expression can be equally seismic; the lyric of New Order's 'Blue Monday' has to be heard to understand the slightness of its role within the song's vast electronic expanse.

Scientists say that each new experience we have dislodges an existing memory, so our bank of memories is continually being drained of nostalgic resources. We forget because we are constantly remembering. Perhaps that phenomenon applies to my experience of lyrics; the more I hear the less I need to know what they mean, what they signify? As Jeff Tweedy writes in his recent autobiography, the lyrics of his songs mean nothing and it doesn't matter, in fact he prefers it that way. Listening to Radiohead's 'Moon Shaped Pool' for the first time in 2015, I was surprised to discover that I had paid no attention to the words; I had been entirely immersed in the colourations of the music, lost in the contours of sound.

Yet still, casting my mind back, as a 15-year-old I went out to my local record store and bought Elvis Costello and The Attractions' *Punch the Clock*, and listened to it all the way through, enjoying every second without understanding much of what he was singing about. Ironically, I had to read a critic's review of 'Shipbuilding' for an explanation of what that lyric meant, what it was intended to convey. And with no disrespect to the High Priest of Pathos, God rest his soul, as a 25-year-old if you had presented me with a choice between Leonard Cohen's 'Hallelujah' and 'La Bamba' by Los Lobos, 99 times out of 100 I would have pressed the button marked 'Fun and excitement this way'. Perhaps nothing has changed.

By the end of this indulgent walk around my own musical block, I find myself strangely calmed. Listening to St Vincent's masterful 'Masseduction' or one of the tracks my son has on by Juice WRLD, I am following everything; the words, the music, the sound – it's a world of colour, gesture and revelation made for the ear to wander around. Like Marvin Gaye's 'What's Going On', the song words are amplified, made taller and louder by the spiritual energy, the sound that brings them into being. On these records the layers of meaning, texture and soul are multiple, the rewards for relistening infinite.

32

Inclusion or Exclusion? The Disconnect Between School Music Programmes and Students' Lived Musical Experiences

Aixa Burgos

Aixa Burgos is a high school music teacher at Passaic Preparatory Academy in New Jersey, USA, where she teaches music technology courses as a career pathway.

In this chapter, the author compares her students' lived musical experiences to the traditional music programme model in her New Jersey, USA school district. The chapter aims to illustrate how music technology programmes can be inclusive for all students regardless of their musical experiences and preferences.

Introduction

When reflecting on the qualities of top university programmes, several characteristics come to mind including inclusivity, excellence, diversity, community engagement, freedom from bias and global-mindedness. Such themes have taken their place in areas such as sociology, mathematics, medicine and in very complex ways, music programmes. Questions such as, 'What can we do to be more inclusive of all students so that they feel valued and see their place in our music programme?' have often led to broad conversations, policy drafts and debates; however, change often takes too long. Too long for the community musician whose chances of acceptance into their dream programme are hindered by their inability to read modern western staff notation. Too long for the talented pop singer who dreams of enrolling at their local university to study voice but is turned away due to their

171

lack of music theory proficiency and inability to perform an eighteenth-century Italian art song. Too long for the successful, self-taught DJ who wishes to expand their career by studying music production at the university level but will not be accepted due to their inexperience on a traditional musical instrument. For this essay, I will be reflecting on the disconnect between traditional music programmes and students' lived musical experiences.

My story

As an avid performer throughout my adolescent and teenage years who found joy in music, I knew for certain that I wanted to be a music teacher. Performing at venues such as the United Palace Theatre in New York City, on air at Fox 5 and at jazz clubs were monumental moments in my life as a young musician. I was convinced that all young musicians needed to have these same experiences and opportunities and I wanted to teach them how. Unfortunately, I was faced with a grim reality when I learned that I had to audition for entrance into a college music programme to become a music teacher. I am a percussionist who specializes in Latin percussion instruments and playing techniques. I was self-taught for many years until I found a few mentors who were touring professionals. My mentors learned just as I did; none of them had formal music training. In other words, no one in my musical circle had gone to college for music but they were all incredibly successful. Since I wanted to be a public-school music teacher, the only way to accomplish that goal would be to attend a collegiate music education programme. I was surprised to learn that I would be required to perform on instruments that were foreign to me – snare drum, timpani and marimba. Not only were the instruments foreign to me but so was the repertoire. To my discouragement, I was unable to matriculate due to my lack of skill in those required areas of proficiency. Areas of proficiency that were set up by a structure that perpetuates the belief that this type of musical training is the standard, therefore all other musical training is not valid for entry.

This realization left me feeling inferior to all those who had had the privilege of learning such elite selections of instruments and elegant repertoires of music. Despite my vast musical experience on several non-classical percussion instruments, my ability to improvise and solo, my endorsement with Latin Percussion® and my many performances, these were not enough to grant me entrance into a music education programme at the collegiate level. Isn't music a 'diverse human practice encompassing many practices, styles, activities, and functions?' (Hess 2019: 40). Apparently music is, but music education is not. I was left out of the narrative when music education admission requirements were established, as were many students with similar backgrounds.

I eventually took private lessons, applied again, and got accepted at the age of 26. My peers, who were 18 or 19 years old, had ten+ years of experience reading music and playing traditional wind band instruments. That is when I realized how disadvantaged I was and how unjust this system can be to people like me. Why were my diverse musical experiences and proficiency in world percussion not enough to grant me admission into a college music education programme, particularly at a time when classical music was less visible and viable in the mainstream, therefore less consumed in comparison to genres such as popular music? The National Endowment for the Arts reported a 3 per cent drop in adults in the United States attending a classical music performance in 2017 compared to 2002 (National Endowment for the Arts 2018).

Music technology as a means of inclusion

A few years into my career as a music educator at the elementary level, I was given the opportunity to teach a high school music technology course. As the school year progressed, I began to realize that my music technology course largely attracted a certain type of student; the student who leads a musical life completely disconnected from whatever traditional school music programmes in the United States have to offer. These students were not interested in wind band, choir or orchestra. They were students who enjoyed making beats to rap over, who DJ'd on the weekend and who enjoyed creating music that they liked to listen to. They were not interested in traditional school music programmes that lacked relevance to their lives. The western canon had no connection to the diverse lives and musical interests of my students. For the first time, there was a place for those students – in our music technology course. A place where genre selections and content choices had a connection with their identity. A place that reflects society's embrace of popular music genres, unlike traditional music programmes. A place where they can pioneer their own thoughts and articulate ideas through digital music creation. My class was filled with students who took music-making into their own hands, becoming active creators of music in a way that suits them socially and culturally.

As someone who also had a musical life completely disconnected from the music programmes my K-12 school had to offer, I understood my students' unique positions and approached my teaching as such. I would share my experiences as a performer and their curiosities led to inspiring conversations about topics such as navigating the music business, marketing and distribution. Students would express how interesting 'this side of music' was in comparison to what they had seen happening in the traditional music programmes at their schools. Students eventually began to initiate their own research into new digital platforms and studio trends, bringing such insightful conversations into the classroom. For many of them, this was the first time they felt excited about the music education they were receiving in school. Students were successful, felt connected, and they were no longer in a classroom where the educator was biased against forms of musical brilliance other than those that the teacher possessed.

Why did it take students entering a high school music technology class for them to finally feel a connection to music education? Some students have been so inspired by what they are learning in music technology that they want to pursue a career in music. But what are the odds of these talented students being accepted into a collegiate music programme with the current admissions requirements? Just as music theory at the collegiate level is dominated by the White male demographic, our current teaching force in K-12 music education consists of White middle-class educators. In light of these facts, I argue that the current system of admissions into music education programmes benefits the White demographic as well. This may not seem alarming to some; however, disadvantaged students whose stories are similar to mine may have a different point of view. I also argue that White dominance in the field may have contributed to the creation and perpetuation of racist policies that disadvantage non-Whites as reflected by the scarcity of quality music education programmes in urban areas. However, this scarcity does not mean that music is not happening in other ways, as evidenced by the students who entered my classroom with unique skill sets not learned in the school music classroom.

There is a need to rethink the approach to music teacher education programmes so that all students can benefit. Diversifying the teaching demographic and broadening the repertoire is a start but we need to do more to challenge the historical dominance of western European practices. When will we finally be inclusive of all forms of musical brilliance? A brilliance tenacious enough to exist against all odds? Or will we continue to exclude those forms of musical brilliance because they do not fit into the standards of western European music?

REFERENCES

Hess, Juliet (2019), *Music Education for Social Change: Constructing an Activist Music Education*, London: Routledge, https://doi.org/10.4324/9780429452000. Accessed 3 March 2022.

National Endowment of the Arts (2018), *U.S Trends in Arts Attendance and Literary Reading: 2002–2017*, https://www.arts.gov/sites/default/files/2017-sppapreviewREV-sept2018.pdf. Accessed 3 March 2022.

33

Finding Her Voice:
A Female DIY Musician's Pedagogical
Spaces and Practices for Popular Tamil Film
Music in Chennai, South India

Nina Menezes

Nina Menezes teaches world music at the University of Tampa and maintains an active voice studio. An internationally acclaimed soprano, her voice features on Bollywood film soundtracks.

This ethnographic chapter chronicles a South Indian female DIY musician's attempts to create pedagogical places and practices for popular Tamil film songs in her quest to discover her musical identity and gain personal and professional freedom.

Spaces and places for popular Tamil film songs

I grew up in Chennai, where popular regional-language Tamil film songs permeate the soundscape of city life. From dawn to dusk, golden oldies waft from transistor radios in coffee stalls. In peak hour traffic, pulsating rhythms of film hits reveberate from car stereos. To ease the monotony of their chores, homemakers croon along to film songs playing on radio or television programmes. No festive gathering is complete without a film song-and-dance session. While such unconscious processes of enculturation shape the musical foundation of film song aficionados, ambitious teenagers adopt more conscious learning strategies by repeatedly listening to and imitating their favorite playback singer's[1] recordings.

175

Since 2006, *Airtel Super Singer*, the longest-running and most popular South Indian music reality television show has provided amateur singers with opportunities to perform film song covers, gain visibility, fame and chances to win lucrative prizes in the form of cash, gold jewelry, cars and real estate. Contestants wear brand-sponsored apparel and perform on a glamorous set, which makes for a visually engaging, high-production-value broadcast. Each performer looks forward to interacting with the panel of judges comprising playback singers, musicians and composers from the film industry. At the end of each season, the winner earns the coveted opportunity of recording a song for a leading film composer's upcoming film, thereby making their debut in Tamil cinema.

Over the last decade, stiff competition among contestants has created a demand for vocal coaching. In the absence of a pedagogical tradition for popular film music, a younger generation of traditional *Carnatic* and *Hindustani* instructors fill the vacuum by experimenting with hybrid practices from traditional and popular music. Some technologically savvy instructors create lucrative business models by equipping their music centres with recording studios. In addition to voice coaching, these students gain recording experience. Moreover, the covers they share on their social media profiles, not only facilitate online visibility, but also allows them to fashion their identities as cover artists. More promising students record demo CDs to distribute among film music directors or producers of music reality shows.

Vandana – A DIY cover artist and vocal coach

During my fieldwork in Chennai in 2016, I encountered Vandana, a 30-year-old female, DIY live and studio cover artist, who had recently established herself as a vocal coach. Vandana resisted formal training in music; she attributed her musical skill and knowledge to her natural abilities, hard work, learning from online sources and trial and error. Although she performed film songs at live events, her work largely centred on assisting amateur singers with recording covers within her family-owned studio. Vandana's experience as a singer and sound producer allowed her to provide clients with vocal and recording tips during their sessions. With the discovery of their singing potential, the high quality of the finished product, and Vandana's knowledge and affable personality, clients started requesting voice lessons with her.

By March 2016, personal and professional differences with her family forced Vandana to leave home; she started residing in a women's hostel.[2] Without access to her family studio, she had to find ways to accommodate her existing students, which was now her primary source of income. In contemporary Chennai, notions

FIGURE 33.1: Vandana teaching female students (left) in their homes and male students in parks (right).

of public and private space still articulate gendered relations. While many women enjoy the freedom to explore public space, not all are free from patriarchal ideological boundaries that still operate when navigating public arenas. Vandana started teaching female students within their domestic spaces, specifically their bedrooms, away from the distraction of domestic activity and areas accessible to male family members (Figure 33.1 – left). Traditional norms of female respectability prevented her from teaching male students in their homes; she chose public locations like parks (Figure 33.1 – right). Between April and June 2016, I observed Vandana's voice lessons within these private and public settings.

Shantha – Vandana's student

Shanta proved to be Vandana's most diligent and promising student. A middle-class woman in her early twenties, Shantha graduated with a computer engineering degree and worked as a programmer in one of Chennai's leading software technology firms. Long working hours made her yearn for a creative life. She learned film songs by listening to recordings of her favourite playback singers and seized every opportunity to participate in singing competitions. In early January 2016, Shantha recorded her first cover, 'Tenu Samjhawan' at Vandana's family-owned studio. Encouraged by the reception she received on her social media profiles, Shantha decided to train her voice with Vandana. She hoped to audition for television music reality shows – a path that would bring her closer to her dream of becoming a playback singer.

From April to June 2016, I witnessed Vandana and Shantha co-create a pedagogy for Tamil film song repertoire. The following section, an excerpt from my fieldnotes, provides a vignette of Shantha's first voice lesson.

Fieldnotes – Shantha's first voice lesson

3 April 2016
1:30 p.m.
I arrive at a four-storey apartment building in Velachery, a residential area in southern Chennai. A narrow staircase leads me to the third floor. Vandana, Shantha and her mother greet me at the door. Shantha's mother, the typical, hospitable Tamil hostess enquires, *'Enna cāppiṭurīṅga?'* ('what will you have to eat or drink?'). It would be an insult to refuse anything, so, as is customary, I ask for a glass of water. In one corner of the living room, film songs blare from the television. In the opposite corner, Shantha's brother is programming at a computer. I gulp the glass of water down. Shantha's mother ushers us into a 100-square foot bedroom, suggesting this would be an ideal place, free from distraction for our lesson. Vandana and I sit on the bed, Shantha slumps into a plastic molded chair.

Although a novice instructor, Vandana assumes confidence in her body language and tone.

VANDANA: So, tell me, how do you start singing?

SHANTHA: [demonstrates knowledge of diaphragmatic breathing]

VANDANA [impressed]: *Seri* ['alright'], very good! Now stand up! When singing, it is important to observe correct posture, only then your singing will come out properly. [Shantha stands up and shifts from one foot to the other. Vandana adjusts her posture; see Figure 33.2].

VANDANA: So, tell me your basic problems with singing.

SHANTHA: I am not able to reach high pitches and sustain long notes

VANDANA: [demonstrates western art music vocal exercises]

SHANTHA: [repeats them]

VANDANA: *Seri* ['alright'], practise these and your range will improve. [For the rest of the hour, Vandana talks about Bollywood film music composers and their musical styles]. Okay, for next class choose a song and work on it. Don't forget to do the exercises for half an hour daily before you sing.

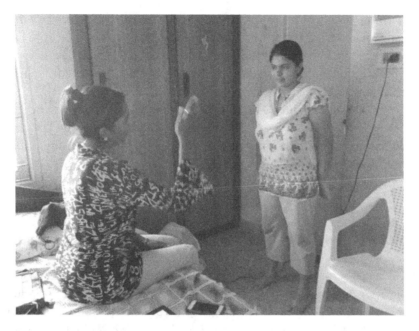

FIGURE 33.2: Vandana adjusts Shantha's posture.

As we leave, Shantha's mother insists we stay for lunch next time.

In the following weeks, Shantha's lessons began with half an hour of vocal warm-ups, an evaluation of her progress, and challenges she encountered during the week. For the remaining hour, Vandana addressed issues with vocal technique pertaining to specific sections in a song. To enhance learning, Vandana prescribed a variety of digital tools and platforms for her students.

Digital tools and spaces for enhanced learning

1. *WhatsApp*: a popular messaging web application facilitated communication outside lessons. During the week, students uploaded homework via the file-sharing feature and received feedback from Vandana.
2. Mobile phone recorders allowed students to record and upload audio clips along with written observations on *WhatsApp* for weekly assignment; this helped hone critical listening and reflection skills.
3. YouTube serves as a repository for film songs and their covers. Vandana and her students relied on these videos for learning. In turn, the covers they produced and shared facilitated visibility, audience interaction and a sense of belonging to a larger online cover scene.

4. *Tanpura Droid*: a phone application, replicates the drone of the *tanpura*, a traditional Indian stringed instrument. Users can select appropriate pitches, speed and volume. Vandana recommended *Tanpura Droid* for vocal warm-ups, pitch support or when students needed to repeatedly rehearse a difficult phrase.

5. VLC Media Audio–Video Player allows users to play an entire or specific section of a song (in MP3 or YouTube video formats) on loop. The reduced speed feature encourages deep, attentive listening when learning a difficult phrase. When Vandana introduced this software, she explained:

> Let me tell you the process of learning a song. When you select a song you like, keep listening to it again and again. *Never, ever* try to sing with the recording. If you sing along, you will imagine you're singing like the singer, but it'll be completely different, and you'll sing that way forever. So, always listen to the song on VLC at reduced tempo, so you'll hear all the notes clearly. Make sure you record practice sessions every time you sing. Listen to the original, then your recording. Note where you sound different. Play the original again on VLC at a slower tempo. Repeat phrases until you learn the song properly. Like this, *neeye kathukelam* ['You can teach yourself'].

Third space pedagogy for Tamil film repertoire

When Vandana said 'you can teach yourself', she was suggesting combining student self-regulated learning with instructor feedback; such a collaborative culture evokes a third space pedagogy (Piazza 2009). It is within the interstitial space between teacher, learner and repertoire where meaning is negotiated and constructed. As Shantha and Vandana worked on repertoire, each understood and made meaning out of what they saw, heard and felt. As Vandana and each of her students built their online communities, they interacted and shared those meanings with their audience.

Forging new pathways

For Shantha, voice lessons brought confidence and fueled her transformation from an amateur singer into a cover artist. By August 2016, Vandana frequently rescheduled lessons in pursuit of other opportunities, forcing Shantha to start training with a traditional *Hindustani* instructor. Shantha continues to learn film songs with the tools and strategies Vandana provided.

Vandana constantly reinvents herself. A year before I met her, Vandana had auditioned for *Airtel Super Singer* but failed to qualify for the televised competition. Pursuing a live and recording career, she created a niche as a vocal coach to amateur singers. In April 2016, exactly a year after her audition, Vandana invited me to the filming set of *Airtel Super Singer* Season 5. A group of semi-finalists from the junior competition were featuring her as guest performer on a special televised segment called the 'Miniseries'. 'People will come to know I am a voice trainer!', she said to me with excitement. At the time, she was yet to realize she was part of something greater – an emerging pedagogical tradition for Tamil film music.

NOTES

1. During the twentieth century, to facilitate the filming process with limited technology, early Indian filmmakers hired traditional theatre actors to sing and dance. However, by the 1940s, playback technology allowed filmmakers to record separate audio-visual tracks. Actors obtained roles on the merits of their appearance and acting skill. And a niche emerged for singers who served as voice surrogates for actors' song-and-dance sequences. During the filming process, singers' pre-recorded tracks were 'played back' over a loudspeaker to enable actors to lip-synch their parts, hence the term 'playback singer'.

2. Traditionally, a Tamil middle-class woman resides with her family until she is married. Hostels typically provide accommodation only to single women who migrate from other towns and cities to work in Chennai. Vandana's unusual circumstances prompted her to exercise agency in her quest for personal and professional freedom.

REFERENCES

Groesbeck, Rolf (2009), 'Disciple and preceptor/performer in Kerala', in R. Wolf (ed.), *Theorizing the Local: Music, Practice, and Experience in South Asia and Beyond*, New York: Oxford University Press, pp. 143–64.

Kumar, Shantha Laxmi (2016), 'Tenu Samjhawan (Hindi – Female version) Cover', YouTube, 10 January, https://www.youtube.com/watch?v=wzAFdJZLGws. Accessed 10 April 2016.

Menezes, Nina (2018), 'One voice, many spaces: A contemporary female self-taught musician's pathways into Tamil film song cover culture in Chennai, South India', Ph.D. dissertation, Gainesville: University of Florida.

Piazza, Susan V. (2009), 'First steps toward third space', *Language Arts Journal of Michigan*, 25:1, pp. 17–21.

Rice, Timothy (2013), 'Time, place, and metaphor in music experience and ethnography', *Ethnomusicology*, 47, pp. 151–79.

Viswanathan, T. and Allen, Matthew Harp (2004), *Music in South India: Experiencing Music, Expressing Culture*, New York: Oxford University Press.

34

Teaching Queer

Mia Ibrahim

Mia Ibrahim is a middle school music teacher in New York City, NY, USA, and a professional clarinetist. She teaches popular music and modern band.

This chapter presents reflections on the author's first-hand experiences and personal perspectives as a gay music teacher in a New York City middle school, working to maintain spaces of agency and empowerment for queer and LGBTQ+ young people.

I just don't want you teaching my daughter how to be gay. You're giving her ideas and now she wants to be gay. That's just not her.

Turning my kid gay

I remember this parent teacher conference night vividly. My sixth grade modern band student had recently joined the Gender Sexuality Alliance (GSA) club that I advise. Soon after, she came out as gay and decided to tell those she loved and trusted, including her foster mom. Her foster mom brought her to conferences that evening with the plan to confront me regarding her concerns about her daughter's sexuality. Throughout my years of music teaching, I've referred to every version of this talk as the 'turning my kid gay' speech and I've been on the receiving end of it many times. The mere mention of queer artists in my music classroom has prompted parents to attempt to pull their children from my music class. Simply incorporating queer identities as part of the rhetoric in my classroom was reason enough to question whether I'm indoctrinating students into ... what do they call it? 'The Lifestyle'? If this were a lifestyle choice, why would anyone be so quick to sign up? Is my student watching her foster mother berate me for my sexuality and finding it all so enticing? Or maybe it was the story I told my GSA about coming out to my Arab parents only to have them initially disown me. Whether it be the protests I attend to maintain basic civil rights or wiping the spit off my face after somebody in the subway called me a 'faggot' and spat in my eye, I am transparent with my students about every pro and con to being out in the world.

Becoming authentically me

I was raised on the traditional North American school music fare of wind band, orchestra, choir (BOC) and took pride in pursuing classical clarinet and music education. I am, after all, great at both. Alongside this growth as an educator and performer I was slowly becoming more comfortable with myself, and I eventually came out of the closet after moving to New York when I was 25 years old. Being happily married to my wife now, I often question, 'What took me so long to come out and be myself?' Those music history textbooks that refer to Clara Schumann as the spouse of Robert Schumann without acknowledging the sexuality or marital status of Francis Poulenc, Leonard Bernstein or Aaron Copland could potentially have been contributing factors. Why link a composer's identity to their marital status while others are not even granted acknowledgment of an integral part of their identity? I'm also the first-generation American and have the additional hurdle of cultural norms to overcome. I deemed coming out necessary enough to derail much of my life in order to live authentically.

Queer in the classroom

I've always set out to be the teacher I wish I'd had growing up. The music room environment I've cultivated is very much a safe space. I welcome conversations about gender dysphoria and I'm patient and empathetic with those who have difficulties understanding various genders and sexualities. I allow students to speak up and discuss these topics with one another or I take the driver's seat of the conversation if requested.

Being in a popular music classroom allows these conversations to come up organically. My students often request repertoire performed by LGBTQ+ artists. Discussing the songwriting, performing and production processes leaves space to also discuss topics of identity. For example, when we perform a Sam Smith song, we must use the proper pronouns when referring to them. This leads to discussions about non-binary identities and trans, gender non-conforming, Intersex (TGNCI) people. Although Sam Smith, and many artists like them, have risen to prominence and fame, many of my students still have questions about their identities and authenticity. I am so grateful for their inquisitive minds, but I have had to explain the biological, neurological, cultural, historical and sociological implications of being queer in so many ways to so many different people at this point I am just exhausted. 'This is something you are born with. Everyone LGBTQ+ comes to realize aspects of their identities on varying timelines. Coming out later in life does not make you any less gay'. Versions of these conversations have happened in all my classes. Again, I am beyond grateful for the discourse, but at a certain point I kind of just want to put down the whiteboard marker and shout, 'JUST LET ME BE ME!'

In the nature-versus-nurture debate, I have encountered many students who directly mirror the views of those around them, especially the adults in their lives. Being around family members and peers who use 'gay' as a slur or insult has perpetuated and solidified the idea that there is something inherently wrong with queerness or nonconformity. I often capitalize on the shock value by stating boldly to my classes that I am the school's 'resident gay' or 'one of the gayest people I know'. Reclaiming these words is important to me and those students in our school who identify as LGBTQ+. We would like to evade ostracization and embrace our identities alongside students who may have used these words as insults in the past.

I am sure to discuss with members of the Gender Sexuality Alliance, or GSA, the best ways to go about this. We have tried normalizing displays of queerness by purchasing swag that students designed with rainbows and trans flags. We hung up flags around my classroom representing many identities, (asexual [ace], pansexual [pan], transgender [trans], pride inclusive, panromantic, bisexual, gay and lesbian). We have even put together presentations for school staff to teach them about the various identities under the LGBTQ+ umbrella and ways they can be more inclusive in their classrooms. And you can always count on my GSA students to request that we perform Todrick Hall or Hayley Kiyoko in music class. Granted, these requests are often shot down with a class vote (you can imagine the song 'Girls Like Girls' is not celebrated in a school setting), but I like that they are at least attempting to diversify exposure to LGBTQ+ repertoire.

The approach I take to teaching popular music is a stark juxtaposition to the restrictive nature of the classical clarinet world I was in for so long. Students wanting to perform in traditional choirs, or even musical theatre productions, are often segregated by gender and pigeonholed into the male/female binary. And when making the brave choice to come out or transition, not all students desire or have access to hormone therapies. Therefore, the gender they identify as may not be reflected in their voice range or physical presentation. Students who fall under the TGNCI umbrella tend to be embraced and comforted by my modern band curriculum. I've heard of many instances in which the student came out and requested to be moved to a different role or voice part and were denied the request. However, in my modern band classroom, if a student singer feels uncomfortable with a gendered voice part, we can usually easily transpose the song or simply choose to perform another artist they are comfortable with.

With the erasure of gendered roles comes the added bonus of no more gendered performance attire. Students can wear what makes them comfortable and we no longer need to conform to dated practices of long black gowns for the girls and tuxes for the boys. My favourite artist, Freddie Mercury, took pride in eccentricity and now, as we perform a Queen set, I get to encourage the same. Finally, I can be certain students are comfortable with the repertoire we perform because much of the time they are writing their own music in my class. My annual protest song unit usually results in many lyrics about LGBTQ+ lives specifically. Students get to perform lyrics that reflect their many identities and write about their feelings around coming out. Here are some excerpts from student songs written throughout the years:

6th Grade, Topic: Gender Identity
'Why I gotta be someone who's not me? Why can't I be me? Why can't I be free being me? I wanna be me. Please don't judge me.'
8th Grade, Topic: LGBTQIA+
'It's the way I feel, I just wanna be real, but whenever I talk about it people make it a big deal.'
10th Grade, Topic: Gay Rights
'I'll fight for my rights, and others in my community as well. Together we unite and fight away all discrimination.'

Freedom

While being the self-proclaimed 'resident gay' is tough work, it is also so liberating! When I got married, I just wanted to tell everyone about my new wife while obnoxiously waving around my left hand like I won a high-stakes pageant. Just as anyone in a heteronormative relationship would have done, I wanted to share the news with my students and celebrate my joy with them. Luckily, my students were so unfazed by the news that I had married a woman in a very loud, rainbow-clad wedding (even my shoes had rainbows) and they had nothing but happiness and excitement for me when I told them.

Who knows how different my classroom would look if I had never gained the confidence to be my loud, boisterous, queer self? There are times students will come to my classroom during their free period just to tinker quietly with a piano in the corner while listening to the free and open queer discourse. They tell me it is one of the few spaces they feel truly safe, and isn't that why I do this?

35

Computer Science && Popular Music Education

Jared O'Leary

Jared O'Leary is the director of education and research at BootUp PD (USA), where they create free computer science curricula and engage in research.

This chapter is written from the perspective of someone with a background in music education who now develops computer science curricula to highlight the intersections of two seemingly disconnected disciplines and to raise questions about the places and purposes of such engagement.

As popular music practices continue to evolve and expand in parallel with technological and social changes, popular music educators can engage in reflective practices that problematize the current curricular offerings and music-making experiences in relation to the ways people engage with music outside of school. My own particular interest when looking at popular music-making practices is to explore music-making and learning that blurs or disrupts disciplinary boundaries and silos. This chapter briefly introduces some of the ways people blur the disciplinary boundaries between popular music and computer science, which raises questions about the places and purposes of such engagement.

Music-making through computer science practices

One way that people make music through computer science practices is through composing. Rather than writing out western staff notation in software such as Sibelius or Finale, people can write lines of code that a computer will use to create music. For example, the following code will play the first two measures of 'Hot Cross Buns' when run on Sonic Pi,[1] which is free software designed to enable music-making with code:

```
play :e, release: 2
sleep 2
play :d, release: 2
sleep 2
play :c, release: 4
sleep 4
```

Although a simple example, the code above can be modified to change the amplitude, pan, attack, decay, sustain, release, pitch, instrument, etc. of each note. As a form of music notation, code can communicate even more information to the computer than western staff notation tends to communicate to human performers.

In addition to composing with code, people also perform live music with code. This practice is often referred to as 'live coding' or as an 'algorave', and is often streamed online or performed in-person in venues with performers displaying their code on a screen so that listeners can not only hear the music they are creating but see the code they are using to create the music. To learn more about this practice, search for terms like 'live coding music' to watch video recordings of performances.

Although the music composition and performance practices above are interesting, they do not necessarily enable ways of making music that is not readily available through other software or practices. However, computer science practices and concepts can augment such forms of music-making and learning by randomizing various aspects of a composition or performance. For example, randomizing which notes or rhythms in a list will be played at a particular time, randomly cycling through a list of potential chord inversions for each chord in a song to add spontaneity to the music, using probability to determine which instrument will play or not at any given moment, creating randomly generated drum kit grooves, etc. In other words, people can use computer science practices to create music that would be otherwise difficult or impossible to create without such practices.

Enabling music-making through computer science practices

Computer science practices can also be used to enable music-making and learning. For example, people can create their own Ableton Live plugins using graphical programming languages like Max[2] to enable new ways of creating or modifying music within digital audio workstations. Although a relatively simple process that integrates with an existing music-making platform, people can create entirely new music-related software for a range of devices, both modern and retro (O'Leary 2018, 2020a). For example, Johan Kotlinski developed the music sequencer known as Little Sound DJ (LSDJ)[3] for the Nintendo Game Boy® to enable music-making with the handheld gaming device.

In addition to modifying and creating software with computer science practices, people can also modify hardware to enable music-making and learning. For example, people who compose or perform music in LSDJ will often modify their Nintendo Game Boy® to enhance the original audio quality of the device. To do this, people will take apart the handheld gaming console and bypass the internal amplifier by rerouting the audio signal to two newly installed 3.5 mm audio ports (O'Leary 2018). This hardware modification enables musicians to record and amplify music created in software like LSDJ with less audio interference and at a higher amplitude than the device's original headphone jack enables. In other words, people can engage in hardware modification practices to enable or enhance their ability to create and share music.

People with an interest in creating music through more complicated computer science hardware practices can also design and build music instruments or interfaces that enable music-making and learning. For example, people will design and build interfaces that allow modern hardware and software to use the sound chip of retro hardware as a MIDI instrument (O'Leary 2018). Other musicians build musical instruments that transcend the possibilities of acoustic instruments. For example, in a YouTube video by Onyx Ashanti,[4] they demonstrate a musical instrument they built that uses saxophone fingerings to send MIDI data to software they designed; pressure-sensitive keys that can change various parameters of each note; joysticks for controlling the octave, volume and other audio effects; accelerometers that enable the angle and movement of a person's hands to shape the audio signal, etc. that runs on open source software that Ashanti developed. This example not only demonstrates how people can use computer science hardware and software practices to enable music-making and learning, it also raises questions about when and where such practices might have a place in popular music education, and for what purposes.

Computer science && popular music education

Before I started working full-time in computer science education, one of the music-related positions I previously held was as a general music and band director for multiple K-6 elementary schools. Over the years in that position, I received numerous requests from teachers who asked me to teach their students some songs from which they would learn various facts about another academic discipline. For example, I was once asked to create and teach a song about maths facts to make maths more interesting to children. My answer was always a firm 'no', because their requests positioned music-making and learning in a subservient relationship to another subject area. In other words, the requests positioned music-making as a medium for learning another subject area without considering the potential for learning and expressing one's self through music.

In many programming languages, programmers can use two ampersands (&&) to indicate that both the condition to the left and to the right of the ampersands need to be 'true' in order for the next line(s) of code to run. If we use this as a metaphor for computer science && popular music education, the kinds of engagement I describe in this chapter are music-related engagement that is not only relevant to popular music educators but to computer science educators. In other words, rather than viewing music or computer science practices as being in a subservient relationship to the other, they demonstrate a place for kids to simultaneously and holistically engage in concepts and practices from both academic disciplines in interesting and meaningful ways.

Although music educators might argue that practices that do not actively create music (e.g. modifying music-related software or hardware) are not relevant to music educators, I argue elsewhere (Benedict and O'Leary 2019; O'Leary 2018, 2020a) that such practices transcend the disciplinary boundaries and standards through purposeful forms of music-related engagement that enable music-making and learning that would be otherwise unavailable – or at the very least constrained – without engaging with and understanding computer science concepts and practices. In other words, people who engage in computer science practices for the purpose of enabling or enhancing music-making capabilities with a particular device are engaging in music-related problem solving and creating that can align with both computer science and music education standards.

This raises a question about where such music-related engagement and problem-solving might occur: a computer science class, popular music class or hybrid class that blurs the boundaries between the two subject areas? The kinds of expertise required to teach the practices briefly described in this chapter require an understanding of two very different subject areas. This presents an opportunity for collaboration or independent study to learn more about both subject areas and how they might intersect in interesting and meaningful ways within the spaces and places we work.

When reflecting on and learning more about these potential connections, I encourage readers to consider not only the potential for children to engage in computer science and popular music practices to create and enable new ways of making music but to do so in a way that disrupts the disciplinary boundaries that exist between two subject areas. That being said, the potential for popular music education to connect symbiotically with other subject areas or academic disciplines is not limited to computer science && popular music education. Rather than using this chapter solely as a springboard for diving into the intersections of computer science && popular music education, I encourage readers to consider other potential intersections and blurred disciplinary boundaries that raise questions about the potential places and purposes of popular music education.

If you are interested in learning more about the intersections of computer science and popular music education, see: Benedict and O'Leary, (2019) and O'Leary (2018, 2020a–c). In addition, the references found within each publication point toward more scholarship on this topic.

NOTES

1. https://sonic-pi.net/. Accessed 2 February 2022.
2. https://www.ableton.com/en/live/max-for-live/. Accessed 2 February 2022.
3. https://www.littlesounddj.com/lsd/index.php. Accessed 2 February 2022.
4. https://youtu.be/8bJsxIeg5iQ. Accessed 2 February 2022.

REFERENCES

Benedict, Cathy and O'Leary, Jared (2019), 'Reconceptualizing "music making": Music technology and freedom in the age of neoliberalism', *Action, Criticism, and Theory for Music Education*, 18:1, pp. 26–43, http://act.maydaygroup.org/volume-18-issue-1/act-18-1-benedict-and-oleary/. Accessed 2 February 2022.

O'Leary, Jared Duane (2018), 'A corpus-assisted discourse analysis of music-related practices discussed within chipmusic.org' (Order No. 10979369), ProQuest Dissertations & Theses Global (2154870828), https://www.proquest.com/openview/1548add5ef2a-cac218c7c0d4a162845f/1?pq-origsite=gscholar&cbl=18750&diss=y. Accessed 3 March 2022.

O'Leary, Jared (2020a), 'Intersections of popular musicianship and computer science practices', *Journal of Popular Music Education*, 4:2, pp. 153–74, https://www.ingentaconnect.com/content/intellect/jpme/2020/00000004/00000002/art00003. Accessed 3 March 2022.

O'Leary, Jared (2020b), 'Hip hot cross buns', in adam patrick bell (ed.), *The Music Technology Cookbook: Ready-Made Recipes for the Classroom*, Oxford: Oxford University Press, pp. 301–09.

O'Leary, Jared (2020c), 'Making music with circuit-bent children's toys', in Frank Abrahams (ed.), *Aligning Music to STEM: Theory and Practice for Middle School General Music*, Chicago: GIA Publications, Inc., pp. 203–8.

36

We Are Music Technology
(and How to Change Us)

adam patrick bell

adam patrick bell is an associate professor of music at Western University, Canada. He teaches and researches music education, music technology, popular music and disability studies.

In this chapter, the author advocates for a reconceptualization of music technology to be understood as a dynamic human-directed process that produces instruments. Music technology is much more than microchips; the things we create to make music are but one node in a network in which humans are interwoven.

Part 1: Instruments are ever-changing

I am tempted to employ the term 'evolution' to describe changes in instrument design over time, but I am also hesitant to use it because for many people evolution implies advancement, and I am not certain that this is always the case. For example, some would argue that the standard width of a piano key at present is too big and that previous designs with smaller widths would enable more people to play octaves and beyond. From this perspective, change is evident but it is not necessarily good change. So, considering this case and others that contradict the notion that instruments are always advancing for the better, I will settle on an assertion that *instruments are ever-changing.*

We musicians just cannot seem to keep ourselves from tinkering with our instruments. Have you heard of the lowboy? It is the precursor to the hi-hat. Essentially, they are the same thing with the notable exception (as their names imply) of their respective heights. The lowboy could only be played with a foot pedal until someone figured out that if the cymbals were raised a few feet off the ground they could be played with a stick, too. This development profoundly changed how the drums are played. In retrospect, this design development seems obviously intuitive, which begs the question: at what point do we give up on an instrument changing at the macro level? Will there be a lowboy-to-hi-hat moment for [insert instrument name here]?

It is also important to consider micro changes: the constant small adjustments we make to instruments in an effort to conform them to our bodies, performance practices, budgets, environments and so on. As a result, fixed instrument designs are an illusion. *Changes to instrument designs may be miniscule and/or incremental, but nevertheless they are happening.*

There is one important caveat to this theory: it only applies if people play the instruments, otherwise the unused instrument will succumb to petrification. It is the interactions between people and their instruments that make them organism-like. These interactions are a two-way street of sorts; *we act on the things we use to make music, but these things act on us, too.* Furthermore, these interactions can take place over long spans of time, in some cases, dating back to the first known instruments used by humans, such as drums. Let's explore this concept with the example of overdubbing, a widely practised music production technique.

Les Paul did not invent overdubbing, but he certainly popularized it in the United States. Prior to the existence of tape recorders, Les Paul honed his overdubbing skills using two recording disk lathes (e.g. listen to 'Brazil' [1948], https://youtu.be/3RkerNaN-v8 [accessed 19 January 2022]). This helps to explain why upon receiving one of the first tape recording machines in the United States (from Bing Crosby), Les Paul modified it to enable overdubbing. The American electronics company Ampex adopted his design, and to this day recorded music is heavily dependent on the overdubbing process. The act of Les Paul retrofitting the tape recorder is the most obvious evidence of changing the instrument, but it is important to recognize how the tape recorder acted upon him as well. Despite never having seen a tape recorder before, Les Paul intuited its capabilities. This is because *we embed our cultural practices into our instruments* and they can be passed along from one thing to another.

Sometimes, it is only when we encounter the physical object that we understand its capability beyond its initially intended use. The objects are communicating to us in a way; it's really just us – people – passing along information through our materials over time. If we can observe an object and say to ourselves, 'Hey, this is just like [name of object], except that it can do this [action], so maybe it *could* do this [action], too', we are being affected by its embedded meanings. Turntablism is a prime example of a musical practice that stems from an object not originally intended to be a musical instrument. Arguably, as reported by Avanti (2013), the same could be said for the saxophone, which apparently started out as a medical inhalation apparatus with an added element of fun – you could play music with it. Lastly, it is worth mentioning that recorded music was not at the top of Edison's list for uses of sound recording when he invented the phonograph. If things had worked out as he envisioned, this would be a chapter on office dictation.

These interactions are the foundation for my observation that *we are music technology*. Rather than using the term 'music technology', my colleague Johannes Ismaiel-Wendt suggests *musikmachdinge*, which translates to 'things we use to make music'. I would add to this that these things we use to make music make *us* make music, too. If this logic seems confusingly circular, you understand perfectly well.

Part 2: A change agent's things-to-do-list

I have argued that change in instrument design is inevitable, but many questions for the future of instrument design remain unanswered (e.g. who, what, where, when, why, how?). I would like to focus on: (1) *who*, by suggesting that the answer should be *you*, and (2) suggest some possible avenues for *how* to go about this. After all, a manifesto needs a call to action!

Use your 'Accumulated Sensibilities'

Paul Theberge uses the term 'accumulated sensibilities' to refer to the idea that we can apply things learned from one context to another. An example of this phenomenon is Tom Morello's turntablism techniques for guitar: https://youtu.be/0W6WZK3AfKE?t=152 (accessed 19 January 2022).

Morello's name often appears on lists of great guitarists because of this innovative practice. He answered the question, 'what if I tried to play my guitar like a DJ?' and this was the result. Similarly, *we can consider our own accumulated sensibilities and change the way we play instruments*, which will inevitably change instruments in the process. The history of any instrument has an accompanying list of innovators, and it is important to be engaged in this process of changing performance practices and changing our instruments accordingly because instruments ought to be democracies, not dictatorships.

Resist designs

We tend to gravitate toward using things to make music that fit with how we conceptualize making music. This helps to explain why there are factions of loyalty to particular companies that make musical instruments. What's better – FL Studio or Ableton Live? The answer to that question depends on whom you ask, and the rationale to the responses are typically rooted in design preferences.

No design is perfect, and *we need to take action to resist static or standard designs*. Sometimes, we have no choice but to take action. For example, in order for David Nabb to continue playing saxophone after having a stroke, he needed a one-handed instrument: https://youtu.be/j2v28JGfphQ (accessed 19 January 2022). David's macro change to the saxophone is an act of resistance to the ableist assumption of instrumentalists not having impairments, which is embedded into most musical instrument designs.

Clearly, such a macro change was needed in David's case, and this design has been and will continue to be useful to others. Beyond the particulars of the design, the idea of one-handed playing more generally will influence other designs. A barrier, physical or conceptual, to an individual making music, may be shared by someone else; if that is indeed the case, what started out as a bespoke solution can morph into a course of change with much broader implications for society (Holmes 2018).

Micro changes may be especially important to demand in the case of software-based instruments such as DAWs. Things such as default settings and presets ought to be resisted if they get in the way of making music. While the makers of instruments have a responsibility to seek out feedback regarding their designs, we, the consumers, should not hesitate to report our dissatisfaction; this is critical to improving instruments for many people.

Finally, if you are dissatisfied with the change or compromise in design, you may be left with no other option than to *become the designer yourself*.

Innovate by mistake (or not)

I often hear sentiments along the lines of 'Anyone can make a song nowadays if they have GarageBand'. There are some issues related to the assertion of 'anyone' that I will bypass here, but I have addressed some of them elsewhere (bell 2015). I take issue with the notion that music-making experiences are bettered by removing challenges (not to be confused with barriers). When we experience something as easy it is because we are standing on the shoulders of giants. We should not take technological advancements for granted. We have a responsibility to avoid falling into a slump of creative complacency; instead, *we can channel the Les Paul spirit of continually seeking new sounds*. We can create (or recreate), as opposed to replicate, which is altogether more challenging and rewarding.

There is a saying I hear repeated often that might be of help in pursuit of new sounds: 'Learn the rules and break them'. See Drake's go-to producer Noah '40' Shebib on this idea: https://youtu.be/ESUHhXgIaos?t=440 (accessed 19 January 2022).

If learning a practice with the aim of later upending it in the name of innovation is unappealing, one alternative is to *make mistakes, and recognize them as innovations*. Throughout the history of music production there are examples of 'happy accidents' – events occurring in the music-making process that were errors but ended up being innovative practices. For example, in the following excerpt, Marley Marl explains how he stumbled across sampling drums:

> One day I was in the studio, and I was working on a Captain Rock record. And what happened, I was actually trying to get a riff off of a record. I made a mistake and got the snare in there before the sound came. I was truncating the vocal part but the snare was playing with the beat – we was truncating while the beat was playing. Thank God the beat was playing, because it probably wouldn't have happened if the beat wasn't playing.
>
> So I was playing it and the snare sounded better than the snare that I had from the drum machine when I was popping it. I was like, 'Yo, hold on'. I started rocking it – and then it just smacked me in the face what just happened. I was like, 'Hold up!' 'This will enable me to take any kick and a snare from any record that people love and make my own beat [...] That means that I can go to my library at home – I've got so many records! I can take the kicks, the snares from everything and make my own patterns!'.
>
> (Muhammad and Kelley 2013: n.pag.)

A happy accident cannot be planned, but places and conceptual spaces can be made for them to happen. And, perhaps, the odds of creating a happy accident can be improved by wilfully resisting our routinized ways and instead employing George Costanza-esque logic of doing the opposite: https://youtu.be/cKUvKE3bQlY?t=133 (accessed 19 January 2022).

REFERENCES

Avanti, Peter (2013), 'Black musics, technology, and modernity: Exhibit A, the drum kit', *Popular Music and Society*, 36:4, pp. 476–504.

bell, adam patrick (2015), 'DAW democracy? The dearth of diversity in "Playing the Studio"', *Journal of Music, Technology & Education*, 8:2, pp. 129–46.

Holmes, Kat (2018), *Mismatch: How Inclusion Shapes Design*, Cambridge: MIT Press.

Muhammad, Ali Shaheed and Kelley, Frannie (2013), 'Marley Marl on the Bridge Wars, LL Cool J and discovering sampling', *Microphone Check* (npr.org), https://www.npr.org/sections/microphonecheck/2013/09/11/221440934/marley-marl-on-the-bridge-wars-ll-cool-j-and-discovering-sampling. Accessed 18 February 2022.

37

Connecting Black Youth to Critical Media Literacy through Hip-Hop Making in the Music Classroom

Jabari Evans

Jabari Evans is assistant professor of race and media at the University of South Carolina in Columbia, SC, USA, where he teaches journalism and mass communication.

This chapter explores the Foundations of Music's Songwriting and Music Production (SWP) programme in Chicago, IL, as a representative case exploring the impact of standardized hip-hop music education programmes toward closing learning equity gaps in low-income communities of colour.

Introduction

Hip-hop-based education (HHBE), or the usage of hip-hop, especially rap songs and lyrics, as curricular resources, has been cited by many as useful for educators seeking to use pedagogy that helps better engage youth with identity formation, prosocial behaviour and critical thinking. Hip-hop, as depicted by many HHBE practitioners in the current literature, is the performance of Black resistance to racism, on the one hand; or, the performance of pathological Blackness, on the other hand. For that reason, there is a fine line to be walked by those school districts, policymakers and researchers that are investigating the idea of formally integrating hip-hop into their classrooms. Given this context, this chapter explores the outcomes observed during my experiences as a researcher and educational consultant for the Songwriting and Production Program (SWP) being delivered in Chicago Public Schools.

HHBE research: A snapshot

Over the last twenty years, researchers have argued social lives of American youth are heavily shaped by hip-hop's cultural practices (Petchauer 2009; Petchauer 2015). Hip-hop culture has consistently been described as an informational medium that Black youth naturally tune into, one that describes the rage of African Americans facing growing oppression, declining opportunities for advancement, changing moods on the streets and everyday life as a matter of sheer survival (Love 2015). Rap music, the most performative and visible product of the culture, is a global phenomenon and a billion-dollar industry that influences the ways in which these youths form their identity, connect with their peers and make meaning of the world around them.

As such, engaged teachers could be well served to expand the concept of literacy in their schools and develop new curricula and pedagogies that involve hip-hop artistic practice. In this essay, I examined youths' developing senses of self in a Connected Learning[1] context, in which young people have increased access to a wider ecology of information, technology and interest-driven learning communities (Ito et al. 2013). As a framework, I fully believe these are the capabilities to provide more pathways for young people of colour to develop deeper identification with a personal interest in school, develop expertise and skill and connection to career and life goals.

Foundations of Music's SWP programme

Using a ten-week project-driven learning format, Foundations of Music's SWP Programme was designed with the aim of teaching young people of colour how to write, produce records and engineer original takes on the contemporary music that they know and love. Intended to appeal to the informal music interests of disengaged students, the ideal SWP classroom emphasized being enabled to 'open up' in educational spaces and authentically share aspects of their hip-hop identity to the world around them. Drawing upon a year of ethnographic field work, this chapter discusses my experiences with the SWP programme at two public schools in Chicago: Shoreline Career Academy and Edwards Community School (both pseudonyms). The participants in this study included 57 Black students aged 10 to 15 years old (35 male and 22 female) who participated in the SWP programme during the 2017–18 school year. Three data sources (song lyrics, participant observations and open-ended interviews) served as my analysis for this study.

Findings

There is a long history of hip-hop oriented media-making by young people, in both formal and informal educational settings. Such work has been led by a variety of philosophies and motivations, ranging from creative 'self expression' through to technical and vocational training. Within the SWP programme, student production was designed as an indispensable aspect of the learning process and was also seen as a valuable means of developing participant social and communication skills. Ultimately, findings indicated participants felt that essential elements of the programme were less about usage of technological tools, but more to do with nurturing hip-hop's cultural capital – that is, with the cultural skills and competencies that are needed to use that technology creatively and productively. Acknowledging these skills and competencies in the classroom also allowed the SWP participants to develop pride in themselves, their peer communities and affirm their identity as authentically belonging in the academic space.

Facilitation of knowledge in small groups can often foster a sense of belonging and pride in one's place in a community. Similarly, within the SWP's tight-knit and free-flowing learning environment, participants were often given opportunities to create, reflect and iterate based on feedback. In many instances, the participants in the SWP programme used their real-life experiences with violence in their musical creations and to process their emotions and think critically about the cause of the conditions in their communities. By interrogating their own music creations and comparing them to that of their favourite artists, participants of the Foundations of Music SWP programme frequently examined socio-political and economic issues happening to themselves, within their families and their communities.

Beyond discussing current events and socio-political issues, SWP participants used their songwriting experiences to choose and critique issues that matter to them personally as related to their communities. SWP students used their lyrics that presented counternarratives that were meant to interrupt and dismantle traditional conceptions of youth in their neighbourhoods as apathetic, underperforming. This suggested to me that the programme's classroom model helped participants to participate in the public sphere through three critical elements: (1) building on youth enthusiasm and interests to foster a desire to learn, (2) emerging in the community for engagement in civic discourse and (3) participation in critical dialogue with internal collaborators to craft for external audiences. By engaging students in this learning environment, SWP students were given an opportunity to hone a craft and authentically develop their hip-hop identity simultaneously while gaining important future-ready skills in language, creative arts and media literacy.

Conclusion and implications for practice

In this chapter, I identified three primary themes of critical media literacy revealed within my observations of the SWP programme: interest-driven learning, critical dialogue and connection to community-based narratives. Youth in this study came from communities deeply affected by the digital divide, but thrived when given the opportunity to create a more professional media artefact with professional tools.

As with all instances where a practice typically seen as 'marginal' draws interest within the 'mainstream', the new attention paid to hip-hop music in education brings with it new tensions. Central among these tensions is the relationship between hands-on music production and larger goals that, in the non-school sphere, are required to relate either to academic achievement (especially critical thinking) or to marketable skills. Using my observations with the Foundations of Music SWP programme, it seems that hip-hop based education (HHBE) programmes often espouse both of these goals at the same time, as well as a range of other objectives related to community development, social change and citizenship.

My experience conducting this study also indicates that HHBE allows students of colour to interrogate their lives and situate their narratives within larger social contexts, students develop a sophisticated vocabulary to address structural inequities, systemic realities and global issues. In addition to the domains of reading, writing and traditional print literacies, hip-hop also seems to bridge an era of technological revolution where educators must develop robust forms of media literacy, computer literacy and multimedia literacies, to support 'multiple literacies' in the restructuring of education. Hip-hop music making creatively uses computer and multimedia technologies to demand novel skills and competencies, and if education is to be relevant to the problems and challenges of contemporary life, engaged teachers must expand the concept of literacy and develop new curricula and pedagogies that involve popular culture. In this sense, hip-hop would appear to work best as a central theme for a modern music education curriculum, particularly one that invites the composition of original lyrics by the participating students.

Hip-hop is considered by many as critical for pursuing social justice through education in the twenty-first century. By failing to consider the lived experiences and 'funds of knowledge' that youth pull from their communities, families and popular culture, a vast majority of schools are missing the opportunity to create class offerings that connect with the desires and aspirations of their youth. HHBE studies, attempt to move beyond gimmicky approaches to using hip-hop culture in the classroom and even more serious culturally relevant approaches by framing as incomplete studies that exploit students' local cultures, knowledges and languages only to 'take them somewhere else', or teach them some curricular standard or canon, without teaching the intrinsic value of students' interest in hip-hop. Ultimately, HHBE classrooms are working toward replacing broad strokes of 'students' cultures' with the more intimately defined strokes of 'students' lives' centralizing students' lives in an effort to reconceptualize the purposes and possibilities of public education.

Seeing music as a pathway to critical media literacy, digital skill acquisition and occupational identity is largely uncharted territory among researchers and policymakers alike. That said, it is my hope that this work will reinvigorate research on HHBE from a new standpoint; one that looks to evaluation in terms of more than academic engagement, standardized testing or psychosocial metrics but rather critical narratives that can show long term occupational success, technological creativity and civic participation.

NOTE

1. Connected Learning is when the intersection of peer cultures and personal interests stimulate learning environments for the combined purposes of professional aspirations, academic achievement and civic engagement (Watkins 2011).

REFERENCES

Gosa, Travis and Fields, Tristan (2012), 'Is hip-hop education another hustle? The (ir)responsible use of hip-hop as pedagogy', in B. J. Porfilio and M. Viola (eds), *Hip-Hop(e): The Cultural Practice and Critical Pedagogy of International Hip-Hop*, New York City, NY: Peter Lang Publishing, pp. 181–96.

Ito, Mimi, Gutiérrez, Kris, Livingstone, Sonia, Penuel, Bill, Rhodes, Jean, Salen, Kate, Sefton-Green, Julian and Watkins, S. Craig (2013), *Connected Learning: An Agenda for Research and Design*, Irvine, CA: Digital Media and Learning Research Hub.

Love, Bettina (2015), 'What is hip-hop-based education doing in nice fields such as early childhood and elementary education?', *Urban Education*, 50:1, pp. 106–31.

Petchauer, Emery (2009), 'Framing and reviewing hip-hop educational research', *Review of Educational Research*, 79:2, pp. 946–78.

Petchauer, Emery (2015), 'Starting with style: Toward a second wave of hip-hop education research and practice', *Urban Education*, 50:1, pp. 78–105.

Watkins, S. Craig (2011), 'Digital divide: Navigating the digital edge', *International Journal of Learning and Media*, 3:2, pp. 1–12.

PART III

HIGHER EDUCATION

This section of the book contains an eclectic set of perspectives and critiques concerning popular music in a range of higher education settings. Authors bring perspectives from Australia, Canada, Germany, Singapore, the United Kingdom and the United States, as faculty, senior leadership and former students. They discuss places and purposes of musical training in relation to policy and employability considerations; the value of popular music and associated pedagogies in music teacher education; admissions requirements for degree programmes; the meaningfulness of a leisure-time faculty rock band; pedagogy for contemporary commercial singers; certification in music technology education; and space and places of music production.

| Brendan Anthony, Queensland Conservatorium | Hussein Boon, University of Westminster | Siew Ling Chua, Singapore Teachers' Academy for the Arts |

Virginia Wayman
Davis,
University of
Texas

James Dekle,
Purdue Univer-
sity Black Cultural
Centre

Heloisa Feichas,
Music School
of the Federal
University of
Minas Gerais

Gemma Hill,
drummer, music
educator and
translator

Jason Huxta-
ble, Leeds Arts
University

Martin Isherwood,
The Liverpool
Institute for
Performing Arts

David Knapp,
Syracuse
University

Candice Daven-
port Mattio,
USC Thornton
School of Music

Lloyd McArton,
University of
Toronto

Richard Smith,
contemporary
musician

Jay Stapley,
session guitarist,
songwriter and
producer

Daniel Walzer,
Indiana
University-Purdue
University

Ana Flavia Zuim,
NYU Steinhardt

38

Crushed by the Wheels of Industry

Martin Isherwood

Martin Isherwood is Head of Music at The Liverpool Institute for Performing Arts, England, where he teaches and leads courses in popular music, songwriting, production and performance.

In this chapter, the author argues that, given the precarious nature of music industry contracts and employment, courses must develop key musical skills for longevity rather than merely providing access to facilities and replicating informal industry practices.

In January 2000, I organized a two-day international conference in partnership with the International Society for Music Education (ISME) at the Liverpool Institute for Performing Arts (LIPA), a new music and performing arts higher education institution (HEI) established in 1995 by Paul McCartney in his old school. *Interactive 2000 – Current Issues in Teaching Popular Music in Higher Education* was attended by 80 delegates from around the world and featured presentations from key popular music education (PME) pioneers. I subsequently published the papers with an introduction summarizing the issues and questions raised (Isherwood 2000). Reviewing that summary twenty years later, it would seem that little progress has been made in addressing those issues. Given the vastness and diversity of musics, practices and industries encompassed within the term popular music and therefore PME, some diversity of purpose and practice amongst educators is unsurprising. However, there still seems to be an issue with the fundamentals, e.g. what is it for, who is it for and how is it different from other types of music education?

Higher popular music education and employment

Since the launch of the first UK popular music degree in 1990, there has been an exponential increase in the number of popular music programmes at established universities and new private sector institutions recruiting thousands of additional popular music students. In 1996, a European Music Office report cited 80 UK popular music programmes in Further Education (FE)[1] and Higher Education (HE) (Laing 1999). In 2020, the UK University and Colleges Admissions Service (UCAS) lists 275 popular music degree programmes with tens of thousands more PME students in FE. There has also been a marked increase in popular music focussed Music Technology (MT) degrees in the UK since the mid 1990s (Born and Devine 2015), with estimates of a 1400 per cent increase in the number of students taking MT degrees up to 2012.

Despite these increases and thousands of new popular music graduates joining the jobs market, estimates show that the music industry and related employment remain a consistently and comparatively small part of the UK economy and that the size of the sector has changed little over the last 25 years. Since Dane (1996) estimated 115,000 full time equivalent (FTE) jobs in the UK music industry there have been similar regular estimates within a narrow range, from 95,010 (Creative Cultural Skills 2007) to 119,000 FTEs (UK Music 2016). In 2019, using a substantially different methodology, UK Music claimed that the music industry 'sustained' 190,935 full time jobs with 72 per cent of these jobs being music creators and self-employed (UK Music 2019). This new figure was achieved by dividing total music UK Gross Value Added (GVA) of £5.2bn by UK average earnings. However, in stark contrast, the then CEO of the Ivors Academy that represents UK music creators, stated in 2017 that fewer than 2000 people in the UK earned above the annual national average salary of £27,600 from their Performing Rights Organization royalties (Bain 2017). An explanation for this discrepancy could be that the 2019 UK Music estimate is distorted by a small number of individuals earning very large sums. Similarly, out of a total UK (GVA) of £1.6 trillion (Office for National Statistics 2015) the £5.2 billion music industry contribution is equal to 0.32 per cent of the UK economy. Employment figures give a similar picture even when using the unusually higher UK Music estimate of 190 thousand FTE jobs in the music industry. Out of a total of 31.75 million people in work (Office for National Statistics 2016), this is equal to 0.6 per cent of the working population.

This lack of growth is perhaps not surprising given the rise of digital piracy, streaming and downloads and the decline in physical sales, but it does contradict commonly held assumptions of music being a major development area for the future economy. Many of the new popular music programmes are specifically marketed as preparing students for careers in the music industry but, given the lack of expansion in employment or even profitable self-employment opportunities, the ability of programmes to fulfil these aims is in doubt. This raises the issue as to whether these new programmes and institutions are preparing students for industry and careers or, in a world of student fees and no government restrictions on numbers of students that can be recruited and funded, whether the providers are an industry unto themselves sustained by unrealistic aspirations of would-be music industry entrants? Around 90 per cent of the increased MT students numbers discussed above were males from 'a relatively lower social class profile', almost 80 per cent appear not to have taken the MT A Level[2], and even fewer have taken a Music A Level (Born and Devine 2015: 153–54). Providing attractive educational opportunities for young men from poor backgrounds is a noble aim but for popular music educators to focus mostly on music industry careers that do not exist is a form of mis-selling and peddling impossible dreams.

Designing PME programmes solely to prepare students for careers in the music industry can lead to adopting informal learning methods close to those that occur in the 'real world'. Given low commercial success rates amongst aspiring rock and pop artists generally, emulating an informal system or 'self-directed learning environment' (Lebler 2008) that clearly fails in securing employment or success in the 'real world' is questionable. PME must add value other than providing access to facilities and serving merely as facilitation and accreditation for what already takes place outside of HE. As Green puts it: 'The benefits of formal music education for young popular musicians must be measured in terms far beyond securing them a position inside the music industry' (2001: 213).

In addition to sustained growth, PME has also undergone a transformation in terms of industry perceptions, and as Head of Music at LIPA I am approached constantly by major label and publishing A&R staff scouting for talent amongst the student body. Despite an increase in scouting, there are still relatively low rates of commercial success reported by HE popular music programmes (Isherwood 2014). PME cannot be merely a 'breeding ground' for a music industry curious to see what education has to offer, but with little to offer back in terms of employment and income. PME must also be an intrinsically valuable learning experience that equips students with a range of musical and transferable skills.

It is easy for PME leaders to set themselves up as imagined gateways to, or as substrata of, the music industry. In doing so, however, they become less concerned with 'education' and more concerned with 'artist development'. The notion that you don't need to be able to read music staff notation or understand music theory to be successful in the music industry is evidently true. It is also prevalent amongst popular music students, many of whom are resistant to engage with such concepts and would rather get lucky and go straight to the record or publishing deal or world arenas tour. It is also common amongst ex-industry professional teaching staff, who can find themselves washed up on the shores of PME but who often cannot engage with music theory beyond a basic level. Predicting what will be successful in an ever-changing music industry is fraught with difficulties and irrespective of how many ex-industry professionals are employed; education

209

institutions will inevitably secure far fewer industry successes than a professional music industry with already terrible success rates. No matter how well educated someone may be, physical beauty, 'natural' ability, confidence, charisma, etc. matter more in the industry.

In a perverse 'aping' of the music industry, popular music HE programmes appear to be offering artists the equivalent of record and publishing company 'development deals'. This analogy works if one considers loans for fees and living costs as 'advances' recoupable from future earnings on a 360-degree basis, but with no commercial releases, publishing contract, synchs, tours, significant Artist & Repertoire staff or industry creative input, or any chance of 'recouping' as a consequence of the HEI's actions.

Creation, performance and production

A distinguishing feature of popular music is that it is principally concerned with the creation of new music, and therefore it is necessary to focus mostly on musical practices: the creation, performance and production of popular music and the skills that directly support these activities. All of these core practices can take a lifetime to master in themselves. However, when the legal, technological, industrial, financial, social and cultural complexities that are associated with the creation, production, distribution and consumption of popular music are also considered, the scale of the potential subject area is enormous. Therefore, whilst some aspects of the intersections with these areas as contextualizing factors should be included, the musical practices must make up the bulk, and be at the core, of any programme of popular music study in higher education.

Since 2001, I have been Head of Music at LIPA. Despite the fact that LIPA only teaches popular, commercial and contemporary music, the term 'popular music' has never featured in the title of the degree programmes, with all of them being variants of a BA (Hons) Music, e.g. Music (Song Writing and Performance) and Music (Song Writing and Production). This was a deliberate decision. I know of no one who would describe themselves as a fan of 'popular music'. Similarly, I know of no one outside of the education sector who would use the term popular music at all in describing the music that they engage with, despite the strong likelihood that the vast majority of that music could be considered 'popular' by one of Middleton's (1990) definitions. Popular music is music and deserves to be included within that broad embrace as much as any other style or genre. In the UK, there is only one Quality Assurance Agency Subject Benchmark: Music.[3] This is more of an important point than it may appear at first glance. If we can accept that PME is principally a *music* education, then many of the issues and questions as to what

PME is and what it should be are resolved at a stroke. A practical music education, whatever the stylistic and repertoire focus, should provide its students with a range of fundamental instrumental, vocal, creative, recreative, aural, technical, technological, theoretical, analytical and critical skills that underpin, and could be applied to, a range of musics. These skills benefit students educationally, artistically and personally, are eminently transferable, and will also ultimately raise the chances of musical employment and creative and technical longevity in the event of any music industry success.

NOTES

1. In England and Wales, Further Education (FE) is tertiary-level education undertaken after completion of secondary school and General Certificate of Secondary Education (GCSE) examinations. Completing a course of FE study is required for admission into Higher Education.

2. Advanced level qualifications (known as A Levels) are subject-based qualifications that can lead to university, further study, training, or work. Students normally take three or more A Levels over two years (UCAS 2020).

3. The Quality Assurance Agency is responsible for setting and monitoring the standards of UK higher education including the development of the UK Quality Code for Higher Education.

> Subject Benchmark Statements describe the nature of study and the academic standards expected of graduates in specific subject areas. They show what graduates might reasonably be expected to know, do and understand at the end of their studies. Subject Benchmark Statements are written by subject specialists [...] They are used as reference points in the design, delivery and review of academic programmes. They provide general guidance but are not intended to represent a national curriculum or to prescribe set approaches [...] Subject Benchmark Statements are available for bachelor's degrees with honours, master's degrees, and professional qualifications.
>
> (QAA 2020: n.pag.)

REFERENCES

Bain, Vick (2017), 'YouTube must not be allowed to benefit from "legalised piracy on an unimaginable scale"', *Music Business Worldwid*, 30 May, https://www.musicbusinessworldwide.com/youtube-must-not-be-allowed-to-benefit-from-legalised-piracy-on-an-unimaginable-scale/. Accessed 3 March 2022.

Born, Georgina and Devine, Kyle (2015), 'Music technology, gender, and class: Digitization, educational and social change in Britain', *Twentieth-Century Music*, 12:2, pp. 135–72.

Creative and Cultural Skills (2007), 'Creative choices – Music impact and footprint 06–07' [online], http://www.data-generator.co.uk. Accessed 29 April 2017.

Dane, Cliff (1996), *The Value of Music: A National Music Council Report Into the Value of the UK Music Industry*, London: National Music Council.

Green, Lucy (2001), *How Popular Musicians Learn*, Aldershot: Ashgate.

Isherwood, Martin (2014), *Sounding Out Songwriting. An Investigation into the Teaching and Assessment of Songwriting in Higher Education*, New York: Higher Education Academy.

Laing, Dave (1999), 'The economic importance of music in the European Union: 6. Music in education', *Journal on Media Culture*, 2 (Summer), http://www.icce.rug.nl/~soundscapes/DATABASES/MIE/Part1chapter06.shtml. Accessed 3 March 2022.

Lebler, Don (2008), 'Popular music pedagogy: Peer learning in practice', *Music Education Research*, http://www98.griffith.edu.au/dspace/bitstream/handle/10072/26123/502421.pdf;-jsessionid=79933D9A4E8BC160F5BC5C63B75F6EAB?sequence=1. Accessed 3 March 2022.

Middleton, Richard (1990), *Studying Popular Music*, Milton Keynes: Open University Press.

Office for National Statistics (2015), 'Statistical bulletin: Regional gross value added (income approach): December 2015', http://www.ons.gov.uk/economy/grossvalueaddedgva/bulletins/regionalgrossvalueaddedincomeapproach/december2015. Accessed 3 March 2022.

Office for National Statistics (2016), 'Statistical bulletin: UK Labour Market: August 2016', [online], http://www.ons.gov.uk/employmentandlabourmarket/peopleinwork/employmentandemployeetypes/. Accessed 3 March 2022.

Quality Assurance Agency (QAA) (2020), 'About us 2020', https://www.qaa.ac.uk/quality-code/subject-benchmark-statements. Accessed 3 March 2022.

UK Music (2016), *Measuring Music 2016*, https://www.ukmusic.org/wp-content/uploads/2020/09/measuring-music-2016.pdf. Accessed 3 March 2022.

UK Music (2019), *Music by Numbers 2019*, https://www.ukmusic.org/wp-content/uploads/2020/08/MusicByNumbers2019Report.pdf. Accessed 3 March 2022.

University and Colleges Admissions Service (2020), 'A Levels', https://www.ucas.com/further-education/post-16-qualifications/qualifications-you-can-take/levels. Accessed 3 March 2022.

39

Towards Popular Music Education as an Institutional Norm

Lloyd McArton

Lloyd McArton is a Ph.D. candidate in music education at the University of Toronto, where he teaches courses in popular music and music education.

This chapter offers a critical appraisal of North American music education degree programmes, suggesting that in order to displace and disrupt their ongoing hegemony, popular music education programmes ought to be established as an institutional norm.

Part of my identity and professional self-conception falls under the guise of 'music teacher' – though I would contend that 'facilitator' or 'mentor' might be a more adequate description of how I help younger and less-experienced musicians along their musical journeys. If you knew me, and somehow also knew nothing of the academic monopoly preserved by western art music's in most institutions offering music studies, you might incorrectly surmise that my formal education was based on popular music: when I perform and create, it is on stages with heavily affected sounds, amplified instruments and loud drummers; and when I facilitate musical learning, it is based on students' existing interests and tastes, which nine-and-a-half times out of ten would be considered 'popular'. Yet, only since beginning my graduate studies have I been able to explore popular music in an academic capacity, and it was only then that I discovered it even existed in universities at all.

In order to become qualified to teach music in public schools, I had to spend an entire degree performing classical music (and jazz, though this was voluntary), learning to teach through courses and classroom placements steeped in the traditions of concert band and choral music. In Canada and the United States, this is not just the norm but effectively the only publicized option. I am reluctant to lend weight to the

213

notion that growing up in a small Canadian town left me with a limited perception of what was 'out there', or that such an upbringing reinforced the financial, geographic and qualificatory pressures that dictated where I would be able to attend university to become a school music teacher. Instead, my typically insurgent and quasi-anarchic outlook urges me to direct the blame towards systems that oppress and discriminate through greedy maintenance of power; the problem was not in my own limitations or my relative isolation from the world's opportunities, but rather that the educational architecture in my country and continent was and continues to be so thoroughly entrenched in archaic notions of 'excellence' that I had no other choice.

Popular music education

My graduate studies have made me highly appreciative of other countries' ongoing efforts and dedicated contributions to the growing presence of higher popular music education, or HPME (Smith 2013; Teague and Smith 2015; Moir 2016, 2017) in performance and, regrettably less common, composition. What continues to disturb me, however, is that no such programme of popular *music education* exists in which students learn and become 'qualified' to facilitate popular music in public schools or educational contexts. The most concerning issue and obstacle in the broader field of popular music education are that the ideas and visions produced therein have not been mobilized towards large-scale change or presence in the system itself. We are in need of real action and upheaval in universities, beyond discussion and considerations.

Smith and Powell observed in the *Journal of Popular Music Education*'s potential demographics a divide between 'two largely separate but far from discrete communities' (2017: 4), which crudely summarized are: (1) music teachers who engage with popular music as one of many tools in the practice of classroom music teaching and (2) popular musicians interested in furthering their skills and understanding through formal education. Such a division, no matter how porous it may become in select forums and other transient settings, prevents wholesale restructuring and can only serve to maintain the dearth of degree programmes that could rightly be described as popular *music education*. Distinct from *popular music* education, which is more representative of the learning undertaken by the second camp outlined above, popular *music education* remains tokenized and underrepresented in the grand scheme of North American music education degree programmes. I propose that one of the chief concerns and functions of our shared and collective disciplines should be to at least partially displace the paradigm of 'bands-as-music-education' (Mantie 2012) and its sovereignty over music teacher training, with the goal of advancing 'popular-music-as-music-education' in that same arena.

The large ensemble paradigm

While academic in their reification, the conversations surrounding the places and purposes of popular music in the 'future of music education' are inherently political, mired in the bureaucracy of university or faculty governance and leadership. Part of me is reluctant to reiterate and echo the numerous scholarly documents suggesting alternatives to the large ensemble paradigm that range from polite tiptoeing to more brazen calls to reform; such is the protocol in the academic dissemination of ideas, that etiquette and formality supersede the desire or need to spread the good word if someone else has already done so. Yet despite others' work in questioning the preservation of large ensemble education in North America, there has been virtually no change at the institutional level. I am privileged to have lived and learned in both the formal and informal, classical and (un)popular worlds of music. Having experienced both, I have lamented over the unfortunate reality that my first five years of university education were wholly unsuited to provide me with the skills, knowledge and understandings required to facilitate students to engage with most music in the twenty-first century. This realization has instilled in me a weight of responsibility to continue to protest wherever and whenever possible in the name of positive change.

I cannot fathom why the default North American degree programme in 'music' continues to model itself after content, skills and philosophies that no longer apply to the musical landscape(s) of the twenty-first century. I am doubly frustrated in considering that music education programmes constructed from the same outdated foundations are responsible for fulfilling students' professional development as both musicians *and* teachers. We ought to re-evaluate what constitutes 'early music' as it pertains to post-secondary studies; universities are supposed to be the research hubs and think tanks of the world, wherein they hypothesize, hone and propagate ideas, methods and solutions towards the betterment of our societies. As they stand, however, university music education programmes are little more than glorified pedagogical museums, who unfortunately own the majority stake in our corner of public education.

As they are designed by necessity to qualify public school music teachers, music education programmes employing large ensembles as the sole model of instruction are professionally negligent for a host of reasons:

- Conducting, as the primary function of a music educator, is pedagogically equivalent to lecturing in other subjects, which would be considered an ancient practice in school classrooms.
- Large ensemble programmes linger despite meaningful and relevant research – sometimes produced by the very same institutions – spelling out their inherent

flaws (see e.g. Allsup and Benedict 2008) and declining enrolment (Fitzpatrick 2013).

- The skills and understandings espoused in the learning of large ensemble music do not include creativity, autonomy or versatility – skills that are integral to the majority of the twenty-first century musicians.
- In the case of concert bands in Canada, the only professional ensembles (four in total) require performers to enlist in the military; all other groups are either community organizations or part of the educational system, whose professional pathways resemble a cult-like propagation of tradition as a teacher/leader.
- School programmes based on the concert band tradition tend to use bribery with 'fun trips' and the 'benefit of being a part of something larger than yourself' to distract students and their families from the squandered time that could have been spent navigating relevant and lasting pathways of musical learning.
- High-school music programmes are virtually incapable of adequately preparing students to successfully audition for a university music degree without supplemental private lessons, which are not economically possible for all families.
- Far and away the largest problem lies in the institutional ubiquity and omnipotence of the large ensemble paradigm, which allow it to determine the processes of auditions, teacher competencies and qualifications and, worst of all, the range of financially accessible experiences available to young musicians. The loftiest purveyors of large ensemble education are irresponsible and embarrassing wardens of music teacher training programmes.

Looking around and ahead

It is important to recognize that *popular music education-ists* are not the only combatants in this conflict, and that other subfields have their own disputes with the conservatory-style practices that I have vilified here. Finding common ground amongst those advocating for change is essential in our shared quest of re-thinking the practices of university music education programmes. It would serve the interests of all to continue supporting our colleagues and allies who are engaging in more explicitly emancipatory work in justice and decolonization.

As I write this (during the pandemic and widespread lockdowns of spring/summer 2020), thousands of music teachers at elementary, secondary and post-secondary schools are likely struggling to navigate virtual music instruction; it will be especially difficult for those for whom concert bands and other large ensembles are their primary musical experience. I wonder how they might respond to this drastic upheaval: will popular music and other currently neglected genres become the new normal out of necessity, as they are far better suited to virtual instruction? Perhaps their time in the spotlight will be only a flash in the pan, with teachers reverting back to typical large ensemble instruction when it is once again safe to congregate in large numbers. Regardless, while we trudge through one of the most devastating and confusing stretches of modern humanity, now is an appropriate time to reflect on what we want to see on the other side of this mess.

As fellow musicians and educators, I implore you to take stock of your beliefs, philosophies and professional integrity, and ask yourselves: what kind of future do you want to see in formal institutions dedicated to the intergenerational proliferation of musical learning? Are you content to stand by while the majority of North American universities preserve large ensemble music as the sole and quasi-official paradigm of music education? Using existing and successful models of HPME programmes being developed haphazardly across the globe, it is easy to imagine what a popular *music education* degree programme would look like, and what impact such programmes might have in disrupting the hegemony perpetuated by the large ensemble paradigm. The cycle is too large a wheel to be stopped by a few sticks in its spokes and will require continued protest and academic action to produce necessary, overdue, lasting and widespread change.

REFERENCES

Allsup, Randall and Benedict, Cathy (2008), 'The problems of band: An inquiry into the future of instrumental music education', *Philosophy of Music Education Review*, 16:2, pp. 156–73.

Fitzpatrick, Laura (2013), 'Factors affecting music education in Ontario secondary schools: Teachers' perspectives', *Electronic Thesis and Dissertation Repository*, Paper 1282, https://ir.lib.uwo.ca/cgi/viewcontent.cgi?article=2549&context=etd. Accessed 3 March 2022.

Mantie, Roger (2012), 'Bands and/as music education: Antinomies and the struggle for legitimacy', *Philosophy of Music Education Review*, 20:1, pp. 63–81.

Moir, Zack (2016), 'Popular music making and young people: Leisure, education, and industry', in R. Mantie and G. Smith (eds), *The Oxford Handbook of Music Making and Leisure*, New York: Oxford University Press, pp. 223–40.

Moir, Zack (2017), 'Learning to create and creating to learn: Considering the value of popular music in higher education', in J. Williams and K. Williams (eds), *The Singer-Songwriter Handbook*, New York: Bloomsbury, pp. 35–50.

Smith, Gareth (2013), 'Seeking "success" in popular music', *Music Education Research International*, 6, pp. 26–37.

Smith, Gareth and Powell, Bryan (2017), 'Welcome to the journal', *Journal of Popular Music Education*, 1:1, pp. 3–8.

Teague, Adele and Smith, Gareth Dylan (2015), 'Portfolio careers and work-life balance among musicians: An initial study into implications for higher music education', *British Journal of Music Education*, 32:2, pp. 177–93.

40

Ideological Extrojection: The De-Neoliberalization of UK Music Education

Jason Huxtable

Jason Huxtable is a senior lecturer in popular music performance at Leeds Arts University and visiting tutor of Percussion and Pedagogy at Royal Birmingham Conservatoire, England.

This chapter explores the idea that, as the neoliberalization of UK higher education (HE) continues, music education faces the 'end-times'. In this provocation, the author considers possibilities for educators to enact decolonizing praxis through reflection upon self-complicity in furthering neoliberal logic, through a Freirian ideological extrojection.

Neoliberal assault

As the assault on UK music education continues, we now head into the 'end-times' where the 'products' of music, culture, the arts and humanities are increasingly viewed as valueless by a society thoroughly corrupted by neoliberal ideology. Consequently, education in these disciplines has been ruthlessly marginalized through conditions of precarity, obedience, fear and complicit subjugation.

The role of education has been systematically re-formed to reflect neoliberal principles, valourizing purely economic outcomes over all other possible conceptions of what societal, cultural, healthful, experiential and environmental 'goods' (Varoufakis 2019) a varied education might provide. This narrowing of values has had the effect of limiting what can, and should, be studied and, consequently, that which is granted modes of cultural capital. This has been done under the guise of 'common sense', rational policy-making within an 'austerity' agenda across the UK, contextualized by a process of insidious neoliberalization. We music educators, practitioners and administrators have obediently carried out this self-fulfilling prophecy, enacted through cultural behaviour and discourse, confirming that there is indeed no alternative to the neoliberal ideology of late capitalism.

The neoliberal project has successfully convinced society that no alternative future exists (Fisher 2009), rendering us impotent to create or even imagine alternative systems of value for the practice of the arts and artistic education. When creation is stunted, death is inevitable; and music education is dying. Our own decay has only been *slowed* through an obedient complicity to the neoliberal system, but this appeasement will not halt it. A new and radical discourse is urgently required.

Neoliberal complicity

When we justify support for music education using the language of the market, according primacy to only economic outcomes, we echo and reinforce dominant discourse. When we justify music education through associated benefits to the more 'useful' disciplines of mathematics and English we marginalize the profession. When we construct a curriculum to function primarily as the development of 'employability' we limit the range of beneficial outcomes viewable. In short, when we enact the discourse of our masters, however well intentioned, we only achieve, at best, a slowing of our own demise. Essentially, the master's tools will never dismantle the master's house. Mere adaptation to the system is the weakest response to hegemony (Freire 1974).

UK higher education (HE) institutions have demonstrated this adaptation to neoliberal principles through adoption of a range of competitive and corporate models. Implementation of neoliberal, 'metricocratic' ratings, such as the Teaching Excellence Framework (TEF),[1] exhibit this subjugation to a system that continues to destroy music education and the arts more broadly. When institutions are pitted against each other as competitors on league tables, more akin to private sports teams than public institutions for knowledge production, dominant ideology becomes fixed and validated. The survival of individual institutions becomes conditional on success in this game of 'meritocracy'. However, the playing field is anything but level when notions of value centre squarely upon graduate earning outcomes. There is no room for misunderstanding when programmes are judged of 'poor value' on this metric and should be 'dropped' by institutions as a result (Hinds 2019). Music education will not survive this game, however 'adaptive' it proves to be.

I agree that music graduates are likely to provide no economic succour when the student debt bubble bursts, but education should never have become a commodity in the first place. Graduates are being subverted into crops to be harvested, units of economic outcome with education functioning as fertilizer; education as a distinctly de-humanizing process. The desperation for graduate economic outcomes is inextricably related to the privatized and heavily interested loans required to fund the UK HE system, an individualistic system disingenuously veiled as providing value for money to the UK tax payer, pitting students against society. We observe limited discontent from dispirited students themselves, well trained through their schooling to apply the logic of neoliberalism to their own situations. Music education has also too readily adapted to mirror the focus upon economic goals of wider society but, even through behaviours of obedient complicity, continues to endure a torturous death by a thousand cuts. Logic is perverted when neoliberalism is the only language available to cure the disease of itself.

Perhaps I have taken a too hyperbolic tone? Not according to the Incorporated Society of Musicians (ISM)'s *Music Education: State of the Nation* report (ISM 2019) which evidences rapid and 'serious decline': 'If the pace continues, music education in England will be restricted to a privileged few within a decade'. The ISM's list of findings indicates a concerted effort to marginalize the entire music education sector.

1. More than 50 per cent of primary schools did not meet music provision curriculum obligations due to accountability pressures for maths and English.
2. Music is no longer taught across Key Stage 3 in more than 50 per cent of state-funded secondary schools.[2]
3. In some schools there is no music provision at all.
4. A drop of twenty per cent in GCSE Music entries since 2014/2015 due to Ebacc marginalzation.[3]
5. Opportunities to sing are being diminished.
6. The skilled workforce is becoming demoralized, leading to skill shortages.
7. There are funding shortages in music education.
8. Music is the fastest disappearing A Level Subject.[4]

As UK HE music programmes face pressures below (through lack of uptake, state support and subject marginalization), above (political mythologizing of neoliberal, meritocratic value systems) and within (continued instrumental corporatization of our supposedly autonomous structures), future collapse is inevitable. As these political and economic strains translate to increasingly ruthless competition, protectionism and individualism across HE music programmes, we are destined to tear ourselves apart through desire to be the last man standing.

It is natural to direct our energies outward, to 'rage against the machine', but I believe the tide will more effectively turn through introspection, a critical engagement with our own contributions to neoliberalism. 'We alone become responsible for the problems we confront when we can no longer conceive how larger forces control or constrain our choices and the lives we are destined to live' (Giroux 2014: 3). After all, power really resides within ourselves, first and foremost – the powers to make change but also those powers which restrict our thoughts and behaviours; the powers which have hold over us. This introspective action should not be mistaken for pacifism; the inward infliction of symbolic violence against powers that bind us is equally brutal, but more subtle than outward protest and force.

Education is symbolic violence, thus it can be used as a weapon to re-culture and, in opposition, as a means to de-culture. We must reflect and question, to what extent are we subjecting our learning communities to the educative process of re-enculturation of neoliberal notions of value in our curriculum and pedagogy? How often do we unquestioningly reinforce the rhetoric of neoliberal value through the lens of education as access to the music business? Are we endorsing systems of faux-meritocracy through competitive, rather than collaborative learning cultures? To what extent are we constructing competitive, hierarchical systems through presentation of ourselves as gate-keepers to the industry? Do we work with our colleagues through loving and supportive interaction or warily suspect (and wage) clandestine manoeuvres through fear of loss of competitive institutional and, therefore, economic capital? Is our research ethically distanced from the neoliberal, instrumental processes of metric based 'excellence' frameworks? Do our pedagogic methods really seek to emancipate and individuate, or look to train graduates to 'survive' within, rather than to question, the 'Hunger Games' of economic Darwinism which inevitably face them?

Escaping neoliberalism

We need to deculture education, to decolonize our curricula away from neoliberal hegemony – education as a practice, or *praxis*, more accurately, of freedom (Freire 1972)! The neoliberalization of music education can be reversed. We need to humanize ourselves through an extrojection of the habitus, to deny the epochal theme of neoliberalism as just an arbitrary mythology which has successfully achieved an unjust fixing of capital and an eradication of cultural experience. '(W)hether or not men [sic] can perceive the epochal themes and above all, how they act upon the reality within which these themes are generated will largely determine their humanization or dehumanization' (Freire 1974: 1). As teachers, musicians and 'culturalists' we are uniquely positioned to re-educate ourselves, conducting processes of ideological reconditioning. If we can extroject our own neoliberalism, ridding our own ideologies from this infection, we can heal, regenerate, renew and recreate. Creation of an alternative future becomes possible.

To do this we need a pedagogy which seeks to clear space to discuss conditions where citizens can attempt to transcend hegemonic situations of unknowing complicity. The transcendence can start with negotiation within and manipulation of the neoliberal order rather than a more radical rejection or explicit rebellion. As a first step, a critical 'integration' (Freire 1974) of neoliberal culture rather than a weak adaptation or unquestioning complicity. To integrate is to unveil – to analyze, to recognize one's own agency within and to take action to transform the self, and therefore the world. This can, and should, be done alongside our students; we are all students/teachers after all!

The process of transformation must come through this re-integration of self within culture; to become a subject of culture rather than a powerless object within it. We begin to transcend our situation when we can view it. We can only view it if we ask questions about ourselves, our own culture, our own systems of values and the meaning of our actions and discourse. Through problem posing, not only our subjective phenomenology to the musical objects and languages of study but also how these act as functions of ideological modes within and without the walls of the institution, we can start to turn the tide. Commonsense assumptions must be put into context, dissected and reconsidered. We have to understand our situationally as a function of our intentionality (Huxtable 2019). We must examine the relationship between micro and meta ideological turns towards an awareness that the world can be changed through the change of self. This process represents a pragmatic step towards critical consciousness and the unveiling of neoliberal mythology.

How we teach is reflective of why we teach, for whom and for what benefits. How we teach reflects the powers at play within ourselves and our students. Let us re-examine our motives, values, complicities and ideological assumptions. Let us review our curricula, pedagogies, departmental structures and contributions to society more fully. We can express value in our own terms and justify our existence not through appeasement of neoliberalism, thereby further neoliberalizing society, but through a new language where music and musicians seek first to integrate and then change society. We are soon to be in the ironically powerful position of having very little left to lose. The future we imagine for music education, society and our students is possible if we can change ourselves. Time is of the essence and we will need to work together.

223

NOTES

1. The Teaching Excellence Framework (TEF) was introduced by the UK Government in 2016. Registered institutions are awarded different status (Gold, Silver, Bronze) through performance against a variety of metrics designed to measure teaching excellence (e.g. graduate earning outcomes). Widely criticized by HE institutions initially, TEF ratings are now routinely used within institutions' marketing materials.

2. Key Stage 3 is the categorization of the three years of secondary schooling known as Year 7, 8 and 9 in England and Wales for students between the ages of 11 and 14.

3. The GCSE, or General Certificate of Secondary Education, is a subject specific qualification taken across England, Wales and Northern Ireland in Years 10 and 11; students aged 14–16. The EBacc is a performance indicator linked to GSCE attainment, similar to a Grade Point Average. Music is not an approved subject and does not count towards the EBacc.

4. A Levels are subject specific academic qualifications offered across the United Kingdom. They are typically studied by students between the ages of 16 and 18 and form the basis of conditional offers made by HE institutions.

REFERENCES

Fisher, Mark (2009), *Capitalist Realism: Is There No Alternative?*, Winchester, UK and Washington D.C.: Zero Books.

Freire, Paulo ([1972] 2007), *Pedagogy of the Oppressed*, Chicago: Penguin Modern Classics.

Freire, Paulo ([1974] 2005), *Freire: Education for Critical Consciousness*, New York: Continuum Books.

Giroux, Henry (2014), *Neoliberalism's War on Higher Education*, Chicago: Haymarket Books.

Hinds, Damien (2019), 'Education Secretary calls for an end to low value degrees', *News Story*, 26 May, https://www.gov.uk/government/news/education-secretary-calls-for-an-end-to-low-value-degrees. Accessed 23 June 2020.

Huxtable, Jason (2019), 'Practice as praxis: A Freirian approach to instrumental practice within the conservatoire', *Leeds Arts University Repository*, 21 May, https://lau.repository.guildhe.ac.uk/17659/. Accessed 23 June 2020.

ISM (2019), *Music Education: State of the Nation, Report by the All-Party Parliamentary Group for Music Education, the Incorporated Society of Musicians and the University of Sussex*, https://www.ism.org/images/images/State-of-the-Nation-Music-Education-WEB.pdf. Accessed 23 June 2020.

Varoufakis, Yanis (2019), *Talking to My Daughter: A Brief History of Capitalism*, London, Vintage.

41

On the Pulse of Change
Through Popular Music
Nourishing Teachers' Professional Identities

Siew Ling Chua

Siew Ling Chua is Principal Master Teacher (music) at the Singapore Teachers' Academy for the Arts, Ministry of Education. She looks after professional development of in-service music teachers.

In this chapter, the author discusses the need for music teachers in Singapore to become familiar with popular music praxes, in order to connect in meaningful, relevant ways with the people they teach in schools.

A plenty has already been said about the importance of popular music education for school-aged students (e.g. Smith et al. 2017). Some literature has shed light on or alluded to the significance of popular music education in pre-service music teacher education (e.g. Davis and Blair 2011; Isbell 2016) and teacher identities (e.g. Welch et al. 2010). There is a need now to turn our attention to the place of popular music education in in-service music teachers' professional development and its implications for music professional development providers and teacher mentors. Given that many in-service music teachers in Singapore received their early musical development in western classical music, popular music education can provide a useful balancing perspective.

In discussing the development of professionalism and the professional identity of music teachers, I enjoy Froehlich's (2007) paradox of professionalism. Froehlich argued that on the one hand, we expect professionals to act professionally, in other words, to act in expected ways that are determined by a body of experts, so that we can trust what they do. On the other hand, professionalism requires professionals to question what they do and discard routinized behaviours and to act flexibly. Apart from the need to question, scholars have also urged music educators to engage in critical pedagogy (e.g. Abrahams 2005; Regelski 1998), and to take cognizance of culturally relevant pedagogies (e.g. Fitzpatrick 2012). Hence, in the professional development of music teachers, in the spirit of professionalism, there is a need for music teachers to continually re-examine their preferences and biases, embrace an openness to diverse kinds of music and be critical of issues surrounding them. Similarly, music teacher educators' and teacher mentors' roles require us to question our understandings continually and to uncover our ignorance. What better place to look than to observe what is changing in our musical environment and contemporary music-making? And what better way to do this than to be immersed in and partake in popular music-making and popular music culture which has become ubiquitous and powerful in its subliminal presence in our daily living?

Changing perspectives and practices, embracing new identities and literacies

Studies in the sociology of music suggest how music 'produces' people since we make sense of a musical experience by taking on subjective and collective identities (Frith 1996: 109). The musical experience is not external to us, but rather it involves experiencing ourselves differently, and these different musical experiences produce different musical identities. Popular musics – from genres such as guitar bands, pop-rock, urban musics, hip-hop and punk, to evolving processes and traditions such as songwriting, music industry, DIY and syncretic ethnic-pop performances in different communities being produced in this digital age – harness the possibilities afforded by technologies to broaden repertoires of sound and how sound is produced and consumed. The remix culture (Lessig 2008) is concerned with re-editing, remixing and mash-ups to the extent that copyright infringement provides the basis for digital creativity as suggested by Brabazon (2011). Most literacies in this digital age are acquired through media, and we have moved from purely listening to 'seeing' music with the advent of YouTube, social media, video games and mobile technologies. Popular musics continue to be created in new ways in response to current issues and lived experiences, such as seen in the surge of virtual performances and COVID-19 inspired songs during the pandemic and lockdowns across the world. Popular music education thus puts us in touch with new literacies, new technologies and the world around us.

With understanding and experience of making current popular musics, music teachers could have sufficient knowledge to (1) function as musicians to guide their students to develop new music literacies, to think and respond musically and (2) function as educators to facilitate students open-mindedly embracing new forms of music-making which may involve new technologies, and expressions that may not have existed in the past, as they grow their identities.

Changing pedagogies, embracing criticality

The proliferation of studies on informal learning as a pedagogy for the music classroom (Green [2002] 2016) has led to a greater understanding of how such informal learning (and non-formal teaching) could be integrated into more formal music learning contexts in Singapore (e.g. Chua and Ho 2013). The digital media in which popular musics are produced, lend themselves well to blended learning approaches. There are new music learning approaches and pedagogical resources such as play-along videos developed by Little Kids Rock (2019) and Musical Futures (2020). These demonstrate fresh perspectives on music learning (e.g. Powell and Burstein 2017) and have been modelled at workshops designed for music educators in different parts of the world including Singapore. For music educators, while these possibilities open up authentic ways for students to be engaged in learning, and give voice to students' musical preferences, I also argue that like any kinds of music, popular musics are not inherently 'good' on their own.

How music education is delivered – along with how music is disseminated, received and consumed – is what determines its effect and its impact on learners. Educators have the power to shape how popular musics can influence, depending on how they are used (or misused) in the classroom. In a similar vein, scholars such as Elliott and Silverman (2014) have cautioned that music education can humanize or dehumanize, depending on whether music educators are educative or not. But instead of censoring popular musics because of a particular fear of their corruptive influence, and denying their pervasive influence, music teachers and teacher–educators need to confront these issues and develop critical discernment in individuals who have been and will continue to engage and participate in the digital world. The notion of an 'activist school music education', where 'music may enable students to navigate the politics of identity, opening up possibilities to embrace, trouble, and explore the intersections of identity' (Hess 2019: 1), shows ways that teaching and learning with popular musics can take place. Popular musics and their associated connections to contemporary issues in our lives and wider society, have the potential to give opportunities for such rich interdisciplinary discourse and explorations.

Toward the growth of music teacher identities

Just as identity is continually shifting, and just as music teachers continuously negotiate their multiple identities in music teaching (e.g. Dolloff 2007), music teachers' musical identities are complex and multi-faceted and will continue to grow and evolve. Therefore, professional development providers and teacher mentors can play a role by engaging in popular music education along with music teachers and be in tune with the contemporary musical environment. I tend to agree with a colleague's view that music teachers respect professional development providers whose world view of music is not just within the classroom, but always trying to go out and see what they can bring into the classroom. As a teacher mentor myself, I have seen how teachers are transformed when finding new ways of engaging their students through harnessing new pedagogies afforded by popular musics. I am reminded of one comment from a music teacher who shared his feelings after experimenting with the informal learning approach with popular music in his music classroom, 'I am a much happier music teacher now, more sold to the music religion' (Chua and Ho 2013: 150).

I argue that the place and purpose of popular music education is significant for developing the professionalism and professional identity of music teachers, professional development providers and teacher mentors. Popular music education is as important as 'world' music education (Campbell 2005) and as important as any music repertoire. We professional development providers and teacher mentors can keep our fingers on the pulse of change through popular musics, seek to understand the contexts and what that constitutes their artistry, and critically evaluate these musics and our mental models. We can also harness these resources and collaborate with other educators with relevant experiences to continually push our visions and practices of good music teaching. Without the inclusion of popular music education in in-service music teachers' professional development experiences, in ways that challenge teachers' frames of thinking, it is a leap to demand of music teachers to be culturally relevant to engage the hearts and minds of our young.

REFERENCES

Abrahams, Frank (2005), 'The application of critical pedagogy to music teaching and learning', *Visions of Research in Music Education*, 6:1, pp. 2–16.

Brabazon, Tara (2011), *Popular Music: Topics, Trends & Trajectories*, London: Sage.

Campbell, Patricia S. (2005), *Cultural Diversity in Music Education*, Bowen Hills: Australian Academic Press.

Chua, Siew L. and Ho, Hui P. (2013), 'Connecting findings, reflections and insights: Student-centricity, musically, creatively', in S. L. Chua and H. P. Ho (eds), *Connecting the Stars: Essays on Student-centric Music Education*, Singapore: Ministry of Education, pp. 143–54.

Davis, Sharon G. and Blair, Deborah V. (2011), 'Popular music in American teacher education: A glimpse into a secondary methods course', *International Journal of Music Education*, 29:2, pp. 124–40.

Dolloff, Lori (2007), 'All the things we are: Balancing our multiple identities in music teaching', *Action, Criticism, and Theory for Music Education*, 6:2, pp. 1–21.

Elliott, David J. and Silverman, Marissa (2014), 'Music, personhood, and *eudaimonia*: Implications for educative and ethical music education', *The Journal for Transdisciplinary Research in Southern Africa*, special edition, 10:2, pp. 57–72.

Frith, Simon (1996), 'Music and identity', *Questions of Cultural Identity*, 1:1, pp. 108–28.

Froehlich, Hildegard (2007), 'Institutional belonging, pedagogic discourse and music teacher education: The paradox of routinization', *Action, Criticism, and Theory for Music Education*, 6:3, pp. 7–21.

Green, Lucy ([2002] 2016), *How Popular Musicians Learn: A Way Ahead for Music Education*, New York: Routledge.

Hess, Juliet (2019), 'Singing our own song: Navigating identity politics through activism in music', *Research Studies in Music Education*, 41:1, pp. 61–80.

Isbell, Daniel S. (2016), 'Apprehensive and excited: Music education students' experience vernacular musicianship', *Journal of Music Teacher Education*, 25:3, pp. 27–38.

Lessig, Lawrence (2008), *Remix: Making Art and Commerce Thrive in the Hybrid Economy*, New York: Penguin.

Little Kids Rock (2019), 'Jam Zone', https://www.littlekidsrock.org/educators-free-resources/. Accessed 13 May 2020.

Musical Futures (2020), 'Who we are and what we do', http://www.musicalfutures.org/who-we-are. Accessed 13 May 2020.

Powell, Bryan and Burstein, Scott (2017), 'Popular music and modern band principles', in G. D. Smith, Z. Moir, M. Brennan, S. Rambrran and P. Kirkman (eds), *The Routledge Research Companion to Popular Music Education*, London: Routledge, pp. 243–54.

Regelski, Thomas A. (1998), 'Critical theory as a basis for critical thinking in music education', *Studies in Music from the University of Western Ontario*, 17:4, pp. 1–21.

Smith, Gareth Dylan, Moir, Zack, Brennan, Matt, Rambarran, S. and Kirkman, Phil (eds) (2017), *The Routledge Research Companion to Popular Music Education*, London: Routledge.

Welch, Graham F., Purves, Ross, Hargreaves, David K. and Marshall, Nigel et al. (2010), 'Reflections on the teacher identities in music education project', *Action, Criticism & Theory for Music Education*, 9:2, pp. 11–32.

42

The Conservatory as Exploratory

Richard Smith

Richard Smith's thirteen solo recordings have established him as a veteran contemporary musician. He is a tenured, full professor at the USC Thornton School of Music.

In this chapter, the author argues that creativity and musical explo-ration are at the core of what it means to be a contemporary musi-cian and student. He urges higher popular music education profes-sionals to embrace an ethos of the conservatory as exploratory.

Going for tenure as an earnest young jazz educator at a major university in the 1990s was rather straightforward. I only had to convince a committee of five classical professors just how much like classical music jazz music was! My case was not very hard to make. In the United States, collegiate jazz education is usually driven by large bands followed by jazz choir and/or smaller ensembles. Classical music is often taught in orchestras, choirs and chamber ensembles. On the surface of it, other aspects look similar as well. Classical and jazz composition and performance both tend to favour virtuosity, and both place an emphasis on precedent and on following the geniuses. But if we focus too much on the similari-ties, we may fail to address essential areas of jazz that are actually not like classical music at all: improvisation, for instance. Work in small jazz ensembles requires a very different set of skills compared to work in classical chamber ensembles. There is the particular way in which rhythm is expressed by a drummer, the amazing elasticity of the art form, and perhaps most importantly, all the cultural diversity that jazz repertoire responds to, absorbs and includes.

Becoming involved with popular music education has given me ample opportu-nity to consider equally distinct and refreshing differences between jazz and popu-lar music. When schools want to add popular music to their offerings, they tend to entrust the jazz department with the task. Based on my experience, this is not an optimal strategy. The place of popular music in the academy is quite different from that of both jazz and classical music, and so should be the way we teach it.

The core of popular music

What generally drives popular music is a hub of freshly inspired, creatively conceived songs that bring together the many 'spokes' in the wheel of which a department of popular music performance is comprised. These spokes can include performance practices (live and studio), repertoire knowledge, rhythm awareness, stage deportment and stagecraft, creativity, technology, recording, collaboration and team building, business, branding, management, fashion, media, marketing and entrepreneurship, wellness, community sing-alongs and many other aspects. These can add a great deal to a traditional conservatory setting and help faculty rethink how a school of music relates to the university and wider community.

Many popular musicians are not fully 'literate' in the traditional sense of being familiar with western staff notation, and may not care as much about instrumental 'mastery' and virtuosity as jazz or classical musicians do. They do not really think of themselves as conservators of a particular tradition or convention. Given these not-so-subtle differences, it would probably be harder to convince a tenure committee of jazz musicians that popular music and jazz music can be judged according to the same criteria – or, for that matter, to convince popular musicians of the same.

At the heart of a popular music programme are the singers/songwriters, the primary content creators. Popular music is generally served and driven by feeding and distilling *creativity*. As we acknowledge this, we need to ask: are students learning what is most likely to support their development as creative artists? Classical, jazz and popular music pedagogues all have certain values, fundamentals and 'must-learns' in their minds. As teachers, our natural, first reflex is to get students to follow our own musical values and learn the 'fundamentals'. But pop students consume, compose, create, absorb and enjoy music differently from how we did at their age, and for pop students in particular, the music business has changed completely, giving rise to a volatile new world in which young musicians must strive to monetize their efforts on their own.

Explore, love, create

What twenty-first-century students of popular music are doing is *exploring* what they love: via YouTube, streaming services or any platform that is available, generally for free. One of the most starkly innovative and forward-thinking composer/performers of our time, Pat Metheny, says this: 'What you love is an incredibly accurate compass that lives inside of you, telling you what you should be doing' (cited in Niles 2009: 93). A fundamental thing I have learned from being a popular music educator is indeed that it is not about teaching something that *I* love, it is more about learning more about what the students love, and getting them to love it more and love it more broadly.

So, do institutions of higher music education give students enough opportunities to explore and work on the music that *they* love? Pop students can listen to more music in one weekend than we listened to in an entire summer when we were their age – music that has just been produced and posted on an array of formats. They have unprecedented access to a staggering mass and variety of musical experiences, with thousands of genres at their fingertips (the website everynoise.com offers a terrific overview). Conservatories do not take this into account as much as they could. In contemporary popular music, 'rules' are constantly changing, and with the media that students have at their fingertips, they can spend *all* of their time following what is new; ingesting, learning from, stealing from and disseminating the intoxicating *current* music from all over the world.

As young artists start making their own music, their creativity and passion are no longer as likely as before to be 'managed' by teachers, record companies or agents who may be a generation or two older. They can freely develop and excel as independent artists in a world of performers, recordists, media and marketing channels, DIY careers and entrepreneurial activity. A conservatory approach that supports the ingrained assumption that young newcomers can only grow by learning from those who have accumulated experience – a gerontocratic paradigm – cannot take popular artists to where they need to be in a mercurial music business that changes (often predatorily) all the time. Popular music practices do not rule out tradition, but they often confront more rigid traditionalism, much as young people have always questioned older generations. This is healthy, and it makes for good art. Popular music also challenges the idea that commercial success is incompatible with quality and originality. Popular musicians can deploy exceptional skill, craft and creativity as they unapologetically search for songs and sounds that can hit an approving response from a massive consumer audience and engage with corporate marketing, promotion, distribution and profit.

Finding one's own way: A lesson from flamenco

Young musicians must often follow their instinct on where to go in order to learn what they need to learn. This is nothing new. One of my first close friendships as a student at the University of Southern California was with Chris, an eccentric DMA classical guitar student and irreverent character assassin with a well-honed cynicism in regard to convention. As part of his doctoral research, Chris had just completed a Fulbright scholarship in Madrid where he, as many others, was encouraged to study the genesis of contrapuntal guitar composition through the Spanish masters. He told me about his experience:

> I flew all the way to Spain and walked into the Madrid library and glanced around the research desks, and all I could see was a room full of snooty-looking college types with horn-rimmed glasses and emery-boarded guitar nails, just like me ... I then realized that the genesis of the modern classical guitar repertoire had probably been researched to death long before I got there. I was suddenly filled with a massive feeling of dread, malaise and loss of purpose. I left the library and drifted around the streets of Madrid, certain that what most of those 'researchers' were up to was academic box-ticking. I needed a beer and a think. Following sounds into a side street, I found the most incredible guitar playing I had ever heard: gitano flamenco artists, busking away in a pub. I felt my soul coming back to me. After talking with some of the artists for a few hours I came up with a plan: I bought the biggest chunk of hashish that I could find and used it to bribe the flamenco troupe to allow me to join their tour, play fourth guitar and pick up whatever I could in the next couple of weeks. I came down from the mountains where they lived just long enough to cash my Fulbright cheque and purchase more 'supplies' for my new friends and teachers.

When Chris came back to Los Angeles, he quickly became recognized as one of the finer flamenco guitarists in the area. He had acquired that elusive depth, passion and cultural magic that are essential in flamenco guitar performance. A clash of educational concepts had brought together the pinnacle of the conservatory tradition, the prestigious Fulbright programme and the 2000-year gitano tradition of learning completely by rote. Nobody could have designed or recommended this unorthodox, transformative learning experience in advance. But ask other flamenco artists and they will talk about the same things: one *must* live in the caves, eat the paella, drink the wine and learn everything by ear, this is *their* tradition.

In conservatories that have developed into strong archival environments, talented and freethinking young musicians like Chris run the risk of feeling that they are being sapped of their vitality. What physical, social, cultural and musical experiences and contexts do they need in order to feel their souls coming back to them? How can formal education support their desire to follow amazing sounds into side streets? Can formative years in higher education help them learn how deep connections are born between musicians and between musicians and their live or online audiences?

233

Exploration as learning

What has brought success to many of my students is sometimes at odds with their conservatory education. Their daily workload may look quite different from what they were trained for. They are immersed in cultures and subcultures of their own; their work is adaptive, not instrument-based, they learn how to serve a song or the situation. They are enthusiastic about business classes, handle technology well, and are generally very skilled at networking and at branding themselves. Outstanding graduates often have clear views of what was substance and what was fluff in their education. My frank and open dialogue with them has been essential to guiding how I teach. Learning from our graduates and other young people who are successfully adapting to and engaging the music world of the present is crucial, for their paths may have included important elements that need to be addressed more strongly in the classroom.

In a music world where entire popular genres and subgenres are created over weekends, we have to be careful as teachers and curriculum builders not to reproduce gerontocratic teaching methods that have worked well for classical and jazz students but may underserve the pop community. Like our students, we must keep experimenting, asking and changing. It is clear that in the 2020s, students of popular music view and use the 'conservatory' curriculum and culture quite differently from how both jazz and classical musicians have viewed and used it. Continuous dialogue and creative thinking are needed in order to find what serves students best and helps them find their own way. For many educators, new practices and expectations are bringing with them plenty of *unexplored* territory. We need to engage our instincts, our research and especially our listening skills to work effectively with each new generation, and we need to assist evolution alongside our students to transform and expand our fundamental approach from that of conservatory to one of *exploratory*.

ACKNOWLEDGEMENTS
The author wish to thank Dr. Cecilia Björck, Åbo Akademi University, Finland, whose keen collaborative sense, inspiring dialogue and clear thinking made this chapter possible. Many thanks also to Dr. Christofer Ashby, who continues to be a source of unorthodox and relevant perspective in a constantly changing musical world.

REFERENCE
Niles, Richard (2009), *The Pat Metheny Interviews*, New York: Hal Leonard Books.

43

Is Higher Popular Music Education Still Relevant?

Gemma Hill

Gemma Hill is a drummer, music educator, translator and former editor of Drummer magazine, who now works for GEWA Drums in Germany.

In this chapter, the author discusses her experiences of and perspective on the relevance of a traditional popular music education when the digital world plays an ever-increasing role in our lives. She draws on experiences of education in the South of England, living in Europe and working across the globe.

About me

My views on this topic are primarily as a drummer and percussionist who has 'studied' in the traditional sense that I took graded exams on my instruments from childhood, studied music A Level[1] at school, went to a music college to get a music degree (in contemporary popular music) and have taken lessons with various instrumental teachers from early childhood to the present day. Ever since graduating from music college, I have worked in the music industry in a variety of ways: as a touring musician, peripatetic teacher, editor of a drum magazine and now as a translator for a German company that distributes and produces musical instruments globally. For me, my 'traditional' route has been extremely beneficial but there are many other non-traditional factors that have helped me along the way. Because of these factors and the amount of educational content that is available online, often even cost-free, I wonder how relevant a traditional popular music education is nowadays and for the future.

Traditional and non-traditional popular music education

What has my traditional music education given me? It taught me how to play using techniques that mean I don't injure myself, how to read and write music notation, how to practice in a disciplined way, how to sight read, how to pitch notes, knowledge of other instruments, how to arrange music and how to approach difficulties on my instruments so that I can overcome them with success. It taught me how to play and appreciate different genres of music, how to work and collaborate with other musicians, how to teach, how to critique music performance, how to write about music in a scholarly way, how to meet deadlines and targets, and about the importance of networking. It gave me an official piece of paper from a recognized institution that said I was qualified in my chosen art-form. That piece of paper has been surprisingly helpful; sometimes, people still want paperwork as proof that you can do something to a certain standard.

What are the 'non-traditional' factors that I mentioned? The main one for me was the art of networking, which I only learned once I got myself 'out there' and amongst other musicians, and which I think has changed in nature over the years. A successful session musician who runs his own session musician agency once told me how he used to drive around London handing out his business card along with the CVs and cassette demos of the musicians he could offer for hire to record labels. Networking is still arguably best done in person, but the internet does give us the chance to instantly make contact with people all over the world, without the effort that was required even ten or twenty years ago.

The more connections I made, the more work I got, which snowballed and has given me sustained contacts and friendships for decades. This networking has involved contacting well-known musicians by email and asking for their advice (without pestering or being a nuisance) and in some cases, offering my help to them in exchange for me picking their brains or getting to know them. In fact, probably the most significant non-traditional factor has been to offer help or a favour to people as often as the situation arises. I've found that people have remembered this for years to come and have thought of me or picked me for a job solely based on me helping them before. Being a positive person brings you more positivity, but that isn't something that can be taught; you have to work on it yourself. Reaching out to other musicians for lessons, especially in areas that you don't feel comfortable in, is another way, as is sharing your own knowledge.

Touring, how to behave with other people on tour, and tips for doing the best possible job on tour, are also non-traditional factors. I found that these weren't covered in my popular music education in school, but I learnt them as I went along with each job. This involved me asking questions of people who had specialist knowledge in areas such as electronics and sound engineering. Having practical knowledge around a band's setup was an advantage so that I could assist my band-mates if necessary, or even just be able to join in conversations to feel included in the band.

Popular music education online and in person

What is available online now that might replace a traditional popular music educa-tion? Content and contacts. You can learn anything from anyone, anywhere in the world. It can range from accredited online courses with curricular material to one-to-one online tuition from musicians of your choice, or practice tips on social media such as Instagram Stories. Social media means we can contact just about anyone in the world and ask questions or make connections. You don't even need to be in the same room as another musician to work with them and create music anymore; session musicians can work from their home studio (which might just be a laptop) and send recordings to other musicians, producers or an audience; Ash Soan, one of the UK's most highly sought-after session drummers, readily talks about working from his own home drum studio, which is a renovated windmill. Stems recorded there can be heard all over the world on chart-topping albums, without the need for Ash and his drums to travel anywhere.

The COVID-19 pandemic lockdowns have meant that bands, choirs and orchestras have sought ways to make music together simultaneously online, using group video platforms such as Zoom to create music together from afar. Perhaps our online existence (and COVID-19 health restrictions) will eventually grow so big that we won't play music together at all anymore, meaning that musicians will have to be taught how to play together in the same space.

A large (and it was considered as 'cutting-edge' at the time) part of my degree course was advice about promoting yourself via a website and creating your own 'brand' as a musician. While I believe a website still looks professional and can still be relevant, you can instantly promote yourself and your skills online now via social media. You can even target an audience and achieve a type of recogni-tion that simply wasn't possible in previous decades, without TV and radio. An example of this is Luke Holland; a drummer who created a YouTube profile for his drum covers and remixes. According to his Wikipedia page, his page had more than 55 million views between 2009 and 2016. In 2019, he toured Europe as a special guest with progressive rock giants, Dream Theater.

What isn't available online? The physical experiences of playing, studying and socializing with other musicians, which are perhaps the most important factors of all. These can still be achieved outside of a traditional popular music education; all you need to do is put in the effort to find ways of achieving them, for example, by attending jam nights, writing and recording music in collaboration with other musicians, taking lessons or advice from other musicians, etc.

While there is still a need for live music (let's hope that survives and thrives!) then there is still a need for musicians to be able to play together live. You can't achieve that by playing on your own in your room to backing tracks or videos online; the skillset for playing live has to be practised and nurtured through live experiences of making music, forming bonds and being humans together with other musicians.

Depending on your desired outcome, I don't think it is necessary to have a traditional music education in order to have a successful career in popular music. It does depend on the individual, their drive and their ability to arm themselves with the necessary tools and skills to work in popular music, but everything is available online and on the 'real' live music scene to be able to connect and prepare oneself for work as a professional musician. In certain fields, such as education, qualifications are almost always advisable to have and therefore, a traditional type of music education will also still be relevant and important for years to come.

NOTE

1. 'A Levels' or 'Advanced Levels' are, in the United Kingdom (except Scotland), qualifications in a specific subject typically taken by school students aged 16–18, at a level above GCSE (General Certificate of Secondary Education).

44

Music Teacher Education in the United States is Failing its Students

Candice Davenport Mattio

Candice Davenport Mattio is assistant professor of music teaching and learning at the University of Southern California's Thornton School of Music.

This chapter draws on the author's experiences as a school and university educator to bring attention to ways in which collegiate music education programmes in the United States are still failing most students by not broadly embracing popular and contemporary music approaches.

Barriers to pursuing popular music in higher education in the United States

Early in my secondary school music teaching career, like many of my colleagues, I relied on the traditional 'standards' of repertoire – the western classics with the occasional institutionalized folk or jazz tune lightly sprinkled throughout. I chose these plans and content not only because I was a novice teacher eager for quick materials but also because this was the content I knew from my training and felt most comfortable teaching. Yet my classrooms, composed mostly of Black students from Chicago's grossly underserved West Side, were largely passive, disinterested and even annoyed. The eyerolls and intentionally audible sighs were constant reminders that I was not engaging them. I knew I had to find a way to create meaningful and enjoyable music education experiences for my students. Music speaks to all of us in different ways, and I desperately needed to make those connections. As time went on, I quickly saw the benefits of incorporating popular music into my curriculum. The students seemed more enthusiastic and invested in their learning and were genuinely interested in what I was teaching.

Although I was experiencing wonderful success and felt an invigoration and renewed passion for teaching, this brought about a new revelation, and one that has deeply troubled me throughout both my secondary public school and higher education teaching careers. One day, several of my most eager students approached me for advice about college majors. These students were brilliant at songwriting, beat-making, production and performing of popular music styles. They fought so many personal battles every day, and music was keeping them in school. They ate music for every meal and breathed it into everything they did. Many wanted to study music in college; some even wanted to teach it!

My insides churned and the hope drained from their faces as I explained the reality of music programmes in colleges in the United States. I explained the landscape of majors, the typical barriers to entry, and expectations of largely classical traditions for which music scholarships are often given. I began to further question my own teaching philosophies and approaches, and whether or not I had done my students a disservice by not forcing a western traditionally focused curriculum down their throats. Had I made an egregious mistake? Did I ruin their futures? Was public school the end of the road for my students who wanted to study music? Is it still the end of the road for most students who do not fit into the mould of Eurocentric traditional paradigms? Years later, when I checked in with one of my former students, Aaron, I discovered that he had pursued a degree in Visual Arts Education, and not in music like he wanted. Aaron explained, 'I really wanted to be a music teacher like you. But I make and edit music on my laptop and can't play another instrument well. No one was going to let me into a music school on a laptop'.

Unfortunately, these situations have not changed much over the past decade (Powell et al. 2019; Larson 2019). Although school music educators are rapidly embracing the movement to incorporate popular music approaches, collegiate music programmes in the United States continue to exist in a bubble of largely classical traditions, holding fast to the archaic barriers to entry and fulfilment. With few exceptions, student applicants are still expected to sight-read western notation and demonstrate sufficient performance skills on classical instruments, in largely classical styles. Even instruments that 'cross over' into more contemporary styles, such as guitar, are funnelled through the classical approaches. Any sense of informal learning practice is lost, and inherently considered unacceptable. Many higher education scholars have argued for the importance of popular music's use, and even problematized the disparity between generalized support for popular music and evidence of its inclusion in music teacher education curricula (Tobias and Barrett 2010). Yet, the vast majority of higher education programmes continue to fixate on the longstanding classical traditions as barriers to access:

> Contemporary musical practices beyond the academy are often centered on creative, cross-cultural engagement and synthesis emblematic of the societies in which those practices flourish; yet contemporary, tertiary-level music study (with interpretive performance and analysis of European classical repertory at its center) remains lodged in a cultural aesthetic, and pedagogical paradigm that is notably out of step with this broader reality.
>
> (Sarath et al. 2017: 55)

A crisis in higher education

Beyond these extreme limitations within collegiate music programmes, higher education in the United States is considered by many to be in a state of crisis. Over the past few decades, cuts in funding for education have caused the cost of college tuition to increase faster than any other goods or services, creating a staggering financial burden of over $1.5 trillion (Friedman 2019). Socially, a general shift in perception of economic value has generated higher demands for industry-focused career training and less demand for a liberal arts education that is often integrated with university matriculation. These stressors, along with intertwined trends in technology development, politics, funding and other issues are pushing for educational reform that requires the academy to be open to new approaches to teaching and learning (Blumenstyk 2015). It would be naïve to think college music programmes are immune from this dilemma. From both economical and moral perspectives, if music programmes are to be more financially self-sufficient and endure these societal shifts, it behooves those of us working in that domain to be more inclusive and responsive to the students being born of these shifts in the school music paradigms. Many also argue that the collegiate system amplifies class, racial and income inequities (Blumenstyk 2015; Smith 2019). Are music programmes exacerbating these issues and questions of relevancy through maintaining an exclusive and singularly classical elitist approach?

A need for change in higher music education

It is well overdue that we revamp higher education approaches to music studies and echo the movements for inclusivity, relevancy and the elimination of systematic inequities being championed by our school music programmes. One major step towards achieving these goals is by authentically and equally embracing the integration of popular music education as valid within the larger higher education paradigm (Larson 2019). The refusal to do so is to blatantly choose a slow but inevitable death as higher education programmes, particularly those in the arts, continue to face serious crises due to rising tuition costs, challenging employment demands and questions of equity, worth and value (Larson 2019; Smith 2019).

This is by no means to suggest that the currently institutionalized approaches to music are not valuable. In fact, the opposite is true. But some argue that the current manner in which collegiate programmes herald the interpretive performance specialization of music of another time is, in fact, antithetical to the classical tradition: 'From this standpoint, the longstanding conventional model of music study in vogue throughout tertiary programmes actually represents a departure away from the European classical tradition' (Sarath et al. 2017: 55). So why then are classical approaches (with some smattering of institutionalized jazz styles) considered the only acceptable boxes to tick in order to receive a collegiate music education? What are we, as the gatekeepers to college music studies, saying to students like mine, when we close the door on the music they do, love, and with which they deeply identify? Is their music not valuable? Not worthy? Are *they* then not valuable or worthy?

Fortunately, higher education has not been completely avoidant of popular music education. Institutions in the United States increasingly offer some form of popular or contemporary music programmes. However, most of these programmes are in private institutions with exorbitant tuition costs and highly selective enrolment, raising the barrier to access for the students most often served by popular music education currently in schools. To further exacerbate the issue, the integration of popular and contemporary music within these programmes varies greatly, particularly for those majoring in music education. Some programmes allow students to study with a mix of classical and contemporary foci, while others require applications to demonstrate classical training on a primary instrument and *then* are allowed to pick up a contemporary minor focus. For various reasons, even schools that offer a popular or contemporary programme may not always 'play nicely' with music education (and vice versa), and thus remain separate entities.

Despite the struggles described, higher education is slowly beginning to experience sprinklings of change, and an apprehensive embracing of the popular music education movement. Organizations such as the Association for Popular Music Education and its conferences, the introduction of the *Journal of Popular Music Education,* the addition of Popular Music Education as Special Research Interest Group (SRIG) at the US National Association for Music Education (NAfME), a Special Interest Group (SIG) at the International Society for Music Education (ISME) and the Modern Band Higher Education Fellowship and Colloquium (sponsored by Little Kids Rock) in the United States have allowed a home for scholars interested in creating change through popular music education. These organizations and events are a credit to their founders and board members and provide a sense of legitimacy and safe spaces of exploration for a growing cohort of practitioners and scholars. Unfortunately, while the research is expanding, it is not enough on its own to change the cultures of college music programmes. Our conversations still, like all areas of specialization in higher education, exist in silos. Unfortunately, changes must also be made at the institutional level, both in terms of curriculum and culture, in order to truly integrate themselves into our programmes.

As the primary training space for the future classroom music teachers in the United States, music education (teacher licensure) programmes are primed for disrupting longstanding norms in higher education. Unfortunately, collegiate programmes, due to reasons beyond the scope of this chapter, generally tend to lag severely behind with regards to curricular change, while shifts in cultures and philosophical stances may take decades. But what if colleges were more responsive to what is happening in school music education? Instead of waiting for teachers like myself to 'figure it out the hard way', imagine the opportunities afforded when popular and contemporary music approaches are embraced in undergraduate training! Imagine the diversity, cultural representation and relevance (not to mention skill sets) of future music educators if those, like my former students, were given a chance to study music in college. What if we were to invite the 'Aarons' of the world to explore music with us, by truly embracing popular music education in the academies? What a world that would be!

REFERENCES

Blumenstyk, Goldie (2015), *American Higher Education in Crises? What Everyone Needs to Know*, New York: Oxford University Press.

Friedman, Zack (2019), 'Student loan debt statistics in 2019: A $1.5 trillion crisis', *Forbes*, 25 February, https://www.forbes.com/sites/zackfriedman/2019/02/25/student-loan-debt-statistics-2019/#2a9545f5133f. Accessed 7 June 2020.

Larson, Robert (2019), 'Popular music in higher education: Finding the balance', *College Music Symposium*, 59:2, pp. 1–14, https://www.jstor.org/stable/26902589. Accessed 3 June 2020.

Powell, Bryan, Smith, Gareth Dylan, West, Chad and Kratus, John (2019), 'Popular music education: A call to action', *Music Educators Journal*, 106:1, pp. 21–24, https://doi.org/10.1177/0027432119861528. Accessed 7 June 2020.

Sarath, Edward W., Myers, David E. and Campbell, Patricia S. (2017), *Redefining Music Studies in An Age of Change: Creativity, Diversity, and Integration*, New York: Routledge.

Smith, Clint (2019), 'Elite colleges constantly tell low-income students that they do not belong', *The Atlantic*, 18 March, https://www.theatlantic.com/education/archive/2019/03/privileged-poor-navigating-elite-university-life/585100/. Accessed 3 June 2020.

Tobias, Evan and Barrett, Janet (2010), 'Counterpoint or remix? A dialogue on popular music and popular culture in music teacher education', in M. Schmidt (ed.), *Collaborative Action for Change: Selected Proceedings from the 2007 Symposium on Music Teacher Education*, Lanham: Rowman & Littlefield, pp. 35–50.

45

Imagining a Credential for Music Technology Education

Daniel Walzer

Daniel Walzer is assistant professor of music and arts technology at Indiana University-Purdue University Indianapolis and co-author (with Dr. Mariana Lopez) of *Audio Education: Theory, Culture, and Practice.*

This chapter explores the possibility of a specialized teaching credential in music technology education (MTE) leading to licensure in the United States. By considering interdisciplinary learning possibilities and emerging digital literacies, the author challenges educators to imagine MTE as a fully realized academic field.

Introduction

Music Technology Education (MTE) is a field without a formal teaching credential. Unlike music education, in which undergraduates prepare for teaching exams and licensure, MTE is a growing area still finding its pedagogical feet. Currently, instructors working in MTE draw on multifaceted backgrounds in music education, music performance, audio engineering, composition and STEM. Triaging music, technology and education as separate entities ostensibly makes perfect sense. Each area draws on art and science, blends theory and practice, and leads to knowledge exchange between different communities. I envision a scenario where music technology education is a complete academic field with its own teaching credential and not just a niche-specific area of study. Accomplishing this vision requires a shift in thinking, philosophy and imagination.

MTE has advanced since Boehm (2005) problematized the proportionality of music and technology more than a decade ago. At the time, music technology suffered from a lack of brand recognition. Boehm questioned how much 'music' and 'technology' constituted a university credential. Advances in teaching, delivery formats and technologies provide instructors today with a plethora of options. The literature on popular music education and assessment in music education grow each year. The obstacle here is that no one seems to position music technology education as a field deserving of its own space. It is as if subject hierarchies have deemed music, technology and education as ubiquitous, and the field of *music technology education* as a subset of music technology or music education ... or perhaps vocational and technology education.

Why does all this matter? Isn't it enough that the three words 'music technology education' live peacefully in existing domains? Is it necessary to navel-gaze and worry about an issue of semantics? Is it not sufficient to recognize the expertise and be done with it? Does the academic community need another credential to validate understanding in a 'new' specialized field? A credential in music technology education is only as valuable as the community that recognizes the knowledge gained during the learning process and after completion. Investing time and resources into building a programme and coursework is a considerable undertaking. Putting aside the more prominent, philosophical issue of what music technology education *might* be, using an imaginative framework, the more practical issue involves a cost-benefit analysis of the credential. Also, analyzing the relationship between music technology education and the growing popular music education field is warranted.

Changing fluencies in music technology education

One advantage of a music technology education credential would be that it would recognize changing literacies in popular music and culture. Competence in music-making, of all kinds, need not overlook playing an instrument, performing as a singer or composing (Tobias 2012). The literacies need not be confined to a definition of reading and writing a notated score. Perhaps a better word than *literacies* is *fluencies*. A credential in music technology education could more closely scrutinize fluencies to include those specific to technology but not *only* utilized with technology.

Another possible advantage of imagining a credential in music technology education is that it would expand canonical possibilities for theory and practice. An MTE critical listening pathway ought to include a deeper immersion into contemporary musical styles. Of course, 'contemporary' is open to interpretation, as is 'popular'. The harmonic possibilities of contemporary classical, jazz and Afro-Cuban music would find a home alongside the rhythmic and production-specific analyses of hip-hop, EDM and styles yet to be discovered. Moreover, if the canon were to expand to include work by more women, composers of colour, LGBTQ+ and gender-non-binary composers, then the listening lists would become more balanced and representative of the diverse world in which our students live; decolonizing the curriculum opens up more opportunities for participation and inclusion.

Listening, composing, written expression and performance (see Butler 2014; Katz 2004) can and do peacefully co-exist. Learning to 'play laptop' or honing expertise on a sampler need not replace the hours spent learning to play an instrument or perfecting the singing voice. The difference from traditional, acoustic forms of music making that I propose, is that of a 'both/and' possibility, rather than an 'either/or' conception. In other words, a philosophy of music technology education that already draws influence from music education by prioritizing creativity, enjoyment, individual and group interaction and technical proficiency. The other significant difference is that faculty members might be drawn from the popular music industry, and guide students to a deeper understanding of music-making possibilities with technology at the fore.

A moment of reflection

Perhaps the most disquieting aspect of this discussion is that as a community, educators might need to look deeply to see if we are truly engaging the broadest population that we can. Do social justice and inclusion inform our curricular and pedagogical choices, or are these decisions rooted in the status quo, neoliberalism and privilege? We can only better understand these issues if we engage in honest conversations with each other.

As noted above, imagining a credential in music technology education starts with considering the balance of human ingenuity, technological mediation, artistic expression and how these elements advance learning. Equally important is ascertaining what the knowledge in music technology education is, both practically and theoretically. In this case, knowledge production must be evaluated outside of a solely technocratic framework and replaced by a more holistic understanding of knowledge that balances the artistic and creative aspects of music, the cognitive aspects of education, and the applied science of technology.

Conclusion

What I am getting at is a richer conception of how the integration of music, technology and education work with each other in contemporary pedagogical matters. The philosophical aim underlying my vision for a credential in music technology education would be fundamentally praxial. The discussion centres on how learners interact with technology, utilize technology, become influenced by technology and produce technologically-mediated output. Instead of seeing technology as a supplement to music-making, technology *is a part* of the musical experience. The skills learned using technology, teaching with technology, performing with technology and composing with technology are similar to the broader academic parts of a music degree – again, with technology as an indispensable aspect of teaching, learning and expression.

Creating an MTE credential would rely heavily on the expertise, contexts and input of local and regional partners. Just as music education curricula are generally prescriptive (e.g. methods courses, conducting, history, ensembles, musicianship, keyboard), MTE degrees might open up the possibilities of a technology-*informed* musicianship using laptops, controllers, DJ equipment and multimedia. In Walzer (2016, 2019, 2020), I describe how educators can build multimedia literacies by incorporating Digital Storytelling (DST) into existing history, 'tech survey' courses and group projects. Other possibilities include teaching opportunities outside of school music contexts. Field experiences might consist of teaching both online and in community programmes. Likewise, MTE might extend its focus on STEM integration, community outreach, and sustainability partnerships and include courses on technology and society's history. History and theory courses might consist of media literacy, theory and popular culture to broaden sociocultural relevance. These are just a few options and could be tailored to fit an institution's needs.

A credential in music technology education ought to give focus to the sociocultural factors that influence how technology is used across different age groups, races, cultures and parts of the world. Perhaps it is not the credential itself that I am most concerned with, but rather a desire to see the fields of music, technology and education combine their assets. I also wish to see the discussion on these matters move forward, and in posing the questions in this essay I take the opportunity to contribute to that dialogue.

REFERENCES

Boehm, Carola (2005), 'Music technology in higher education', *Probing the Boundaries of Higher Education*, 12:1, pp. 85–90.

Butler, Mark (2014), *Playing with Something that Runs: Technology, Improvisation, and Composition in DJ and Laptop Performance*, Oxford: Oxford University Press.

Katz, Mark (2004), *Capturing Sound: How Technology has Changed Music*, Berkley: University of California Press.

Tobias, Evan S. (2012), 'Hybrid spaces and hyphenated musicians: Secondary students' musical engagement in a songwriting and technology course', *Music Education Research*, 14:3, pp. 329–46, https://doi.org/10.1080/14613808.2012.685459. Accessed 5 February 2022.

Walzer, Daniel (2016), 'Digital storytelling in music and audio education: Inspiring modern reflective practice with relevant technology', *TOPICS for Music Education Praxis*, 3, pp. 46–76, http://topics.maydaygroup.org/articles/2016/Walzer2016.pdf. Accessed 5 February 2022.

Walzer, Daniel (2019), 'Digital storytelling, reflective teacher inquiry, and student learning: Action research via media technology', in Z. Moir, B. Powell and G. D. Smith (eds), *The Bloomsbury Handbook of Popular Music Education: Perspectives and Practices*, London: Bloomsbury, pp. 429–40, https://www.bloomsbury.com/us/the-bloomsbury-handbook-of-popular-music-education-9781350049437/. Accessed 5 February 2022.

Walzer, Daniel (2020), 'Twenty-first-century implications for media literacy and music education', in J. Waldron, J. S. Horsley and K. Veblen (eds), *The Oxford Handbook of Social Media and Music Learning*, Oxford: Oxford University Press, pp. 1–21, https://doi.org/10.1093/oxfordhb/9780190660772.013.8. Accessed 5 February 2022.

46

The Price of Admission: Amateurism, Serious Leisure and the Faculty Band

Virginia Wayman Davis

Virginia Wayman Davis is a professor of music education at the University of Texas Rio Grande Valley, USA. She teaches general music education and popular music.

In this chapter, the author reflects on how academic professors embraced amateur music-making by learning popular music instruments and performing among students in their South Texas community. By approaching music with beginners' eyes, we (re)discovered how important it can be – and how good it can feel – to do something badly.

In the fall of 2019, I finally succeeded in doing something I'd been fantasizing about for years: starting a faculty pop/rock band at my university. My faculty band, appropriately named The Minör Revisiöns (requisite röck umlauts and all), is made up of 'academic' faculty: two music theorists, a musicologist, a philosophy professor and me, a professor of music education. The only non-professor band member was a graduate student, a guitarist and music educator. The fact that the band is made up of music scholars is significant because this band is not (in either conception or reality) a polished, professional-sounding group of seasoned experts. Although we may have entered the field as performers, we now spend most of our professional lives listening, analyzing, writing and talking about music while finding that we may go days and weeks at a stretch without playing a note! This band represented a way to both return to our roots as performers while also trying something new – approaching new musical instruments and genres as amateurs.

Amateurism (or *amateuring*, as coined by Booth [1999] and extended by Regelski 2007) is an approach to an activity which emphasizes a 'vigorous, demanding human pursuit practiced for the love of the pursuit itself rather than for any practical use or payoff' (10). Far from indicating a lack of ability or a careless approach to the activity, amateuring instead embodies what Kratus (2019) reminds us is the original etymology of the word, 'the Latin *amator*, meaning "lover"' (32).

In this spirit of amateuring, we gathered in an empty classroom and picked up instruments that, for most of us, were unfamiliar. A music theorist who could play a few chords strapped on an electric guitar. A percussionist taught a musicologist and a theorist how to play bass and drums. A philosophy professor dusted off his keyboard. And while my primary instrument is percussion, I sat down behind a drum kit (similar in nature to classical percussion while also being worlds away), continuing on my yearlong journey of (re)discovering what, if any, chops I may possess (Davis 2018). I also stepped up to the vocal mic, as did several of my colleagues.

We looked fantastic. We sounded terrible. We kept playing. As we did, we tried to remind ourselves that learning, not perfection, was the goal. Andrés,[1] musicologist and fledgling bassist and drummer, found 'the idea of amateurism both challenging and comforting. I enjoy being a beginner. I enjoy the "pass" it gives me for making mistakes and growing' (Amado 2019: n.pag.). As Chesterton famously noted, 'if a thing is worth doing, it is worth doing badly' (1912: 320). The musical output of those first jam sessions was very, very bad yet we experienced a curious pleasure at slowly, painstakingly rooting out each difficulty and helping each other correct it. Rachel, theorist and horn player transformed into guitarist and singer, noted that 'until I started attending regular rehearsals again, I didn't realize how much I missed playing in a group, making music, and sharing that experience with others' (Mann 2019: n.pag.). We occupied a unique place along the continuum of amateur and professional (Kaplan 1956): professionals, yes, but not on these instruments; not at this genre of music; not in this informal, conductor-less structure.

Noted Andrés, 'approximating a good performance can be both frustrating (as we realize we are falling short) and exhilarating (as we realize we are getting close)' (Amado 2019: n.pag.). Stebbins (1982) described this phenomenon using the wonderfully oxymoronic phrase, 'serious leisure' (251). The word 'serious' in this case refers to qualities such as sincerity and carefulness, rather than joylessness or solemnity as well as 'the occasional need to persevere at it' (Stebbins 1982: 256). Even at the (almost certain) risk of public and professional embarrassment, we persevered and did so more than occasionally – paying, in a phrase I borrow from advice columnist Savage, 'the price of admission' (2013: 56). Loosely defined, the price of admission is what you are willing to put up with in order to obtain the thing you want. Sounding terrible is the price of admission to the possible future one imagines (Henley 2016). Frustration is the price of admission. Embarrassment is the price of admission.

But *why* do we amateurs persist, keep paying that price of admission? Numerous researchers have found that amateur musicking by adults can impart numerous social and musical rewards (Jellison 2000; Kaplan 1963), but working together at something like music just *feels* good. Regelski referred to these benefits as '*good time*, not in the sense of effortless or spontaneous fun ... but in the sense of time well spent, even where it requires strenuous effort!' (2007: 31, orginal emphasis). Noted Rachel:

> It would be expected that after only three months of learning, our performance would not be perfect; it would likely be dirty, gritty, grungy, maybe even a bit off-kilter. The great thing about [it] is that this is all ultimately ok.
>
> (Mann 2019: n.pag.)

As the date of our first gig approached, the thought of a public performance was both exciting and alarming. Challenges, such as a rehearsal schedule that could be attended by six busy adults, were everywhere. I also discovered that it was much easier to allow imperfection in others than in myself. Andrés, too, noticed a change in tone from lowkey experimentation to goal-oriented rehearsal, though he didn't find it to be a negative:

> Once we had a gig and we were preparing for a performance I feel the dynamic changed a bit, for me personally. I started treating the band with the formality I would treat any other ensemble [...] This didn't make rehearsals any less fun, since part of the enjoyment of playing music is also to create a musically satisfactory experience. I tried to apply my professionalism and musical training more seriously, and I enjoyed the results.
>
> (Amado 2019: n.pag.)

Between rehearsals, we kept up a constant stream of chatter through e-mails and group texts, enjoying the camaraderie and the deepening of existing friendships as well as the break from our professional roles and responsibilities, also noted by Regelski (2007) and Booth (1999) among others. According to philosophy professor and keyboardist Anthony, 'it's such a nice respite from the constant totally-cerebral grind of my academic work' (De Santis 2019: n.pag.). We were keeping *good time*, even though sour notes and dropped beats; every time we rehearsed, we found 'band member' was developing as an important feature of our identities (Henley 2016; Rathunde and Isabella 2016) alongside 'scholar', 'music professor' and others. We began to talk up the group, starting sentences with 'So, I'm in this rock band ...'

Many colleagues seemed bemused, a few reeked disapproval, but why did this feel so subversive? We were just making music in a School of Music, after all. Still, the activity did have the sensation of going against the grain some-how. Mid-semester, some faculty adjacent to our rehearsal room complained about the 'noise', forcing our department head to barter a compromise stating that popular music ensembles could practice only after 3 p.m. and on week-ends. (One of my student bands cheekily responded by naming their group 'Not Until After Three'.) Kratus (2019) would likely not be surprised, noting that 'in many collegiate music buildings, strumming a guitar and singing a song can get you kicked out of a practice room' (35). Luckily, I can confirm that this is most definitely not the case at my institution (as long as it is after 3 p.m.).

This tension between the old guard and more inclusive practices is common. Collegiate music programmes face ongoing pressure to change with the times but remain resistant (Moore 2018). Not all faculty resist: according to Rachel,

> I've already shared what I've learned in my own classroom; I have found myself drawing connections between chord progressions of rock songs I've learned and musical examples from the common-practice period, and I plan to use more rock band examples in my ear training courses as well.
>
> (Mann 2019: n.pag.)

Rock bands and pop progressions in theory class are not enough to trigger wide-spread change, however. In order to successfully transition tertiary music study into the twenty-first century, the only solution may be a complete re-design that de-centres western classical music and instead focuses on amateuring.

And indeed, on a balmy South Texas night in early December, four bands of varying experience took to the stage in front of 50 or so students, colleagues, family members and friends in a joyful celebration of communal music making. If success in this endeavour is defined by the feeling of playing music with friends on stage, the laugh-ter between sets, and the pleasurable exhaustion afterward (and I believe it is), then our first attempt at pop music as serious leisure was wildly successful. Recalls Andrés:

> A student came up to me after the performance and engaged me in conversation for several minutes. Evidently, our performance shattered many of his preconceptions of what it means to be a professor, a music scholar, and to learn and play music. He was puzzled, amazed, confused. 'I thought professors were always busy. How did you manage the time to learn to play a new instrument? And how did you get so proficient in only two months?' And then (hilariously), 'I had no idea you had a social life outside of school!'
>
> (Amado 2019: n.pag.)

The biggest success of the faculty band for me, though, was the feeling of break-ing down some of the barriers between the faculty and the students as all of us just wanted to enjoy the evening and make some music. Andrés agreed, recalling that after we played:

> [A]nother colleague (said) she cannot think of many institutions where students and teachers would create such an environment of equal partnership and collaboration as what she was witnessing. There's a special synergy between students and teachers that is hard to explain; the roles of teachers and students still exist, and they still honor those roles and pay the corresponding respect that go along with them, while also interacting in more equalitarian or less hierarchical ways.
>
> (Amado 2019: n.pag.)

And if that is the ultimate outcome of the experience, the payoff of all the effort, then for me it was absolutely worth the price of admission.

NOTE
1.   Band members' real names are used by permission.

REFERENCES

Amado, Andrés (2019), 'Re: Quotes', email received by Virginia Davis, 19 December.

Booth, Wayne C. (1999), *For the Love of It: Amateuring and Its Rivals*, Chicago: University of Chicago Press.

Chesterton, Gilbert K. (1912), *What's Wrong with the World*, London: Cassell.

Davis, Virginia W. (2018), 'Higher ed rocks: Don't fret the small stuff', *Journal of Popular Music Education*, 2:3, pp. 283–88.

De Santis, Anthony (2019), 'Re: Quotes', email received by Virginia Davis, 17 December.

Henley, Jennie (2016), 'The musical lives of self-confessed nonmusicians', in R. Mantie and G. D. Smith (eds), *The Oxford Handbook of Music Making and Leisure*, Oxford: Oxford University Press, pp. 203–22.

Jellison, Judith (2000), 'How can all people continue to be involved in meaningful music education?', in Clifford K. Madsen (ed.), *Vision 2020: The Housewright Symposium on the Future of Music Education*, Reston: MENC—The National Association for Music Education, pp. 109–37.

Kaplan, Max (1956), 'Music, community, and social change', *Music Educators Journal*, 43:1, pp. 64–67.

Kaplan, Max (1963), 'Music education and national goals', *Music Educators Journal*, 49:5, pp. 33–36.

Kratus, John (2019), 'A return to amateurism in music education', *Music Educators Journal*, 106:1, pp. 31–37.

Mann, Rachel (2019), 'Re: Quotes', email received by Virginia Davis, 20 December.

Rathunde, Kevin and Isabella, Russell (2016), 'Playing music and identity development in middle Adulthood', in R. Mantie and G. D. Smith (eds), *The Oxford Handbook of Music Making and Leisure*, Oxford: Oxford University Press, pp. 131–49.

Regelski, Thomas A. (2007), 'Amateuring in music and its rivals,' *Action, Criticism, and Theory for Music Education*, 6:3, pp. 22–50.

Savage, Daniel (2013), *American Savage: Insights, Slights, and Fights on Faith, Sex, Love, and Politics*, New York: Dutton.

Stebbins, Robert A. (1982), 'Serious leisure: A conceptual statement', *Pacific Sociological Review*, 25:2, pp. 251–72.

47

Vocal Diversity and Evolving Contemporary Voice Pedagogy

Ana Flavia Zuim

Ana Flavia Zuim is assistant music professor and director of vocal performance at NYU Steinhardt, New York, NY, USA, where she teaches graduate and undergraduate courses.

This chapter brings considerations for rethinking vocal pedagogy in a way that is inclusive of the vocal diversity it requires.

Introduction and context

The diversity found in contemporary vocal performance includes styles such as pop, rock, country, folk, R&B and others. This richness of genres has created a need for systematic and effective training across categories. However, the evolving academic field of vocal training currently in its infancy. Pedagogical considerations can help vocal teachers guide singers towards an optimal level of vocal coordination and promote vocal efficiency. Furthermore, an increased scientific understanding of style-specific vocal production can help the field destigmatize and decatastrophize voice injury among the contemporary voice population. Terminology used by vocal pedagogues can be confusing and misleading, both in regard to specific voice terms used during training, as well as in regard to the meaning of the words 'popular' and 'contemporary'. Contemporary commercial music (CCM) is the term most commonly used in the field, encompassing all contemporary commercial music including musical theatre. Currently, the majority of higher education voice programmes in the United States focus on classical voice studies. The majority of programmes that offer singing training in contemporary styles are geared towards training the musical theatre performer, with only a few focusing on the development of a sustainable technique for singing other contemporary and popular styles. The level of knowledge and experience among instructors varies widely among the few contemporary commercial musical pedagogy programmes that teach the full range of popular and contemporary commercial singing styles.

Considering that the field of contemporary voice in academia is still in its infancy, the majority of contemporary voice pedagogues learned how to teach these styles from experience or using methodologies and techniques passed on from person to person outside the academic setting. In a profession where credentialing is not required for opening a private voice studio, genre-specific instruction with a vocal pedagogue who received academic training in that genre can be hard to find. Consequently, students may seek out training from teachers with limited knowledge about the application of vocal pedagogy to a specific vocal genre. In a survey of university, high school and private voice instructors, Lovetri and Means found that 45 per cent of respondents who teach musical theatre did not have any specific pedagogical training in the genre (2003). It is not uncommon for training methodologies that are effective in one style/genre to be inappropriately generalised to another style/genre that requires a different tone quality and needs alternative acoustical strategies to be produced effectively.

Accounting for vocal diversity in singing training requires an understanding of the specificity in the sound production of each genre and style. As such, the search for additional scientific knowledge and understanding of the vocal adjustments necessary to produce the desired vocal quality continues, and vocal pedagogues are increasingly interested in merging science and art. A systematic understanding of the scientific underpinnings of voice production, the dissemination of genre-specific methodologies, and considerations of the cause of voice injuries can help minimise the stigma surrounding vocal injuries among the contemporary voice population.

Teaching CCM singers

Chapman (2017) stated that teachers who prepare singers for musical theatre and CCM rely upon a firm understanding of anatomy, physiology and vocal acoustics while accounting for the stylistic needs of a particular piece of music for a student to succeed. In preparing these 'vocal athletes' for the 'marathon' of a stage performance, the teacher guides the process of vocal coordination of each singer. The foundational pillars for vocal production (posture and alignment, breath management, resonance, embouchure shapes/vowel choices and level of vocal fold adduction, among others) are similar across singing styles; however, they are employed differently from one style to another. Thus, there is a need to develop style-specific vocal coordination. For example, a singer may employ good posture and utilize breath management efficiently, while lacking resonance due to a lack of coordination between the valving mechanism of the folds (pressed phonation) and embouchure shape (too spread for the style at a certain note across the range). Coordination of these factors can be honed via repetitive motor learning tasks. When a singer has achieved an optimal level of vocal coordination of the many foundational pillars, the result will include what James McKinney ([1994] 2005: 77) identified as the eight characteristics of good vocal production: 'a freely produced voice; pleasant to hear; loud enough to be heard easily; rich, vibrant and resonant; with an energy that flows smoothly from note to note; consistently produced; vibrant, dynamic and alive; expressively flexible'. These characteristics serve as the basis for many styles of singing, with some exceptions such as screamo growling styles and others taking into account technology and microphone use.

Cleveland (1998) identified a difference in breathing techniques in classical versus non-classical singers. Country singers, for instance, used breathing patterns more closely related to those used in speech rather than to the breath management technique utilized by classical singers. Titze (2011) shows how embouchure shapes play a role in the source of vocal tract interactions in classical versus belting strategies. Different styles of singing call for different embouchure shapes, as well as different levels of subglottic pressure and airflow. Through the study of vocal acoustics, pedagogues are able to understand the basic differences between vowels and help singers be mindful of embouchure choices/vowel modifications that are style-specific at different points in their vocal range. This produces vocal inertance, which is a result of the source-filter interaction that occurs when a formant aligns slightly above a harmonic, producing a boost of energy that then returns to the vocal folds. This creates a balance between the subglottic and supraglottic pressures of the vocal folds and aids the self-oscillatory pattern of the folds. Understanding such concepts can richly impact a vocal pedagogue's effectiveness, especially when navigating the new field of contemporary voice. By applying vocal acoustic principles, vocal pedagogues help singers develop vocal coordination that promotes efficient, style-specific vocal production via an optimal source-filter interaction.

While classical singing is traditionally known for consistent use of vibrato, musical theatre and CCM styles vary. Musical theatre belters often employ a straight tone for a long-sustained note, followed by the addition of vibrato towards the end of that note. It is also common to hear a predominantly straight-tone style of singing in pop, country and other similar CCM styles. However, it is not uncommon for young singers to be inefficient in their breath management, resulting in a vibrato neither consistent nor appropriate to the style in question.

While singers are considered an at-risk population for voice injury due to increased vocal usage in comparison to non-singers, the vocal health stigma is highly intensified when the singer in question sings mainly contemporary styles. The stigma around the vocal injury as a catastrophic and potentially career-ending event has been strengthened by anecdotal information and has been trauma-inducing for many singers who experienced a vocal pathology at some point in their career. Voice care professionals are no stranger to the stigma and scepticism. As Dr. Paul Kwak said in an essay published at Schmopera: 'we who care for singers are certainly not unused to the chatter, the gossip, the verbal bile that can flow so freely and unbidden in these circles' (2017: n.pag.). However, as the field progresses through a deeper understanding of vocal pedagogy based on voice science, anatomy and physiology, voice care professionals will be increasingly equipped to contribute to the destigmatization surrounding contemporary voice and voice injury. Furthermore, they will be prepared to train singers to prevent injuries and cope better during recovery processes. Much work is still needed in this field to help further decatastrophize voice injury while solidifying vocal methodologies giving successful artists sustainable and efficient vocal techniques.

Contemporary singers rely on amplification and microphones, replacing what McKinney identified as the third characteristics of good vocal production: 'loud enough to be heard easily' ([1994] 2005: 77). Understanding how each type of microphone (e.g. dynamic or condenser, etc.) best suits their unique instrument can be of great advantage in both live recording contexts. As described by Edwards and Hoch (2018: 186), 'commercial artists often view the microphone as an extension of their instrument'. Therefore, including information and the practice of using a microphone become crucial components of CCM singing training.

Conclusions

Considering that each human voice has unique acoustic characteristics due to the structure and size of their resonant cavities (i.e. neck, mouth and throat), it is important for vocal pedagogues to account for how such uniqueness during the vocal coordination journey with students. Vocal training brings the unique challenge of discovering how each rare and unique instrument functions, and while there is a general understanding of how the voice works, teaching a singer how to play *their* own unique instrument can be an exciting and challenging journey. An appreciation of each distinctive voice allows singers to find *their* voices instead of resorting to imitating the vocal choices made by a singer they admire. Furthermore, understanding the innate characteristics of each singer's vocal instrument (formants) can help pedagogues train their students to increase resonance by boosting frequencies that will give them the desired sound quality with greater efficiency. By producing a good tone quality unamplified, singers can then add the amplification and microphone of choice to enhance certain frequencies rather than relying on technological tools alone to produce the desired tone quality. It is therefore vital for vocal pedagogues to be comfortable with and knowledgeable about how technology functions and to consider its effects on the singer's vocal production in order to guide them in making good vocal choices.

In contemporary vocal styles, the use of yodel (as well as other stylized vocal flips, e.g. the shift from full voice to a pop-falsetto) is common, acceptable and desirable. Such specific techniques require specific coordination and therefore need to be both considered and taught in the study of contemporary singing styles. Developing a technique required to execute such nuances is of great importance so that singers can rely on vocal coordination rather than isolated vocal effects after having explored and developed a level of mastery and vocal flexibility over their instrument.

While contemporary styles of singing have enjoyed popularity in society for longer than the relatively new field of contemporary voice has been embraced by academia, the nuances that make these popular vocal styles unique must be accounted for at the university level. While it is possible for all singers to enjoy vocal freedom and flexibility, the path to style-specific vocal coordination must take account of the desired sonority. Taking into account differences in breath management, embouchure shapes/vowel choices, usage of technology, appropriateness of vibrato and other style-specific considerations is an important step in promoting sustainability and efficiency for contemporary singers. Knowledge of vocal anatomy, physiology, functionality and acoustics are vital components for vocal pedagogues seeking to help contemporary singers find their voice based on their instruments' natural qualities.

REFERENCES

Chapman, Janice L. (2017), *Singing and Teaching Singing: A Holistic Approach to Classical Voice*, San Diego: Plural Publishing.

Cleveland, Thomas (1998), 'A comparison of breath management strategies in classical and nonclassical singers: Part 3', *Journal of Singing*, 55:2, pp. 53–55.

Edwards, Matthew and Hoch, Matthew (2018), 'CCM versus music theater: A comparison', *Journal of Singing*, 75:2, pp. 183–90.

Kwak, Paul (2017), 'Stop shaming Adele', *Schmopera*, 5 July, https://www.schmopera.com/stop-shaming-adele/. Accessed 3 February 2022.

McKinney, James ([1994] 2005), *The Diagnosis and Correction of Vocal Faults: A Manual for Teachers of Singing & for Choir Directors*, Long Grove, IL: Waveland Press.

Titze, Ingo, Albert Worley and Brad Story (2011), 'Source-vocal tract interaction in female operatic singing and theater belting', *Journal of Singing*, 65:5, pp. 561–72.

48

Student and Tutor Life Worlds and Impossible Standards in Higher Popular Music Education

Hussein Boon

Hussein Boon is a principal lecturer at the University of Westminster, London, UK, where he teaches popular music, performance, songwriting, music technology and music business.

This chapter challenges educators to examine their assumptions and the music production realities faced by students. Bringing the tutor into closer alignment with the student 'lifeworld' is a spirited call, using 'old knowledge' in service of the new, expanding artistic musical outputs at the institution.

Introduction

Given the number of music and video uploads to services such as Spotify, YouTube, Apple Music and Bandcamp, one could be struck with the impression that perhaps the world of music creation has never been quite so populous and productive – democratized to a point where access to both creation and dissemination are within reach of all. However, some music commentators will tell us the world of music has gone to 'hell in a hand basket' (Guardian Music 2015: n.pag.), that music isn't as good as it used to be and if only they followed 'my plan', then the world of music would be better for it.

The 'my plan' brigade tends to consist of alt-rock producers leaning toward indie and punk ideologies, with the opinion that other styles of music lack appropriate creative foundation and cannot be considered creative due to having a commercial imperative. Producers such as Albini and Bienhorn have been part of some highly successful albums made with iconic artists and yet ironically 'their' music would also have been on the receiving end of similar criticism from the previous generation. Added to this is Albini's questionable Rapeman project, which should still be a part of popular music education discourse when considering any of his observations on music, culture and creativity.

With more diversity and difference in the demography of the music making, we might expect a shift of focus in a number of areas, whether songwriting, production or performance (Rosenberg 2010: 48). Gates draws our attention to an area of concern where 'the student's life world and the teacher's practice begin to take different paths' (Gates 2009: xxvi). This affects popular music education as well as the wider music education landscape (Juuti and Littleton 2012: 8). Borrowing from Warner's highlighting of issues and causes of why student writing was not good enough, I propose that two of his observations are directly applicable to popular music education. First, that students are held to 'wrong or unreasonable' standards (Warner 2019: 14) and secondly, that teachers overestimate their own 'past proficiency' (Warner 2019: 13). In the context of music teaching, it follows to ask when 'correctness' kicks in for recorded or performed works.

Life worlds in music or correctness in teaching

If self-expression is an assumed core attribute of much popular music, which may also include elements of not getting it right and going against orthodoxy, then where are the spaces for this in courses of instruction? Matters are further complicated when one takes into account aspects of representation and voice. For example, when we consider gender fluid artists and their use of voice/pitch quantizers and formant manipulation to represent their 'voice', then this is also a site of emancipation. How might we accommodate these practices in teaching and learning contexts? Should students' attempts be discouraged due to a lack of 'conformity', what I refer to as part of the 'shadow realities' (Boon 2020) of Higher Education Institutions? Another example of a shadow reality is what Philip Ewell terms the 'White racial frame':

> On the one hand, music theory, as a field, states that it supports diversity and inclusivity, and with it one presumes racial diversity and inclusivity. But on the other hand, 98.3% of the music that we choose to represent the entire field to our undergraduate students in our textbooks is written by composers who are white.
>
> (Ewell 2020: 5)

As a student, I had jazz tutor who did not like guitarists, which posed a problem for me – a guitarist. Being mixed heritage, in a class of White students, coupled with my instrument being publicly 'rejected' by the tutor, made for a level of discomfort that the University did not want to deal with.

In popular music education we need to balance ideas of tradition, skills, self-expression and creativity whilst adhering to the expectations of a degree. This places real issues at the heart of education in terms of which aspects require instruction, which correction and which facilitation and/or encouragement, and how these are framed and communicated both in the academy and to the wider world. The choice of model is important as we should avoid a turn towards orthodoxy (Beinhorn 2020), leading to a level of disconnect with current conditions. Clearly there are issues that educational practitioners face, especially in regard to how to avoid canon formation especially if used to diminish and/or devalue students' music practices or life worlds. Rosenberg suggests solutions for music theory education including repertoire consisting of 'student-chosen works' (Rosenberg 2010: 49), ensuring that the educator and materials remain a mix of current and 'classic'. Doing so also provides opportunities for educators to engage with the student life worlds outside of the classroom.

Production life worlds

With personal ownership of the means of production and access to markets, the possibility of different voices emerging through these mechanisms means that the world of music is going to be more diverse in sound and thought. Given opportunities of access afforded by more widely available music technology, the function and purpose of music will be different and differently purposed from those of previous generations, which will have an influence on student work. When we consider contemporary music purely as audio then we also overlook visual representation. Artists use video or still images as integral to audio works, extending their work into other domains of understanding and appreciation for audiences, as tools of discovery and, for some artists, as acts of resistance.

At best, discussions of impoverishment and lack of music quality can demonstrate a fixed mindset approach with a vision of artistic development and/or recording that is both narrow and careless. As an attitude it refers back to the historical issues of autocratic and patriarchal behaviour that beset producers and the world of production especially. Educators should be mindful not to reinforce nor commit similar acts, in what Western (2018) describes as 'aural bordering':

> It no longer makes sense to think of borders only as lines on maps or physical barriers that separate nation-states. Borders, instead, are technologies of social

circulation; and societies are the products of bordering, rather than the other way around.

(481)

If one were to approach a problem such as bordering differently, i.e. from a position of empowerment not just of the student but also the teacher, then one could consider the problem from a number of learning situations and perspectives. These could include problem-solving, self-advocacy and efficacy (of the self and the production method/approach) coupled with improvements in academic and critical thinking skills. Doing so would close some of the 'gap' identified by Gates (2009) and would depend less on supportive 'outcast teachers' (Juuti and Littleton 2012: 8). This is by no means the only solution, but would allow teachers to bypass potential reliance on 'comfortable' and 'reassuring' teaching examples, opening the door to more pragmatism in discursive and evaluative situations:

> This view of the sources of content knowledge necessarily implies that the teacher must have not only depth of understanding with respect to the particular subjects taught, but also a broad liberal education that serves as a framework of old knowledge and as a facilitator for new understanding.
>
> (Shulman 1999: 65)

An area primed for realignment, especially since COVID-19, is the location of production teaching in the 'bedroom studio'. This is the primary site for production, songwriting and video making that can be considered the student life world. This is the life world and not Abbey Road! Think basements and bedrooms, possibly with foam on the wall as DIY sound treatment; laptops on public transportation and headphone mixes, all whilst adhering to social distancing guidelines! In many ways, educators have got to be 'logic flippers'. They need to flip their own logic and question benchmarking music made under bedroom conditions against that made under different circumstances, especially where methods and contexts have changed so much. Educators should ask ourselves: what's the lesson, what do we want the students to learn and how are we best going to demonstrate this using our own work?

Old knowledge, new understanding

Working contexts have changed; in fact they are always changing. Popular music educators should recognize this, seeing opportunities to improve and develop practice in their teaching and curricula. I mentioned the established alt-rock producers above, in part to highlight flaws in arguments of music quality and representation. They are demonstrative of a 'locked-in' ideology that does not acknowledge change as having happened, and this lack of acknowledgement can thrive in education. My jazz tutor obviously made their mind up before I had even walked in the room. Whilst I had not been party to this, I was the recipient of their legacy decision. What are students to do when educators have made such decisions that have remained fixed for many years, irrespective of changing contexts and circumstances? By formulating music production, performance and songwriting as a purely North American/western European practice, educators encourage canon formation, even if informally (Rosenberg 2010: 48), creating situations where students are expected to adhere to 'unreasonable' standards (Warner 2019). This forces practitioner difference and multiplicity of working methods into a flattening of identity expression (Boon 2020). It is the job of educators and institutions to look past narrow and restricting visions of music, where the music made by younger musicians is deemed inadequate at best, and where even those who are successful, but still young, are deemed to be merely adequate and not comparable to any music or musicians from the past. This new music might well express a 'lived in' context of which a tutor has no knowledge or experience. Relocating the recording process to a bedroom studio challenges educators to deal with the fundamental reality faced by students and brings the life worlds closer together. Yes, this is a challenge, but one that is not unreasonable to meet. Here are opportunities to influence the construction of very different musical outputs supported and encouraged by the ways educators interface and interact with their students, ensuring they are allies and advocates for diverse musical expression.

REFERENCES

Beinhorn, Michael (2020), 'The problems facing the music industry & how to improve them', YouTube, 23 June, https://www.youtube.com/watch?v=CbhtHJcz-g&feature=youtu. be&t=4094. Accessed 3 February 2022.

Boon, Hussein (2020), 'The ways of making, dissemination and reception have changed, so what should we do about it?', *Equality, Diversity and Inclusion in Music Higher Education*, City University, London, 24 January.

Ewell, Philip A. (2020), 'Music theory and the white racial frame', *Music Theory Online*, 26:2, September, https://mtosmt.org/issues/mto.20.26.2/mto.20.26.2.ewell.pdf. Accessed 3 February 2022.

Gates, J. Terry (2009), 'Grounding music education in changing times', in T. Regelski and J. T. Gates (eds), *Music Education for Changing Times - Guiding Visions for Practice*, New York: Springer, pp. 19–30.

Guardian Music (2015), 'Steve Albini rant about dance music turned into billboard', *The Guardian*, 30 September, https://www.theguardian.com/music/2015/sep/30/steve-albini-rant-about-dance-music-turned-into-billboard. Accessed 3 February 2022.

Juuti, Sini and Littleton, Karen (2012), 'Tracing the transition from study to a contemporary creative working life: The trajectories of professional musicians', *Vocations and Learning: Studies in Vocational and Professional Education*, 5:1, pp. 5–21.

Rosenberg, Nancy (2010), 'Popular music in the college music theory class: Rhythm and meter', in N. Biamonte (ed.), *Pop-Culture Pedagogy in the Music Classroom: Teaching Tools from American Idol to YouTube*, Maryland: Scarecrow Press.

Shulman, Lee (1999), 'Sometimes one word is worth a thousand pictures', in J. Leach and R. Moon (eds), *Learners & Pedagogy* (Learning, Curriculum and Assessment Series), London: Paul Chapman Educational Publishing, pp. 61–77.

Warner, John (2019), *Why They Can't Write: Killing the Five-Paragraph Essay and Other Necessities* [Kindle], Baltimore: Johns Hopkins University Press.

Western, Tom (2018), 'Aural borders, aural bordering', in F. Scheding (ed.), *'Who Is British Music?' Placing Migrants in National Music History, Twentieth-Century Music*, Cambridge: Cambridge University Press, 15:3, pp. 439–92.

49

Places and Spaces of Popular Music Production Pedagogy in Higher Education

Brendan Anthony

Brendan Anthony is a senior lecturer at the Queensland Conservatorium, Griffith University, Australia where he teaches popular music production and performance to popular music and music technology cohorts.

In this chapter, the author uses the concepts of place and space to compare the profession and its practitioners with higher education and its students. Findings illuminate methods that support the development of graduates who are socially equipped, musically skilled practitioners.

As popular music educators, we seek out concepts that interconnect our pedagogical disciplines (production, performance, songwriting) and bridge the educational experience to professional contexts. We do this to expand the diversity of student practice and engage them in the realities of the profession to which they aspire. When designing popular music production pedagogy, the affordances of the profession and its practitioners can be considered and compared alongside those of higher education. With particular reference to popular music production, in this article, I use the concepts of *place* and *space* to facilitate this comparison. Place and space have fluid meanings that link cognitive processes with practical applications and they prove useful when comparing students with professional practitioners.

Defining place and space

In Tuan's (1979) work, meanings of place and space often merge. Tuan positions place as 'centres of felt value' where human needs are satisfied (4). He suggests: 'What begins as undifferentiated space becomes place as we get to know it better and endow it with value' (Tuan 1979: 6). For Tuan, 'space' is more abstract than 'place'. Within the context of music production these terms have a similar relationship. Toynbee (2000) uses the term *technospheres* to describe 'an imagined space of communicative potentialities and constraints' (xxii) when discussing the creative space technology affords a producer. Space is also considered within the spatiality of a mix (Gibson 2008), or when describing a person's state of mind, their thoughts, feelings, emotions or *headspace*.

Places

Professional music producers work in diverse places: various countries, cities, towns and remote locations. Often these places have distinguishing factors: ghettos, beaches, rolling hills or fast paced cities. They engage with different cultures and languages; have vast arrays of food, sport, music and nightlife. Subsequently, the characteristics of these places have a deterministic impact on musical creativity (Gibson 2005: 193) and the music production cultures in which musicians operate (Anthony 2019; Pras and Guastavino 2011). They inspire conversations and the social atmosphere of a session and influence the music that is conceived, written and recorded (Gibson 2005). Often these places are strategically chosen by the producer in an attempt to transfer a type of *feel* (e.g. relaxed, angry, happy) to the recording. Additionally, since the invention of the internet and the Digital Audio Workstation (DAW) large recording studios are less common. More-so, small studios (renovated houses) and home studios (bedrooms) are used regularly by modern music makers. These places have unique dimensional characteristics, architecture and acoustics, and they produce individualized atmospheres.

There are similarities to music making places of higher education because universities are located in diverse geographical locations and are encapsulated within various cultures. However, university campuses have institution-like architecture, where *teaching* is often prioritized over *learning* or *doing,* and the sterile atmosphere of lecture rooms and computer labs is pervasive. Music production is also commonly taught within replicas of large format recording studios and with their associated technological affordances. The use of one DAW software like Pro Tools is often prioritized. But with a large percentage of popular music now being produced in home studios, one wonders about the relevance of such practices. Most graduates will begin their careers in bedroom studios; therefore, music production educators must also ensure that large recording studios and expensive equipment are not the only resources used. Many graduates may never encounter these, so home studios and entry-level audio equipment should also be utilized in classes.

Metaphorical place is often considered during music production and song-writing. Lyrics that describe a 'dark sky', for example, can represent a sad or ominous place. Music producers often encourage artists to take themselves to these metaphorical places in their minds whilst performing. This process influences a performer's mood and the character of their performance, and artists often clear the room of occupants so as to allow solitude for these meaningful moments to occur. These actions all target the generation of an emotive performance and the interconnectedness of place (metaphorical) and space (headspace) is obvious here.

These activities can prove challenging in pedagogical landscapes. Whilst students may be encouraged to engage with metaphorical places whilst perform-ing, emptying classrooms when students sing is problematic. A profession-based context is important, but in practice, learning is better framed as a collaborative journey where students engage, discuss, reflect and unpack together how it feels to attempt such practices and then use these processes in autonomous work. There are also the social influences of the greater university context (place) that may transfer into the class setting. Bullying, friendships, personal relationships and sacked band members may be present whilst students perform and subsequently some students may be hesitant to fully engage. Despite such pedagogical challenges, facilitating a student's connection to a suitable metaphorical place during creative practice does much to locate the student in a profession-based context – a *professional place*.

Spaces

Professional producers choose the technology they use on a project to project basis, affording them various *technospheres* (Toynbee 2000) within which to work. These are musical, technological, communicative and social potentialities and constraints – a specific *music making space*. A *tracker producer* and *top-line* writer, for example, work together to produce and compose music within the DAW (Auvinen 2017). Within these productions, the use of samples, soft sounds, quantization, Auto-Tune and mass editing shapes the musical work. Songwriting, pre-production and mixing can occur concurrently and often all of this can be done via online collaboration where the top-liner and producer transfer files, work independently and rarely engage in face-to-face contact. Many contemporary, folk and rock artists, however, still hunger for live acoustic recordings, where the individual human nuances of performance and sound generation come together in a linear performance. Stalwarts of this process covet minimal editing and audio processing, and this culminates in a recorded work that the listener associates with

269

a band playing at a gig. A producer's agency is therefore often constrained by the technological and musical spaces in which they work.

University educators should aspire to develop graduates capable of working in many of these spaces. In the past, much pedagogy has been centred on acoustic music production processes (Thompson and Stevenson 2017) because music programming and electronic music production are often solitary practices that prove difficult to facilitate in group contexts. However, it is imperative that popular music students engage with diverse music production tasks similar to the tracker/top-line model (Anthony et al. 2020). This will ensure students are pushed outside their comfort zones, engage with diverse forms of technology, experience the communicative and musical realities of many types of music production and work in music-making spaces both familiar and foreign to them. This would promote graduates with diverse attributes, capable of achieving career longevity.

Some of the most challenging work music producers do is with headspace; producers envision music production from a holistic perspective where the music is the result of collective efforts (Lefford 2015). Producers consider musicality, performance, songwriting, instrumentation, communication and psychological engagements as stringently as sonic design, sound engineering and technological application. With the continued blurring of the producer/musician role (Anthony 2017), it is important to ingrain a similar holistic approach in popular music production pedagogy. Professionals also ardently consider the song's message and the emotional response they want to generate from listeners. To achieve this, professionals engage with emotion whilst recording (Howlett 2007) and they place musicians in situations that can take them to the necessary emotional headspace. These processes are influenced by the song's message and can engage feelings of anger, frailty, happiness etc.; there can also be sexual connotations. By working with known genres (places) professionals become more familiar with the necessary creative 'vibe' (space) needed for specific types of music and the artists with whom they are working.

Pedagogical applications of place and space

There are obvious difficulties in a pedagogical landscape when contemplating these processes, including a major challenge faced by educators: often students do not view university work as professional practice. In these situations, *student accountability* is a headspace issue. I often tell students that every time they make music needs to be treated like it is their profession. Student headspace can be challenged and nurtured through mentorships and by inviting external professionals into collaborative music making classes.

Finally, the educator's headspace can have an effect on the pedagogical environment. It is advantageous if popular music production educators are experienced industry professionals so they have an in-depth understanding of music production as a form of cognitive and practical agency. Yet music production is also fundamentally learned through doing (Anthony 2015; Bell 2019), therefore, if educators release ownership of classes appropriately, students can become responsible for the music making and take control of their learning. This enables the pedagogical experience to replicate professional practice; students can make mistakes, learn from these and are not over-nurtured, better enabling them to thrive. By considering concepts of place and space, popular music production educators can aspire to develop graduates who are socially equipped, musically skilled practitioners ready for the transition into the industry.

REFERENCES

Anthony, Brendan (2015), 'Creative conceptualisation: Nurturing creative practice through the popular music pedagogy of live recording production', *International Association for the Study of Popular Music*, 5:1, pp. 139–56.

Anthony, Brendan (2017), 'A final guiding hand: A practice-based study into the evolving role of third party mixers', *International Association for the Study of Popular Music*, 7:2, pp. 41–47.

Anthony, Brendan (2019), *Perspectives on Learning Popular Music Production in Higher Education From Both Sides of the Glass (Doctorate of Education)*, Brisbane: Griffith University.

Anthony, Brendan, Auvinen, Tuomas and Thompson, Paul (2020), 'Learning to be a "Tracker": A pedagogical case study of learning collaborative music production', *Journal of Popular Music and Education*, 4:2, pp. 211–35.

Auvinen, Tuomas (2017), 'A new breed of home studio producer?: Agency and the idea "Tracker" in contemporary home studio music production', *Journal on the Art of Record Production*, 11, https://www.arpjournal.com/asarpwp/a-new-breed-of-home-studio-producer-agency-and-the-idea-tracker-in-contemporary-home-studio-music-production/. Accessed 1 December 2018.

bell, adam patrick (2019), 'Of trackers and top-liners: Learning producing and producing learning', in Z. Moir, B. Powell and G. D. Smith (eds), *The Bloomsbury Handbook of Popular Music Education: Perspectives and Practices*, New York: Bloomsbury, pp. 171–85.

Gibson, Chris (2005), 'Recording studios: Relational spaces of creativity in the city', *Built Environment*, 31:3, pp. 192–207.

Gibson, David (2008), *The Art of Mixing: A Visual Guide to Recording, Engineering, and Production*, Boston: Thomson Course Technology.

Howlett, Mike (2007), 'Fixing the volatile studio: Studio vocal performance techniques', paper presented at the *3rd Art of Record Production Conference*, Brisbane: Queensland University of Technology, 10–11 December, http://eprints.qut.edu.au/33275/. Accessed 1 January 2016.

Lefford, Nyssim (2015), 'The sound of coordinated efforts: Music producers, boundary objects and trading zones', *Journal on the Art of Record Production*, 10, http://arpjournal.com/the-sound-of-coordinated-efforts-music-producers-boundary-objects-and-trading-zones/. Accessed 1 January 2017.

Pras, Amandine and Guastavino, Catherine (2011), 'The role of music producers and sound engineers in the current recording context, as perceived by young professionals', *Musicae Scientiae*, 15:1, pp. 73–95.

Thompson, Paul and Stevenson, Alex (2017), 'Missing a beat: Exploring experiences, perceptions and reflections of popular electronic musicians in UK higher education institutions', in G. D. Smith, Z. Moir, M. Brennan, S. Ramabaran and P. Kirkman (eds), *The Routledge Research Companion to Popular Music Education*, New York: Routledge, pp. 203–16.

Toynbee, Jason (2000), *Making Popular Music: Musicians, Creativity and Institutions*, New York: Arnold.

Tuan, Yi-Fu (1979), *Space and Place: The Perspective of Experience*, Minneapolis: University of Minnesota Press.

50

Fostering a Sense of Belonging in the Recruitment of Underrepresented Students at Purdue University

James Dekle

James Dekle is the artist-in-residence at the Purdue University Black Cultural Centre and serves as the director for the Black Voices of Inspiration choir and The Purdue Express.

This chapter describes the Purdue Express, a performance recruitment ensemble founded at Purdue University to recruit underrepresented student populations through a 30-minute musical presentation. This paper shares information regarding the mission of the Purdue Express and how popular music can foster a sense of belonging in potential students.

Introduction

Racial tensions are escalating throughout America, and many universities in the United States are addressing the realities of racism and the dynamics of the race on their campuses. Considering this climate, diversity officers across the country have taken the opportunity to create task forces on their campuses which include administrators, faculty and other university personnel. The purpose of such task forces is to gather the best ideas to fight racism and other social justice issues. Such is the case at Purdue University, a large public research university located in northwestern Indiana, United States.

The Chief Diversity Officer at Purdue introduced the Diversity Transformation Award to provide faculty and staff the opportunity to develop programmes that would increase diversity on campus. The award specifically targets the areas of recruitment and retention of underrepresented students and faculty. Each proposal submitted had the opportunity to earn funding up to $250,000. In the autumn semester of 2015, I proposed a music performance recruitment group – The Purdue Express.

During the proposal phase, grant supervisors were most concerned about the effectiveness of a 'music show' to advance the university priorities of increasing cultural diversity and inclusion. The following question laid the foundation for the intense vetting process: 'Why should we fund a music project to recruit underrepresented students?' As music educators, it is common to face such questions when proposing music as a catalyst for a significant change in educational institutions. This was especially the case at Purdue because of the strong focus on Science, Technology, Engineering and Math (STEM) and has heralded Purdue a stellar global reputation. Therefore, successfully advocating for funding of a music project required me to defend a music ensemble's ability to recruit underrepresented students. At the time of the proposal, Purdue didn't have a music major and this further complicated the notion of a music ensemble being utilized to recruit STEM students. Nevertheless, after an intense proposal process, *The Purdue Express* received an award of $250,000. In this chapter, I highlight the concept of the music performance recruitment group and the role of popular music in the group's effectiveness to introduce a sense of belonging with potential students from underrepresented cultural backgrounds.

Why fund the Purdue Express?

When presented with the question, 'Why should we fund a music project?', my response was simple. The Purdue Express music project was, and is worthy of funding because it serves as a catalyst to foster a sense of belonging in potential students. Successful recruitment of underrepresented students requires these students to feel the possibility of belonging. Although belonging will mean something different for every student, educational institutions need frequently to assess their culture and its impacts on belonging. In their study to identify tools to increase the college enrolment of African American men, Tolliver et al. (2020) share that 'community expectancy' frames the outlook of underrepresented students' life decisions, and is developed from an individual's experiences; this helps a person determine the behaviours required to belong within a social group (431). A significant concern among underrepresented students is negotiating themselves in an environment of social isolation. Acclaimed somatic racial trauma therapist and bestselling author Resmaa Menakem, states, 'more than anything, culture creates a sense of belonging – and belonging makes our bodies feel safe' (2017: 246). If an educational institution desires to foster a better sense of belonging among under-represented students, then broadening campus culture should be a priority. The first step in broadening culture is to recruit more students from diverse cultures. How do you recruit more students from diverse cultures? One way is to empower current students who are currently underrepresented. Baumeister and Leary (1995) suggest that effective recruitment of underrepresented students requires recurrent positive social interaction. The Purdue Express initiates positive interactions with potential students in high schools and college recruitment fairs and seeks to moti-vate potential students to campus for additional positive interactions that will ultimately influence their college decision.

The Purdue Express

The Purdue Express is a fifteen–sixteen-member performance ensemble that prior-itizes membership from students who self-identify with underrepresented cultures on campus, primarily Black students. The cast consists of ten–twelve stage perform-ers and a three–four-piece band. Together, these students perform a 30-minute action-packed stage show telling the story of Purdue University by interweaving various styles and genres of popular music with Purdue's history, admissions process, academics and campus life. The mission of The Purdue Express is to travel throughout the state of Indiana, the United States and abroad to tell this story from an underrepresented cultural perspective. The administrative team consists of the director, assistant director and choreographer. As a director, I write the show, serve as music director, and oversee all administration functions for the ensemble.

The performance consists of five music selections and concludes with a medley of songs that students perform choreographed and freestyle dance to, without sing-ing. Each season the show comes to life during an intense six-day retreat (before the semester begins) which closes with a private preview show for local media and recruitment stakeholders. The group performs eight–ten shows during the fall recruitment season, scheduled with the Office of Admissions, which helps deter-mine the high schools and recruitment events that will yield the best opportunity to engage potential underrepresented student populations.

The intent is to share elements of the Purdue student experience including favourite hangout spots on campus and the variety of food options available at the all-you-can-eat dining courts. One song we featured was Flo Rida's 'Welcome to My House'.[1] The lyrics in the hook provided the perfect context to discuss campus life. Because the song was on continuous radio rotation at the time, students immediately made the connection between the song's lyrics and our intent to contextualize Purdue as a future home for prospective students. One of the most electrifying elements of the show is the dance routine, where cast members execute popular dances in hip-hop culture. The dance routine always concludes the show and the audience response is immediate. As soon as the music begins some members in the audience shout song lyrics, as well as joining in dancing. Popular dances featured include 'Stanky Legg',[2] 'Dougie'[3] and 'Whip/Nae Nae'.[4] I intentionally placed the dance routine at the end of the show to create a lasting impression, leaving the audience wanting more.

During the genesis of The Purdue Express, every member had to accept the responsibility of being a student cultural ambassador for Purdue University. This was not easy for some members, and I knew I would have to earn their trust. One student made this very clear when they shared with me, 'I do not want to be part of anything that is going to have me shuckin' and jivin",[5] i.e. making the university *appear* diverse with no real intention of changing the culture. So, what makes The Purdue Express different?

Student members of The Purdue Express communicate through music that is meaningful to *them* and represents *their* values. As such, my role in this group is to challenge and collaborate with student members to determine musical selections that are contextually appropriate and well-known. For example, we programmed Bruno Mars' '24k Magic' and 'Finesse'. Cast members wanted these songs included because of the songs' popularity. However, because some lyrics were not suitable for educational audiences, we replaced them with lyrics about Purdue, retaining the original hook. These songs were great suggestions from the cast members, and they enjoyed every moment of creating our version of the songs. Student ownership in the creative process is essential because student members are the cultural representatives that potential students will observe. Providing them a voice in the creative process increases the relatability of show contents to prospective students. If The Purdue Express is to be successful in introducing a sense of belonging, it will be because of the prioritization of the ensemble members' musical interests and on campus experiences. College Administrators often control the narrative of the student experience during recruitment, instead of students sharing their realities of the university experience. If The Purdue Express is to avoid shuckin' and jivin', students' real experiences help determine the authenticity of our performance.

The show

The setting of the show is an imaginary passenger train with nonstop service to Purdue University. The train is symbolic of Purdue's nickname, the Boilermakers.

The show begins with a voiceover telling all passengers to have their application, test scores and personal essay available as they board the train. Then the drummer provides a rim shot and the music begins. The cast takes the stage for our opener, 'The Purdue Express Theme Song'. During the song, the cast members introduce themselves to the audience sharing their name, programme concentration/major and hometown. This sets the tone for the entire show, because audience members begin to see the performers as students, not just entertainers.

The theme song immediately transitions into an up-tempo contemporary pop tune. Each song begins with singing and choreography before the music abruptly breaks down to a soft dynamic, creating background mood music on this imaginary train ride. Cast members take turns sharing details about the campus experience. The show continues in this format, seeking to provide a nonstop, engaging experience while bringing to life details that are often overlooked on university websites and informational brochures. Because the show interweaves music and speaking, our song selections need to support the information that we are sharing about the University. I believe the synergy between the music selections and information provides the key ingredient to making a lasting impression for potential students. Through meaningful music engagement, The Purdue Express seeks to inform, recruit, and display cultural inclusion in ways that resonate with our teenage audiences.

Conclusion

Through the constantly evolving nature of popular music, The Purdue Express continues to create engaging experiences for potential students and remains a valuable part of Purdue's recruitment efforts. Through collaborative planning, The Purdue Express prioritizes meaningful experiences where a sense of belonging can be realized. The goal is to positively impact the community expectancy of inspiring students, allowing them to see Purdue as their home away from home. Consequently, underrepresented students need positive social interaction to feel they belong, and The Purdue Express provides a creative way to achieve that result.

NOTES

1. Flo Rida is an African American rapper singer, songwriter from the Miami, Florida metropolitan area. 'Welcome to My House' was released in 2015 and was nominated for a Teen Choice Award, which is sponsored by Fox television network.

2. Stanky Legg: popular dance associated with the rap song 'Stanky Legg' by hip-hop group the GS Boyz. The song was released in 2009.

3. Dougie: popular dance associated with the rap song 'Teach Me How To Dougie' by hip-hop group Cali Swag District. The song was released in 2011.
4. Whip/Nae Nae: is a popular dance associated with the rap song 'Watch Me (Whip/Nae Nae)' by American rapper Silentó. The song was released in 2015.
5. Shuckin' and jivin' is a phrase associated with African American culture that describes misleading or deceptive talk or behaviour.

REFERENCES

Baumeister, Roy F. and Leary, Mark R. (1995), 'The need to belong: Desire for interpersonal attachments as a fundamental human motivation', *Psychological Bulletin*, 117:3, pp. 497–529, https://doi.org/10.1037/0033-2909.117.3.497. Accessed 12 December 2020.

Menakem, Resmaa (2017), *My Grandmother's Hands: Racialized Trauma and the Pathway to Mending our Hearts and Bodies*, Las Vegas: Central Recovery Press.

Tolliver, David V., Kacirek, Kit and Miller, Michael T. (2020), 'Getting to and through college: African American adult men talk about increasing underrepresented student participation', *College Student Journal*, 53:4, pp. 430–39.

51

Awakening Spirituality in
Brazilian Higher Music Education

Heloisa Feichas

Heloisa Feichas is an assistant professor of music education at the Music School of the Federal University of Minas Gerais in Belo Horizonte, Brazil, where she teaches music education.

In this chapter, the author discusses a humanist pedagogical approach focused on popular songs with spiritual values. The author draws on her experience teaching optional courses about spirituality for undergraduate students at the Music School of the Federal University of Minas Gerais, Belo Horizonte, in the southeast of Brazil.

Introduction

This work discusses some aspects of an optional course called 'Spirituality in Music Education' at the Music School of the Federal University of Minas Gerais in Brazil. One of the pillars of this course has been a 'playlist' based on popular songs whose lyrics are connected to spiritual values. The concept of spirituality in this context is related to the development of human values such as respect, tolerance, patience and loving attitudes towards oneself and others. It is also related to a sense of aliveness and interconnectedness: a connection with oneself and with the world, searching for a meaning in life (Merwe and Habron 2015; Tolliver and Tisdell 2006). In this way, it has to do with awakening one's purpose in life, making it valuable and internally rich (Tolle 2004, 2005). It also intersects with the search for emotional wellbeing which in turn is related to positive feelings, such as acceptance, gratitude, peace and contentment, among others (Kabat-Zinn 2016). The choice of popular songs with spiritual meaning is the trigger point for many creative activities and discussions which lead to reflexive and collaborative attitudes within the group. The pedagogical approach in this course is humanist, and it is concerned with a holistic education, which considers the realm of affections, bringing the notion of education that links heart and mind (Freire 2011).

Concepts of spirituality

Defining spirituality for a discussion in music education is challenging. Research studies about spirituality are normally found within philosophy, psychology, religious studies, health and medicine fields. As Merwe and Habron (2015: 48) realized in their research about a conceptual model for spirituality in music education, 'there has been a recent surge in the study of spirituality within academic discourse beyond the disciplines of theology and religious studies'. Some pioneering and important work for spirituality and music education includes the work of Boyce-Tillman (2007, 2016). She has developed a phenomenography of the musical experience, broadening its concept with implications in music education. In her model, Boyce-Tillman (2016) seeks to restore the notion of spirituality, linking it to four domains (Materials, Construction, Expression and Values) of musical experience, which will ultimately promote an inner contact with oneself and with others in a musical context (Boyce-Tillman 2016).

Merwe and Habron (2015: 54) developed a conceptual model working with the idea of music as a holistic experience and music as drawing on body, space, time and relationships to offer an experience of the sacred. They used four 'lifeworld existentials', which comprise different categories: *corporeality* as an expression of spirituality including *embodiment, sensory experience, creativity* and *breath*; *relationality* 'refers to the connections that exist between people as well as the relationships between individuals and communities, the natural world, cosmos, and the divine. It also includes the relationship with the self' (Merwe and Habron 2015: 55–57). The categories within relationality are *connection, inter- and intra-personal relationships, meaning and spiritual virtues* and *vices* (Merwe and Habron 2015: 59). *Spatiality* includes *awareness, awe and wonder, transcendence, ecstasies,* and *suprarationality* (Merwe and Habron 2015: 59).

This resonates with studies of *mindfulness* (Kabat-Zinn 2001) and other spiritualist writers like Eckart Tolle (2004, 2005). These texts all say that when we are aware and present in the now, or mindful, we have a different experience of ourselves and others. It creates a different way of connecting to others and to the divine, which is a transcendent or metaphysical experience. The last 'lifeworld existential' is *temporality*, which includes the notion of *journey*, indicating movement through time and space (Merwe and Habron 2015: 60). Another category linked to temporality is *joy* related to the emotional quality of the present moment and altered perceptions of time, which is ultimately connected to the concept of *flow,* as theorized by Csikszentmihalyi (1990). As Merwe and Habron (2015: 61) point out, 'the notions of fulfilment through challenge and the seeming alteration of time through joy are both aspects of the psychological state of flow'. Flow has also a characteristic of dissolving dualities because there is little distinction between self and environment, or between past, present and future (Bogdan 2003 cited in Merwe and Habron 2015: 62). The authors conclude that their conceptual model could be beneficial for music educators to 'develop sensitivity to and holistic aware-ness of the potential for spirituality in their own and their students' experiences. This potential is important since spirituality has been shown to be a determinant of wellbeing' (Merwe and Habron 2015: 63).

Besides works in music education and spirituality, there are some researchers within higher education looking for a more holistic approach, with a less individu-alistic focus, integrating multiple ways of knowing. From their experiences in adult education, Tolliver and Tisdell (2006) noticed a presence of spiritual aspects in the classroom advocating in favour of transformative learning (Tolliver and Tisdell 2006: 37). For transformative learning to really happen, it would be necessary to engage affective, intuitive and spiritual domains which actually help the rational ideas to be anchored (Tolliver and Tisdell 2006: 39). They also focused on the 'exploration of individual and communal dimensions of cultural and other dimen-sions of identity and collaborative work that envisions and presents manifestations of multiple dimensions of learning and strategies for change' (Tolliver and Tisdell, 2006: 41). Although putting all these components into practice might be challeng-ing, it can be a way of fostering spirituality in the higher education classroom.

Putting spiritual values into practice: Working with popular songs

At the Music School of the Federal University of Minas Gerais, besides compulsory subjects, undergraduate music students need to register in several optional courses throughout their academic path. I have been responsible for offering some of these optional subjects. One of these is 'Spirituality in Music Education'. In search-ing for content and teaching methods suitable for such a new topic area, I have found a rich resource in a collection of Brazilian popular songs as there are many songwriters who have written true poems with meaningful and inspiring lyrics. I first started looking for particular songs with spiritual meaning in their lyrics. Having chosen a few songs, I brought them to the classroom and worked together with students in a creative and collaborative way (Freire 2011; Renshaw 2011).

281

In this context students are heard and invited to contribute with their own 'play-list' of 'spiritual songs'. They are also encouraged to engage within the class through group activities, such as making new arrangements for the chosen songs and performing them.

As I aim to create a good environment for working with 'spiritual songs' I do a different 'warm-up' at the beginning of class: short meditations from different approaches, starting always with closing the eyes, breathing in and out, until reaching a peaceful state. Some meditations come from mindfulness techniques; others come from the Hindu tradition, and others from modern spiritualist authors (Tolle 2004). After some minutes it is common to see students describing their state as calmer, more balanced and grounded. Then we start working with the chosen songs. In order to fulfil the tasks, they first need to analyze the lyrics deeply and discuss them collectively. Normally these 'spiritual songs' have different themes related to spiritual values, such as respect for each other, awareness about nature and its conservation, the need for working together for the sake of all, faith, hope, friendship, trust, patience, creating peace and love. Ideas for musical arrangement arise in different ways through students' interactions. While dealing with the analysis of lyrics, new images come out motivating the students in creating musical ideas, exploring all resources available such as voices, instruments and even body percussion.

This pedagogical experience has a holistic view and fits well in the model proposed by Merwe and Habron (2015) so far as it contains elements of corporeality, relationality, spatiality and temporality. At the core of this holistic approach there is a focus on effective and intuitive dimensions which goes beyond the rational and mental perspectives. This approach is also based on Freire's (2011) ideas of humanist education which are dialogical, collaborative, culturally inclusive and concerned with linking head to heart, that is, intellectual to emotional domains. It also made me think about theories of intelligence as per Gardner's categorization. In his reframed multiple intelligences, he defines existential intelligence as 'a concern with ultimate life issues', such as why we are here, what is the meaning of life, describing the core ability of this intelligence as the related capacity to locate oneself with respect to existential features of the human condition (Gardner 1999: 60). In this sense, existential intelligence involves one's ability to understand others and the world around through intuition and collective values.

The students' experiences shared within the class were illuminating, showing the great potential of 'spirituality in music education'. For the assessment at the end of the semester students were asked to write a report about the course. Some of these reports were quite interesting, illustrating the impact of the activities, such as:

> This course has been an oasis in the desert! It is such a pleasure and joy that I don't feel time passing [...] it is like time stops [...]

I never pay attention to lyrics when I listen to songs [...] normally I listen to the music, the instrumentation, voice, but never the words [...] it was wonderful to realise how many songs with lyrics that made us think about life, about the meaning of being here [...]

Working together collaboratively was great! We don't have that much during the undergraduate course! We work too much individually [...] I learnt a lot about relationships!

Final thoughts

This chapter is an attempt to reflect upon a dimension of human beings that has not been widely acknowledged in musical pedagogy: the spiritual. Expanding curricula to include wellbeing experiences as well as working with spiritual values should be an important step towards a humanizing education. Perhaps we could talk about pedagogy of spirituality, based on the idea of a holistic human being with body, mind, emotions and soul; also based on collective, respectful and loving values, rather than individualistic ones. It is time to encourage communion instead of isolation. In doing this, we will touch on our spiritual dimension, encouraging contact with our inner selves, so that we may engage with others in deeper ways, with a real sense of community. More research is needed on spirituality in music education. It is also imperative to create a new ground where the seeds of spiritual values can be planted, nurturing human relationships for the development of aware citizens based on loving attitudes. Then we will make our difference in the world in which we live.

REFERENCES

Boyce-Tillman, June (2007), 'Spirituality in the musical experience', in L. Bresler (ed.), *International Handbook of Research in Arts Education*, New York: Springer, pp. 1405–22.

Boyce-Tillman, June (2016), *Experiencing Music: Restoring the Spiritual*, Bern: Peter Lang AG, International Academic Publishers.

Csikszentmihalyi, Mihaly (1990), *Flow: The Psychology of Optimal Experience*, New York: Harper and Row.

Freire, Paulo (2011), *Pedagogia da Autonomia: Saberes Necessários à Prática Educativa*, 43rd ed., São Paulo: Editora Paz e Terra Ltda.

Gardner, Howard (1999), *Intelligence Reframed: Multiple Intelligences for the 21st Century*, New York: Basic Books.

Kabat-Zinn, Jon (2016), *Mindfulness for Beginners: Reclaiming the Present Moment and Your Life*, Boulder: Sounds True.

Merwe, Liesl and Habron, John (2015), 'A conceptual model of spirituality in music education', *Journal of Research in Music Education*, 63:1, pp. 47–69.

Renshaw, Peter (2011), *Working Together: An Enquiry into Creative Collaborative Learning Across the Barbican-Guildhall Campus*, London: Barbican Centre and Guildhall School of Music & Drama.

Tolle, Eckhart (2004), *The Power of Now: A Guide for Spiritual Enlightenment*, Vancouver: Namaste Publishing.

Tolle, Eckhart (2005), *A New Earth: Awakening to Your Life's Purpose*, New York: Penguin Books.

Tolliver, Derise E. and Tisdell, Elizabeth (2006), 'Engaging spirituality in the transformative higher education classroom', *New Directions for Adult and Continuing Education*, 109, pp. 37–47.

52

Embracing Innocence, Uncertainty and Presence in Popular Music Performance

Jay Stapley

Jay Stapley is a session guitarist, songwriter and producer from England. His session credits include Roger Waters, Mike Oldfield, Scott Walker, Toyah, Shakin' Stevens and Westernhagen.

In this chapter, the author reflects on experiences teaching popular music performance in higher education. He emphasizes how important it is for aspiring professional musicians to embrace innocence, creativity and spontaneity as they create live music. The author wrote the following after a conversation with a bassist and fellow teacher at a festival in the summer of 2017 ...

That was an interesting (despite being alcohol-fuelled ... or maybe because of it) discussion about the mental processes involved in playing music. I've had it many times in an academic context and it always seems to founder on the requirements of academic rigour. The notion that conclusions can only be drawn from consistently repeatable and communally observed phenomena does not sit well in an activity which is rigorously non-rigorous and repeatedly unrepeatable (although it is communally observable, and a surprisingly solid consensus on quality usually emerges among audiences). Much academic practice is based on the premise that its observations are only valid when consistent application of input *x* results consistently in output *y*: nothing could be further than the reality of an activity which is never the same twice and in which there are so many variables. When I discuss the same theme with non-academic practitioners, the conversation flows much more smoothly ... as indeed should the music.

Innocence

I refer throughout this piece to what I call 'vernacular music', the broad spectrum of music produced and performed originally by 'non-experts', and herein lies one of the main problems with applying formalized education to such music. As soon as it becomes professionalized, it loses its innocence and is no longer vernacular. As a teacher, I often found myself asking eighteen-year-old guitar students who they listened to. Right up to the present day, they always answer with the same names – the pantheon of the 1960s, 1970s and the occasional 1980s guitarists such as Hendrix, Beck, Clapton, Iommi, Blackmore, etc. Mention any of the more modern guitarists such as Johnny Marr or The Edge, and they scoff. I believe that the reason for this is that many musicians in those earlier eras took to music in order to *avoid* having a career, and that innocence of intent is transmitted through their musicality. These days, musicians come to colleges and universities in order to *have* a career in music: the results are very different. I must confess to taking great delight in the fact that the most successful guitarist to come out of the college where I was teaching had studied on the songwriting programme, not the guitar programme and had no idea about scales, fretboard knowledge, or indeed any of the styles and techniques which form the bulk of the curriculum on all the guitar courses I've ever seen. What he did have was a glorious innocence which led him to just use his ears. His band is called Daughter and his guitar soundscapes are wonderful.

The central theme of the discussion which prompted this article was around the value in giving students a set of instructions in live performance workshops (LPWs).[1] 'Play metronomically but stay human' is an example of a fairly typical (and impossible because contradictory) instruction, guaranteed to fill a student's mind with anxiety and fear, where what is really required is for the student to know the material's broad shape rather than in intricate detail, and be relaxed, free from worry, and sitting on the cutting edge of reality (aka 'in the moment'). Sufficient technical competence to be able to think on your instrument is also required, and this is where technical studies should be aimed. Helping students to develop and express their own dynamic 'mind's ear' rather than slavishly recreating someone else's should be the aim of such study.

The story behind writing *The Inner Game of Tennis* (Gallwey 1972) is instructive: the writer was a tennis coach, and anyone who has ever had a tennis lesson knows that the first thing the instructor does is ... instruct. A stream of orders are issued,

> racket back, weight on the back foot, stand sideways to the ball, watch the ball, swing the racket (keep your wrist stiff!) through the path of the ball, transfer your

weight onto the front foot, follow through the stroke and finish with your racket higher than when you hit the ball ...

The student stands there, paralyzed with fear, trying to remember and perform this sequential list of actions. One day, the coach decided to just tell the student 'Hit the ball over the net into that big box behind me'. To his astonishment, the student (who had never been instructed before) performed all the requisite actions and hit a perfect topspin forehand into the court. The coach went home and had a long think. The book was the result of his thinking, and it was adapted for golfers, musicians etc.

Uncertainty principle

So: if we are not to think about trying to obey a list of instructions when playing music (or giving them when we teach), what are we to do? Most performers I've discussed this with, (musicians, actors, public speakers) shy away from verbalizing their mental processes during the performance, mumbling things like 'I don't really think about it' or 'no idea: my mind is blank when I'm playing'. These comments are simultaneously the most annoying and the most useful, and also the ones I've found in my own experience to be closest to the truth. I once gave a young musician who was trying desperately hard to be brilliant in rehearsal, over-thinking the parts and trying to play as though we were on stage, the following advice:

> Learn the chords, play the simplest thing possible, quiet your busy mind, and trust that your musicality, your 'mind's ear', will supply you with the 'right' thing to play when we are on stage in front of a live audience. Rehearsals are just for the musicians to find out where the furniture is.

The situation which pertains in most live performance workshops is further complicated by the applicability of the Uncertainty Principle: one interpretation of this suggests that because the energy used to observe an event changes that event, any observations are rendered invalid. The instruction to 'be creative' gives rise to a sort of porno-creativity, in which the motivation or intent behind the creative act is perverted, the act being performed for 'impure' reasons rather than for the pure joy of it.

Add to that the dreaded 'authenticity' trap ... no instruction makes less sense than 'be authentic'. Authenticity only means something when it refers to something already in existence, which precludes originality and produces safe, timid art. And authentic to what? The original recorded performance? How can the students be expected to recreate a recording which was almost always done as a series of overdubs in a state-of-the-art recording studio? Do the students have exactly the same equipment? The same engineer? Or are they supposed to be authentic to a style or genre? Many styles arose primarily by vernacular performers being *in*authentic, thus allowing existing styles to mutate and grow. If Bluegrass musicians had remained authentic, country music would not have developed, and if country musicians had remained authentic, the wonderful hybrid of country and jazz known as western swing would never have happened, and to paraphrase Nietzsche, life without western swing would be a mistake.

Taking the above into account, it's no wonder the poor student is either frozen with fear or delivers a soulless technical performance, when what is really required from a performer is transmission to the audience of the performer's own pleasure, the excitement of playing something as it comes into the mind's ear, the exhilaration of riding the moment which at its peak is like being strapped to the front of a 747 on its take-off run. That's why audiences pay significant sums to attend performances by great performers: they aren't interested in the performers' technical competence; indeed, they don't even know about the technicalities, and neither should they.

Assessment

However, as the old saying goes: you've got to play the hand that's dealt you, and as teachers we are required to deliver some sort of assessment. How do we assess live performance? Again, the Uncertainty Principle applies, but this time it's the educators who are bitten rather than the performers. The fact that we are listening critically means that we are not responding innocently to the performance. We have matters such as technique, authenticity, sound quality and so forth to consider. No audience ever attends a performance with such a mental checklist in their minds: they simply react in a pure and naïve manner to what is happening in the room. They are much more qualified to assess the performance than we are, and their assessment is simple and immediate. As soon as learning outcomes and grading criteria are introduced, we are prone to end up with porno assessment: our reactions to the performance are perverted by the very factors that are required to fulfil academic rigour.

What to do? I've used peer assessment in the past, but it's not valid academically unless the peers know about the learning outcomes and grading criteria, which renders them as 'perverted' as the tutors. Self-assessment is another option, best performed in conjunction with peer assessment, but the same caveats apply. How about no assessment at all? What most closely mirrors the reality of performance is if the act is performed for its own sake rather than to fulfil some other requirement. It would be a brave programme leader who proposed to the validation panel that the team would not assess the central activity of a performance-based programme and I'm afraid I can offer no more persuasive arguments than the ones included here. Good luck ...

NOTE

1. A live performance workshop is a class in which vocal, drum, bass and guitar students are given a piece to play as a band. A chart and recording are supplied ahead of time, and student groups take it in turns to perform the piece. Tutors provide guidance and feedback.

REFERENCE

Gallwey, Timothy (1974), *The Inner Game of Tennis: The Ultimate Guide to the Mental Side of Peak Performance*, London: Pan.

53

How I Relearned to Give a Shit

David Knapp

David Knapp is an assistant professor of music education at Syracuse University, where he teaches modern band and directs the Music in Community programme at SU.

In this chapter, the author discusses how punk and Blackness could be more central to music making and music learning in the context of education in the United States, where practices and norms appear entrenched in oppressive practices from the past.

My vision

I have a recurring vision for music education that involves the Russian punk rock collective Pussy Riot. A young woman attending a music performance assessment has dutifully written the eighteenth century Italian aria 'Caro mio ben' on her judging sheet. She enters the room with a confident posture and hands the sheet to the judge. With her accompanist behind her, she walks to the piano's crook and stands attentively. The judge gives her a nod and she brings her hands to a clasp in front of her body. She then takes in a long breath when suddenly her accompanist loudly pounds out block chords. She begins to sing, or maybe it is a scream? It is hard to make out her words, exactly; perhaps something about bodily autonomy and consent. At the first sound, the judge and audience startle. As the performance continues, they look around more nervously, not sure what is happening. She remains focused and pushes forward for the duration of her verses and chorus. She has prepared for this moment for months.

When the last chord is played and the last words are sung – maybe it's 'me too', or maybe because she's inspired by the vulgarity of Pussy Riot it's something more provocative ...

Well, I'm not sure what happens next. I'm not sure I understand this moment outside the bookends of the performance. And it's my vision! Was her music teacher aware of what was going to happen? Is the judge able to process the performance with her afterwards? Is she evicted from the festival?

I'm unable to bring this moment into clear focus because this kind of music making is beyond the borders of our field. The music education profession, at least as it has been practiced for the last century or so in the United States, is premised on re-creating music devoid of context and human experience. Nevertheless, a version of the profession that allows for this moment is exciting to think about! Even imagining a young person courageously and musically expressing themselves gives me goosebumps! But what would a version of music education that allows for this kind of moment look like, and how might we get there?

I should admit here that this vision was inspired by an interview I heard on the radio programme *Radiolab* with a young man named Ryan Wash. In the episode, Wash – a queer, Black, first-generation college student – recounts his journey in competitive debate. He talks about the overwhelming Whiteness he experienced the first time he attended a competition. He recounts the loneliness he felt in not feeling welcomed by a community that did not include him. And, defiantly, he tells the story of how he and his debate partner bent the entire competitive debate scene to confront its systemic racism. When I heard this episode, Donald J. Trump had just been elected President of the United States. Jews were being murdered. Muslims were being banned. And Black men, women and children were being killed by the state. Meanwhile, I'm talking to my students about the edTPA.[1]

Colour-blind music education

I wasn't sure how to find edification through work. More than any other truth I hold for our profession, I believe in the connection between human experience and music making. As I looked around me, I didn't see our field reflecting on this connection. I didn't see *myself* reflecting this connection. That year NAfME released the poster shown in Figure 53.1.

Was this a moment of clarity? Was this the moment our field responded to a society in crisis and reinvigorated our democracy through musical engagement? Was this NAfME echoing anti-authoritarian movements that – from Moscow's Cathedral of Christ the Saviour to Cairo's Tahrir Square – used music to galvanize youth around the world for a better, more equitable world?

Of course not. It was NAfME engaging in light jingoism, with a thin veneer of relevancy. After Colin Kaepernick forced a national conversation about Black lives and police violence, NAfME was keen to demonstrate its relevance. 'Bringing

FIGURE 53.1: Advocacy poster, National Association for Music Education, 2016.

a nation to its feet' accomplishes this, but by recasting the heroic action as standing – instead of kneeling – NAfME avoids upsetting their upper-middle-class White constituency. It really was a perfect sentiment for the organization, and whoever coined this phrase deserves a raise.

Yet, one wonders why we are standing, or where we are going. The slogan doesn't provide direction, but instead merely stokes some generalized claim of music's power. It is provocative without provoking. It entirely ignores the realities of our nation: the escalating authoritarianism, the political killings, the fascism, and of course the everyday structural racism that is part of the fabric of our imperfect union. NAfME wants us to reflect on the power of music to engage our nation, but it conspicuously avoids having an opinion about what we should do with this power.

To be fair, NAfME recently penned a statement on Black Lives Matter shortly after the murder of George Floyd and prominently placed it on their landing page (2020). Though for an organization that purports to be responsive to the nation, you might ask why it took so long to do the bare minimum. You might ask where they were after Michael Brown's murder in 2014. Or Freddie Gray's. Or Sandra Bland's. Or the many other times in the last seven years that the murder of Black people has brought this topic to the centre of American social discourse.

When NAfME says music education 'can bring a nation to its feet', they want parents and teachers in the suburbs to feel roused; to be proud their well-rounded neighbourhood school is contributing to the liberal Democracy envisioned by Dewey, without heeding the reconstructivist activism of Du Bois. What they absolutely don't want is to promote a version of music education that confronts the truth that pluralism is murky and difficult. By authentically engaging in this dissensus of values and musics – by providing space for non-upper-middle-class White experiences – NAfME would risk alienating its racialized and classist base.

On 6 February 2016, Beyoncé released the track 'Formation'. Along with the track, an evocative music video was also surprise released that depicted police violence, the abandonment of Black communities during Hurricane Katrina, and Black feminist strength in response to these struggles. The next evening she appeared at the Super Bowl alongside a legion of women dancers wearing Black Panther berets and showing raised Black fists. In short, 'Formation' was just really feminist and Black. Black as fuck. Blacker than most people in White America, including myself, were accustomed to. It was also a major fucking hit. Outlets including *Rolling Stone* and *Billboard* listed 'Formation' as among the best songs of the year and won a Grammy for Best Music Video. Simply put, it dominated the cultural landscape in 2016. Saturday Night Live, the barometer of American zeitgeist, even performed a sketch about the song's Blackness.

The video to 'Formation' hit me hard. Even though I am not a woman and am not Black – or maybe precisely *because* I am not those things – it really struck me. Something about Black women talking about the world on their own terms and just altogether ignoring Whiteness. I wasn't prepared to see that. It's four years later and I'm still shocked by it. I watch 'Formation' every few months or so and cry every time.

As best I can tell this landmark of American culture was entirely ignored by NAfME. 'Formation' *did* bring a nation to its feet (or at least some of the nation), and the organization that touts the centrality of music education in the lives of Americans didn't engage with it. Four years later and the only reference to Beyoncé that I can find on NAfME's website is an earlier discussion board post that complains about pop music performers lip syncing during performances.

The music education imaginary and ourselves

What would it be like to participate in a field that engaged the difficult and inspiring complexities of American life? What would it feel like to have music education practices that interrogated musical meanings and reflected the moment? That allowed for America's multiple and sometimes competing consciousnesses? What would it be like if music education not only tolerated but also created an American Pussy Riot? These questions are rhetorical because I of course don't know the answers. I'm asking them because I want us to see the expanse that's beyond our self-imposed borders. I want us to stake the claim that there are untested feasibilities in our field that allow for the real work of liberation, and then I want to go out and explore them! I want us to finally admit to each other that 'Caro mio ben' probably shouldn't be performed anymore.

Since I can't provide any answers, I'll return back to where I started by discussing my professional ennui and speak briefly about how I relearned to give a shit. Before my current job, I had some experiences in community music and popular (vernacular) music education. When I arrived here, I knew I wanted to do something that combined popular music and the kinds of extramusical outcomes that often accompany community music activities. Because my city has a relatively large refugee population (approximately 10,000 people; or, roughly 8 per cent of the city's people), I decided to start a band at a neighbourhood refugee centre. The kids in the programme are from all over: Congo, Syria, Nepal, Sri Lanka, to name a few. And though they come from different places, they share some similar experiences that relate to dislocation and trauma. Our band – The New American All-Stars – performs covers typical for their age cohort, like John Legend's 'All of Me', as well as regional popular music like Abdulrahman Mohamed's أصابكعشق ('Craziness').

But members of the band were also voracious in writing their own music. The band has since become a place for members to musically encode their past experiences as well as their present lives as American teenagers; a place to interrogate the world around them. Even more, members collaboratively contest these meanings through the music-making process.

As an example, the band has unofficially released its first music video to the tune 'I'll Come Back For You', by front person Emmanuel Makengera (The New American All-Stars 2020).[2] (It would be official, but we're waiting on the pandemic to be over to have our launch party.). Emmanuel wrote the song in response to saying goodbye to his family and friends when he immigrated here. Though it remains unspoken in the music, Emmanuel lost his father and brother when he came to the United States to violence and disease. His brother was his best friend and principal musical collaborator. When he sings the titular lyrics, it remains unspoken that he will never see them again and never had the chance to say goodbye.

Yet, the song is upbeat and positive. In the verses, Emmanuel reflects on the fond memories he has of loved ones, and in the chorus imagines being able to see them once again. Even though Emmanuel penned this very personal song, it was opened up to the band to make sense of it – what does it mean to say goodbye, what role does grief play in our lives, how does one create hope after a loss – and map this sense to musical elements like tempo, rhythm and phrasing. They eventually decided on something bright sounding that celebrated relationships and looked to the future, without being unduly cloying.

The band meets every Thursday, and it is without a doubt the most joyful part of my week. There is also an extra lab day when members can play around on their own, experiment with recording equipment, or, in the case of one of the band members, learn to use professional video production and editing gear. I also spend some time helping them with non-musical things, like college applications or driving them to job interviews. It has become a family of sorts.

Though the status of the bands' members as refugees may be somewhat specific to this community, the band's focus on authentically connecting with each other and musically engaging our lives is not. Music programmes across this country, both in and out of school, can have real relevance and rigour as soon as they stop asking their students to sing songs like 'Caro mio ben'. Sure, the intrepid voice teacher may ham-fistedly attempt to relate this many-centuries-old aria to the lives of their students by drawing upon the universal experience of heartbreak. But unless we celebrate and centre the vernacular of our students, we will continue to fail them.

I wholeheartedly thank those of you within organizations – NAfME and otherwise – pushing for something more important. And maybe my cursory analysis of the organization here is lacking. However, when I read what has come out of the organization, from the *Music Supervisors' Journal* to the *Music Educators Journal*, I see a field perpetually mired in the status quo, punctuated by periodic calls for change that go unheard. Expecting our profession to lead seems like a losing bet. So, let's get out there and do the work ourselves. We are the only ones that can realize the imaginary. It is up to us to no longer languish in the irrelevance of past practices. Instead of '*Languische il cor*', let's have our students exclaim: 'I came to slay, bitch!'

NOTE

1.   edTPA is a teacher assessment required in some states for teacher licensure.

REFERENCE

The New American All-Stars (2020), 'I'll Come Back For You', Music Video, Morgan Mbuli (dir.), https://youtu.be/8XvArbsh1c. Accessed 27 October 2020 [no longer available].

PART IV

POLITICS AND IDEOLOGY

Politics and ideology are omnipresent in music education and become visible if one looks just beneath the surface. In this final section, the authors from Brazil, Hong Kong, India, the United Kingdom and the United States consider topics pertinent to their work as scholars, teachers and leaders in their respective contexts. Issues under discussion include colonial structures in music education, neo-colonial practices of the UK higher education sector; invisibility and neutrality of societal values; ability, disability and sexuality; state government involvement and intervention in music teaching and learning; quick-fix professional development; the potential of popular music education for social transformation; and Black feminist thought.

Warren Churchill,
NYU Abu Dhabi

Radio Cremata,
Ithaca College

Saurav Ghosh,
drummer and a
music edu-preneur

Jasmine Hines,
Kent State
University

Wai-Chung Ho,
Hong Kong
Baptist University

Nathan Holder,
musician, author
and music educa-
tion consultant

Noah Karvelis,
University of
Wisconsin-
Madison

Adriel E. Miles,
University of
Bristol

Zack Moir,
Edinburgh Napier
University

Flávia Narita,
Universidade de
Brasília

Bryan Powell,
Montclair State
University

Jesse Rathgeber,
Augustana College

Ed Sarath,
University of
Michigan

Scott R. Sheehan,
educator, leader,
advocate,
Hollidaysburg, PA

Gareth Dylan
Smith, Boston
University

Nilesh Thomas,
Vijaybhoomi
University

Martin Urbach,
drummer, music
educator

David Wish,
Little Kids Rock

54

We Are Not Neutral:
Popular Music Education, Creativity
and the Active Creation of a
Graduate Precariat

Zack Moir

Zack Moir is an associate professor of music at Edinburgh Napier University, UK, where he is the programme leader of the MA Music programme.

In this chapter, the author argues that music educators have a responsibility to recognize their agency as political actors and the impact this has on students. He argues that music educators are not socially or politically neutral and that education can be a potent force in challenging the problematic status quo.

Introduction

In this chapter, I argue that the purpose of popular music education (PME) should not be to blindly and unquestioningly perpetuate the market-driven, employment-focussed, capitalist ideologies that have shaped many areas of PME in higher education (HE) in recent decades. The impact of such pervasive ideologies goes far beyond merely influencing curricular content encountered by the relatively small number of students who choose to study popular music in HE, with clear links between the values, beliefs and behaviours that such approaches to education promote, and the myriad social, political, economic and environmental problems we face internationally.

We are not neutral, and we need to stop pretending

In some areas of the academy – the arts perhaps being a key example – there is a view that many subjects, and the institutions in which they are studied, are 'neutral' when it comes to social and political influence on students. Some would say that teaching people to play a musical instrument, to operate a recording studio or write songs, for example, is not political in the way of sociology or political science, for instance, which have explicit political focus. I disagree and argue that such thinking is problematic and dangerous on a number of levels and fails to acknowledge the broader picture of the social, political and economic landscape in which HE operates. Woodford (2018) observes that:

> In too many cases, intellectual curiosity and political Interests are extinguished in schools and universities because those institutions portray themselves as technological, politically neutral, and socially abstract and thus value-free when nothing can be farther from the truth!
>
> (2)

Indeed, the idea that any education could be considered as politically neutral or value-free is preposterous because neutrality favours and upholds the social and political status quo, which is inherently value-laden. To fail to acknowledge the intrinsic political functions of HE is to tacitly accept the way things are and to perpetuate current conditions. By clinging to the illusion of neutrality, some HE educators have abandoned their responsibility to be the facilitators of critical consciousness within their students. As Giroux (2010) states: 'Education cannot be neutral. It is always directive in its attempt to teach students to inhabit a particular mode of agency, enable them to understand the larger world and one's role in it in a specific way' (718). Educators unequivocally *not* neutral and those who peddle myths of neutrality feed students the convenient falsehood that the current way of being is 'common-sense' and the way things should be, have always been, and is immutable – or worse that this is the *best* that things can be. Such educators are effectively complicit in stripping education of its social function, foregrounding an instrumentalist approach to education that favours individualistic gains over collective responsibility and societal benefits. This embrace of false neutrality prevents students from 'looking behind the curtain' and considering the ideological function of education in the production and perpetuation of certain forms of power, knowledge, attitudes and comprehension of the ways in which the world works and their places in it.

In the context of the pervasive employability agenda (a key preoccupation of the many universities in which popular music programmes proliferate), we see

302

HE having a function and meaning that many, including myself, see as oppressive. A problem faced by PME, however, is that many educators and students alike find it difficult to consider such criticisms, struggling to see how studying music could be considered as anything other than expressive and creative, for example. Some people do not wish to consider that such seemingly virtuous artistic pursuits could have anything to do with wider socio-political and economic injustices. In this case, part of the problem is the use of the term 'creative'.

'Creativity' as euphemism

There is a tendency to assume that the purpose of popular music in higher education is to prepare students for employment in the 'creative industries'. This is problematic for a number of reasons. As Woodford (2018) states: 'If [universities] are thought to have any political purpose at all – they now serve primarily capitalist purposes [...] often in collusion with business in confusing job training with education' (2). Linking the word 'creative' so explicitly to the notion of 'industry' is a clear indicator that industry preparation is a key aim in many areas of HE. It follows, as Mould (2009) suggests, that when we use the term 'creativity' we do so as a convenient, euphemistic shorthand for 'capitalistic creativity' – doing or creating services or things deemed necessary for their exchange value by our neoliberal, market-driven, consumerist society.

Links between arts education and the 'creative industries' are not simply means for universities to appear attractive to prospective students (Moir 2017). As is discussed in detail by (Banks and Hesmondhalgh 2009): 'A long-held ambition of the UK Labour government [...] has been to make Britain the world's creative capital [...] and the creative industries have been identified as the basis of this goal' (415–16). The UK's Department for Culture, Media and Sport made it explicit in their publication 'Creative Britain' (DCMS 2008: 25) that their aim is 'to ensure that academia is equipping students with skills to make the most effective contribution they can to the creative economy'. The incentive to engage in such work is often framed by universities and the government in terms of vocationalism. Effectively, students are assured that there is glamour and joy in being able to make a living from 'doing the things you really love' (e.g. being a musician, photographer or designer), and that life can be great when you are flexible and 'your own boss' or an entrepreneur.[1] Doing the things you love, being in charge of your own working practices, and having relative flexibility in your work (compared to 9–5 'office workers', for example) are appealing to many. However, such flexibility and autonomy usually come at a cost, with a great deal of employment activity for 'creative entrepreneurs' being project-based and low-paid, short-term and precarious, highly competitive (thus subject to negotiation on price) and exclusive of benefits such as sick-pay or pension contributions.

We find ourselves in a position in which many universities effectively validate and endorse this type of lifestyle. In PME within HE, the idea is often posed that if we teach students to be able to tap into and channel their inner creativity and 'entrepreneurship', then they will be able to survive in the creative industries. This, again, is clearly not neutral as the world in which we live is one shaped by the political and economic policies of austerity (Blyth 2013), following the global financial crash of 2008. Thus, we risk instructing students to adhere to the status quo and use their skills for individual gain within a hostile 'free' market environment and submit to the prevailing context of the industries that our sector blindly venerates, rather than encouraging them to critique the world around them.

Creating a graduate precariat

Most PME programmes that I am aware of across the HE sector explicitly profess, at least in part, to train graduates for employment in the ways noted above. However, the aforementioned precarious 'entrepreneurship' and unstable labour, often go hand-in-hand with uncertain living conditions based on insecurity, and with little or no access to non-wage benefits. Not only does this lead to a situation in which people are conditioned to believe that they should dedicate considerable amounts of their 'non-employment' time to finding work – thus effectively working for free to secure employment – it also risks significant negative effects on their health and mental wellbeing. Standing (2011) writes about the notion of the 'precariatised mind' (18) noting that this is associated with:

> Anxiety – chronic insecurity associated not only with teetering on the edge, knowing that one mistake or one piece of bad luck could tip the balance between modest dignity and being a bag lady [sic] [...] People are insecure in the mind and stressed, at the same time 'underemployed' and 'overemployed'. They are alienated from their labour and work, and are anomic, uncertain and desperate in their behaviour. People who fear losing what they have are constantly frustrated ... The precariatised mind is fed by fear and is motivated by fear.
>
> (21)

We educators need to ask ourselves whether or not we support the status quo. If we find ourselves positioned uncomfortably with the current socio-economic situation and the inequalities and injustices it creates for the majority of people in our societies, and if we struggle morally and philosophically with the way in which many forms of education bolster and perpetuate that situation, then we need to strongly consider the potency of our influence and examine our own educational practices. Again, 'there are no neutral educators' (Freire 1985: 180). We need to ask ourselves what we are doing to either support or disrupt this situation. The more that educators encourage people towards a precariatized life, often by perpetuating the myth that 'this is how it has to be' or by selling this as the aim for musicians, the greater the disservice we do our students and wider society, by framing education as preparing students for labour over humanization.

Of course, some people want to do this type of work and many may find it exciting and engaging.[2] Nonetheless, educators have a responsibility to engage with the inherently political situation in which we work, and to encourage students and colleagues to be aware of it. We should alert those with whom we work and teach to the illusion of neutrality and help them to read the world so they can critically reflect on the wider social, political and economic situation and their place within it. For me, education is about creating a formative culture that breeds the ideas and values of the future. Thus, we educators need to facilitate the creation of a critical culture which ensures that PME is not simply a mechanism for the tacit perpetuation and rationalization of an unjust social, political and economic reality. Educators are not neutral, our disciplines are not neutral, and failing to acknowledge the implicit influence our actions have on our students, their view of the world and their place within it, is a dereliction of our duty.

NOTES

1. As I write this in 2020, the world is in the midst of the COVID-19 global pandemic. I am having conversations with many of my students and recent graduates who make their living in this precarious way in the creative industries. For many, income through gigs and private teaching has just completely disappeared, and the supposed virtue of flexibility and 'being your own boss' is entirely meaningless in a world where they have been effectively trained into a position of precarity and conditioned, through the normative narrative of neoliberal HE, that this should be the goal of education. If our education system is primarily focussed on replicating capitalist norms by way of equipping students to contribute to the economy (as per explicit governmental statements) then what happens when this version of the economy fails?

2. I would like to make it clear that this is not an attack on any individual that chooses to engage with this way of working. As a young musician I found this way of working to be hugely appealing and was able to support myself and pay for my postgraduate studies by existing in this way. I was undoubtedly indoctrinated by my undergraduate studies in popular music performance, and my professional practice in this area, and it took a number of years of critical reflection on what and how I was taught as an undergraduate

to understand that my experience was clearly shaped by economic and political forces that I profoundly disagree with.

REFERENCES

Banks, Mark and Hesmondhalgh, David (2009), 'Looking for work in creative industries policy', *International Journal of Cultural Policy*, 15:4, pp. 415–30, https://doi.org/10.1080/10286630902923323. Accessed 3 March 2022.

Blyth, Mark (2013), *Austerity: The History of a Dangerous Idea*, Oxford: Oxford University Press.

Department for Culture, Media and Sport (DCMS) (2008), *Creative Britain: New Talents for the New Economy*, https://static.a-n.co.uk/wp-content/uploads/2016/12/Creative-Britain-new-talents-for-the-new-economy.pdf. Accessed 10 May 2022.

Freire, Paulo (1985), *The Politics of Education: Culture, Power and Liberation*, London: Bergin & Garvey.

Giroux, Henry A. (2010), 'Rethinking education as the practice of freedom: Paulo Freire and the promise of critical pedagogy', *Policy Futures in Education*, 8:6, pp. 715–21.

Moir, Zack (2017), 'Learning to create and creating to learn: Considering the value of popular music in higher education', in J. Williams and K. Williams (eds), *The Singer-Songwriter Handbook*, London: Bloomsbury, pp. 35–49.

Mould, Oli (2009), *Against Creativity*, New York: Verso.

Standing, Guy (2011), *The Precariat: The New Dangerous Class*, London: Bloomsbury Academic.

Woodford, P. G. (2018), *Music Education in an Age of Virtuality and Post-Truth*, New York: Taylor & Francis.

55

Toward the Political Philosophy of Hip-Hop Education and Positive Energy in China

Wai-Chung Ho

Wai-Chung Ho is a professor at Hong Kong Baptist University in the Hong Kong Special Administrative Region, where she teaches sociology of music and music education.

This chapter draws on the author's personal perspective to examine under-researched relationships between Chinese political philosophy and hip-hop education. The author discusses how China's political philosophy has integrated hip-hop education and the culture of positive energy to shape and consolidate the Chinese state's authority.

Introduction

China has witnessed great political, economic, societal and educational changes since its reform and opening up in 1978. Economic reforms and openness to popular music in China have induced radical changes in the country's educational and political ideology. Globalization is an important phenomenon that has affected popular music education in China's schools and its community. It has also produced values education such as social morals, resolving the apparent contradiction between national unity and national identity in the ever-changing interplay in the Mainland. Artists and writers are expected to promote a popular online catchphrase – 'positive energy' (*zheng nengliang*, a popular social byword used in Chinese political discourse since 2012) – that encompasses socialist values, through which China can transform itself with a collective focus on its political philosophy (see Chen and Wang 2020; Triggs 2019). In this context, this chapter will argue that the promotion of hip-hop education has been dynamic in its spread of positive energy that expresses love for the Communist Party of China (CPC) and the territorial integrity of China during the era of President Xi Jinping.

Theme of the chapter

As the People's Republic of China (PRC) entered 2021, questions regarding political developments and propaganda songs have come to the fore as the nation has made tremendous progress in its transformation to a socialist market economy. Far from parroting official orthodoxy, Chinese politicians since the turn of the twenty-first century have embraced emerging popular media – such as the internet and social media – by featuring a vast range of positive energy associated articles, films, books, songs, videos, quotations and more. Core socialist values are the soul of cultural soft power.

Given the vast scope of the subject, this brief chapter focuses on selected representative examples of general trends, which will help delineate the relationship between Chinese political philosophy and hip-hop in present-day China within the broader studies of politics and popular music education. In response to political developments and hip-hop education, this chapter was shaped by the ideological significance of positive energy in maintaining the importance of state control by encouraging a common interest in the CPC, with a focus on the following two central issues inside and outside China, respectively:

1. The use of hip-hop to celebrate the CPC and PRC authorities with new Party-backed rap songs; and
2. To fuel China's geopolitical and ideological propaganda wars against the recent Hong Kong protests.

Using rap music to spread state propaganda in Mainland

In this recent decade, waves of online nationalism (also known as cyber-nationalism) in China continue to shape the sociopolitical landscape. President Xi's fondness of using 'positive energy' represents a remarkable case of the Chinese party-state's intervention in educating people through online media discourse. According to a study on Chinese opinion surveys conducted by Alastair Johnson at Harvard

308

University from 2007 to 2015, nationalist sentiments diminished after the 2008 Beijing Olympics, and it was found that younger respondents were less nationalistic than older ones (Fang 2019). In 2015, only about 25 per cent of those in the 'post-1980s' and 'post-1990s' generations aged between 15- and 30-years-old strongly agreed with the statement 'I prefer to be a Chinese citizen' (Fang 2019: n.pag.). To address this concern, the CPC has attempted to engage Chinese youths through a number of new propaganda efforts using rap songs, WeChat stickers (simple gestures from the emoji collection of animated stickers stored on China's messaging and social media platform WeChat), and comics, with the integration of celebrity power. For example, Sina Weibo (often referred to as Weibo) has emerged in Twitter's shadow as an innovative Chinese microblog that CPC authorities use as a tool to unify the Chinese people under a shared sense of Chinese nationalism and positive energy.

When President Xi came to power in 2013, the Ministry of Culture (now the Ministry of Culture and Tourism) blacklisted more than 120 songs, including many Chinese hip-hop classics that were criticized for blasting rebellious opinions. Despite the official crackdown on hip-hop culture in the mainstream media, hip-hop (which first appeared in China in the early 1990s) is a movement for change that has promoted China's state reforms. The CPC and the state media have adopted a new strategy of using rap songs to get its message across, not only to the nation but also around the globe, and to deliver President Xi's words. In December 2015, in an effort to reach out to the smartphone generation, the state-run China Central Television (CCTV) released a rap cartoon to mark the second anniversary of the Central Leading Group for Comprehensively Deepening Reforms (a high-powered committee founded and chaired by President Xi), extolling a long list of achievements, with President Xi's contribution of backing vocals in the form of samples from some of his speeches.[1] To introduce the 13th Five-Year Plan, in February 2016, China's state news agency released a new cartoon rap video titled 'Four Comprehensives' to explain and to promote China's long-term development plan, such as environmental protection, fighting corruption, and education for all citizens, with lyrics in multiple languages including Chinese, English, Arabic, French, German, Japanese, Korean, Russian and Spanish.[2] In early May 2016, to attract young people, the People's Liberation Army (PLA) released a new hip-hop recruitment music video titled 'Battle Declaration', filled with masculine lyrics and images of advanced weapons, on the PLA Daily's website.[3] China's state media also promoted a new rap song titled 'Marx is a post-90' released in March 2016 that praised Karl Marx to reengage young people and to leverage popular culture in support of the ruling Communist Party.[4]

English is an important part of establishing China's propaganda overseas, and the CPC authorities continue to use rap to cultivate patriotism in Chinese youths. In 2016, the Communist Youth league (CYL) promoted the English-language rap song 'This Is China', sung by the hip-hop group Chengdu Revolution (also known as CD Rev) (a Chinese government-sponsored rap group), on YouTube and Facebook.[5] 'This Is China', regarded as a campaign by the PRC Government to soften its image in the world, was performed in English in an attempt to change westerners' perceptions of China. The song 'This Is China' repeated the following lyrics several times throughout: 'We love the country, we the Chi-phenomena'. Toward the end of the video, the group rapped about red dragons, peace and love. The group was also prominent for attacking Taiwanese President Tsai Ing-wen in their 'The Force of Red' song, and the lyrics about embracing the one-China principle were in English, which included the line 'There's only one China, HK, Taipei, they are my fellas', along with expletives aimed at President Tsai and her government. The group's lyrics are an assertion that the people's 'Chinese Dream' will come true, but they also do not shy away from China's problems, such as air pollution. In December 2017, the Xinhua News Agency (an official state-run press agency of the PRC) released a new video titled 'Another Day in China' sung in English for foreign residents as a loving ode to China in the form of propaganda rap by critics.[6]

In 2019, an English-language propaganda rap video was produced to highlight the annual 'Two Sessions' Chinese legislative gathering held in March of that year. The music video, sung by the Chinese rapper Su Han and posted by the state media agency Xinhua, was titled 'Two Sessions'. The lyrics, 'I got elation from inspiration writing a compliment song for a nation while I'm talking about "two sessions"', are sung while the camera pans over Beijing's Great Hall of the People, where the National People's Congress gathered for the political meeting; they continue by celebrating China's recent developments, including its moon lander and its battles against pollution and poverty.[7] In April 2019, China launched a public welfare programme sponsored by the Central Committee of the CYL to promote hip-hop dance in schools in impoverished areas with a view to boosting students' fitness and self-confidence. This officially approved hip-hop culture has become a political acknowledgement of its inclusion in educational materials for Chinese youths.

Propaganda rap for condemning Hong Kong's protests and anti-US sentiment

Outside China, the Chinese government has embarked on a propaganda campaign to portray Hong Kong's protesters as extreme and violent. Anti-government protests in Hong Kong, which started out as demonstrations against a now-suspended extradition bill, took place in 2019. On the one hand, Hong Kong protest songs have included Christian hymns and Cantonese pop hits, which protesters have used to express their frustration and solidarity through singing. On the other hand,

Beijing has found a new way to intensify the pro-democracy protests in Hong Kong through its communication of the positive energy of socialist values. Over the summer of 2019, some of China's most prominent rappers took to social media to voice their politics. Big-name rappers in China lined up to back the establishment after an attack on a journalist from the Mainland by anti-government protesters at Hong Kong International Airport. A number of Chinese hip-hop stars, ranging from international crossover artists Higher Brothers to rising rappers and the long-standing collective CD Rev, all stood up for the Chinese authorities. They called out the ongoing pro-democracy protests in Hong Kong and shared a meme originally posted by the CPC mouthpiece *People's Daily* on 14 August 2019 that bore the words 'I support Hong Kong police, you can hit me' in traditional Chinese characters on a red background, with 'what a shame for Hong Kong' written in English underneath. PG One (the co-champion of the first Chinese hip-hop music variety show *The Rap of China*) re-posted the meme on *People's Daily* and Weibo, with the following caption: 'Support Hong Kong police, resist violence atrocities!!! I hope everyone is safe and secure' (Navlakha 2019: n.pag.). Vava, who also rose to fame with her performance on the television show *The Rap of China* and has been called China's Rihanna, posted the meme to her over 300,000 Instagram followers with the English caption, 'Hong Kong is part of China forever' (Navlakha 2019: n.pag.). As of 21 August 2019, seven of China's biggest rap artists have condemned the Hong Kong protesters and some of them used their art to send a tranquil larger anti-Hong Kong message (Wright 2019). Their response became part of an ample online patriotic movement in the Mainland, which mushroomed following a state-led propaganda campaign to discredit protesters in Hong Kong.

Chinese rap songs were adopted to boost the image of China abroad, with the intent of using Chinese societal resources to generate soft power in hip-hop education. One rap song, 'Hong Kong's Fall' by CD Rev, featured Donald Trump, with lyrics rapped in both English and Putonghua (the official language of the PRC) about the ongoing protests in Hong Kong. The song included a remix of President Donald Trump's statement on August 1 that 'Hong Kong is a part of China. They'll have to deal with that themselves. They don't need advice' (Borger 2019: n.pag.). The song demanded an end to the protests and suggested that the Chinese military could use tanks and soldiers to terminate the protests. The *People's Daily*, *China Daily*, and China Global Television Network (an international media organization launched by CCTV) simultaneously shared CD Rev's song on Twitter in August 2019. Another rap video, 'Hey Democracy' by CD Rev, overlaid clips of Hong Kong protesters clashing with police and breaking into Hong Kong's legislative offices, with the lyrics, 'Hey democracy! Once I heard you be found in the Middle East, people were throwing bombs across the city streets' in English. Another rap song, 'Wrong Way', promoted by the state-led media, pleaded with the Hong Kong protesters in both Cantonese and Putonghua to 'stop' and 'calm down' before 'turning Hong Kong into heaven and violence' (Chen 2019: n.pag.). These rap songs served as attempts to inject strong positive energy into regional and national security, thus making a contribution to the Chinese community through the shared Chinese political philosophy of hip-hop education.

Final remarks

Propaganda hip-hop and rap are promoted and shared using cutting-edge popular culture to cultivate a political philosophy and officially approved positive energy via cyber culture in China's territory. In this regard, although rap songs and patriotic campaigns have increased national support for the Communist regime, the revival of Chinese nationalism is also a cultural image constructed by a collective act of the CPC's rule and has both controlling and emancipating capacities, generated and cultivated in a specific time and space. These rap songs signify Chinese positive energy for a political philosophy that intends to bring about political unity and social stability promoted through cultural media to bolster the nationalist's claim as the legal and cultural representative of the PRC. Following top-down orders from President Xi Jinping, the rap songs are dynamic, constantly recasting and reinvoking national memories to address the collective needs of the Chinese authorities and sustain their contemporary political rule. Tension may exist between the Chinese people's experiences with nationalism or populist nationalism, and praise for the CPC found in the rap songs. As China is a one-party state dominated by the CPC, many putatively patriotic songs are, in reality, songs praising the CPC, Chairman Mao, Marxism and President Xi. Hoping to boost the image of CPC authorities and President Xi, the recent rap songs are part of an ongoing plan aimed at young people. The question that remains for the CPC, however, is whether and how song campaigns and rap songs can restore public confidence and national spirit and perpetuate various kinds of positive energy spins on the CPC's achievements in the long run. Further research is, therefore, needed to explain how the promotion of rap songs in response to domestic and external changes has mediated Chinese politics to affect the construction and recycling of positive energy in China. Research should further explore the extent of popular propaganda songs such as rap songs as a means to reorganize propaganda efforts at home and abroad in China's popular music education.

ACKNOWLEDGEMENT
The author wishes to acknowledge the generous support of the Hong Kong Research Grants Council who funds this project (HKBU 12608618).

NOTES

1. The music video can be viewed at: https://www.youtube.com/watch?v=xhU8C5RCbBs&t=27s. Accessed 27 October 2020.

2. The rap video sung in multiple languages, can be viewed at: https://www.youtube.com/watch?v=EUYJKtfnAyA&t=27s. Accessed 27 October 2020.

3. The music video can be viewed at: https://www.youtube.com/watch?v=rTdOnDSPZQ&t=6s. Accessed 27 October 2020.

4. The music video can be viewed at: https://www.youtube.com/watch?v=jN2UBLb7U70. Accessed 27 October 2020.

5. The music video, with English subtitles, can be viewed at: https://www.youtube.com/watch?v=HCm3sbujB8g. Accessed 27 October 2020.

6. The music video, with Chinese and English subtitles, can be viewed at: https://www.youtube.com/watch?v=YQtHY3QWxjY. Accessed 27 October 2020.

7. The music video, with English subtitles, can be viewed at: https://www.youtube.com/watch?v=a5rvO5e-rik&t=10s. Accessed 27 October 2020.

REFERENCES

Borger, Julian (2019), 'Trump promised China US silence on Hong Kong protests during trade talks', *The Guardian*, 4 October, https://www.theguardian.com/world/2019/oct/04/trump-china-hong-kong-protests-xi-jinping-trade-talks. Accessed 10 May 2022.

Chen, Qin (2019), 'Rap songs fuel China's propaganda war on Hong Kong protests', *Inkstone*, 22 August, https://www.inkstonenews.com/politics/rap-songs-fuel-chinas-propaganda-war-hong-kong-protests/article/3023932. Accessed 27 October 2020.

Chen, Zifeng and Wang, Clyde Yicheng (2020), 'The discipline of happiness: The Foucauldian use of the "positive energy" discourse in China's ideological works', *Journal of Current Chinese Affairs*, 48:2, pp. 201–25.

Fang, Kecheng (2019), 'Is cyber-nationalism on the rise in China?', *Echowall*, 25 September, https://www.echo-wall.eu/chinese-whispers/cyber-nationalism-rise-china. Accessed 27 October 2020.

Navlakha, Meera (2019), 'China's patriotic rap stars are blasting the Hong Kong protests on social media', *Vice*, 22 August, https://www.vice.com/en/article/xwex5z/chinas-patriotic-rap-stars-are-blasting-the-hong-kong-protests-on-social-media. Accessed 27 October 2020.

Triggs, Francesca (2019), 'The ideological function of "positive energy" discourse: A People's Daily analysis', *British Journal of Chinese Studies*, 9:2, pp. 83–112.

Wright, Adam (2019), 'How Chinese rappers are selling out hip hop by slamming Hong Kong protesters and supporting police', *South China Morning Post*, 21 August, https://www.scmp.com/lifestyle/entertainment/article/3023712/how-chinese-rappers-are-selling-out-hip-hop-slamming-hong. Accessed 27 October 2020.

56

Structural and Cultural Barriers to Relevant Popular Music Education in India

Nilesh Thomas and Saurav Ghosh

Nilesh Thomas serves as Dean of the True School of Music at Vijaybhoomi University. He has two decades' experience in designing higher music education programmes.

Saurav Ghosh is a drummer and a music edu-preneur working to democratize music education for young learners by leveraging the power of technology.

In this chapter, the authors shed light on current practices, shortcomings and the potential for popular music education in India. India is on course to become one of the fastest growing music and entertainment markets, while music education, particularly popular music education, largely continues to be brushed aside as a hobby.

Popular music in India

The term 'popular music' faces a bit of an identity crisis in India at present (Cashman 2013). The terms *contemporary music* and *popular music* are often used to refer to western contemporary music, which in most cases is a reference to western popular music styles, especially in the context of education. However, from the context of the genre of music that most appeals to the majority of the Indian population, popular music is Bollywood music and music from regional language films. New Bollywood songs are #1 on the list of favourite genres in India, followed by old Bollywood songs and other regional music, while pop music is at #5, and hip-hop/rap is at #6 (International Federation of the Phonographic Industry

2019: 25). International music accounted for only 18 per cent of what Indians listened to in 2018–19, while Bollywood alone, excluding regional language music topped the chart at 50 per cent of the market share (Forbes India 2019: 3).

There is consistent influence and influx of western popular music elements in the musical construction of new Bollywood songs, particularly stylistic characteristics in compositions, use of harmony and widespread use of western musical instruments. Contemporary Bollywood music producers have pioneered the art of combining western popular music with Indian rhythms, melodic motives and Indian musical instruments that evoke cultural connections to shape a unique genre of music that appeals to the evolving taste of Indian audiences. The primary purpose of popular music education in India, therefore, should be to further this craft by creating versatile popular music practitioners and thought leaders capable of continuous musical innovation that connects India seamlessly with the rest of the world.

Popular music education in schools

The unique characteristics of India's popular music – an amalgamation of a wide variety of musical styles and influences from across the globe underpinned by Indian classical music roots – present an immense challenge and scope to popular music education in the Indian context. Popular music education has been long neglected in India, with no meaningful efforts to introduce music, let alone popular music studies in the school system that caters to roughly 250 million students. While India's National Curriculum Framework specifies that music must be an integral part of the school curriculum (NCERT 2005: 55), research indicates that music education is not available in most schools, and there is a severe dearth of qualified music teachers, relevant curriculum and infrastructure (Vishal 2015: 5). In the limited number of schools where music is included in the curriculum, high priority is given to Indian classical music and only traditional Indian musical instruments are made available, leading to a rather limited awareness of the wider subgenres and style idioms within popular music among students (Vishal 2015: 6–7).

The absence of a centralized, comprehensive popular music education programme in schools has created a vacuum of comprehensive curriculum and meaningful music skill building among students, especially within the public school system, and some private music education providers have stepped in with attempts to fill some of this void through music teaching in select schools. While the intent is mostly well placed, the music curriculum and delivery standards are often diluted to fit other priorities in schools, and the music programme often amounts to being merely a poster boy for extra-curricular activities, meant only to increase a school's social reputation. There is a pressing need to focus on finding a meaningful, sustainable and scalable popular music education model for schools that, most importantly, allows students to express themselves through music.

A parallel western art music learning ecosystem exists in India for school going children through a network of private music teachers, private music academies and examination bodies such as the ABRSM, Trinity and Yamaha. Increasingly, contemporary western music pathways such as Trinity Rock & Pop and Rockschool that extend learning to domains such as music production and contemporary music theory have gained popularity among students and parents. Private popular music academies that offer their own custom learning pathways incorporating music performance, music theory and music technology have emerged in most metropolises. While this trend is encouraging, it serves only a very small fraction of learners since the access is restricted both due to geographical limits and the cost of tuition. And most importantly, it addresses only one part of India's popular music learning equation, which is western contemporary music, while ignoring the Bollywood and traditional music elements.

Popular music in higher education

A similar plight exists for popular music in India's higher education ecosystem consisting of nearly 900 universities and 49,000 colleges, with only a couple of undergraduate programmes that focus on the key aspects of popular music, i.e., songwriting, music production and engineering, music performance, music business or music education. It is intriguing to note that the $790 million Indian popular music industry sustains itself, innovates and is forecasted to grow at a CAGR of 13.5 per cent to reach $1.5 billion by 2023 to become one of the top music markets in the world (PricewaterhouseCoopers 2019), with very little contribution from the country's formal education sector.

Tertiary education in popular music remains entirely with private institutions in India, with practically no contribution or accreditation from national or state level higher education bodies. These 'institutes' operate outside the realm of the university and college system,[1] and have been generally successful in developing popular music courses focusing on employability and enterprise. Three institutions, The True School of Music in Mumbai, Global Music Institute in Delhi and the KM Music Conservatory in Chennai offer structured popular music programmes from one to three years in duration. Several other smaller institutions across the country offer independent 'short professional courses' focusing on specific aspects of popular music such as electronic music production (EDM), sound engineering, songwriting and music performance.

Most of the leading popular music education institutes in India began operations in response to a rising demand for contemporary western music education in the country, and looking up to the small but promising independent music scene fuelled by the growing affluence of the middle class. Many started in the early 2010s as training grounds for grooming performing musicians and singer-songwriters for the independent music scene by introducing contemporary music programmes focussed on jazz, rock, pop, hip-hop and R&B. Some others focused solely on music production, sound engineering and DJ training, adopting more of a vocational training approach in view of India's booming digital media industry. There have been very few attempts to bridge the gap between this contemporary western-focused music education and the demands of India's popular music, which requires a unique set of skills and expertise that traverses Indian and western music genres, styles and influences. Academic leaders and other relevant stakeholders must explore innovative and hybrid approaches integrating Indian music fundamentals, western contemporary music practice and modern music production techniques to develop a coherent set of popular music education programmes relevant to India. Such an approach is likely to guarantee far-reaching outcomes more than merely trying to mimic globalized practices in western popular music education as an alternative to studying abroad.

One of the major challenges from the onset for India's popular music institutes during the early 2010s was the lack of qualified popular music educators in the country, which continues today. Many institutes are still sourcing faculty from abroad to fill the gap in local teaching talent (Cashman 2013). While recruitment of expatriate faculty solves the issue of sourcing qualified western contemporary music practitioners, it presents a multitude of other challenges. Maintaining an expatriate teaching team has a direct impact on tuition fees, and students are left with little choice but to pay relatively higher fees. While the fees charged by leading popular music institutes in India are still only a fraction of the fees charged by US and UK counterparts, they are high in comparison to professional courses in STEM, business or law. The lack of sufficient professional industry experience within India and exposure to Bollywood music among expatriate faculty poses another challenge to designing and delivering courses that cross over from western contemporary music to Indian popular music. Academic heads usually attempt to mitigate this challenge by integrating local music industry experts in the academic team, mostly as adjunct faculty, consulting curriculum advisors or masterclass facilitators.

Popular music education in India is still at a nascent stage. With increasing exposure to western media and the increasingly apparent career opportunities in music and media, Indian parents are slowly warming up to the idea of alternative career options such as music for their children. However, a terminal qualification on paper still remains a very important aspect for many, often valued more than employable skills, therefore the lack of formal undergraduate qualifications in popular music within India remains a serious roadblock to the proliferation of popular music education in the country. Most private popular music institutes rely on international degree granting university partners from the UK or the US to offer degrees via articulation agreements that require students to complete the final leg of their studies abroad. While this provides a reasonable option for some students, it is not a preferred choice for many due to the additional costs involved. Lack of locally accredited undergraduate study options also severely limits funding options for students who wish to pursue a career in popular music since student loans are not easily available to those taking courses outside of the Indian university system.

Towards the future

In 2014, the Indian government established a new Ministry of Skill Development and Entrepreneurship and various sector skill councils under it to boost employability and enterprise. This has given much needed traction to the establishment of skill qualifications within the media and entertainment sector in India, under which music is recognized as an independent skill domain. The Media and Entertainment Skills Council of India (MESC) published the first set of National Occupational Standards and Qualification Packs for music programmer, music producer and music composer/director mapped to National Skills Qualification Framework (NSQF) levels 5, 6 and 7 (equivalent to undergraduate years one, two and three) in 2019, paving the way for formalizing further skill qualifications in popular music with an India focus. The True School of Music, Mumbai was the first to offer career-oriented popular music programmes in music production, music performance and sound engineering with integrated skill certification from MESC. True School also established articulation agreements with UK universities as an alternative route to address the lack of local undergraduate qualifications, allowing its students a continuous learning pathway to earn a UK undergraduate or master's degree in popular music practice.

Introducing centralized and structured popular music education within the K-12 system in India is going to be a complex task owing to the sheer size of the country, involvement of a number of overlapping regulatory bodies between central and state education boards, infrastructure requirements, and, most importantly, the availability of trained music teachers for 1.4 million schools. India's Ministry of Human Resource Development began working with MESC in 2019 to encourage universities and colleges to integrate media and entertainment skill training into undergraduate courses. India's New Education Policy (NEP) 2020 has proposed radical changes to the school education system and tertiary learning framework, including choice-based education that suit individual learners and their aspirations instead of the forced fit into a fixed learning pathway. These could turn positive for the future of popular music education in India since it is expected to foster an environment that promotes learning diversity, acceptance of alternative careers, academia, thought leadership and innovation that can usher a new era of music education from early years to tertiary studies.

NOTE

1. These institutions (institutes) do not have degree awarding powers, a choice often made in view of the extreme complexities within the local higher education system. However, these institutions remain the top choice among music students due to their curricular integrity, teaching excellence and sate of the art learning infrastructure. Ultimately they serve the purpose of preparing students for a career.

REFERENCES

Balani, Aditya (2018), 'How music education is still evolving in India', *Entrepreneur India Edition*, January, https://www.entrepreneur.com/article/307603. Accessed 28 November 2019.

Cashman, David (2013), 'Foundation studies: Contemporary music education in India', *Ethnomusicology Review*, 18, https://www.ethnomusicologyreview.ucla.edu/content/foundation-studies-contemporary-music-education-india. Accessed on 28 November 2019.

Forbes India (2019), 'How the Indian music industry makes money', *Forbes India*, http://www.forbesindia.com/article/special/how-the-indian-music-industry-makes-money/55099/1. Accessed 3 December 2019.

International Federation of the Phonographic Industry (2019), *Music Listening 2019*, https://www.ifpi.org/downloads/Music-Listening-2019.pdf Accessed 3 December 2019.

National Council for Educational Research and Training (India) (2005), *National Curriculum Framework-2005*, http://www.ncert.nic.in/rightside/links/pdf/framework/english/nf2005.pdf. Accessed 3 December 2019.

PricewaterhouseCoopers (2019), 'India's entertainment and media industry to clock over INR 451,373Cr by 2023: PwC Report' [Press release], https://www.pwc.in/press-releases/2019/global-entertainment-and-media-outlook-2019-2023.html. Accessed on 28 November 2019.

Vishal, Dr. (2015), 'The face of music education in schools in India', presented at the *International Gandhi Jayanti Conference 2015*, New Delhi, India, https://www.researchgate.net/publication/282843648. Accessed 28 November 2019.

57

Popular Music Education as a Liberating Education

Flávia Narita

Flávia Motoyama Narita has been a lecturer at the Universidade de Brasília (UnB), Brazil since 2006, teaching graduate and undergraduate courses in music education.

This chapter presents educational concerts of popular music as an outreach activity with undergraduate music students of Universidade de Brasília, Brazil. Before the COVID-19 pandemic, the author supervised that activity aiming at developing conscientization of democratic issues alongside musical skills whilst planning interactions with pupils during concerts in schools.

Introduction

In 2019, following the elected conservative president coming to power in Brazil, Brazilians witnessed government policies undermining education, especially those related to government-funded higher education institutions. In less than two years, we have had four ministers of education privileging the hard sciences and private institutions.[1] One previous minister used to attack universities through social media, claiming without proof that some universities were sites of extensive cannabis plantations[2] and that universities instilled Marxist indoctrination and disorder and did not conduct research.[3] The current minister may not be as belligerent as the last but views education as a 'factory' to mould professionals for industry and business, rather than a place for the development of full human beings.

In such a threatening scenario, it is worth recalling Paulo Freire's reminder that education is politics and once we gain consciousness that we are beings in the world, interacting with the world and with others, we 'cannot escape ethical responsibility for [our] moving through the world' (Freire 2005: 99). Thus, being ethically responsible for our actions means we face the consequences of our choices. 'As a consequence of thinking in favor of whom, in favor of what, in favor of what dream I am teaching, I will have to think against whom, against what, against what dream I am teaching' (Freire 2016: 21). Hence, when I position myself against these attacks on education, against a type of teaching that does not take into account students' voices, I am in favour of an education that can liberate students and teachers to think autonomously, so that we can critically develop our own reasoning, regardless of who or which political party is in power.

Freire used to remind us that a truly liberating education is also a humanizing education. Despite difficulties we might face, Freire (2005: 100) always hopefully believed that changing is possible because we are unfinished beings, conscious of our unfinished nature and thus have the potential to make things different. It is this possibility of trying new routes that is in tune with my (re)search into a humanizing education through music that instigates my interest in popular music education, in particular what Lucy Green (2008a) identified as the informal learning practices of popular musicians.

When introducing the *Journal of Popular Music Education*, Smith and Powell (2017: 4) noted that there were two different groups of the prospective audience for that journal: one that considers popular music education as 'one part of the jigsaw puzzle of a schoolteacher's diverse portfolio of approaches to learning, teaching and assessment', and another whose 'goal is to learn (about) popular music'. I belong to the first group and subscribe to the idea that Green's (2008a, 2008b) informal learning approach to music education is in tune with Freire's ([1970] 2005: 79) liberating and humanizing education. In this chapter, I briefly discuss popular music education through informal learning practices and in educational concerts, dialoguing with Freire's ideas.

Music teacher education and informal learning practices

In informal learning practices, learners' choice of musical repertoire and the use of 'real' music (Green 2009: 129, original emphasis), that 'exists in the world *beyond* education, as well as, or instead of, the world *of* education', can be paralleled to Freire's ([1970] 2005: 106) generative themes, which 'can only be apprehended in the human–world relationship'. The generative themes were a result of people thinking about their realities and people's actions upon those realities. In addition, the dialogical strategy in which teachers and students can learn from each other is found in both Green's and Freire's educational approaches. In musical practices, this dialogical approach 'permits the equal/unequal relationship between teacher and student to be rebalanced by allowing students to be in control of the music and the learning' (Wright 2014: 32). Ruth Wright (2017: 20) also points out that 'mainstream popular music is a space which [students] feel safe to inhabit alongside their peers and one in which they can develop and maintain at least one of their outward facing identities'.

As a music teacher–educator, I can promote such informal learning practices with undergraduates, who can later implement those practices in school settings. Although all of them already play at least one musical instrument and know how to read music staff notation, many are not used to playing by ear. Moreover, many are not used to a dialogical approach to education and reproduce what Freire termed 'banking education', a kind of approach that disempowers learners since they passively receive and reproduce teachers' valued, deposited knowledge. Therefore, popular music education experienced through informal learning practices in music teacher education modules can help future music teachers not only to promote practices of music making through aural learning but also to develop a dialogical approach to teaching. This is key to develop a more critical stance on the roles of education and of educators.

University outreach: Educational concerts

Another place of popular music education I have explored of late is the university outreach activity of educational concerts. Recently I supervised an undergraduate musical band of five male students. All of these five music students have their own bands outside the university and, therefore, are used to playing to and interacting with their audiences as any popular group does in concerts. Similarly to their informal learning outside the university, they conducted their rehearsals autonomously, deciding the structure of each song and directing their own learning (Lebler 2008: 194; Green 2008b: 178). However, practising for an educational concert required music undergraduates doing more than getting the repertoire ready for their audiences. They had to plan appropriate interactions with young pupils in schools. My role in the rehearsals was to give this group of undergraduates some ideas about how they could interact with school pupils.

As Green (2009: 127) reminds us, 'pupils' engagement as producers – in whatever style of music – is the key to opening out their ears as listeners, most particularly when production involves an amount of aural work'. In the concerts we played, we did not manage to involve school pupils in what Green (2002: 24) termed 'purposive and attentive listening' tasks. Their engagement as producers involved more visual than aural work and included looking at one of the band members and imitating a pentatonic riff on the keyboard, clapping a rhythmic ostinato, creating a specific soundscape using body percussion and singing. The repertoire included Brazilian popular and folk musics that were part of an interdisciplinary examination that selects applicants to enter the Universidade de Brasília, a government-funded university. Some of the songs were familiar to the pupils, who usually sang along with recordings.

As part of the educational side of the concerts, band members skilfully demonstrated differences among musical genres such as rock, bossa-nova, reggae, waltz, pop, baião, sertanejo and caipira music. They also talked about their instruments (bass guitar, acoustic guitar, drums, viola caipira and voice) and gave information about melody, rhythm, harmony, pitch, duration, tempo and timbre. In addition, they discussed issues related to the lyrics. These included domestic violence, consumerism, race and cultural blending, and access of Black people to societal goods. Such discussion topics had the potential to raise pupils' awareness about power relations and, through musics that sounded familiar to most of them, develop what Freire ([1970] 2005a: 119) called conscientization, which refers to critical consciousness 'of a situation, [and] [...] action [that] prepares men [and women] for the struggle against the obstacles to their humanization'.

Opening up spaces for (popular) music education

In Brazil, higher education institutions still have the autonomy to decide the criteria of their admissions processes. At the Universidade de Brasília, there are three main routes that applicants may take to enter university. The first is to sit for an exam prepared by the institution to assess applicants' general academic knowledge at the end of their secondary education. The second is to use the scores of a national exam taken at the end of secondary school to apply for a course. The third is to sit for an exam prepared by the institution at the end of each year of the last three years of secondary school. In the first two types of exams, information about art and of some musical genres and instruments might be asked, but it is in the third type of the admission process that music is found more often. There is a list of a broad music repertoire for each year of the examination and applicants are required to connect that repertoire to other subject knowledges in an interdisciplinary study. That undergraduate musical band I supervised, focused on the popular music repertoire for that type of exam.

Music lessons in Brazil are not implemented in every school, despite the law that made it mandatory as curricular content in 2008 and another law that included other arts in 2016. Due to this, educational concerts and other university outreach activities can be a means to broaden school pupils' repertoire and information about music that could help them in the examinations to enter the public university. Ideally, we would also provide pupils more experiences of music making during the concerts, so that some pupils could play along with the band.

In 2020, however, the pandemic scenario caused by the COVID-19 has transformed our musical practices. Peer-learning and the hands-on experience of music making frequently found in informal learning practices had to be reinvented during these times of social distancing. Technology has been essential to keep us connected through video lessons, apps and video calls but access to internet has also been a concern in a country with so many inequalities. Popular music education through engagement in musical experiences that open up spaces for various apps, interactions and discussions about digital inclusion/exclusion, may develop both school pupils' and music undergraduates' awareness of the power of (popular) music to disseminate harmony, hatred, ideals and values. If they achieve Freire's conscientization, that awareness will instigate them to take action. In the current time, under a conservative government that tries to silence dialogue, the fight for education should be on everyone's agendas. Popular music education may be a powerful weapon in that fight.

NOTES

1. https://www.universityworldnews.com/post.php?story=20201113063532958. Accessed 29 November 2020.
2. https://www.web24.news/u/2020/06/six-controversies-that-marked-the-administration-of-abraham-weintraub-in-the-ministry-of-education.html. Accessed on 29 November 2020.
3. https://www.brasildefato.com.br/2019/05/21/cuts-will-impact-more-than-30-of-budget-in-half-of-brazils-federal-universities/. Accessed 2 November 2020.

REFERENCES

Freire, Paulo ([1970] 2005), *Pedagogy of the Oppressed* (trans. M. Bergman Ramos), 30th anniversary ed., New York: Continuum.

Freire, Paulo (2005), *Pedagogy of Indignation*, Boulder: Routledge.

Freire, Paulo (2016), 'Pedagogy of solidarity', in P. Freire, A. M. Araújo Freire and W. de Oliveira (eds), *Pedagogy of Solidarity*, Walnut Creek: Routledge, pp. 15–34.

Green, Lucy (2002), *How Popular Musicians Learn: A Way Ahead for Music Education*, Aldershot: Ashgate.

Green, Lucy (2008a), *Music, Informal Learning and the School: A New Classroom Pedagogy*, Aldershot: Ashgate.

Green, Lucy (2008b), 'Group cooperation, inclusion and disaffected pupils: Some responses to informal learning in the music classroom', presented at the *RIME Conference 2007*, Exeter, UK, *Music Education Research*, 10:2, pp. 177–92, https://doi.org/10.1080/14613800802079049. Accessed 1 January 2020.

Green, Lucy (2009), 'Response to special issue of "Action, criticism and theory for music education" concerning music, informal learning and the school: A new classroom pedagogy', *Action, Criticism, and Theory for Music Education*, 8:2, pp. 120–32.

Lebler, Don (2008), 'Popular music pedagogy: Peer learning in practice', *Music Education Research*, 10:2, pp. 193–213.

Smith, Gareth Dylan and Powell, Bryan (2017), 'Welcome to the journal', *Journal of Popular Music Education*, 1:1, pp. 3–8.

Wright, Ruth (2014), 'The fourth sociology and music education: Towards a sociology of integration', *Action, Criticism, and Theory for Music Education*, 13:1, pp. 12–39.

Wright, Ruth (2017), 'The longer revolution: The rise of vernacular musics as "new channels of general learning"', *Journal of Popular Music Education*, 1:1, pp. 9–24.

58

Young, Gifted and Black Q.U.E.E.N.: Nuancing Black Feminist Thought within Music Education

Jasmine Hines

Jasmine Hines is an assistant professor of music education at Kent State University in Ohio, USA, where she teaches contemporary and traditional choral methods courses.

In this chapter, the author aims to provide culturally reflective insight towards how Black women's contributions within popular music can be utilized in all levels of the music education classroom in hopes of connecting with and listening to young Black girls who have personal aspirations in music and music education.

In an age of social justice advocacy within education, the work of Black womxn continues to be excluded from the hegemonic educational canon despite the long history of Black feminists advocating for the eradication of systematic oppression in education. By examining livelihoods and music created by Black feminist musicians, music educators may reflect on how Black womxn's positionalities within society have had a direct influence on the music they created within a White culturally dominant society. Distinguished University Professor Emerita of Sociology, Patricia Hill Collins (2000) stated:

> Developing Black feminist thought as critical social theory involves including the ideas of Black women not previously considered intellectuals – many of whom may be working-class women with jobs outside academia – Musicians, vocalists, poets, writers, and other artists constitute another group from which Black women intellectuals have emerged. Building on African-influenced oral traditions,

musicians, in particular, have enjoyed close association with the larger community of African-American women constituting their audience.

(16–17)

Black feminist musicians have historically used music as an educative tool to create and disseminate cultural knowledge while simultaneously providing sociocultural and sociopolitical commentary. Thus, the incorporation of Black feminist musicians within the pedagogical, philosophical and musical canon of music education not only provides educational representation for other young Black female musicians but also disrupts monolithic or stereotypical perceptions others may have about Black womxn in music. Therefore, I find it imperative to highlight two outspoken popular Black female musicians who have a legacy of disrupting their respective canons: Nina Simone and Janelle Monáe.

Young gifted and black Q.U.E.E.N. – Nina Simone and Janelle Monáe

Many of Nina Simone's songs spoke the lived realities of Black women and Black girls. Nina Simone centralized the collective Black American experience in songs such as 'Four Women' (Simone 1966), 'To Be Young, Gifted, and Black' (Simone 1967), Simone's cover of 'Strange Fruit' (1965) and 'Mississippi Goddam' (1964). Nina Simone's expression of her musicality often depicted the pleasures and devastating realities many Black women faced at the intersection of racism, sexism, sexual discrimination and classism.

Dick Gregory, a Black American comedian and civil rights activist, strongly admired Simone's sharp tongue on White supremacy and institutions that benefitted from the social constructions of race and gender (Lee 2015). Nina Simone's unapologetic commentary can also be seen within some of her most famous musical performances. Nina Simone often showcased her skill of balancing the playfulness and buoyancy often found within Eurocentric historical children's songs or showtune-like music along with lyrics that criticize society's actions or reactions towards racism and sexism in the United States. This expression of intersectional musicality allowed for Nina Simone's music to cross racial and gender boundaries within her respective cultural climate.

Janelle Monáe, the 34-year-old Black, nonbinary,[1] pansexual, singer, songwriter and Oscar- and Grammy-nominated activist, has been a prominent figure in popular music over the past decade. Their journey with Hollywood beauty standards, expectations of her sexuality and displaying her early struggles with classism can easily be seen as resistance towards a myopic understanding of what it means to be a successful Black female musician. This outward personification

327

of intersectionality has not only relegated Monáe to a level of crossover stardom, but the intersectional musicality of their music has left Monáe in an undefined music genre (Tran 2020). Monáe is an intersectional musician who consistently centres their intersectional identity within her work. She initially embodied an androgynous look, performed dance moves that resembled those of Michael Jackson and James Brown, and played with her vocal range and ability on several recordings. While some praised the uniqueness of her image and music, others found it difficult to pigeonhole Monáe according to socially constructed expectations the society typically aligns with a darker-skinned young Black woman (Wortham 2018).

Monáe, a Black, queer woman from an economically poor background, created music reflexive of her own experiences while also critiquing systematic structures that impact the lives of Black womxn and girls. Black feminist musicians continue to uphold the responsibility of reflecting the sociocultural and sociopolitical times through their music. Analyzing lyrics of popular Black feminist musicians – such as Nina Simone and Janelle Monáe – within music education can provide a glimpse in what it means to create, perform and even exist as Black womxn.

An artist's duty

In Netflix's *What Happened, Miss Nina Simone?* (Garbus 2015), Nina Simone spoke about the responsibilities of an artist; she stated:

> An artist's duty [...] is to reflect the times. I think that is true of painters, sculptors, poets, musicians. [...] it's their choice, but I choose to reflect on the times and situations in which I find myself. That, to me, is my duty.

Black feminist writers have written similar statements. Hill Collins (2000: xi) stated, 'I have always seen organic links between Black feminism as a social justice project and Black feminist thought as its intellectual center'. Black feminists have historically been extremely vocal about eradicating all forms of oppression (Combahee River Collective 1986; Hill Collins 2000). Thus, it is not uncommon for Black feminists and Black feminist musicians to provide reflexive lyrics about oppressive systems and societal structures in songs like 'Mississippi Goddam', 'To Be Young Gifted and Black' and 'Strange Fruit'. While Simone's musical commentary was provocative and progressive, due to cultural morality of the United States during the 1960s and 1970s, she did not provide contextual information by way of music or interviews on her views of the LGBTQIA+ community (Simone and Cleary 1992). However, Simone's call to action, understood in her reflections towards an artist's duty, provided theoretical support for future Black LGBTQIA+ individuals to creatively share their stories and experiences through music.

Janelle Monáe has also been seen as a musician-activist. In a 2018 *New York Times* feature, she elaborated, 'I've always understood the responsibility of an artist – but I feel it even greater now' (Wortham 2018: n.pag.). Her activism as a mainstream artist continues to be unexpected, as she went off script and had her mic cut off during a *Good Morning America* interview (Pengelly 2015). Before she was censored, she publicly stated:

> God bless America. God bless all, all the lost lives to police brutality. We want White America to know that we stand tall today. We want Black America to know that we stand tall today. We will not be silenced.
>
> (Pengelly 2015)

It is important to state that while we can certainly see similarities of activism between Simone and Monáe, they are not outliers or spectacles. Black women have a history of calling for social justice. All we have to do is simply listen.

Monáe's activism in the form of lyrical representation can be seen in her 2013 hit single 'Q.U.E.E.N.', featuring Erykah Badu. Her 2018 *Rolling Stone* interview (Monáe 2018: n.pag.) claimed, '[t]he original title of "Q.U.E.E.N.", she noted, was Q.U.E.E.R., and you can still hear the word on the track's background harmonies'. Although Monáe chose the alternate title of Q.U.E.E.N. over Q.U.E.E.R., Q.U.E.E.N. stands for 'Queer community, untouchables, emigrants, excommunicated, negroid' (Monáe 2018: n.pag.). While the title was changed, some lyrics hinting at sexual attraction are still seen within the lyrics, such as '[a]m I a freak because I love watching Mary?' (Monáe 2013).

Just as adolescents of any demographic, young Black girls go through periods of questioning. They question their aesthetic beauty, their worth in society, the sensuality and the perception of their sexuality – as Black girls are often highly sexualized at a very young age (Hill Collins 2000). However, many Black girls suffer in silence because no aspect of their identities has been normalized within society or, therefore, at school. Monáe's discography is filled with moments of reflexivity about her sexuality, from this episode of questioning in Q.U.E.E.N. to her more recent single 'PYNK' – an ode to femininity. The positionality of a young Black womxn openly questioning her sense of attraction throughout her discography, consistently encouraging her listeners to become more critical of systems of oppression, and fighting for equity, while also attempting to normalize aspects of her intersectionality through her music and videos, show Janelle Monáe to be a viable figure to lean on concerning social justice advocacy within popular music education.

Conclusion

Through Nina Simone and Janelle Monáe we can begin to understand how Black feminist musicians have crafted stories and messages within their lyrics and musical choices. However, they are not the only ones. By understanding the intersectional musicality of Black female musicians, we can recognize and continue to validate the experiences – such as racism, sex or gender oppression, economic disadvantages and other social constructs – that Black womxn and Black feminist artists attempt to reflect within their art. By adhering to an understanding of intersectional musicality, one can begin to understand how Black female musicians hold their cultural background and identity of Blackness constant within a music industry that is dominated by Whiteness. However, that is not to say that the Black women's experiences can be essentialized. Due to the societal consequences of being Black and a woman, Black womxn provide insights into the complexities of obtaining true social justice. As the Combahee River Collective stated, '[i]f Black women are free, it would mean that everyone else would have to be free since our freedom would necessitate the destruction of all systems of oppression' (Combahee River Collective 1986: 215).

Nina Simone's sociopolitical and cultural commentary through music provides music education practitioners with additional resources and insight that may be beneficial to the intrinsic motivation of Black girls in music education programmes. Highlighting Black womxn musicians who balance sociopolitical and sociocultural critiques through reflexive lyrics and intersectional musical choices disrupts the stereotypical and often monolithic perspectives of Black women within music education, the popular music industry and society. Nina Simone, along with Janelle Monáe's history of queering the music industry for Black women in popular music, can serve as an example – to future Black female musicians in music classrooms – of how to carve out true self-definitions for themselves and of how music education can validate and support the identity, musicianship and experiences of Black girls (Lorde 2007). Through intersectional musicality, students can begin to develop deeper understandings of their own layered identities, with music as their guide.

NOTE

1. In July 2020, Janelle Monae disclosed that they identify as non-binary. She alternates between the pronouns she, her, they, and them.

REFERENCES

Arthur, Kate (2020), 'Janelle Monae sings, acts and knows how to master an escape room. Her next challenge: Directing', *Variety*, 15 July, https://variety.com/2020/tv/news/janelle-monae-interview-escape-room-1234635504/. Accessed 14 March 2022.

Combahee River Collective (1986), *The Combahee River Collective Statement: Black Feminist Organizing in the Seventies and Eighties*, New York: Kitchen Table Press.

Garbus, Liz (2015), *What Happened, Miss Nina Simone?* (Documentary), USA: Netflix.

Hill Collins, Patricia (2000), *Black Feminist Thought: Knowledge, Consciousness and the Politics of Empowerment*, 2nd ed., New York: Routledge.

Lee, Christina (2015), '10 things we learned from new Nina Simone Doc', *Rolling Stone*, 29 June, https://www.rollingstone.com/movies/movienews/10-things-we-learned-from-new-nina-simone-doc-59571/. Accessed 14 June 2020.

Lorde, Audre (2007), *Sister Outsider: Essays and Speeches*, New York: Crossing Press.

Monáe, Janelle (2018), 'Interviewed by B. Monáe', *Rolling Stone*, https://www.rollingstone.com/music/music-features/janelle-Monáe-freesherself-629204/. Accessed 18 January 2019.

Monáe, Janelle and Badu, Erykah (2013), 'Q.U.E.E.N.' (composed by J. Monáe), *Electric Lady*, CD, Atlanta: Wondaland Records.

Pengelly, Martin (2015), 'NBC appears to silence Janelle Monáe during Black Lives Matter speech', *The Guardian*, 16 August, https://www.theguardian.com/music/2015/aug/16/nbc-today-show-janelle-Monae-cut-off-blacklives-matter. Accessed 18 January 2019.

Simone, Nina (1964), 'Mississippi Goddam', *Nina Simone in Concert*, CD, Amsterdam: Phillip Records.

Simone, Nina (1965), 'Strange Fruit', *Pastel Blues*, CD, Amsterdam: Phillip Records.

Simone, Nina (1966), 'Four Women', *Wild Is the Wind*, CD, Amsterdam: Phillip Records.

Simone, Nina (1967), 'To Be Young, Gifted and Black', *Little Girl Blue*, CD, New York: Bethlehem High Fidelity.

Simone, Nina and Cleary, Stephen (1992), *I Put a Spell on You: The Autobiography of Nina Simone*, Cambridge: Da Capo Press.

Tran, Viet (2020), 'HRC to honor Janelle Monáe at the 2020 LA dinner', Human Rights Campaign, 23 January, https://www.hrc.org/blog/hrcto-honor-genre-bending-artist-janelle-Monae-with-the-hrc-equalityaward/. Accessed 18 January 2019.

Wortham, Jenna (2018), 'How Janelle Monáe found her voice', *New York Times*, 20 April, https://nyti.ms/2JX2fAl. Accessed 18 January 2019.

59

Decolonizing Higher Music Education: Person Versus Persona

Adriel E. Miles

Adriel Miles is a doctoral researcher in the Department of Music at the University of Bristol in England, studying decolonial methods for music curriculum design.

In this chapter, popular music education is presented as a space where Black musical achievements are celebrated, contrasted with the typical higher music education curricula of America and Britain. This contrast is explored as a potential hindrance to Black musicianship in academic spaces and a contributing factor to academic underrepresentation.

Background

When I consider my past experiences as a composer within both undergraduate and postgraduate academic spaces, in both the United States and the United Kingdom, I often wonder if higher music education (HME) institutions truly welcome the participation of Black people and the inclusion of their perspectives. In the United Kingdom, the lamentable statistics on the number of Black academic faculty members speak volumes (Advance HE 2018: 133–34), and anecdotally this seems to be the case even in universities in London, where the Black population is significantly higher than in the rest of the United Kingdom. In the United States, the situation is marginally better, where Black people comprise 6 per cent of full-time faculty in postsecondary institutions (McFarland et al. 2019), though one in eight people in the United States identify as Black.

As a postsecondary music student, it was always clear to me that my skin made me an anomaly within the walls of HME institutions, and this experience was intensified by my choosing to study composition. I was dedicating myself to a discipline where it would be exceedingly difficult to find relatable cultural role models. Despite a relatively healthy cohort of Black peers, Black people were almost entirely absent from the required music curriculum and the school's faculty. Except for one valiant attempt at an equitable, cosmopolitan first-year music history course, the nearest I got to learning about Black influence in classical music was learning about George Gershwin. As observed by William Robin in a 2014 *New York Times* article: 'The influence of African-Americans on the orchestral tradition is represented more often by Gershwin's "Rhapsody in Blue" than William Grant Still's "Afro-American Symphony"' (Robin 2014: n.pag.).

Person and persona

Phenomena such as these have led me to describe a distinction that I believe is key when discussing issues of diversity: that between 'person' and 'persona'. In this context, person means the physical aspects of a human being (age, weight, sex, gender, etc.), and persona describes a collection of aspects constituting a discrete facet of a person's identity, a facet that is presented to or is perceivable by an observer. So, the admittance of Black bodies within my alma mater speaks to a desire for diversity of person, but these bodies were invariably expected to perform within the confines of the classical music canon which explicitly resists intrusion by the perspectives of Black musicians. This restriction of academically acceptable personae seemingly requires Black composers – and indeed composers of many nonwhite or othered identities – to adopt an artificial, academic persona that eschews their cultural connections as an explicit part of their practice, either because space has not been made in the curriculum to discuss these connections or because the composer wants to avoid being two-dimensionalized as an artist. In my experience, this can lead to a sort of existential crisis where a composer does not know how to avoid writing music that would be viewed with scorn or discomfort on a racial basis.

The great tragedy of Robin's supposition about Gershwin versus Still is that during his lifetime, Still was about as celebrated as a Black classical composer could expect to be. I hazard it would be a challenge to find undergraduate music students today who are aware of his contributions at all. Despite having studied composition in the United States, I am not sure I was fully aware of any African American classical composers until after I had finished my undergraduate degree. It is unclear to me whether or not my teachers were even aware of these composers. It was only once I pursued instruction in jazz composition, arranging and improvisation later on in my undergraduate programme that I began to hear regularly about the academic and aesthetic contributions of Black musicians within an academic space.

Popular music education represents a space wherein the contributions of Black musicians are not wholly minimized or two-dimensionalized on an untenable aesthetic basis. This is not to say that racial disparities in popular music education faculty do not exist; they certainly do, yet popular music education still understands, whether implicitly or explicitly, that some of the most widely appreciated and influential genres of music in the world today – and certainly in the so-called 'western world' – are of Black origin, with hip-hop arguably one of the most popular by some metrics in the United States in recent years (Nielsen Company 2019: 29). It celebrates that these musics are worthy of study, of unpacking and deciphering, and it builds theoretical and pedagogical strategies that allow for their comprehension and appreciation. I find it fascinating how popular music's pedagogical structures readily allow connections between itself and other music pedagogies. For instance, drawing pedagogical parallels between track mixing and orchestration allows for a richer number of resources to be used to illustrate these interrelated ideas. I recognize this desire to make connections as a possible decolonization strategy for the higher music education curriculum.

Juliet Hess shows how music academics and curriculum designers can look across disciplines, such as to women's studies, for curricular models that 'describe the manner in which "other" subject material is engaged in the curriculum' (2015: 336). She proposes a comparative model that seeks to make connections between currently included and marginalized musics, highlighting the interrelated, discursive nature of musical techniques, their aesthetics and their surrounding cultures. Such a comparative model may well prove successful in achieving greater academic parity, with the caveat of rejecting current hierarchies of aesthetic perspectives. Otherwise, such a model runs the risk of having all musics be compared to western classical music as the acme of musical thought, rather than being compared on equal footing.

So, like many Black composers, I indulge my desire to invoke musical traditions that fall outside the explicit domain of classical music and to establish connections between my vernacular influences and my art music practice. Composers have long drawn upon vernacular musical traditions to inspire classical compositional output. Criticism seems to arise specifically from the nature and cultural origins of the musics being drawn upon. I posit that the overwhelming majority of Black musicians who have been recognized for their musical output have received this recognition from outside the domain of the classical music institution, almost exclusively from the popular or vernacular domains. Whether this is because popular music aesthetics are more responsive to typical Black compositional and performative practices like Signifyin(g) (Floyd 1996), or whether this is because composers like Duke Ellington, for instance, have found themselves restricted from classical musical spaces, is unclear. However, the reality of Black musicians more typically finding recognition outside classical music prompts me as a Black composer to devote much of my attention to musical spaces where Black perspectives and personae are already viewed as legitimate, while also championing the achievements of my musical and cultural progenitors within classical spaces.

The need to effect change

I will highlight two areas needing immediate intervention. The first area pertains to reforming institutional hiring practices, which requires White academics and administrators to abdicate their positions of power to the underrepresented, and the fragility of these parties (DiAngelo 2011) manifests in a number of resistant behaviours. Nevertheless, African American students on US campuses are acutely aware of the lack of faculty diversity (Steele 2010: 19, 25), and it is likely that the same is true among Black British students. This lack of visible diversity contributes to Black students' anxieties about marginalization of their interests and about their sense of belonging to the academic community, which can contribute to academic underperformance or lack of attainment. These stressors can also contribute to Black (and variously othered) musicians not realizing their full artistic potential by denying them relevant sources of artistic inspiration. To reform hiring practices, human resources administrators need novel, more involved approaches. Institutions must actively seek out the diversity they wish to foster; they cannot expect it to wander through their doors at their convenience.

Of course, the physical presence of diverse bodies is not itself a sufficient solution, and this leads to the second area of focus: decentring and decolonizing HME curricula to benefit all students. In the typical HME institution today, pedagogical schemata are neither able to discuss nor respond to the cultural and social relevancies of their students, and because of this, students whose identities are not already privileged can be subjected to academic and artistic harm. This can be particularly damaging when viewed alongside the concept of 'stereotype threat' (Steele 2010). Steele posits that students of all identities (both majority and minority) who are placed in environments wherein the threat of being stereotyped is contingent upon their identity can experience a measurable detriment to academic performance unrelated to their actual ability, particularly when faced with tasks at the extremes of their ability. It can be reasoned, then, that assumptions about who Black musicians are, and expectations of their aesthetics, skills and capabilities can present as hindrances to their confidence and success. In an effort to refute specifically negative stereotypes, Black musicians may resort to what I call 'persona restriction' – an intentional refusal, denial or sequestering of one or more facets of a person that conform to the stereotype. The amount of energy and focus a Black musician has to devote to persona restriction, coupled with the denial of some of their artistic inspirations, can impede their ability to complete assignments or to take full advantage of career-building opportunities, and it may discourage other Black people from participating in these environments as well, leading them to seek more inclusive and fostering spaces such as those focused on popular music education.

Higher popular music education (HPME) is not a perfect haven for underrepresented perspectives. However, HPME programmes and institutions typically do better than traditional conservatoires and universities at hiring diverse faculty and fostering the diverse perspectives of these faculty and their students. The dramatic change in perspective parity I personally noticed within the sphere of popular music education still inspires my current philosophy as a classical composer. It is absolutely important to champion composers like Still, Florence B. Price, George Walker and many others within the sphere of classical music to remind ourselves that Black people have made notable and continuing contributions to the classical tradition. Additionally, though, I have come to understand intimately that looking outside this sphere to other musical disciplines, traditions and histories can produce moments of enlightenment and revelation that are invaluable to classical musicians who do not yet see themselves represented within higher music education.

REFERENCES

Advance HE (2018), 'Equality in higher education: Staff statistical report 2018', https://www.advance-he.ac.uk/knowledge-hub/equality-higher-education-statistical-report-2018. Accessed 20 March 2020.

DiAngelo, Robin (2011), 'White fragility', *International Journal of Critical Pedagogy*, 3:3, pp. 54–70.

Floyd, Samuel A. (1996), *The Power of Black Music: Interpreting Its History from Africa to the United States*, New York: Oxford University Press.

Hess, Juliet (2015), 'Decolonizing music education: Moving beyond tokenism', *International Journal of Music Education*, 33:3, pp. 336–47, https://doi.org/10.1177/0255761415581283. Accessed 3 March 2022.

McFarland, Joel, Hussar, Bill, Zhang, Jijun, Wang, Xiaolei, Wang, Ke, Hein, Sarah, Diliberti, Melissa, Forrest Cataldi, Emily, Bullock Mann, Farrah and Barmer, Amy (2019), *The Condition of Education 2019*, NCES 2019-144, Washington: National Center for Education Statistics, https://nces.ed.gov/pubsearch/pubsinfo.asp?pubid=2019144. Accessed 21 March 2020.

Nielsen Company (2019), 'Nielsen music mid-year report U.S. 2019', https://www.nielsen.com/wp-content/uploads/sites/3/2019/06/nielsen-us-music-mid-year-report-2019.pdf. Accessed 20 March 2020.

Robin, William (2014), 'Great Divide at the Concert Hall', *New York Times*, 10 August, AR8, https://www.nytimes.com/2014/08/10/arts/music/black-composers-discuss-the-role-of-race.html. Accessed 3 March 2022.

Steele, Claude M. (2010), *Whistling Vivaldi: How Stereotypes Affect Us and What We Can Do*, New York: W. W. Norton.

60

My Vision for Popular Music Education

Nathan Holder

Nathan Holder is a musician, author and music education consultant currently serving as International Chair of Music Education at the Royal Northern College of Music.

In this chapter, the author considers questions such as 'What is "popular"?' and 'Who defines what "popular" is?' Drawing on the European Impressionist painting, the author considers what makes something popular, and how the redistribution of power can increase student autonomy, diversity and inclusivity.

The word 'popular' is a strange word in music circles. We often fail to distinguish 'pop music' which has stylistically ranged from Madonna's *Like a Prayer* (1984) to Psy's *Gangnam Style* (2012), from 'popular music', which indicates cultural and individual taste(s) or preferences. The sound of mostly pentatonic melodies, mixed with the relatable ('Complicated' by Avril Lavigne) and the fanciful ('Miami' – Will Smith) for example, have been pop and popular for many over the last 50 years. When we think about 'popular music' in education there is one question that comes to mind. Who defines what is popular?

In his book *Hit Makers*, Derek Thompson floats the idea that instead of all of us individually and independently arriving at the opinion that one particular song is 'good', there are taste makers who, purposefully or unwittingly, tell us what to think about something. Thompson's example in the book is taken from the late nineteenth century world of European impressionist painting, where he points out that the seven core impressionist painters where in fact, not the result of many Europeans individually and independently coming to the conclusion that Cezanne, Degas, Renoir, Monet, Manet, Pissarro and Sisley were the crème de la crème. The core canon of impressionist painters was in fact the only seven painters whose works were requested to be displayed by the Musée du Luxembourg in a will written by a man convinced that he would die young. Three years after this wealthy Parisian named Gustav Caillebotte died at the age of 45, the Musée du Luxembourg granted his request and hung Caillebotte's suggested paintings on the wall in a new wing of the museum. The public flocked to the exhibition. These painters and their works began to be displayed and analyzed constantly, and to this day, the most popular impressionist painters are the seven aforementioned. Were these paintings and painters the objective 'best'? Or were they simply the result of a famous museum displaying art which, at that time, wasn't very popular? Did I mention that Caillebotte was not only an art collector but also an acquaintance of all seven?

Aside from the obvious nepotism, to not be aware of these paintings, their creators and cultural significance suggest a naivety at best, or complete ignorance at worst. These painters and their work have been preserved and used to indicate a level of sophistication and/or cultural understanding. The Caillebotte seven were, and have remained as popular as late nineteenth century impressionism can be – but not for everyone. That's what The Beatles were like for me. I didn't grow up listening to The Beatles. I remember the words 'we all live in a yellow submarine' from my childhood, but I couldn't have told you how I knew those lyrics or where they came from. The lyrics and the song were a part of wider British culture; salient for some, irrelevant for others. Probably until the age of fourteen, I couldn't have named one single Beatles album. The only reason I could at that age was because of Jay-Z.

In 2004, the producer Danger Mouse remixed Jay-Z's *Black Album* (2003) with The Beatles' *White Album* (1968), which became *The Grey Album*. I was heavily into Jay-Z back then, but also other popular rappers at that time. Nas, Ludacris, Busta Rhymes and others were always on my CD-RW's; that's what was popular for me. My own and some of my friends' musical tastes were being shaped by MTV Base, and not the top ten hits of 2004 which featured Eric Prydz's 'Call On Me' and DJ Casper's 'Cha Cha Slide'. The UK singles charts were like the Musée du Luxembourg.

'Now who's hot, who not?
Tell me who rock, who sell out in the stores?' – Ma$e (1997)

Even though the artists we loved were popular, they weren't popular enough to even be mentioned in class. Entering into the school musical environment only emphasized the fact that my musical tastes were of little relevance to the world of music education. The music wasn't implicitly deemed to be of enough value to be studied, or even to be listened to for fun in class. The reason for this may either stem from my teachers' own musical tastes, or from them having to stick to what they felt would best prepare us to enter external examinations. This resulted in a disconnect; not only between us and the music we had to study but also from our teachers. I don't think we ever really got to know them musically, what they enjoyed, or what they regarded as popular. One can only speculate whether or not they felt disconnected from their own musical tastes and what they had to teach us. Those who designed and enforced the curriculum decided what was to be popular in our music classroom. The school curricula were like the UK singles charts.

My Yé is different to your Yé

One of the results of colonization is a top-down approach to education. Lecturers and teachers are charged with inputting valued information into students' minds, and often the music which forms set curricula is not heavily influenced by their own tastes but is handed down by the same top-down colonial practices. Our teen years are pivotal for shaping our musical tastes which explain why, years later, those artists in my CD collection still rank as some of my favourite musicians and lyricists. Daniel Levitin argues that musical tastes are generally formed in our late teens, and will have been shaped by the people around us, those with 'whom we want to be like, or whom we believe we have something in common with' (Levitin 2006: 232). If educators were truly in charge of what is to be taught, would we study less Beethoven and more Björk? Less Mozart and more MJ?

The musical knowledge and repertoire learned by students in universities and schools, often trump personal ideas about what music is, and means for themselves, changing through time and life experiences. It stands to reason that not only are many teachers' tastes shaped by the people around them but also by those who taught them what and how to teach. If those people stem from similar cultural, social and economic backgrounds, the tastes, and therefore ideas about what's worthy of being taught and what's not, will quickly become fairly homogenized. Not only what music is taught, but how it is analyzed and the language used in which to do so, slowly becomes uniform.

If I were a racist,
I'd teach children that talking about music means,
Texture, timbre and tempo.
If you can't use these words, you're not a musician.

(Holder 2020: n.pag.)

Increasing ethnic and gender diversity in the workforce not only provides young people with new potential role models but also allows for those who didn't grow up with The Beatles to teach texture, timbre and tempo through the beats of Timbaland or music of Guns n' Roses for example. It's no wonder that in 2020, given the lethargic movements towards diverse teaching staff and curricula across music education, that many students turn away from formal music education in favour of following their own paths. Although decolonization includes diversity initiatives, it's how popular music is taught opposed to who is teaching it that I want to address.

'Come as You Are' – Nirvana (1991)

YouTube, Instagram and TikTok are all platforms which young people have turned to, to express themselves, and to learn from others who share similar tastes. As Bryan Powell (2011) writes, many talented young musicians fail to see a correlation between their personal tastes and the music they have to study in school. The colonial input model, in which information was disseminated and produced by a few, is being rejected in favour of a contemporary 'Pick 'n' Mix' model, in which young people are no longer restricted by limited time in music lessons, or the knowledge or ideas of only one teacher.

One of the ways I believe that we can amend colonial structures of popular music education is to dismantle the traditional 'teacher talk, student listen' hierarchical model, and introduce a student led approach to learning. Emdin (2016: 87) proposes a 'reality pedagogy-based version of coteaching'. This approach 'requires a redistribution of power in the classroom that returns to the essence of teaching – privileging the voice of the student'. Not only does this require flexibility and reflexivity on the part of the teacher but also a reimagined curriculum and assessment process. One in which the first impressionist exhibition at the Musée du Luxembourg is not the fixed vision of one White man, but a revolving door of abstract impressionism, cubism, surrealism, and everything else in between.

The key phrase, 'redistribution of power', is an important concept in decolonization. Knowing that for centuries, power has been the preserve of those with a particular ethno-socio-economic standing in society (not even limited to their own), the redistribution of that power is key in reforming how we not only think about studying popular music but also the very idea about what is popular in the first place. Gustav Caillebotte's wealth and connections allowed his request to be approved by the Musée du Luxembourg. If it wasn't for his ethno-socio-economic status (and dare I say self-identification as a man), his request would have been scoffed at and perhaps the Caillebotte seven and the impressionist canon would not be what they are today. If the construction of music education were not rooted in White supremacy, perhaps the musical canon would not be what it is today. If 'the popular' is understood to be individual, perhaps popular music education would not be what it is today.

By students having a greater level of autonomy in what they choose to study, the power that teachers and exam boards have to define set works and set precise marking criteria would need a complete overhaul. Perhaps it would mean the formation of networks between faculties from different campus' and universities from around the world, pairing students with lecturers who not only have theoretical knowledge of certain musics but also a yearning to stay relevant and connect with a younger generation for whom 2004 and CD-RWs are now their year of birth and Spotify. Where the students start out on a path of self-discovery, rather than attempting to find themselves inside prescribed curricula and stagnant reading lists. Where a recent album can be discussed, and Twitter can be cited as a source of knowledge and inspiration.

'Wouldn't it be nice?' – The Beach Boys (1966).

REFERENCES

Emdin, Christopher (2016), *For White Folks Who Teach in the Hood … and the Rest of Y'all Too: Reality Pedagogy and Urban Education*, Boston: Beacon Press.

Holder, Nathan (2020), 'If I Were A Racist …' *#DecoloniseMusicEd*, 8 July, https://www.nateholdermusic.com/post/if-i-were-a-racist. Accessed 16 March 2022.

Levitin, Daniel (2006), *This is Your Brain on Music: The Science of a Human Obsession*, London: Penguin.

Powell, Bryan (2011), *Popular Music Ensembles in Post-Secondary Contexts: A Case Study of Two College Music Ensembles*, Boston: Boston University.

61

External Examining:
An Insider Perspective on
a Neocolonial Practice

Gareth Dylan Smith

Gareth Dylan Smith is an assistant professor in the music education department at Boston University, Boston, USA, where he teaches graduate and undergraduate courses in music education.

In this chapter, the author describes his experiences of, and subsequent reflection upon, his work on behalf of a British university for whom he assessed and reported on music education programmes and courses in Asia. He problematizes this work as a neocolonial practice.

This short chapter is a reflection on my reviling and revelling in a moderately glamorous episode in my life as a seagull academic.[1] Below, I briefly define the terms, 'external examining' and 'neocolonialism', describe some of my roles in sustaining both systems, and suggest possibilities for addressing a problem endemic to higher music education. If you are titillated sufficiently by what follows, note the further reading suggestions at the end.

Wherefore external examining?

External examining, under the auspices of the Quality Assurance Agency (QAA),[2] is intended to help ensure parity in quality of teaching, learning outcomes and assessment practices across the diverse higher education sector in the United Kingdom. Of course, it achieves nothing of the sort, but along with a raft of similar managerialist matrices, including the Teaching Excellence Framework,[3] its neoliberal bullshit provides competing vendors in the higher education market-place with a thin veneer of faux accountability. Every single-degree programme in the UK needs an external examiner, and with positions rotating every four years there is ample nepotism, mutual back-scratching and theft (ahem, 'sharing best practices'). External examining works hand-in-glove with degree validation, whereby when a small college does not have degree-awarding powers ('DAP' in the lingo), for the right price a 'real' university will bestow the certifications. So, for instance, students who *study* at London's Institute of Contemporary Music Performance *receive degrees* from the University of East London.

Capitalism and neocolonialism

Capitalism is an economic and political system that has long been the domi-nant ideological force worldwide. European capitalists' compulsion for resource exploitation led to colonialism – the theft of entire continents, widespread geno-cide, and cultural and economic domination of indigenous peoples. White Euro-peans and their descendants have for centuries dominated globalized trade and culture, and while the imperial rule of colonialism has been largely dismantled over the last 100 years, western powers strive to maintain dominance through continuous usurpation of indigenous knowledge and traditions; this is neocoloni-alism. External examining practices enter neocolonial territory when UK universi-ties stamp their approval on degree programmes abroad and send in the requisite external examiners to check up on things. Thus capitalists' obsessive measuring and bean-counting sustain jobs for thousands of middle managers in exported UK higher education.

Imperial ambassador

In mid 2014, I applied and was approved to be external examiner for Colonial University (a pseudonym), not actually in the city where it is located but on Colonial University's behalf at the Asian Music College (AMC) (a pseudonym) in Kuala Lumpur, Malaysia, a school specializing in preparing young people for careers in popular music. AMC's BA in Professional Music was validated by Colonial University so every six months I needed to review and report back to the University on how students' work and staff's assessment and administrative processes – *in Malaysia (!!)* – compared with my expectations of programmes in the United Kingdom. The most important foci for me, according to QAA guidelines, were AMC's assessment processes. Equating educational 'quality' with adherence to protocols is of course absurd, but, per the capitalist-colonial obsession with profit and efficiency, it is measurable – the McNamara Fallacy[4] in full swing. AMC leadership was well organized, and everything was clearly accounted for. Marking (grading) was broadly fine. Students' work was mostly decent, sometimes subpar, and occasionally spectacular. My repeated critical observation was that students' 10,000-word dissertations were not really of the standard I would hope for from final-year undergraduate students earning a degree from a UK university. *Quelle surprise!* They were written by a diverse international population of undergraduates studying on a vocational programme to become professional musicians throughout Asia, forced to pen over-long scholarly essays in order for their studies to count as degree-worthy according to a subcontractor employed by a regional university taking full advantage of the three or four nights of five-star hotel accommodation provided to me through the partnership fee AMC paid the University.

My work at AMC consisted of spending a handful of hours – although never before 10 a.m. – skimming through piles of essays and big band arrangements, sampling audio recordings of student compositions and watching videos of performances, all in a windowless room with climate control options of arctic wasteland or tropical nightmare. Mid-way through the day, my host would take me for a spicy lunch at a local hole-in-the-wall (or sometimes to the McDonald's on the corner, since it was closer). I would then fight the urge to nap in the airless room, hastily finalize my checks, and head upstairs with a handful of teaching staff (notably all male) to the fancy, wood-panelled, stained-glassed room (replete with encased silver sceptre) to enjoy a short Skype call with colleagues back in England. During the proceedings, I would utter up to 100 complimentary words, assuring everyone present that all was above board and kosher. Sometimes I would pass out from jet lag and lunch, jerking awake either shortly before or immediately after it was my turn to join the discussion. We would congratulate one another on another job well done, I would take a taxi back to my hotel and avail myself of the excellent gym, sauna and swimming pool facilities for a few hours before heading to dinner followed by a few overpriced Belgian beers with my AMC host and maybe a co-worker. I would close the night in the hotel bar, reading with a glass of red wine and free snacks.

The following morning, I would rise early, work out hard, steam myself for no reason and swim again before spending as long as possible eating all the breakfast curries, fruit and breads on offer at the buffet. After breakfast, there were always signs by the elevators, directing young musicians to the piano and violin exams taking place on the fourth floor with the Associated Board of the Royal Schools of Music; this next-level neo-colonial gas lighting by the British establishment probably accounts for why I didn't feel *quite* so bad in my own capacity carrying out the slightly subtler imperialist agenda of the more working-class Colonial University (and at least I was only dealing in *popular* music!). I would spend the rest of my final day in Kuala Lumpur writing or editing a book project over tasty cappuccinos in the hotel lobby, before taking the KL Express train back to the airport and settling in for the twelve-hour flight back to England. On the plane, I would write my external examiner report, including enough friendly critique to justify my position, with praise adequate to warrant continuation of the lucrative (and, for me, thoroughly enjoyable) financial and academic partnership. I would then imbibe ample free wine and an action movie and sleep in my seat till breakfast.

Colonial University saw fit to hire me for a handful of other post-imperial examining jollies, including a 30-hour round-trip to check in on an MBA programme at a business college in Cochin, India and a four-day whirlwind tour of board meetings and liquid lunches to oversee approval of a single English language learning module at a large technical college in Wuhan, China. I saw things on one of these visits that I dare not commit to paper. I can neither confirm nor deny that my initial report on the Wuhan visit was returned to me, heavily redacted, with a reminder that mine was a non-judgemental observer role, along with a request for more of a seal-of-approval.

Antiracism as a way forward

I look back with a modicum of disgust at my joyous complicity in this whole external examining racket. I tried applying the Nuremberg Defence, but that hardly holds. It is expected that academics in the United Kingdom will do some external examining, and I did it with alacrity for the travel, food, moderately exotic experiences, and extra cash. The obscene lack of necessity (flying to Malaysia for four days to join a one-hour Skype call back to England?!) reeks of colonial-capitalist privilege and excess. One year in the middle of it all, I used a website to calculate that it would require the material resources of seven planets for each person on Earth to travel as abusively as I was doing. And throughout my trips, there were discomfortable reminders of Malaysia's past as a British colony – power sockets were the United Kingdom style, cars drove on the left, just about everyone I met spoke English, and the whole BA in Professional Music was taught, learned and assessed in English. Probably it makes sense, at a place like Asian Music College, to have students develop fluency in an international language, and to make music that conforms to global vanilla pop-rock norms. But still, there is something inherently – and intentionally – wrong about all of it.

Setting aside my distaste for the Quality Assurance Agency, and bureaucrats' success in hollowing out UK higher education to a wizened husk, forcing and an increasingly exhausted, deflated scholarly workforce to pound the hamster wheel in pursuit of relentless productivity, what bothers me most is the absence of any public conversation about the ethics of UK Universities swanning around, 'validating' and awarding degrees in southeast Asia like silver-tongued spivs and grifters. I resent being hoodwinked into going along with it too (but I would probably return in a heartbeat to use the gym, sauna and pool and to avail myself of that epic breakfast buffet because I am a hedonist and a hypocrite). I am glad I worked as an external examiner. I am also disappointed in myself for not initially seeing of what I was a part.

UK higher education's quality assurance sector perpetuates endless pointless busywork to justify its own existence. It is the poster child of neoliberal managerialism. And when it operates internationally, it perpetuates a perniciously neocolonial and therefore racist, enterprise. I understand that there are likely manifold benefits to different stakeholders in the programme-validation and external examining game; groups and individuals learn from one another's expertise, mistakes and cultural differences, and there is undoubtedly kudos attached to a programme stamped with the kitemark of a British university – but therein lies the problem. Higher music education presumably affords learners things that other (lower?) music education cannot, but that does not mean it needs to do so as part of a neocolonial project.

There is a huge amount to untangle here – logistically, economically, politically and epistemologically. We in the music education profession must address conscious and unconscious assumptions and perpetuation of 'West is best' cultural and epistemological superiority. This necessary work begins at the personal level, whence it translates into decisions and actions on departmental and school-wide committees. It implicates policy makers in government and at quangos like the Quality Assurance Agency. We all need to think hard about what we are measuring, how, why, and the impacts this has and on whom. To grant the benefit of the doubt, I think many working in higher education in the United Kingdom are unconsciously complicit in the sector's neocolonial ways. But it is past time to acknowledge the bigger picture, the imperial subtext. As Ibram X. Kendi tells us, the only way we can hope to end systemic racism (including neocolonial practices) is deliberately to build and enact policies that are explicitly anti-racist. Thus, we can begin to undo the inequitable power dynamics of neocolonialism and afford more musicians and educators what ISME President Emily Akuno called a *visible voice*.

NOTES

1. Periodically swoop in, crap on everything, fly off to a safe distance, re-fuel, repeat.
2. See also Martin Isherwood's chapter in this book.

3. See the Office for Students website: https://www.officeforstudents.org.uk/advice-and-guidance/teaching/about-the-tef/. Accessed 19 January 2022.

4. The McNamara Fallacy – named after Robert McNamara, U.S. Secretary of Defense – holds that everything of value can be measured, and therefore anything that cannot be measured is unimportant.

REFERENCE

Smith, Gareth Dylan and Moir, Zack (2021), 'Popular music, policy, and education', in S. Homan (ed.), *The Bloomsbury Handbook on Popular Music Policy*, London: Bloomsbury, pp. 91–107.

62

Cripping Popular Music Education

Jesse Rathgeber

Jesse Rathgeber, Ph.D., is an assistant professor of music education at Augustana College, Rock Island, Illinois, USA. He researches disability, inclusion and professional vision.

In this chapter, the author discusses the need for music educators to focus on the real (rather than the perceived) needs of students learning music with a range of impairments and disabilities.

Contemporary approaches to working with disabled persons/persons with disabilities (DP/PwDs) focus on mainstreaming,[1] assistive/adaptive technology,[2] differentiated instruction,[3] universal design,[4] working with support personnel[5] and special educational laws/policies.[6] While powerful in shaping equitable practices, these approaches to inclusion presume that (1) DP/PwDs, generally, long to be included into settings built for and primarily by nondisabled persons/typical learners and that (2) settings and practices for and by non-disabled persons are neutral, regular and/or the norm. Yet, DP/PwDs who are artists, musicians, poets, community leaders and scholars call for practices and settings built *with* them from the ground up that value the different approaches to music learning, experiencing music and music-making. Such practices and settings are not reactively inclusive and in need of adaptation for each new participant, as may be the case with current inclusive approaches, but rooted in innovation and accommodation. In this chapter, I draw on the concepts of these DP/PwDs 'to crip'[7] popular music education (PME), opening up pedagogies, musical practices, musical products and aesthetics that value difference over conformity.

Aesthetics of difference

Imagine yourself walking into a space filled with sounds of violins, electric guitars, power drills, vibrating toys and incomprehensible vocalizations. The sounds mix in cacophony and then harmony, to a swung beat and alternating in free rhythm. The sounds alone might make one imagine an exploratory music class, an open jam session or an avant-garde premiere. Such sounds might come from the Amplified Elephants (see Hullick 2013), a sonic art group consisting primarily of musicians diagnosed with intellectual disabilities. The work of these musicians, who are occasionally joined by non-disabled musicians, calls into question problematic assumptions about what a musician or sound arts is and can be. Their work demonstrates a dedication to amplifying and catalyzing difference to crack open mores of music-making that centre non-disability. The Amplified Elephants' work reflects an aesthetic of difference, an aesthetic not grounded upon non-disabled mores and replicative approaches. Such an aesthetic is less than predictable, requires a continually evolving set of practices and necessitates a commitment to collaborative accommodation to open up sonic and communal possibilities.

The aesthetics of difference on display though the Amplified Elephants reject non-disability as the basis for what can be deemed normal, natural and possible. Such an aesthetic is grounded upon an acceptance of disability as an affirmative position that enriches and complicates accepted notions of the nature of artistic production and product (Siebers 2010). Centring disability opens up space for difference, for non-conformity. Disability presents nearly infinite aesthetic processes, products and positions. Centring disability in such a way presents an aesthetics of difference that values iteration and innovation, adaptation and accommodation and 'revision and re-contextualization' (Smith et al. 2018: 2). But what could centring disability and embracing an aesthetics of difference entail? Below I explore three lessons for cripping PME.

Lesson 1: Embrace complexity

Disability and the lives of DP/PwDs are far more complicated than many assume, as is the case with stereotypes applied to populations seen as marginal. Many people have an aversion to the word 'disability', favouring euphemisms such as 'special needs', 'differently-abled', 'persons with exceptionalities' or 'handicapable'. Yet, many *disabled persons* – people who identify as disabled or see disability as central to their sense of self – reclaim 'disability', positioning it as a positive and complex, type of personhood: 'Disability is not a brave struggle or courage in the face of adversity. Disability is an art. It's an ingenious way to live' (Marcus 1993: n.pag.).

Many disabled persons recoil at negative conceptions of disability and the nondisabled compulsion to fix and simplify disabled life. Disabled persons may reject disability euphemisms, seeing them as microaggressions serving non-disabled persons' fragile comfort (i.e. Sinclair 2013). While some DP/PwDs may prefer euphemisms, it is important to understand that terminologies are as various and complex as disabled identities and lives.

Lesson 2: Focusing on agency and self-accommodation

Embracing the complexity and positivity of disability requires a critique of language and approaches to music-making. Therefore, it is vital that we ask DP/PwDs their preferred terminologies and meet their needs, desires and differences rather than forcing a nondisabled-centred frame. We must foster DP/PwDs' agency as musical beings, as with all learners. Preferred language and self-identification are but low-hanging fruit concerning agency.

DP/PwD express their agency through identity, connections and actions. How DP/PwDs preferentially use musical instruments and navigate techniques provide other avenues for forwarding agency. When music educators treat technique as codified and universal, rather than as socially constructed and continuously negotiated (Lubet 2011), they work against difference and police non-disabled conformity. It may be useful to keep in mind that many now-accepted techniques came from the self-accommodating innovations of musicians who were/are DP/PwDs. Django Reinhardt's two-finger playing, Tony Iommi's dropped tuning and self-developed finger caps, Jeff Healey's dulcimer-like chording/strumming and Joni Mitchell's open tunings, among others, have impacted popular music technique. Self-accommodation – valuing personal agency – for these guitar heroes opened up new options, approaches and music for everyone. Music educators can crip PME by meeting DP/PwDs and learning from/with their agentic, innovative and self-adaptive approaches.

Music teachers can begin by exploring how DP/PwD – and, indeed, all learners – interact with instruments, rather than beginning with the process of conforming learners to established techniques. Interestingly, handedness with string instruments can be a site for non-disability centring, where all-too-many people view right-handedness the 'norm'. Nevertheless, countless artists, from Jimi Hendrix to Joanna Wang and from Elizabeth Cotten to Paul McCartney, have bucked right-hand-dominant techniques to form their highly emulated styles. We need not police handedness but should encourage all learners to explore how different approaches to handedness bring affordances and constraints.

My point here is that music teachers should frame technique as a matter of personal agency as well as a matter of tradition. If we are to teach in ways that embrace the DIY and rebellious spirits of popular music past, centring the agency of DP/PwDs' may encourage all learners to be innovative and self-accommodative and help them branch out and challenge themselves.

Lesson 3: Embracing DP/PwD representation and identity

Disability, as a social construct and identity, challenges non-disabled normality. The challenge to conformity is often central to popular music approaches and products and, perhaps, disability is central to popular music. Scholars have demonstrated how disability is central to rock music (e.g. McKay 2013) and hip-hop (e.g. Hinto 2017; Porco 2014). Disability and disabled representations are already embedded within popular music practices. As such, we might do well to help all learners challenge ableist assumptions by referencing and exploring current and past disabled musicians. For example:

- What can we all learn about genre formation from examining Ian Dury's (1981) 'Spasticus (Autisticus)', a formative work in new wave and post-punk?
- What can we learn about how identity, experience and authenticity inform lyrics and beat making by analysing Wheelchair Sport Camps' (2016) 'Teeth' in which queer, disabled MC Kalyn Heffernan, spits, 'Most would not anticipate, the shit I say, and flee the scene in disarray, Watch the haters dissipate, here's my ass kiss away'?
- What might we learn about storytelling, sound painting, wider timbral choices, and self-accommodation from folk singer and violinist Gaelynn Lea? Few musical phrases cut to our shared concern of the temporal nature of life than Lea (2016) singing, 'Don't tell me we've got time, the subtle thief of life, It slips away when we pay no mind'.
- What might we learn about how to structure a song and how to play with texture than through a careful exploration of Brian Wilson's modular songwriting and overinclusive wall-of-sound arranging, all of which are coloured by his experiences through schizoaffective disorder?
- What can we learn about innovations in music-making through considering the luminary work of Kendrick Lamar, Les Paul, Missy Elliott, Captain Beefheart, David Byrne, Rick Allen, among other musicians for whom disability was/is an important facet of their lives?

Centring disability to make space and foster place

We music educators may gain more by working beyond the 'inclusion' framework. We can do more than adapt existing settings based on some non-existent, non-disabled norm. In this chapter, I have advocated for a change in thinking that (1) centres disability, (2) builds on musical processes and products of DP/PwD and (3) opens up popular music learning settings to an aesthetic of difference. My point may seem commonsensical, yet the conceptual shifts and heightened reflexivity required to crip PME may be far more difficult than one may assume. Cripping PME requires consciously challenging the non-disabled-centric ways of knowing and being; it requires questioning reductionistic understandings of disability and the lives of DP/PwDs. This work is personal, requiring individual reflexivity and it is social, necessitating constant collaborative restructuring of teaching, learning, making and experiencing music. By cripping PME, we can make popular music learning settings become not just spaces, but places in which *all* learners can encounter equitable music-making and learning experiences.

NOTES

1. Kochhar, West and Taymans (2000), working to educate DP/PwDs in settings with and using adapted approaches for 'typical' learners.
2. 'Equipment [...] used to increase, maintain, or improve functional capabilities of a child with a disability' (U.S. Government Printing Office 2004: n.pag.).
3. An approach that starts with learners' needs rather than a curricular guide (Tomlinson 1999) through developing multiple experiences or tiers of curricular structure.
4. An approach to curricular design inspired by the work of architect Ron Mace's philosophy and approach to proactively address and remediate barriers to participation (see Universal Design for Learning n.d.; Rose and Meyer 2000; McCord et al. 2014).
5. Such as paraprofessionals, social workers, psychologists and special education team members, among others.
6. See, for example: Malawi Handicapped Person Act of 1972, the Individuals with Disabilities Education Act in the United States, China's Regulation on the Education of the Disabled, Special Education Needs and Disability Act in the United Kingdom, the work of the Colombian Division of Special Education, as well as the education policies outlined in the United Nations Convention on the Rights of Persons with Disabilities.
7. I use the re-claimed term 'crip' here to align with contemporary disability justice practices, adopting this 'once-negative discourse to positively embrace the concerns of disabled subjects, much as the word queer has been similarly rehabilitated' (Ginsburg and Rapp 2017: 182). Turning the subject position of 'the crip' into an active term. 'To crip' or 'cripping' involves centering disability to call attention to points of exclusion and demonstrate a multitude of ways to be, to connect and to make music.

REFERENCES

Ginsburg, Faye and Rapp, Rayna (2017), 'Cripping the new normal: Making disability count', *Alter*, 11:3, pp. 179–92.

Drury, Ian (1981), 'Spasticus (Autisticus)', *Lord Upminster*, CD, New Providence, The Bahamas: Compass Point Studios.

Hinton, Anna (2017), '"And So I Bust Back": Violence, race, and disability in hip-hop', *CLA Journal*, 60:3, pp. 290–304.

Hullick, James (2013), 'The rise of the amplified elephants', *International Journal of Community Music*, 6:2, pp. 219–33.

Kochhar, Carol, West, Lynda L. and Taymans, Juliana M. (2000), *Successful Inclusion: Practical Strategies for a Shared Responsibility*, Upper Saddle River: Merrill.

Lea, Gaelyn (2016), 'Someday We'll Linger in the Sun" by Gaelynn Lea (2016 Tiny Desk concert submission)', YouTube, 28 January, https://www.youtube.com/watch?v=jb1oC-jiIu9M. Accessed 10 December 2020.

Lubet, Alex (2011), *Music, Disability, and Society*, Philadelphia: Temple University Press.

Marcus, Neil (1993), 'Disability social history project', Disability Social History Project, http://www.disabilityhistory.org/dshp.html. Accessed 2 April 2008.

McCord, Kimberly, Gruben, Amy and Rathgeber, Jesse (2014), *Accessing Music: Enhancing Student Learning in the General Music Classroom Using UDL*, Van Nuys: Alfred Music.

McKay, George (2013), *Shakin' All Over: Popular Music and Disability*, Ann Abor: University of Michigan Press.

Porco, Alex S. (2014), 'Throw yo' voice out: Disability as a desirable practice in hip-hop vocal performance', *Disability Studies Quarterly*, 34:4, https://dsq-sds.org/article/view/3822/3790. Accessed 3 March 2022.

Rose, David H. and Meyer, Anne (2000), 'Universal design for learning', *Journal of Special Education Technology*, 15:1, pp. 67–70.

Siebers, Tobin (2010), *Disability Aesthetics*, Ann Arbor: University of Michigan Press.

Sinclair, Jim (2013), 'Why I dislike "person first" language', *Autonomy, the Critical Journal of Interdisciplinary Autism Studies*, 1:2, pp. 1–2.

Smith, Gareth Dylan, Powell, Bryan, Fish, David Lee, Kornfeld, Irwin and Reinhert, Kat (2018), 'Popular music education: A white paper by the Association for Popular Music Education', *Journal of Popular Music Education*, 2:3, pp. 289–98.

Tomlinson, Carol Ann (1999), *The Differentiated Classroom: Responding to the Needs of All Learners*, Alexandria: Association for Supervision and Curriculum Development.

Universal Design for Learning (n.d.), 'About Universal Design for Learning', https://www.cast.org/impact/universal-design-for-learning-udl. Accessed 10 May 2022.

U.S. Government Printing Office (2004), 'Individuals with Disabilities Education Act', https://www.govinfo.gov/content/pkg/PLAW-108publ446/html/PLAW-108publ446.html. Accessed 10 May 2022.

Wheelchair Sports Camp (2016), 'Teeth', *No Big Deal*, CD, Providence: Strange Famous Records.

63

Excessive Pedagogical Moments: A Deaf-Gay Intersectional Duet

Warren Churchill

Warren Churchill is a lecturer of music at NYU Abu Dhabi, UAE, where he teaches courses in musical performance and disabilities in musical contexts.

In this chapter, the author offers a personal reflection about popular music, identity and curriculum. Although popular music was largely absent from his formal educational training, he recognizes its identity-affirming potentials in informal spaces. Applying the idea of 'pedagogical excess', he considers subversive identities as potentially resisting histories of oppression.

In this short self-reflection, I consider how popular music has become more central to my teaching practice over the past three decades. My thinking is inspired by approaches to curriculum theorizing that engage with autobiographical writing.[1] As such, I look back to certain experiences of popular music at various moments to see how these might have influenced my present teaching practices. Of course, classical music, jazz and other musical genres are woven into all of this as well. However, I suspect that foregrounding popular music will afford me greater freedom to speak to certain identity issues that have shaped my subjective experiences. I should make it clear that I do not claim to be an expert on popular music, but as a musically eclectic 'jack of all trades', I hope that what I share here might usefully connect with current conversations about popular music in our field.

Navigating classical and popular musics in education

In September of 2020, I received an unexpected text message from one of my former students from the New York City public schools:

> Hello Mr. Churchill. You might not remember me, but I was one of your students in elementary school. You were my fourth and fifth grade music teacher. I played the drums and I still do. I wanted to let you know that I'm applying for Berklee College of Music this year. You were one of the reasons that I started taking drums seriously and I wanted to thank you for that. Your positive attitude and your ability to make music fun for me have motivated me to make drumming and music part of my livelihood. Thank you so much![2]

How could I possibly forget this talented and courteous young man? Indeed, Paulo[3] had started percussion lessons with me back in 2013. He was a very keen young musician who excelled in his studies. By the fifth grade, Paulo started playing the drum kit. And seeing how much progress he had made during the year, I invited Paulo and a fellow student guitarist to join me in accompanying the entire fifth grade in a rousing rendition of Led Zeppelin's 'Stairway to Heaven'. Obviously, I am biased, but every one of those fifth graders gave us an electrifying performance that evening! However, I think that Paulo deserves much of the credit on account of how his drumming skills brought our ensemble together.

A few months later, Paulo reached out again, this time to inform me that he had been accepted into Berklee – on scholarship, no less. Elated for him, I recalled the excitement I felt upon receiving my acceptance letter from the Crane School of Music 35 years prior. In those days, our required musicianship sequence and performance studio courses were based on western classical music. Voice majors were expected to learn *bel canto* technique and to perform art songs in several foreign languages. Although my peers and I certainly listened to Queen, Duran Duran, Madonna and so forth, none of this music was included in our formal studies. Likewise, our teaching methods courses introduced us to child-friendly, seemingly anodyne songs and activities to use during our student teaching practicums.

In November 1989, I was assigned to work with a very experienced teacher who taught elementary general music in a fairly affluent suburban school district. We readily talked about our favourite music, and I noticed she had the sheet music for Bonnie Tyler's 'Total Eclipse of the Heart' on her desk. However, she did not share this kind of music with her students. In that particular educational setting, a simple choral arrangement of 'Part of Your World' from Disney's *The Little Mermaid* would have been the limit of 'popular' acceptability. In those days, the Disney princess trope did not receive the same critical attention it would today.

And thinking beyond the usual heteronormative critique, Leland G. Spencer (2014) reads Hans Christian Anderson's *The Little Mermaid* as a narrative performance of transgender identity (Leland and Spencer 2014). Today, and under the right circumstances, should one discuss the possible metaphorical meanings of Ariel's desire for feet instead of fins? Or is it best to avoid divisive topics altogether? As Alexis Kallio observes, 'music teachers assume a degree of social responsibility in navigating diversity and difference in ethical ways, to be able to justify the exclusion of certain musics, expressions, or practices in relation to the pursuit of a common good' (2020: 2).

I am left to wonder whether, or indeed how the exclusion of popular music from my undergraduate education served the common good. Popular music was clearly evident in the domain of our personal lives in the residence halls and off-campus and I am convinced it fulfilled various needs for *personal good*. Likewise, I suspect that Bonnie Tyler's angst-ridden song resonated with my sponsor teacher in ways that she kept private. Hidden curricular moments such as this reinforced for me the idea that popular music should be kept separate from my formal teaching practice. In retrospect, I realize that popular music provides an affirming vernacular-of-self for many people. Reflecting upon the educational marginalization of popular music that I experienced, I draw a connection between Alexis Kallio's observation about the ethical pursuit of the common good and Janet L. Miller's idea of 'pedagogical excess'. This has to do with moments that exceed the norm by resisting the constraints of educational discourses, such as when a student brings a potentially taboo topic into a class discussion. Miller characterizes such excessive moments as 'a symptom of histories of repression and the interests associated with those histories' Miller (2005: 111). I would then surmise that popular musical genres, particularly those associated with subversive identities, represent a threatening excess for music educators who pursue more conservative visions of the common good.

During my undergraduate years, I witnessed several peers engage in various forms of musical resistance against the constraints of educational discourses. For instance, I recall one of my voice studio peers performing impressive rock vocals at a coffeehouse event. It was apparent that this style of singing was far more uplifting for him than the formal singing we did in class each week. And during my third year at college, another voice major, who was gay and proudly out, performed a cover of Erasure's anthemic song, 'A Little Respect'. Given the stigma connected to homosexuality and AIDS at that time, I thought this was incredibly brave of him. Furthermore, his performance offered resistance against the heteronormative songs we were expected to perform in our vocal studio. Clearly, his public demand for 'a little respect' was significant for him.

Coincidently, my roommate had introduced me to Erasure just a few months prior to this. And I listened to Andy Bell's vocals on *The Innocents* album obsessively:

Yes it was you, my love, that made me turn around.
Yes it was you, mein Herr, that turned me upside down.

(1988)[4]

Did that mean what I thought it did? My roommate assured me it did. I suspect he was trying to gently nudge me out of the closet. However, I was not able to openly acknowledge being gay until my mid 20s. As a professor today, I have to admit to having felt some envy toward one of my undergraduate students who spoke so freely in class about how Lady Gaga's music helped him navigate this aspect of his identity.

Hearing disablement as an intersectional factor

Another important aspect of my identity is connected with my hearing. As a toddler, I suffered a bout of meningitis, which left me deaf in one ear and gave me considerable difficulty hearing certain frequencies in the other. I suspect this may have contributed to some vocal technique issues I struggled with during my undergraduate years. Although I was serious about my studies, meeting the expectations of my classical singing studio was not easy for me. In fact, I generally find popular music to be more aurally accessible than many kinds of classical music. I suspect this is due to the fact that popular music tends to be recorded using a more compressed dynamic range than classical music (Kirchberger and Russo 2016), which is more favourable for my hearing. In contrast, I recall moments during my undergraduate conducting courses where melodies that I could clearly read in the score were completely inaudible to me in recordings. Further, I learned that having stereo hearing is a necessary ability for the aspiring conductor. As a consequence, I tended to seek out ways of engaging with music that felt more affirming.

Why do I share these personal issues so publicly? Disability scholar, Tobin Siebers, uses the term 'complex embodiment' (Siebers 2008) to refer to the unique perspective of individuals whose experience is shaped by unpleasant, inconvenient and sometimes painful particulars of their impairment or debility. In the same way, my way of hearing provides a unique vantage on music that is not usually experienced by those with normative hearing. As such, I might frame my present reflections as a form of pedagogical excess. In other words, I am 'coming out' about a disability that is often seen as antithetical to music as a way of resisting histories of ableist oppression. My hope is that reframing disablement in this way might be useful for working with students who are facing their own personal challenges.

In conclusion

I return to the ideas of popular music, pedagogy, difference and the common good. Recalling one of my elementary school experiences might usefully bring these ideas together. I remember that our fifth-grade classroom teacher would invite us to bring in our own records to play during choice time. Towards the end of the 1970s, disco was waning in popularity as more aggressive rock music came into vogue. Although I enjoyed songs by Donna Summer and Blondie, the other boys would make derogatory comments about my music – 'disco is for faggots!' Meanwhile, I fiercely disliked their music. Unfortunately, choice time eventually became dominated by hard-rock songs like 'Do You Love Me?' by Kiss. In retrospect, I can now appreciate the irony of four straight men dressed in 1970s rocker drag performing songs of sexual hedonism. But as a fifth-grader, the collision of popular musical tastes in my classroom was deeply upsetting and alerted me that I was somehow different from the other boys.

What pedagogical insights might music educators take from all of this? First, although popular music can potentially create liberating openings and foster inclusion, it is important to be aware that popular music has the potential to marginalize as well. What might seem popular for some students might not resonate so affirmingly for others. As my story above may illustrate, the reasons might not be immediately obvious. Second, music educators should be alert to potential classroom tensions that might arise in relation to popular music. Nobody deserves to be bullied on account of their music preferences. As such, music educators might best serve the common good by helping students to understand why they prefer certain kinds of music over others, which could lead to a greater appreciation of other musical styles. And finally, I am convinced that popular music can spark necessary excessive pedagogical moments. Rather than censoring difference, music educators might ethically engage difference as the basis of the common good.

NOTES

1. Examples include William F. Pinar (1994), *Autobiography, Politics and Sexuality: Essays in Curriculum Theory 1972–92* and Janet L. Miller (2005), *Sounds of Silence Breaking: Women, Autobiography, Curriculum.*
2. Cited from Facebook Messenger with permission (9 September 2020).
3. Paulo is a pseudonym.
4. Originally recorded fall 1987 and released 10 April 1988.

REFERENCES

Erasure (1988), 'Witch in the Ditch', Track 10, *The Innocents*, USA: Sire and Reprise Records.

Kallio, Alexis Anja (ed.) (2020), *Difference and Division in Music Education*, London: Routledge.

Kirchberger, Martin and Frank A. Russo (2016), 'Dynamic range across music genres and the perception of dynamic compression in hearing-impaired listeners', *Trends in Hearing*, February, https://doi.org/10.1177/2331216516630549. Accessed 10 May 2022.

Miller, Janet L. (2005), *Sounds of Silence Breaking: Women, Autobiography, Curriculum*, vol. 1, Bern: Peter Lang.

Pinar, William F. (1994), *Autobiography, Politics and Sexuality: Essays in Curriculum Theory 1972–92*, New York: Peter Lang.

Siebers, Tobin (2008), *Disability Theory*, Michigan: University of Michigan Press.

Spencer, Leland G. (2014), 'Performing transgender identity in the little mermaid: From Andersen to Disney', *Communication Studies*, 65:1, pp. 112–27, https://doi.org/10.1080/105109 74.2013.832691. Accessed 10 May 2022.

64

Race, Caste, American Democracy and Popular Music Education

David Wish

David Wish is the founder and CEO of the music education non-profit, Little Kids Rock in the United States. He first coined the term 'modern band' in 2012.

In this chapter, the author explores ways in which resistance to popular music education in schools is a central manifestation of systemic racism, while also highlighting how including popular music education helps to dismantle racism within the field.

The persistence of caste and race hostility, and the defensiveness about anti-black sentiment in particular, make it literally unspeakable to many [...] You cannot solve anything that you do not admit exists, which could be why some people may not want to talk about it: it might get solved.

(Isabel Wilkerson 2020: 385)

America has race issues. George Floyd's killing sparked protests which were among the largest in our country's history (Buchanan et al. 2020). Floyd's killing was just one of the latest in a long, painful string of moments of racial reckoning which stretch back through the centuries. We are living the latest chapter of a great, American paradox: the same men who declared in 1776 that all men were created equal also supported chattel slavery on the new, national American stage.

But what has this to do with our newer and decidedly smaller stage of American *music education*?

American music education also has race issues. This is according to NAfME, the leading trade organization for music educators in the United States. In an email from NAfME's President Mackie Spradley sent to members on 4 January 2021,

Spradley wrote, 'Given the history of our country, systemic racism is embedded in all facets of our life including education. NAfME, with its 113-year history, is no exception [...] a difficult reality for us to face.' This candid acknowledgement is good news for our field; we cannot solve a problem we cannot admit exists.

This chapter unearths how resistance to popular music education in schools is a central manifestation of systemic racism. It also highlights how including popular music education helps to dismantle racism within the field while reinforcing the best parts of our nation's democratic norms.

Writing for the Smithsonian, Steven Lewis once noted that the Black influence on American music has been so fundamental that there would *be no American music without it* (Lewis 2016). The most popular music genres in the United States today are rap, rock, pop, Latin, R&B (which account for a whopping 76 per cent of what Americans listen to) and each of these genres originated in Black and Brown communities (Buzz Angle Music 2017). Music is just a product of culture and these Black musical forms, like jazz and blues before them, have become the musical lingua franca of not just the United States but much of our modern world.

Our embrace of Black music has roots in slavery. Beyond forced labour in the fields or in domestic settings, entertainment was the only role open to the enslaved. Wilkerson (2020) notes that from the days of minstrelsy through our present moment, White America's taste for Black music has been facilitated by stereotypes. Racist beliefs in Black earthiness based on animal instinct rather than human creativity allay any threats of to the dominant-caste's own perceived supremacy in leadership and intellect. Even now, seventeen of the top twenty richest Black Americans – from Oprah Winfrey to Jay-Z – made their wealth in the entertainment industry or in sports (Wilkerson 2020). Nevertheless, Black music has subverted racial segregation and White supremacist beliefs from the jazz age forward.

In the 1950s, Black artists started playing rock 'n' roll, a new musical form that quickly swept the nation. While civil rights advocates were being beaten and killed for attempting to desegregate lunch counters and city buses, musicians like Chuck Berry and Sister Rosetta Tharpe were forced to play to segregated crowds. Many venues had actual lines painted on the floor to separate audiences by race. However, a curious thing began happening at rock concerts. They became so boisterously biracial that it was sometimes impossible for officials to fully segregate the audiences. Some recall the cops simply throwing up their hands. 'A lot of places had the line when we first walked in, and after we started playing, they let them cross the line', recalled Leon Hughes of The Coasters (Knopper 2017). The imaginary line separating Black music from school music programmes would prove harder to cross. 1967s 'Summer of Love' was a cultural moment with racial justice and music at its core. That June, our Supreme Court legalized marriage between races, ending legally enforced endogamy. The language of the Court's decision in Loving v. Virginia was stirring; 'The freedom to marry has long been recognized as one of the vital personal rights essential to the orderly pursuit of happiness' (United States Supreme Court 1967). That July, America's music education establishment issued stirring words of its own. The famed Tanglewood Declaration of 1967 boldly declared 'Music for every child and every child for music'. It also stressed the importance of teaching rock or 'popular teenager music' in schools (Choate 1967: 78).

Over a half-century has passed since the Summer of Love. America has changed dramatically and has also remained disappointingly the same. Our first Black President finished his second term four years ago, but he was succeeded by a White President who gleefully stirred the pot of racial animus. George Wallace is no longer swinging his axe at the top of the steps to Alabama University[1] but a disparate mob of White supremacist insurrectionists surged up the steps of the Capitol Building as this piece was being written.

It is not surprising that music education remains riven by its racist foundations. In 2016, NAfME's Executive Director, Michael Butera explained that racial progress had been slow but not for a lack of trying. He lamented what he called 'the enormous complexity of the issue' and as an example of this complexity offered that Blacks and Latinos lacked the piano skills needed to become music teachers (Cooper 2017). While the ensuing uproar led to Butera's resignation, change remains elusive. A 2019 study by a firm specializing in unconscious bias concluded that foundational barriers to diversity, equity and inclusion persist at NAfME (Cook Ross 2019).

But why?

Popular music instruction remains largely absent from school music programmes despite its continuing ubiquity in American cultural life. The fact that this remains a 'hot button' issue in music education (Byo 2018) is reflective of enduring systemic racism in education. The same US school system that, until 1952, used legal segregation to close its doors to Black and Brown students' bodies still closes doors *today* on 'their' music. That this music is the central soundtrack of the United States and countries the world over makes its general exclusion from school music education all the more disturbing.

At a conference dedicated to the promotion of popular music education in US schools, Dr. Ruth Wright of Western University offered the following critique:

> Could it be that our previous largely unquestioning acceptance of the superiority of western art music, its ensembles, canons, and pedagogies, has excluded students who

can't recognize themselves, their music, or their ways of learning in these offerings? [If] so, previous models of music education might be seen as structures of oppression and exclusion. In other words, they are institutional causes of harm.

(Wright 2017)

Whether the music education establishment sees this or not, the negative impact on our children's joy, well-being and understanding of democracy is the same. That our schools heavily favour western classical, jazz, folk, world and children's music may also harm students' economic prospects. These genres represent just 6 per cent of the music that Americans consume (Buzz Angle Music 2017). From a career readiness perspective, 94 per cent of the jobs in our nation's $21.5 billion music industry appear to lie elsewhere (Statista 2021).

The over-representation of culturally distant music and its pedagogies, methodologies and curricula is likely one of the primary contributing factors to the fact that music education struggles to reach what they commonly refer to as the 'other 80 per cent'. It is a well-established phenomenon that the vast majority of children quit music as soon as it becomes a school elective or shortly thereafter (Williams 2019). How can we be surprised by this when we consider that over three-quarters of the music that our kids listen to is not embraced in school and that the majority of our children today are people of colour?

I coined the term 'modern band' in 2012 to redress the implicit and explicit biases of US music education. The term been has gaining currency ever since (Wish 2020). On the surface, modern band is simply a new category of music education that joins existing programmes such as marching band or jazz band and which focuses on the popular music genres of today. On a foundational level, I conceived modern band as an educational reform movement aimed at breaking up the logjam of hegemonic, largely White, Eurocentric and exclusionary educational practices that our forebears at Tanglewood sought to disrupt in 1967. It is long past due that we do so. The inclusion of popular music education in our schools is a means of both instilling and supporting democratic norms in our academic institutions and is beneficial to all of our children.

Our national character rests on a foundation that is at once deeply racist yet democratic. No wonder then that our history has been defined by a see-sawing struggle of Black resistance and progress followed by White anger and backlash. It is no secret that these forces continue to struggle today. As the world watched the Confederate flag paraded through the Capitol Building on 6 January 2021, we were reminded in stark terms that the poisonous sins of America's founding may yet kill the world's longest-running experiment in representative democracy. Experiments can and do fail. Living citizens in Germany, Venezuela, Peru and elsewhere can confirm this.

The world has yet to see a truly multi-ethnic democracy in which no particular ethnic group is in the majority and where political, social and economic power sharing have been achieved (Allen 2017). The United States can still become the first nation on Earth to solve this problem but only if we can admit that this problem exists. The microcosm of music education cannot solve these problems alone. Yet, if our field can solve its own problems, the impact would be tremendous. Music punches far above its weight as a force shaping cultural norms. Just ask the late Representative John Lewis of Georgia.

Lewis came to prominence when he dared set foot on the Edmund Pettus Bridge which was named in honour of a Grand Wizard of the Ku Klux Klan. Lewis crossed the bridge with hundreds of others to ask America for the vote. America responded by gassing them and beating them bloody. Lewis marched successfully for another half-century yet died knowing his work was unfinished. Toward the end, he made an observation we music educators would do well to remember as we consider our work.

Without music, the civil rights movement would have been like a bird without wings.

(Representative John Lewis)

NOTE

1. On 11 June 1963, George Wallace, the Governor of Alabama, stood in the doorway of Foster Auditorium to prevent the entrance of two Black students who were seeking to register to attend the university.

REFERENCES

Allen, Danielle (2017), 'Charlottesville is not the continuation of an old fight. It is something new', *Washington Post*, 13 August, https://www.washingtonpost.com/opinions/charlottesville-is-not-the-continuation-of-an-old-fight-it-is-something-new/2017/08/13/971812f6-8029-11e7-b359-15a3617c767b_story.html. Accessed 10 May 2022.

Buchanan, Larry, Bui, Quoctrung and Patel, Jugal K. (2020), 'Black lives matter may be the largest movement in US History', *New York Times*, 3 July, https://www.nytimes.com/interactive/2020/07/03/us/george-floyd-protests-crowd-size.html. Accessed 10 May 2022

Buzz Angle Music (2017), *Buzz Angle Music 2017 US Report*, https://www.buzzanglemusic.com/wp-content/uploads/BuzzAngle-Music-2017-US-Report.pdf. Accessed 11 January 2020.

Byo, James L. (2018), '"Modern Band" as school music: A case study', *International Journal of Music Education*, 36:2, pp. 259–69.

Choate, Robert (1967), 'The Tanglewood symposium: Music in American society', *Music Educators Journal*, 54:3, pp. 1–33.

Cook Ross (2019), *Diversity, Equity, Inclusion, & Access – Current State Study-Findings & Recommendations Report*, October, https://nafme.org/wp-content/uploads/2020/01/NAfME_DEIA_Executive-Summary_2019.pdf. Accessed 10 May 2022.

Cooper, Michael (2016), 'Music education group's leader departs after remarks on diversity', *New York Times*, 12 May, https://www.nytimes.com/2016/05/13/arts/music/music-education-groups-leader-departs-after-remarks-on-diversity.html. Accessed 10 May 2022.

Knopper, Steve (2017), 'The rope: The forgotten history of segregated rock & roll concerts', *Rolling Stone*, https://www.rollingstone.com/music/music-features/the-rope-the-forgotten-history-of-segregated-rock-roll-concerts-126235/. Accessed 9 January 2020.

Lewis, Steven (2016), 'Musical crossroads: African American influence on American music', *Smithsonian*, https://music.si.edu/story/musical-crossroads. Accessed 9 January 2020.

Spradley, Mackie (2021), 'Re: January 11: Last all-member virtual NAfME town hall', email communication to NAfME membership, 4 January.

United States Supreme Court (1967), 'Loving v. Virginia', 388 U.S. 1.

Wilkerson, Isabel (2020), *Caste: The Origins of Our Discontents*, New York: Random House Publishing Group.

Williams, David (2019), *A Different Paradigm in Music Education: Re-examining the profession*, New York: Routledge.

Wish, David (2020), 'Popular music education and American democracy: Why I coined the term "modern band" and the road ahead', *Journal of Popular Music Education*, 4:1, pp. 117–25.

Wright, Ruth (2017), Keynote address, Modern Band Summit, Fort Collins, CO, USA, 30 July.

65

The Problem of Conversion in Music Teacher Education in the United States

Radio Cremata

Radio Cremata is associate professor and chair of music education at Ithaca College, NY, USA, where he teaches graduate and undergraduate courses in music education.

In this chapter, the author problematizes popular music education by considering challenges associated with converting pre- and in-service music educators. He considers some entwined complexities of neophytes and profiteers, and discusses a sincere desire to maintain elements of authenticity to the popular music learning and making experience.

The context and need for conversion

The music education profession in the United States continues to call for reform and is currently experiencing an increased interest in popular music education. Some have dubbed this the modern band movement. The movement is being driven by several components including reactions to preservationist practices, responses to contemporary culture and other rethinking regarding the future direction of the profession. Leading the charge of the modern band movement are popular music advocates who promote the poignant and provocative potential of popular music education to the masses. While not always the case, often the promotion of modern band can engage and be undertaken by inexperienced newcomers. Implicit to this are problems centring on conversion.

Music education students in the United States often have very little or no background making or learning popular music. Additionally, they have likely

367

been admitted to tertiary music education programmes in large part due to their skills, experiences and interest in western art music practices. In that context, pre-service music educators are often introduced to and asked to learn something additional about popular music education with modest to little depth of exposure. The college and university music education students are often exposed to elements of popular music by music education faculty members who also have little experience with popular music themselves. There are also in-service music educators who, for various reasons, seek a change in their practice, and despite their lack of experience as popular musicians, are willing to switch approaches and begin teaching popular music in schools. These cases of conversion are complex because converted people inherently lack foundational knowledge and deep experience of (in this case) modern band. To ignore the issue of conversion would be to turn a blind eye to a problem that could fester and negatively impact the modern band movement, thereby missing opportunities to broaden music education offerings to large swaths of marginalized student populations.

Modern band, Little Kids Rock and popular music education

Modern band, as its name suggests, is an outgrowth of, and a response to, current music education practices, frequently referred to in North America as 'traditional' school band or wind band. Modern band involves the elements of rock/pop bands including drums, bass, guitar, keyboards, vocals and technology. At the heart of the movement are what the progenitor of the term modern band and its affiliated charitable organization, Little Kids Rock (LKR), which describes as its three P's: Pioneering, Preparing and Providing. While it may be the case that these guiding principles are not entirely at play in all of the work LKR does, they do serve to help the promotion of the modern band movement. Little Kids Rock claims first to *Pioneer* innovative teaching methods; next, they *Prepare* teachers to disseminate methods and materials; lastly, they *Provide* musical instruments and training to schools affected by budget cuts. LKR is not alone in this. They have several dozen higher education partners as well as other stakeholders interested in pioneering, preparing, providing and promoting popular music education. As a modern band and popular music education become increasingly popular, they are gaining traction in the music education establishment, evidenced by its inclusion in many school districts across the United States, a dedicated All National Honor Ensemble at the annual conference of the National Association for Music Education (NAfME), a Popular Music Education NAfME Special Research Interest Group, and a recent special issue on popular music education in the widely read and distributed *Music Educators Journal*.

While increased interest in popular music education is encouraging, it is not without its challenges, including the issue of conversion. Conversion is both dynamic and disruptive. Conversion is a response to the tight-knit, curatorial and exclusive nature of music teacher education culture. As new modern band culture is created out of existing traditions, the newly converted naturally require additional support and ongoing development. The depth and richness of that support can be insufficient at best and improbable at worst. It is important to note that conversion happens in response to the rigidity and immobility of traditions, and thus, sudden conversion seems to be not only needed but also a natural progression of disruption in a dysfunctional inbred school music culture.

As noted earlier, the modern band refers to school-based popular music education and not all forms of popular music education. Important to the distinction is that modern band involves licensed (some may say trained), certified music teachers. Additionally, modern band involves school classrooms and an entrenched context for codified/curricularized, structured learning. With that in mind, the modern band is at the nexus of two independent cultures: popular music culture and school music culture. One might wonder whether tertiary music education programmes are sufficiently capable of providing rich and prolonged popular music education experiences for their students, given rigid institutional cultures of certifications, music school requirements and traditions associated with degrees. At this stage, given the limits and challenges of undergraduate degree curricula, the modern band may, in most cases, fit best as an add-on to required course offerings. As schools of music evolve and admissions standards change, perhaps modern band experiences may become more integral to undergraduate music teacher education offerings.

Problems with conversion and converts

Due to rigid admissions standards in undergraduate music programmes that often marginalize popular musicians, music teachers who graduate music teacher education programmes will likely have limited backgrounds in popular music. Should they be interested in teaching popular music, where will they turn to for professional development? Unfortunately, there is currently an insufficient amount of professional development offerings. The LKR-sponsored modern band workshops typically last an afternoon or a few days. These brief experiences are not sufficient for a richly informed modern band culture. Consequently, we may be placing the future of popular music education in the hands of poorly informed neophytes. One does not have to look too far to witness neophytes at work in the modern band. NAfME, state music educator association conferences, and the Modern

Band Summit are meccas for converted modern band practitioners seeking tips and tricks to enrich their popular music pedagogies.

The music merchant market has also responded to this. Hal Leonard recently released a series of method books for the modern band as curriculum guides. Additionally, and independently, there are web resources such as LKR's Jam Zone,[1] to help modern band teachers structure what they do. While these resources can be helpful particularly to neophytes, they are also problematic because popular music learning and the cultures associated with it in non-school environments have largely leveraged informal learning models that intentionally avoid curricula, structure, guided instruction and sequential learning. That is to say, school cultures and the converted impose an ill-fitting formality upon popular music learning processes.

The newly converted modern band teacher might feel safer with a familiar pre-set/turnkey approach to music education. Converts might innocently buy, teach from and recommend prescribed popular music methods materials resembling the already saturated band method book market. Music merchants can be predatory and their interests are profit driven. Additionally, methods can function as forms of indoctrination that espouse singular approaches that perpetuate cultures of domination and oppression. Typically, each method is singular in that it presents *one method* and *one approach* to transmitting knowledge. Methods are oppressive in that they are written and published by people positioned to benefit from their purchase, propagation and consumption. Music merchants who codify modern band materials often ignore cultural and psychological understandings that are essential to maintaining the authenticity of popular music learning. Even if the modern band methods that make their way into the hands of converts are intended as suggestions and adaptable resources, their very nature can inevitably steer the modern band movement towards the schoolified establishment that modern band and LKR purportedly seek to augment or disrupt. While outwardly appearing harmless, these method books (which are not the same as reference resources or textbooks) are motivated by profiteering music merchants to stabilize a sense of safety, fill gaps of knowledge, and regiment practice for neophyte modern band students and teachers.

Music educators who propagate modern bands seek to be inclusive and broaden opportunities for music learning in school music cultures. Neophytes who grasp for help in curriculum, method books and other teaching tools may do more to alienate students than to include them, particularly those who are attracted to the freedoms associated with more typical, discovery-based popular music learning. Schoolified experiences drive some learners away from the modern band, as those students may be repulsed by standardized school-oriented practices. Prefabbed methods can essentially strip out the natural/organic experiences of popular music making, favouring a curated, microwavable, made-to-order, schoolified approach prepped for schoolroom contexts that are governed by policies that at times may be at odds with the music and the culture from which it comes.

Conversion leads to an additional problem associated with monetization. Musical artists and record companies may need to work together with modern band publishers balancing matters related to age- and school-appropriateness. Additionally, the shelf-life of popular music may need to be factored into the often-slow process of publishing bound books and other school friendly resources. This could potentially further marginalize some popular musics by either excluding them, and/or deteriorating and degrading the authenticity and provocative nature of those musics. Music teachers, as a profession, ought to guard against this and remain aware of publishers' powers to deepen the consumer-dependent culture that so often dominates the popular music marketplace neglecting the many facets of popular musics.

Dealing with the issue of conversion

Music education has a long history of oppressive, autocratic and dictatorial practices. Conductors often stand on podiums, waive batons, silence student voice, and ignore student musical preferences. In recent decades, the profession has found something new to consider related democratic learning practices. The profession has work to do going beyond vaguely understood notions of facilitated instruction, democratic exchanges and informal learning. Converts may need help understanding how these processes actually work since they may lack experiences in them.

Conversion is a problem that might not be that easy to resolve, but one solution could be for music teacher education programmes to recruit students and teachers with strong popular music backgrounds. Having them work together with 'traditional' students would deepen possibilities and diversify experiences. There is room in music teacher education for more than one culture. The highly systematized, method-dominated approaches of band, choir and orchestra alongside informal learning and the music habits of popular musicians are richly fertile ground for future music teachers to cohabit. In-service music educators looking for a change in their practice might consider significantly deepening their understanding of popular music prior to any encounters promoting and exchanging it with their students. Neophyte modern band in-service teachers should be encouraged to add modern band gradually to their practice.

If popular music education is to be included as an equal member of the profession, then some of its practitioners would be well-served to be more fully versed in popular musics, popular musicianship and the teaching and learning models associated with popular music. In addition, as popular music continues to evolve and the instruments, hardware and software that mediate it evolve in conjunction, the conversion problem will presumably remain. It is up to modern band music educators to stay aware of and connected to ongoing developments in how popular musics are created, recorded, shared and performed. If it is to remain contemporary, relevant and reflective of popular music cultures, and not serve a preservationist whitewashed role influenced by biased profiteering curators, then the modern band will require teamwork between newly-converted, non-converted, versatile and highly adept musicians, educators and students at all levels.

NOTE

1. https://jamzone.littlekidsrock.org. Accessed 19 January 2022.

66

Expanding the Reach of Music Education through Modern Band

Scott R. Sheehan

Scott Sheehan is a music educator and department chair at the Hollidaysburg Area Senior High School in Pennsylvania, USA. He is the NAfME President-Elect.

Music education in the United States is on the threshold of a revolution in the way teachers regard inclusive, student-centred teaching practices. Modern band expands opportunities by giving students a voice and choice as they create, perform, respond and connect through popular music styles in culturally relevant and engaging ways.

Introduction and background

This narrative is built upon the perspective that all children have a right to a culturally responsive music education that is sequential, appropriate and provides depth and breadth in opportunities to create, perform, respond and connect through and with music. As I share my thoughts and ideas here, I recognize the privilege I have had to lead, educate and make music, and I recognize that my voice has been part of discussions that have impacted programmes at a local and national level in the United States. I have served on numerous committees and boards at local and state levels, served on the National Executive Board for the National Association for Music Education (NAfME) for six years and acted as the Programme Chair for the NAfME All-National Honor Ensembles. I do not take these responsibilities lightly, and I truly value all music and its power to change lives. So, with this in mind I offer my views on expanding music education's reach.

I believe music education is on the threshold of a revolution, or perhaps in the midst of an evolution, in the way many music educators regard student learning and growth. Receding are the days of the 'sage on the stage' (King 1993) where the teacher expounds wisdom in front of the room while students sit and receive all they need to know. Today, many, if not most teachers facilitate learning as a 'guide on the side' by helping students discover and unpack concepts and develop skills through a variety of learning strategies. These teachers empower students to take ownership and be more involved with decision making. The National Core Music Standards place students at the centre of each of the artistic processes and state that in order to achieve the highest levels of musical skill and understanding, students should be involved in the process of selecting music and repertoire, creation and refinement of new musical ideas, and development of criteria for responding to music. Practices such as flipped classrooms, blended learning and backwards design (Wiggins and McTighe 2005) encourage teachers to focus on student outcomes before designing lesson plans and instructional strategies. Additionally, Domain three in the Danielson Framework for Teaching (The Danielson Group 2019) focuses on high levels of student engagement and calls for students to take part in the development of questions and contribute to their learning. Also, social–emotional learning, student wellness and growth mindset initiatives in schools further demonstrate an emphasis on student-centred practices.

Every student comes to school with their own background and their own story. Their individuality may be obvious in part through their ethnicity, race or gender. Other differences may be less clear, such as socio-economic status, sexual identity or spiritual beliefs. Musical abilities, as well as physical, academic and social abilities also vary with every child. All of these factors contribute to each student's uniqueness and are part of each child's culture. The support for student-focused learning referenced above suggests that students need to be an integral part of their educational decision-making processes in order to best learn, grow and achieve. For many music teachers, this type of teaching and learning may be very different from their own experiences in school. It may not be intuitive for some teachers to ask students what they are interested in knowing or the preferred mode of instruction for learning a new concept. It may have never occurred to some teachers to give their students input about what music might be studied and performed. Knowing how to meet the many needs and desires of diverse student populations may be challenging; however, when the differences that each student brings to our classes are combined, the result is a vibrant culture unique to each ensemble, music room and school. It is through approaching our teaching with this type of student-centred and culturally responsive lens that we may find answers to questions about how to ensure all children can access relevant and meaningful music education.

Responsiveness to and inclusion of the culture of each student form the crux of discussions about educational reform (evolution, revolution – you choose). For the past several decades, music education associations have used the advocacy message of 'Music for All' and encouraged music educators to work to reach the 80 per cent of students who are not part of high school music programmes (Elpus and Abril, 2011). However, when parents, administrators and/or the community at large sees 'Music for All', what does this really mean? How do music educators or music education associations uncover all the implications of this statement? How do we go about achieving this lofty goal? What is the metric to know how we're doing? There are many questions that need to be asked and factors to be considered by each individual teacher; the first is 'Why are more students not participating in the music classes offered at my school?' which should be followed by 'Do students have access to music opportunities in my school that include their culture?' Obviously, many factors may contribute to answering these questions; however, a close comparison of teachers' curricula with their personal values and beliefs may uncover solutions for enhancing the appeal and impact of music programmes.

Modern band

One movement in music education I have witnessed in recent years making considerable progress in addressing some of the aforementioned questions is a modern band. I see it expanding the footprint of music education, especially for some ordinarily underrepresented student populations. The tenets and constructs supporting modern band resonate with many music educators because the basic premise is to bring vernacular music into the classroom and give students an opportunity to connect with music they already enjoy. The goal of the modern band is not necessarily to produce huge rock concerts or dazzle enormous audiences with the sounds of today's pop culture (although that would be pretty cool), but rather to immerse students in the fundamentals of music through melodies and beats with which they are familiar and provide them with voice and choice in what they learn.

As a high school music educator, I have observed that meaningful musical experiences can happen in many ways, and modern band may be a more authentic approach for students to experience certain styles and genres of music. After participating in two levels of training with Little Kids Rock (non-profit purveyor of modern band practices, and progenitor of the term 'modern band'), I am much more comfortable with taking risks to provide these opportunities for my students. The decision to incorporate modern band into my own music curricula did not feel like a risk. The experiences for my high school students have been extremely positive when introducing modern band concepts and practices into the guitar classes

I teach, and our music department has plans to offer a new modern band elective in the near future. I have witnessed students' eagerness to try something new and their enjoyment figuring out a cool bass riff or sitting down at a drum kit and creating a groove to go along with a tune we are learning. They thrive on the collaborative processes this approach offers, and each player is excited to add to the overall sound of their group's creation. My colleagues and I have observed that some students in our wind band, chorus and orchestra programmes have been drawn towards modern band opportunities simply to have another chance to make music with their peers. Due to the impact, we are seeing at the high school, we plan to add more modern bands into our curriculum at elementary and junior high levels.

The addition of modern band to the 2019 NAfME All-National Honor Ensemble Programme was intended as a significant step in showcasing outcomes of this type of collaborative music making process to music educators across the country, and to serve as an example of how the artistic processes outlined in the National Core Music Standards transcend musical genre and type of ensemble. From the very beginning, the students in the inaugural All-National Modern Band had input into the pieces of music they would perform and how those pieces would be arranged and nuanced for their unique performance. The students collaborated to create a new song that would be premiered at the All-National concert. They advanced their abilities to critique and refine their individual performance skills, as well as how to respond to bandmates as a cohesive ensemble. The collaboration was highly student-driven, and the 'directors' assisted with the technical and production aspects of the experience. It was very clear that the musical decisions came from the students, and the musical growth that the ensemble and individuals experienced in just three days was remarkable. It seemed as though a new culture was created by adding the modern band to the NAfME programme. The students in the other ensembles were eager to listen to rehearsals and to cheer on their new friends during the concert, and some people were out of their seats, dancing in the aisles. The overall programme felt more complete by adding modern music to the established sounds of the choir, orchestra, wind band, jazz and guitar styles.

Another important aspect of NAfME's commitment to add the modern band to the National Ensembles was to increase access for students' eligible to apply for this experience. Currently, there are no states with an All-State modern band, which is a pre-requisite for the other NAfME All-National ensembles. For the modern band, the door is wide open for all students to apply as long as their director is a NAfME member; and thanks to financial support from music education non-profit Little Kids Rock, students are able to apply for scholarships to assist with costs. NAfME is committed to increasing access and equity for students to have a meaningful music education, and the modern band as a National Ensemble has become an example of those beliefs and values in action.

National and state programmes are two ways to showcase or promote the importance of music education on a large scale; however, each individual music educator has a greater direct impact on the experiences and culture of students. As teachers, we make hundreds of choices about what happens in classrooms every day. These decisions range from instructional strategies and assessments to the colour of t-shirts for a concert, where to go on the next field trip, what is on the bulletin board and many others. We also choose what musical opportunities our students will have, both in and out of the classroom. With these choices comes the great responsibility to be culturally responsive to our students about what, when, why and how they learn and engage in music making. We must recognize that every decision is informed by unconscious bias from our own beliefs. I can attest that my own beliefs and values have been expanded through a deeper understanding of the modern band approach. I see this as a 'yes/and' proposition; I believe that there is room in music curricula for large ensembles *and* experiences with popular music, each in their own authentic and meaningful ways. As we all strive to expand our reach and provide life-changing musical opportunities for more students, the modern band can serve as a means to engage with students who otherwise may not find a place in our classrooms. Our work is far from over; however, harnessing the power of music to build community in schools through new and creative ensembles and platforms will help us move closer toward achieving the mission of 'Music for All'.

REFERENCES

The Danielson Group (2019), *The Framework for Teaching* [online], https://danielsongroup. org/framework/framework-teaching. Accessed 15 October 2019.

Elpus, K. and Abril, C. (2011), 'High school music ensemble students in the United States: A demographic profile', *Journal of Research in Music Education*, 59:2, pp. 128–45.

King, Alison (1993), 'From sage on the stage to guide on the side', *College Teaching*, 41:1, pp. 30–35.

National Association for Music Education (2014), 'Overview of 2014 music standards', https:// nafme.org/overview-of-2014-music-standards/. Accessed 3 March 2022.

Wiggins, Grant P. and McTighe, Jay (2005), *Understanding by Design*, Alexandria: Association for Supervision & Curriculum Development.

67

Lessons from Community
Music and Music Therapy:
Beyond Familiar Comparisons

Bryan Powell

Bryan Powell is an assistant professor of music education and music technology at Montclair State University, NJ, USA, where he teaches popular music and music technology courses.

In this chapter, the author examines tendencies to justify the inclusion of popular music education by comparing it with approaches to concert band, choir and orchestra programmes. He discusses practices common in music therapy and community music settings to suggest ways in which popular music education can continue to evolve.

Comparisons in popular music education advocacy

As the presence of popular music education (PME) in United States K-12 schools (ages 5–18) continues to expand (Clauhs et al. 2020), many of the discussions about the benefits of PME seem to be couched in comparisons to more traditional music ensemble approaches. These comparisons usually centre on the same familiar ideas: concert bands do not compose that often (or at all), and PME can allow for songwriting; the director usually chooses the repertoire in band, choir and orchestra, but PME allows the students to have an active role in the selection of songs; PME allows students to play rock band instruments and use technology that they might prefer over traditional concert band instruments like the trombone and clarinet; PME promotes life-long music making in ways that marching band does not; etc. I could go on and on with these 'comparison' arguments, and I have certainly used them in the past.

While it is perhaps initially useful to differentiate PME from teaching approaches for concert band, choir and orchestras, much of the advocacy around PME in K-12 schools seems to focus on how PME might be 'better' than, or at least 'attractively different' from what already exists in school music programmes. Most advocates for K-12 PME promote it as an addition to, rather than a replacement of, more traditional approaches. Yet when it comes to advocacy, it seems that most efforts are focused not on being the best version of PME, but on contrasting what popular music educators do compared to band, choir and orchestra music teachers.

For a long time, popular music educators have been fighting for a seat at the school music table. With the expansion of modern band programmes across the United States and the establishment of a NAfME[1] All-National Ensemble for Modern Band as well as a Special Research Interest Group for Popular Music Education, it seems that PME is now, at the very least, 'seat-adjacent'. But now that we are here, what are we going to do? If PME is going to reach its potential for relevant music education that is inclusive and accessible, popular music educators need to stop being so fixated on comparing what they do to other established approaches and instead explore other musical fields of practice to see what lessons might be learned. This expanded view includes examining the compelling examples of popular music education that have been happening in the fields of community music and music therapy for decades. Let us briefly explore the practices of community music (CM) and music therapy (MT), not to compare them with PME but to see what opportunities might exist for PME.

Music therapy

I am fortunate to teach courses in music education, popular music and music technology at Montclair State University (MSU) in New Jersey. MSU also has a respected music therapy programme that is one of the oldest in the United States. Inevitably, whenever I walk down the hallways past a music therapy class, they are doing cool, interesting and relevant things. Each week, the music therapy students engage with popular music technologies using hardware such as Abelton Push and Akai MPCs. They are writing songs and creating music. Their discussions focus on inclusion and access as core tenets of their practice. And they are engaging with participant-preferred musics including hip-hop, EDM and other culturally relevant genres. And social and emotional growth which has recently moved into the spotlight in music education circles has been a core principle of music therapy for decades. The music therapy students are also some of the most accomplished multi-instrumentalists within the school of music. Instead of focusing on mastering one instrument, these students often have broad musicalities on guitar, keyboard, vocals and a range of technologies that will serve them well throughout their careers.

Community music

Community music (CM) is another area of theory and practice that often embodies PME ideals. Higgins (2012: 3) discussed three broad perspectives for CM: CM as the 'music of a community', CM as 'communal music making', and CM as an 'active intervention between a music leader or leaders and participants'. This third perspective of CM as an intentional intervention involves 'skilled music leaders who facilitate group music-making experiences in environments that do not have set curricula' (Higgins 2012: 3–4). The leader in a community music intervention works more as a facilitator than a director, and within this perspective, community music facilitators are committed to the idea that everybody has the right and ability to make, create and enjoy their own music. CM facilitators put an emphasis on the variety and diversity of musics that reflect and enrich the cultural life of the community, the locality and individual participants, while acknowledging both individual and group ownership of the music (Higgins 2012).

Many community music interventions offer 'unconditional hospitality' (Higgins 2012) to participants without the need for prior musical experience. For the CM facilitator, the social welfare of the participants is as important as the end result of the music-making. Participant-preferred musics are often the focus of community music interventions, and musical activities are often collaboratively developed to prioritize the goals and desires of participants. CM interventions also seek to engage meaningfully with participants to address societal concerns and work toward individual and community empowerment.

Facilitation

In both CM and MT settings, the skills possessed by music facilitators align with the skills that I want my PME students to have as they enter the teaching profession. Price (2010) described areas of competence that facilitators may have, including interpersonal skills, social and political awareness, organizational skills, motivational skills, 'musical tastelessness' (able to value all forms of music), fluency in many musical languages, facilitation skills and technological skills (332). Rogers (1993) outlined three attitudinal attributes necessary for facilitative practice: *realness* – the teacher is being themselves with awareness of their feelings; *prizing, acceptance, trust* – the facilitator cares about the students and values their feelings; and *empathy* – understanding the perspectives of the students. These aspects of a facilitator are also integral to the work of a K-12 PME facilitator.

I recognize that PME in schools is subject to certain limitations and requirements that CM and MT are not. Issues of assessment, evaluation and expectations from school administrators are all concerns that CM and MT practitioners do not have to deal with. Nonetheless, my point in providing this provocation is to encourage popular music educators to avoid falling into the trap of comparing our practice to traditional school approaches to music education as a way of positioning PME as 'superior'. Doing so provides a blinkered focus on being 'better' than something else, as opposed to growing the field of PME in meaningful ways while critically examining our own practices.

Expanding approaches to popular music education

So, what might a 'widened' view of PME look like that taps into elements of MT and CM practices? There would certainly be an increased focus on social justice and issues relevant to the community as part of 'music-making as ethical action' (Elliott 2012: 22). There would also be an increased spirit of unconditional hospitality that welcomes all musicians regardless of musical skills or (dis)ability. This welcome would embrace 'a return to amateurism' (Kratus 2019) in a way that removes any stigma that term might have in music education circles. Participants preferred musics and the musical goals of the students would take precedence over learning a traditional canon of popular music songs (Powell and Smith 2019), and the presence of hegemonic instrumentation that favours guitar, bass, drums and keyboards would give way to music making more focussed on instrumentation and technologies relevant to the students and their communities.

This view of PME is not all that radical. And it seems eminently doable. As popular music practices in K-12 schools are becoming more solidified through the development of curricula and method books, it is important for popular music educators to not settle into a sense of complacency. Widening our view to areas of musical practice outside of school-based music education will allow us to recognize and embrace compelling forms of PME happening within community music interventions and music therapy practices.

NOTE

1. The National Association for Music Education (NAfME) is the largest organization of school music educators in the United States.

REFERENCES

Clauhs, Matthew, Powell, Bryan and Clements, Ann C. (2020), *Popular Music Pedagogies: A Practical Guide for Music Teachers*, London: Routledge.

Elliott, David (2012), 'Another perspective: Music education as/for artistic citizenship', *Music Educators Journal*, 99:1, pp. 21–27.

Higgins, Lee (2012), *Community Music: In Theory and in Practice*, Oxford: Oxford University Press.

Kratus, John (2019), 'A return to amateurism in music education', *Music Educators Journal*, 106:1, pp. 31–37.

Powell, Bryan (2021), 'Community music interventions, popular music education and eudaimonia', *International Journal of Community Music*, 15:1, pp 3–25.

Powell, Bryan and Smith, Gareth Dylan (2019), 'Philosophy of assessment in popular music education', in D. J. Elliott, M. Silverman and G. E. McPherson (eds), *The Oxford Handbook of Philosophical and Qualitative Assessment in Music Education*, New York: Oxford University Press, pp. 347–63.

Price, David (2010), 'A view from the workshop floor: What skills and qualities are demanded of today's community music workers and how can they best be taught?', *International Journal of Community Music*, 3:3, pp. 331–36.

Rogers, Carl R. (1993), 'The interpersonal relationship in the facilitation of learning', *Culture and Processes of Adult Learning*, 1, pp. 228–42.

68

Adolescence, Education and Citizenship: Tracing Intersecting Histories and Reimagining Popular Music Pedagogies

Noah Karvelis

Noah Karvelis is a Ph.D. student at the University of Wisconsin-Madison where he studies the histories and epistemologies of teacher activism and music education.

In this chapter, the author presents a critical, historical engagement with the object of citizenship education as it relates to popular music pedagogy.

Citizenship and popular music pedagogy?

The concept of teaching citizenship has recently been offered as a potential purpose of teaching popular music (Smith et al. 2018; Wish 2020). While the beginning of a discussion on citizenship and popular music learning is encouraging, I am interested in considering what epistemologies may inform such a notion. In doing so, I hope that we, popular music pedagogues, question: What exactly is a citizen? Where does the idea of producing citizens through education come from? And, if popular music education is a distinct set of practices with distinct conceptions of citizenship, how do we intend to depart from historical conceptions of citizenship in order to establish such a distinction? My intent is not to offer 'solutions' or 'better' ways of teaching citizenship. Rather it is to question the processes of citizenship development through schooling in the hope of moving beyond the historical conceptualizations and constraints of such a notion. To do so potentially draws us towards an actualization of alternative potentialities of being and thinking both within and beyond popular music pedagogy.

Panoptical time, adolescence and the historical object of 'citizen'

The citizen is not real. Rather it is made 'real' through specific language, ways of conceptualizing the world and relations of power. In order to understand how the citizen becomes a real, actionable object within education, we can perhaps begin by investigating how an idea entangled with the citizen – adolescence – was created. As Nancy Lesko (2001) shows, the idea of adolescence, like the citizen, is produced. It is a particular way of thinking about the transition from childhood to adulthood that serves to determine who possesses the virtues necessary for being a good citizen. Importantly, it also becomes a way of thinking about who does not possess those virtues and, importantly, the ways in which that child can be acted upon in order to instil such qualities. This way of thinking about the child, Lesko argues, is not natural but instead made possible through biological sciences, a fear 'that the future will be diminished, dragged down by teenagers' failures to act in civilized or responsible ways' (Lesko 2001: 37) and particular conceptions of time. In regard to time, her primary focus, Lesko (2001) states that adolescence became standardized as a period of

> always 'becoming', a situation that provoked endless watching, monitoring, and evaluating. As time was made and marked in public, standardized ways, the modern scientific adolescent became a multifaceted social site for talk about the productive use of time, the glorious future, and, sometimes, the inglorious past. Slow, careful development-in-time was identified as the safest path.
>
> (38)

Through this fixation on development, productive use of time and eventual becoming, a particular framework of time, panoptical time, became 'a dominant aspect of the discourse on adolescence' (Lesko 2001: 41). Utilizing McClintock's (1995: 37) definition of the term, Lesko understands panoptical time as 'a condensed, commodified time built upon global hierarchies of gender, race and class and understood at a glance as natural' (MacClintock 1995: 37 cited in Lesko 2001: 40). Within panoptical time, it then becomes possible to regard the adolescent as not simply 'always becoming' or in need of intervention to secure a glorious future and avoid the inglorious past. Rather, it becomes possible to place the adolescent in a condensed, surveilling framework of time that serves to forward such a project of transforming the child. It is this way of conceptualizing the adolescent, particularly within panoptical time, 'that compels us – scholars, educators, parents, and teenagers – to attend to progress, precocity, arrest, or decline' (Lesko 2001: 37) by acting upon the developing child.

As Popkewitz et al. (2001) explain, developing nations began actualizing such a possibility of attending to progress through producing children as something other, namely citizens, prior to the establishment of adolescence and as early as the end of the eighteenth century. While different across contexts, the republics of France and the United States mobilized the school as a vehicle which could create the citizens the republic would need. Importantly, though, it was not simply that the citizen was produced. Rather, certain technologies which mobilized specific epistemologies made such a project possible. For example, ideas such as religious salvation, republican cultures, modern science and shifting forms of government contributed toward determining who exactly the citizen should and would be. In this way, 'the pedagogy of the school embodied and brought together a variety of social and political changes as it was reconstituted at the level of transforming the self and organizing the problems of personal life' (Tröhler et al. 2001: 22).

Adolescence eventually becomes one such 'change' which informs the pedagogy of the school and the transformation of the self. In the late nineteenth and early twentieth centuries, following its establishment, adolescence became dominant within the field of education theory (Ramos 2001: 71). It is through this dominance and the consequent reconceptualization of the student as an adolescent that the work of making citizens through education begins to shift. During this period, through the convergence of notions of the citizen, the future, and the adolescent, 'a vision of the child with a mouldable soul who would learn to act as a self-motivated, self-responsible individual in the name of public interest' (Ramos 2001: 71) begins to be developed and actively produced through schooling.

While such an understanding of the citizen is of course specific to particular times and spaces, Popkewitz, Labaree and Tröhler make clear that such ideas have travelled. They explain that 'what became possible as modern schooling entailed the assembly, connections, and disconnections of different historical phenomena that are never neutral, but about who the child is and should be' (Tröhler et al. 2001: 22). It is largely through this assembly that it becomes possible to conceive of education as capable of transforming children into 'good' citizens. With this entanglement of citizenship, schooling, the state and conceptions of adolescence in mind, perhaps we can begin to shift toward a questioning of how the idea of popular music citizenship becomes constituted.

Tracing the traveling notion of making citizens

Drawing from Thomas Popkewitz and Ruth Gustafson's (2002) work, I under-stand music education as an 'alchemy' which is historically not solely about music but instead occupied also with making and marking citizens in specific ways. I suggest that due to this history, as well as the history of adolescence and the making of citizens through education, perhaps such notions have become taken up within popular music education discourse. In pursuit of such under-standings, we can consider Smith et al.'s (2018) conceptualization of the artis-tic citizen who is developed through popular music learning. In my reading, the authors' artistic, popular music citizen is developed primarily through learning 'to believe in themselves' (19), a possibility actualized through inclusion in popu-lar music programmes, specifically the modern band programme proliferated by the non-profit organization, Little Kids Rock. The authors suggest that through including students in popular musical learning, 'we empower them to have voice and be heard', ultimately creating the conditions to transform their lives (Smith et al. 2018: 19). Citing Linton (2015), they also seem hopeful that by doing so 'these young students can participate in reshaping the musical landscape within the school setting' (cited in Smith et al. 2018: 311).

While Smith, Gramm and Wagner's goals are certainly laudable, I question if such a view of citizenship makes visible a negotiation between the multiplicity of forms of citizenship within popular music-making and the histories surrounding the idea of creating a 'good' citizen through education. The concept of giving a student a voice, for example, perhaps implies a general lack of inherent agency within youth as well as a fear that without our intervention the adolescent may not become a productive member of society. Questioning the histories which poten-tially inform this conceptualization of youth allows us to consider where such a notion develops. Is it drawn solely from popular music practices? Or is it also indebted to other epistemologies such as those surrounding a belief that adoles-cents will fail to 'act in civilized or responsible ways' (Lesko 2001: 37), necessi-tating our intervention as scholars and educators?

Further, conceptualizing the student as without voice and in need of transfor-mation potentially fixates on the final product that the student will one day become and, through this, invites the use of panoptic time. By focusing on the final product, the student as empowered in this case, we potentially relocate the student within the surveilling, temporally condensed logics of panoptic time which patrol the path toward such a state. What likely becomes difficult in this conception of time is the embrace of alternative forms of making and marking time, participation and being which are beyond the boundaries of panoptical time, yet perhaps present in popular music practices. For example, music-making practices which profoundly challenge or even entirely do away with notions of 'order' or demonstrable 'development' potentially become possible when we move beyond the logics of panoptical time. Finally, empowering students with a stated goal of shifting the landscape of music teaching and learning (Smith et al. 2018: 18) draws into question whose goals are being pursued. Are they those of the students? Or are they goals defined as valid by the entity which does the educating, relegating the adolescent to a position of being educated and empowered through the 'conditions to transform lives' (Smith et al. 2018: 19) which we have created in order to achieve a 'glorious future'?

Towards popular music citizenship

To be clear, I am not suggesting that such notions of teaching citizenship through popular music are inherently bad or inauthentic. Rather, I invite questioning about whence we draw these notions in order to fundamentally reimagine what a pedagogy of popular music citizenship might entail. This essay has engaged primarily with the histories of adolescence and the production of citizens rather than literature in citizenship education in order to highlight the existence of the citizen and adolescent as unnatural, produced categories in the hope of inviting such a reimagining. By making strange and consequently departing from the historical notions of what the student is and how they can be transformed into the ideal citizen through education, we can potentially develop an epistemology of being which is unbounded by such notions. I suggest that if we believe popular music education is a distinct, specific practice and that popular music citizenship is a consequently distinct way of being, then our pedagogies and epistemologies must begin from such a departure and consequent reimagining in order to establish that difference.

REFERENCES

Lesko, Nancy (2001), 'Time matters in adolescence', in K. Hultqvist and G. D (eds), *Governing the Child in the New Millennium*, New York: Routledge Falmer, pp. 35–67.

MacClintock, Anne (1995), *Imperial Leather: Race, Gender and Sexuality in Colonial Context*, New York: Routledge.

Popkewitz, Thomas S. and Gustafson, Ruth (2002), 'Standards of music education and the easily administered child/citizen: The alchemy of pedagogy and social inclusion/exclusion', *Philosophy of Music Education Review*, 10:2, pp. 80–91.

Ramos, Jorge, (2001), 'Republican deliveries for the modernization of secondary education of Portugal in the 19th Century', in T. D. Labaree and T. Popkewitz (ed.), *Schooling and the Making of Citizens in the Long Nineteenth Century: Comparative Visions*, New York: Routledge, pp. 70–93.

Smith, Gareth Dylan, Gramm, Warren G. and Wagner, Kenrick (2018), 'Music education for social change in the United States: Towards artistic citizenship through Little Kids Rock', *International Journal of Pedagogy, Innovation and New Technologies*, 5:2, pp. 11–21.

Tröhler, Daniel, Popkewitz, Thomas S. and Labaree, David F. (2011), *Schooling and the Making of Citizens in the Long Nineteenth Century: Comparative Visions*, New York: Routledge.

Wish, Dave, (2020), 'Popular music education and American democracy: Why I coined the term "modern band" and the road ahead', *Journal of Popular Music Education*, 4:1, pp. 117–25.

69

#SongsOfBlackLivesMatter: Co-creating and Developing an Activist Music Education Praxis Alongside Youth

Martin Urbach

Martin Urbach is a White Latino Jewish immigrant drummer from Bolivia. He is a music teacher and youth organizer in New York City, USA.

In this chapter, the author draws on his experience as music teacher, drummer and youth organizer to describe activist music making with high school students in New York City, NY, United States.

As a music educator, activist and researcher, I yearn to teach music in ways that go beyond schooling and toward education for liberation. As a musician, I am deeply inspired by socially conscious artists such as Janelle Monaé, Nina Simone and Olodum, who use their songs 'HellYouTalmbout', 'Mississippi Goddam' and 'They Don't Really Care About Us', respectively, to address topics of police brutality, race and racism, making powerful and unapologetic statements about the role of music(ians) in the struggle towards collective liberation. The struggle for social justice across the world has always featured music inspiring people to question the status quo, and to rise up together demanding freedom by bringing the voice(s) of the oppressed together. In times when Black men like Eric Garner[1] are killed at the hands of police, and when White police officers like Daniel Pantaleo[2] are not charged for their deaths, it is instrumental (pun intended) that the curricula I choose to create for my students reflect the realities that affect them.

In this essay, I propose the creation and implementation of a new school course: #SongsOfBlackLivesMatter. In this course, students would analyse, respond to, create (compose), perform and reflect on music/songs within social, cultural, historical and political contexts. Obviously, this course would be developed per research on developmentally appropriate ways of teaching complex topics as well as the musical skills that will be needed for such a course to succeed. Musically speaking, the curriculum would consist of the study of such building blocks of Black American popular music as syncopated rhythms, verse/chorus song forms and pentatonic melodies. This course would be planned and facilitated through a combination of drumming and singing circles, musicking (Small 1999), Freirean Culture Circles (Freire 1970; Souto-Manning 2010) and Youth Participatory Action Research (YPAR), which would be used as methods for democratic curriculum development (Cammarota and Fine 2008).

Musicking

Christopher Small writes about music being a verb instead of a noun, a social action in which one participates: 'The meaning of musicking lies in the relationships that are established between the participants by the performance' (Small 1999: 9). Musicking is about making sense of the living world by developing relationships and learning from direct experiences. When students engage in musicking, they can combine their musical, cultural and historical knowledge to create a body of knowledge that is both deep and wide.

Culture circles

Culture circles are informal learning spaces, developed by Brazilian educator and philosopher Paulo Freire during the 1950s as examples of participatory, democratic and critical pedagogy. In a culture circle, the community learns skills and topics with and from one another by the process of being in that community and by putting information in cultural, social and political contexts relevant to them. Culture circles rely on 'generative themes', things that the community experiences, that define an epoch, and that keep coming back; one such theme in this proposed class would be racism at the hands of police. Participants then codify these themes through pictures, songs and other media as a way to invite students to talk about difficult themes like police brutality without having to disclose personal experiences if they do not want to, thus making the experience less threatening while still engaging in dialogue.

Drumming and singing circles

Drum circles promote collaboration, risk taking and enjoyment. Drummer Babatunde Olatunji professed: 'Drumming is the simplest thing that we can do to bring us together' (Hull 2007: 84). Musically and socially, rhythm is a powerful unifying force. Musicians and audiences can synchronize with one another by both performing or listening to music together. Rhythm can bring a community (closer) together, physically and spiritually. The symbiotic relationship between critical pedagogy and music education is rooted in music's power to bind people to one another. These new ways of being allow for healthier, deeper discussions about the political nature education, which is one of the tenets of critical pedagogy. Moreover, rhyming and rhythmic chanting have been forms of communication and therapy for oppressed people for centuries; shamans in Mongolia, Minianka healers in Mali, enslaved Africans in Cuba and street drummers in New Orleans have used rhythm, melody and chant to communicate with one another – often in code – as well as for maintaining physical, mental and spiritual health.

Youth Participatory Action Research (YPAR)

YPAR is an approach to youth and community development where youth are trained to co-research, co-create and co-disseminate knowledge based on topics that affect them as a community. YPAR is a way to redistribute access to power, resources and voice to youth, while developing young people's socio-political and psychological empowerment. All stakeholders have individual and collective roles and responsibilities in deciding on all of the elements that they research, from planning to action, evaluation and dissemination of their learning. These processes would be embedded in creating and implementing the #SongsOfBlackLivesMatter course.

Figure 69.1 is not intended to prescribe a process; rather, I include it to help conceptualize the amalgamation of the Freirean culture circle and a drumming circle in the context of the proposed music course. Discussions make connections to music, and the music connects to discussions. For example, when learning chord progressions, students will be exposed to traditional western tonal harmony (major/minor keys) as well as African, African American and Latinx uses of harmony, especially with the I–IV–V blues form and the minor seventh additions to diatonic chord triads.

Cogens (co-generative dialogue),[3] not handbooks: Co-designing planning and instruction alongside students.

391

FIGURE 69.1: Drum circles as culture circles (Urbach 2018).

1. *Drumming, singing and chanting together* sets the stage for participants to build relationships and to share culture and musical skills. This serves to decolonize the ways in which people are introduced to one another in formal settings like schools. For far too long, schools have demanded students learn in Eurocentric, 'proper' (read: racist) ways, and to only use some of their intelligences while erasing and silencing others. Tara J. Yosso[4] speaks about cultural wealth and cultural capital, reminding us that dancing can be an academic epistemology. Smith (forthcoming) reminds us one can be a drummer and an academic and that one can and must inform the other. Students can make sense of their world, as Freire (1980) reminds us to read the world as well as the word. Combining rhythm and speech in call-and-response drumming/chanting ice-breaker games is not only an effective way to learn people's names but it also engages learners' multiple intelligences (Gardner 1983).

2. *Themes* can first be introduced by the teacher working as a 'facilitator',[5] planting seeds for the community to *feel invited in*; to do the same. As a provocation/question, the facilitator might ask: How can we use musicking to celebrate and to protest? I identify as a facilitator rather than a teacher. Though for some it might be a difference in semantics only, for me, to be a facilitator, is to help make things easier, to facilitate an experience, to help someone(s) through something they have yet to see/live/experience/do.

392

3. *Problem posing*: A teacher-as-facilitator might ask: What are some shared themes people might celebrate or protest across the group? What are songs some songs that speak truth to power about these issues? As we 'problematize' the world, it is important people tell their stories and not someone else's. This can help the community members find a sense of belonging and position in this ever-changing world. Students and facilitators might decide to research collectively issues such as 'why are the bathrooms always locked in our school?', or 'how come our high school in a wealthy district does not have metal detectors but the middle school I attended in an underfunded neighbourhood had multiple metal detectors?' In problem posing, students engage in ethnographic data collection, they interview peers, staff and community members. They also look at music and art that speaks about the demonization of youth, the school to prison pipeline, and the racialization of who is and is not afforded free bathroom use in their schools. The central question in Marvin Gaye's 'What's Going On?' still applies today in the schoolhouse.

4. *Dialogue in rhythm*: Based on the findings from their research, the class uses group drumming to explore and communicate the feelings that they have regarding the themes being explored. Students can do multimedia research about how other teenage musicians might respond to similar themes as well as gather drumming-based music, or other music of resistance from around the world. Students can present their findings to the class, which can into new music.

5. *Problem solving plan*: Students decide on a plan to disseminate their findings and present their musical work to the community or communities they choose. Students have full agency to choose to perform, for example, an in-class 'informance' for students in a younger grade, a full school assembly, a showcase at the university next door or even a takeover of City Hall, depending on what problem they aim to solve and who the audience and stakeholders are. They also decide on the format, such as live performance, pre-recorded music video or an interactive teach-in.

6. *Action/performance*: Presentations of such projects can systemically transform schoolhouses into fertile spaces where naming the world, pushing against the status quo and fighting alongside one another for justice are the norm.

7. *Reflection*: Although good teaching/facilitation teaches us that reflection should happen throughout a project and not just at the end, having a few sessions to meet, debrief and reflect after the actions would be vital to this proposed course. This intentional and unrushed time for reflection affords participants the chance to affirm one another, to name what they learned from preparing and presenting the project and thus make new connections to and through teaching and learning.

In conclusion

Through the development and implementation of #SongsOfBlackLivesMatter as a culturally relevant school music course that is co-created alongside students, I yearn to effect change in our school in a way that activates, connects and inspires our students to become vehicles of social change in their communities, like Pete Seeger, Mahalia Jackson and Common,[6] at the same time transforming our field of music education systemically, away from a system focused on music for music's sake and toward a system of education for liberation.

NOTES

1. https://www.nytimes.com/2015/06/14/nyregion/eric-garner-police-chokehold-staten-island.html. Accessed 3 March 2022.

2. https://time.com/5642648/eric-garner-death-daniel-pantaleo-suspended/. Accessed 3 March 2022.

3. http://www.ascd.org/publications/educational-leadership/sept16/vol74/num01/Seven-Cs-for-Effective-Teaching.aspx. Accessed 3 March 2022.

4. https://www.tandfonline.com/doi/abs/10.1080/1361332052000341006. Accessed 3 March 2022.

5. http://adriennemareebrown.net/2013/12/14/principles-of-emergent-processes-in-facilitation/. Accessed 3 March 2022.

6. https://www.grammy.com/grammys/news/aretha-franklin-public-enemy-heres-how-artists-have-amplified-social-justice-movements. Accessed 3 March 2022.

REFERENCES

Cammarota, Julio and Fine, Michele (eds) (2008), *Revolutionizing Education: Youth Participatory Action Research in Motion*, New York: Routledge.

Freire, Paulo (1985), *The Politics of Education: Culture, Power, and Liberation*, South Hadley and Hadley: Bergin & Garvey.

Freire, Paulo (2000), *Pedagogy of the Oppressed: 30th Anniversary Edition*, New York: Bloomsbury Academic.

Gardner, Howard (1983), *Frames of Mind: The Theory of Multiple Intelligences*, New York: Basic Books.

Hess, Juliet (2015), 'Decolonizing music education: Moving beyond tokenism', *International Journal of Music Education*, 33:3, pp. 336–47, https://doi.org/10.1177/0255761415581283. Accessed 3 March 2022.

Small, Christopher (1999), 'Musicking – the meanings of performing and listening' [a lecture], *Music Education Research*, 1:1, pp. 9–22, https://doi.org/10.1080/1461380990010102. Accessed 3 March 2022.

Smith, Gareth Dylan (forthcoming), *A Philosophy of Playing Drum Kit: Magical Nexus*, Cambridge: Cambridge University Press.

Souto-Manning, Mariana (2010), *Freire, Teaching, and Learning: Culture Circles Across Contexts*, New York: Peter Lang.

70

From Black Lives Matter
to Black Music Matters:
Crossing the Rhetorical Divide

Ed Sarath

Ed Sarath is a professor of music and director, program in creativity and consciousness at the University of Michigan. He is a
flugelhornist, composer, recording artist and author.

*In this chapter, the author discusses the centrality of Black music
and its improvisatory roots to US American culture and musics.
He urges foundational, rather than token reform measues around
these premises in order to render music studies more socially and
artistically just.*

As heartening as the newfound wave of racial justice discourse that has gripped
music schools across the nation may be, I still find myself yearning for new kinds
of conversation and action.

In short; while there is no dearth of declarations that 'Black Lives Matter', a huge
gulf remains when it comes to a key anti-racism threshold for music studies – that
'Black Music Matters'. Indeed, if my book of that title was timely when it made its
2018 appearance, it is all the more so now. In no way do I mean to disparage recent
intensified efforts to incorporate BIPOC works in existing curricular and ensemble
formats (Sarath 2018). However, until these attempts are recognized as addressing but
the tip of a hegemonic iceberg that extends deep into music studies' frigid and fore-
boding hegemonic waters, the field will only become more entrenched in its racism.

Systemic pathology calls for systemic healing: There is no middle ground.

Shortly after *Black Music Matters* appeared, I founded the Alliance for
the Transformation of Musical Academe (ATMA) in hopes of galvanizing

movement to circumvent what I viewed as a longstanding impasse in music studies progressivism.[1] Now, just a couple of years later, perhaps I might reflect on what I believe the book, and the organization, have to offer. While I frame my thoughts through an American lens, I believe much of what I propose applies across wide-ranging cultural boundaries and thus recognize the importance of multi-national efforts to these ends.

Combining a visionary perspective with an activist tone, *Black Music Matters* develops three basic premises. First is that jazz and Black music warrant a foundational place in a new paradigm for twenty-first century musical training that, at once, provides American musicians grounding in a core facet of their cultural heritage while also yielding an unprecedented skill set for cross-cultural navigation. Jazz – construed as writ large – is the central site through which the Contemporary Improviser Composer Performer (CICP) profile that prevailed in earlier eras of the classical tradition (e.g. Bach, Mozart, Beethoven and many of their contemporaries were CICPs, as are today's jazz musicians) makes its return, laying groundwork for new levels of achievement.

The second premise is that, if movement in this direction is to transpire, music studies progressivism (let alone conservativism) needs to take a hard look at itself, and particularly (for progressives) the half-century of reform discourse that I argue has eluded critical interrogation. In particular is what I call 'lingering aversion to musical blackness (Sarath 2018: 50) that has manifested itself in a variety of ways, even amid an ever-increasing crescendo of diversity rhetoric. As I have argued in ATMA circles (and elicited no small degree of ire from some of the most fervent activists), change conversation remains constrained by a 1960s kind of Tanglewood-era thinking, despite new wrinkles that would take hold over the decades. The failure to acknowledge that in Black American Music, our nation has an extraordinary musical treasure in its midst, is a primary casualty. We see this oversight in – among other places – K-12 teacher education programmes, core curricular reform, popular music pedagogy and literature that routinely evade the African American foundations of most pop music, and in the recent spate of racial justice proclamations that began in spring 2020.

Third entails an evolutionary vision, whereby wholesale overhaul of the field atop Black American Music (BAM) foundations (not to be conflated with a BAM-centric model) has the capacity to catalyze a transformative continuum that not only impacts music studies but also education and society at large. Invoking principles of an emergent worldview called Integral Theory, I frame this as an arts-driven revolution in creativity and consciousness, where we – species *homo sapiens sapiens* – fundamentally transform our experience and understanding of ourselves in relationship to one another, our natural environment, the innermost dimensions of the soul, and the furthest regions of the cosmic wholeness. I devote considerable attention in the book to the mystical dimensions of jazz and the Black music pantheon as further reservoirs to be tapped from America's own heritage for broader transformation, with burgeoning contemplative and consciousness-studies movements in higher education cited as promising, however preliminary, glimpses of this possibility.

But there is no mincing words about the amount of work required were this vision to be realized, and neither the book nor ATMA, are for the faint of heart.

Music studies may be among the most racist disciplines in the history of the academy, and nothing short of wholesale reconstruction of the field from its curricular and cultural core on up will suffice.

I conclude by emphasizing the confluence of Black American Music studies and Music Education (K-12 teacher education) areas as a particularly powerful catalyst for the racial justice/artistic justice leadership so urgently needed in today's world.

NOTE

1.　For more information, see https://atma.jazzcosmos.com. Accessed 10 May 2022.

REFERENCE

Sarath, Ed (2018), *Black Music Matters: Jazz and the Transformation of Music Studies*, New York: Rowman and Littlefield.

Notes on Contributors

Sᴇʀɢɪᴏ Aʟᴏɴsᴏ is a high school and community music educator in San Fernando, CA, USA, where he teaches mariachi music.

* * * * *

Bʀᴇɴᴅᴀɴ Aɴᴛʜᴏɴʏ is a senior lecturer at the Queensland Conservatorium, Griffith University, Australia where he teaches popular music production and performance to popular music and music technology cohorts.

* * * * *

Kʀʏsᴛᴀʟ Pʀɪᴍᴇ Bᴀɴꜰɪᴇʟᴅ is Vice President for Education Outreach, Social Entrepreneurship at Berklee College of Music in Massachusetts, USA, and supervises Berklee's international creative youth development programme, Berklee City Music.

* * * * *

ᴀᴅᴀᴍ ᴘᴀᴛʀɪᴄᴋ ʙᴇʟʟ is an associate professor of music at the Western University, Canada. He teaches and researches music education, music technology, popular music and disability studies.

* * * * *

Nᴀᴛᴀʟɪᴇ Bᴇᴛᴛs is a music and creative arts lecturer for Weston College. She teaches a non-accredited music course at Her Majesty's Prison and Young Offenders Institute Portland, England.

* * * * *

HUSSEIN BOON is a principal lecturer at University of Westminster, London, UK where he teaches popular music, performance, songwriting, music technology and music business.

* * * * *

AIXA BURGOS is a high school music teacher at Passaic Preparatory Academy in New Jersey, United States, where she teaches music technology courses as a career pathway.

* * * * *

CHRISTOPHER CAYARI's (he/they) research focuses on mediated musical performance, YouTube, informal music learning, virtual communities, video game music, and online identity

* * * * *

SIEW LING CHUA is Principal Master Teacher (music) at the Singapore Teachers' Academy for the Arts, Ministry of Education. She looks after professional development of in-service music teachers.

* * * * *

WARREN CHURCHILL is a lecturer of music at NYU Abu Dhabi, UAE, where he teaches courses in musical performance and disabilities in musical contexts.

* * * * *

MATTHEW CLAUHS is an assistant professor of music education at Ithaca College in Ithaca, NY, USA, where he teaches courses in music education and instrumental methods.

* * * * *

SHANE COLQUHOUN, Ph.D. is a Grammy-nominated music educator. He currently teaches band and general music at Loachapoka High School located in Auburn, AL, USA.

* * * * *

RADIO CREMATA is an associate professor and chair of music education at Ithaca College, NY, USA, where he teaches graduate and undergraduate courses in music education.

* * * * *

ABIGAIL D'AMORE is an independent consultant specializing in music education, youth voice, professional development of teachers and musicians, evaluation and impact and strategic planning.

* * * * *

JAMES DEKLE is the artist-in-residence at the Purdue University Black Cultural Centre and serves as the director for the Black Voices of Inspiration choir and The Purdue Express.

* * * * *

SHEENA DHAMSANIA has taught elementary music, songwriting and rock band in Wyoming for ten years. She is in the composer duo No Such Thing As Noise.

* * * * *

EVA J. EGOLF earned a Ph.D. from New York University. She lives in Bronx, New York, United States where she teaches music in school and university settings.

* * * * *

JABARI EVANS is an assistant professor of race and media at the University of South Carolina in Columbia, SC, USA, where he teaches journalism and mass communication.

* * * * *

HELOISA FEICHAS is an assistant professor of music education at Music School of the Federal University of Minas Gerais in Belo Horizonte, Brazil, where she teaches music education.

* * * * *

JAMES FRANKEL, EdD, is a life-long musician, music educator and very proud Deadhead. He is the Founder and Director of MusicFirst.

* * * * *

SAURAV GHOSH is a drummer and a music edu-preneur working to democ-ratize music education for young learners by leveraging the power of technology.

* * * * *

FELIX GRAHAM (singwithdrfelix.com) is an NYC-based educator whose practice focuses on vocal health and retraining, while guiding clients in reconciling their voice and personal identity.

* * * * *

JASON HANLEY is Vice President of Education and Visitor Engagement at the Rock and Roll Hall of Fame in Cleveland, Ohio, USA, where he oversees the museum's award-winning programmes.

* * * * *

GEMMA HILL is a drummer, music educator, translator and former editor of *Drummer* magazine, who now works for GEWA Drums in Germany.

* * * * *

JASMINE HINES is an assistant professor of music education at Kent State Univer-sity in Ohio, USA where she teaches contemporary and traditional choral methods courses.

* * * * *

WAI-CHUNG HO is a professor at Hong Kong Baptist University in the Hong Kong Special Administrative Region, where she teaches sociology of music and music education.

* * * * *

NATHAN HOLDER is a musician, author and music education consultant currently serving as International Chair of Music Education at the Royal Northern College of Music.

* * * * *

STEVE HOLLEY is a Ph.D. candidate in music learning and teaching at Arizona State University. His research focuses on experiences of professional musicians-come-teachers in popular music classrooms.

* * * * *

JASON HUXTABLE is a senior lecturer in popular music performance at Leeds Arts University and visiting tutor of percussion and pedagogy at Royal Birmingham Conservatoire, England.

* * * * *

MIA IBRAHIM is a middle-school music teacher in New York City, NY, USA and a professional clarinetist. She teaches popular music and modern band.

* * * * *

MARTIN ISHERWOOD is Head of Music at The Liverpool Institute for Performing Arts, England, where he teaches and leads courses in popular music, songwriting, production and performance.

* * * * *

NOAH KARVELIS is a Ph.D. student at the University of Wisconsin-Madison where he studies the histories and epistemologies of teacher activism and music education.

* * * * *

DAVID KNAPP is an assistant professor of music education at Syracuse University, where he teaches modern band and directs the Music in Community programme at SU.

* * * * *

NIKLAS LINDHOLM is the co-founder and CEO of Rockway Ltd and has taught music technology and video-based pedagogy courses in Arcada and Metropolia Universities of Applied Science.

* * * * *

ERIK LUNDAHL is an assistant principal and music teacher at the aesthetic programme at Ystad Gymnasium in Ystad, Sweden where he teaches the EDI and other music courses.

* * * * *

TOBIAS MALM is a Ph.D. in education at Stockholm University and Royal College of Music in Stockholm, Sweden, where he teaches learning and organization theory, and teacher training courses.

* * * * *

ROGER MANTIE is an associate professor at the University of Toronto Scarborough. His teaching and research focus on music, education and leisure.

* * * * *

CANDICE DAVENPORT MATTIO is an assistant professor of music teaching and learning at the University of Southern California's Thornton School of Music.

* * * * *

LLOYD MCARTON is a Ph.D. candidate in music education at the University of Toronto, where he teaches courses in popular music and music education.

* * * * *

NINA MENEZES teaches world music at the University of Tampa and maintains an active voice studio. An internationally acclaimed soprano, her voice features on Bollywood film soundtracks.

* * * * *

BRYCE MERRILL is the music programmes director at Bohemian Foundation in Fort Collins, Colorado. He is a musician and advocates for popular music as a public good in his free time.

* * * * *

SOL ELISA MARTINEZ MISSENA is a DMA student and research assistant in Music Education at Boston University, from Asuncion, Paraguay. Her work experience includes teaching piano, accompanying and choral conducting.

* * * * *

ADRIEL MILES is a doctoral researcher in the Department of Music at the University of Bristol in England, studying decolonial methods for music curriculum design.

* * * * *

STUART MOIR is a bicentennial education fellow at Moray House School of Education and Sport, University of Edinburgh, where he teaches on the community education programmes.

* * * * *

ZACK MOIR is an associate professor of music at Edinburgh Napier University, UK where he is the programme leader of the MA Music programme.

* * * * *

FLÁVIA MOTOYAMA NARITA has been a lecturer at the Universidade de Brasília (UnB), Brazil since 2006, teaching graduate and undergraduate courses in music education.

* * * * *

JARED O'LEARY is the director of education and research at BootUp PD (USA), where they create free computer science curricula and engage in research.

* * * * *

JOSEPH MICHAEL PIGNATO, professor at the State University of New York, Oneonta, teaches music industry, beat production, experimental music and improvised rock.

* * * * *

ROSHI NASEHI is a Welsh-born, London-based musician of Iranian parentage with a track record in performance, theatre, recording, cross arts collaboration workshops, public art and social intervention projects.

* * * * *

BRYAN POWELL is an assistant professor of music education and music technology at Montclair State University, NJ, USA where he teaches popular music and music technology courses.

* * * * *

ELEANOR RASHID works as a freelance music practitioner, songwriter and performer throughout London, England. She founded and presents On Repeat, a weekly podcast that explores genre and music hierarchy.

* * * * *

JESSE RATHGEBER, Ph.D., is an assistant professor of music education at Augustana College, Rock Island, IL, USA. He researches disability, inclusion and professional vision.

* * * * *

TIGER ROBISON, Ph.D., is an assistant professor of music education at the University of Wyoming. Tiger writes about classroom management and plays electric bass.

* * * * *

KAYLA RUSH is an anthropologist and a Marie Skłodowska-Curie research fellow based at Dublin City University. Her current work examines private, fees-based rock music schools.

* * * * *

MARTIN RYAN is a music educator from Limerick, Ireland who specializes in teaching popular music through technology. He is a doctoral student of music education at Kent State University.

* * * * *

ED SARATH is a professor of music and director, program in creativity and consciousness at the University of Michigan. He is a flugelhornist, composer, recording artist and author.

* * * * *

TOM SCHARF is a novelist, painter and working musician in Denver, Colorado. He runs rivers, and sometimes they chase him.

* * * * *

MEGHAN K. SHEEHY is an assistant professor and director of music education at Hartwick College in New York, USA. She loves playing horn, piano and singing to her son!

* * * * *

SCOTT SHEEHAN is a music educator and department chair at the Holli-daysburg Area Senior High School in Pennsylvania, USA. He is the NAfME President-Elect.

* * * * *

GARETH DYLAN SMITH is an assistant professor in the music education department at Boston University, Boston, USA, where he teaches graduate and undergraduate courses in music education.

* * * * *

RICHARD SMITH's 13 solo recordings have established him as a veteran contemporary musician. He is a tenured, full professor at the USC Thornton School of Music.

* * * * *

JAY STAPLEY is a session guitarist, songwriter and producer from England. His session credits include Roger Waters, Mike Oldfield, Scott Walker, Toyah, Shakin' Stevens and Westernhagen.

* * * * *

NILESH THOMAS serves as Dean of the True School of Music at Vijaybhoomi University. He has two decades' experience in designing higher music education programmes.

* * * * *

MARTIN URBACH is a White Latino Jewish immigrant drummer from Bolivia. He is a music teacher and youth organizer in New York City, USA.

* * * * *

SHREE LAKSHMI VAIDYANATHAN teaches kindergarten music at a private school and is a part-time faculty member at The Bangalore School of Music in Bangalore, India.

* * * * *

MARTINA VASIL is an associate professor of music education at the University of Kentucky, USA, and is president of The Association for Popular Music Education.

* * * * *

KENRICK WAGNER is a social entrepreneur and hip-hop artist with over fifteen years of professional musical experience as a music educator, performer, recording artist, published author and producer.

* * * * *

DANIEL WALZER is an assistant professor of music and arts technology at Indiana University-Purdue University Indianapolis and co-author (with Dr. Mariana Lopez) of *Audio Education: Theory, Culture and Practice*.

* * * * *

VIRGINIA WAYMAN DAVIS is a professor of music education at the University of Texas Rio Grande Valley, USA. She teaches general music education and popular music.

* * * * *

ANDY WEST is a professor at Leeds Conservatoire, where he is the head of post-graduate studies and oversees the MA Music programme.

* * * * *

DAVID WISH is the founder and CEO of the music education non-profit, Little Kids Rock in the United States. He first coined the term 'modern band' in 2012.

* * * * *

ANA FLAVIA ZUIM is an assistant music professor and director of vocal performance at NYU Steinhardt, New York, NY, USA, where she teaches graduate and undergraduate courses.

Index

411